*Colonial Migrants at the Heart of Empire*

AMERICAN CROSSROADS

*Edited by Earl Lewis, George Lipsitz, George Sánchez, Dana Takagi, Laura Briggs, and Nikhil Pal Singh*

# Colonial Migrants at the Heart of Empire

PUERTO RICAN WORKERS ON U.S. FARMS

*Ismael García-Colón*

UNIVERSITY OF CALIFORNIA PRESS

University of California Press
Oakland, California

© 2020 by Ismael García-Colón

Library of Congress Cataloging-in-Publication Data

Names: García-Colón, Ismael, author.
Title: Colonial Migrants at the Heart of Empire : Puerto Rican Workers on
    U.S. Farms / Ismael García-Colón.
Description: Oakland, California : University of California Press, [2020] |
    Series: American crossroads ; 57 | Includes bibliographical references
    and index.
Identifiers: LCCN 2019040635 (print) | LCCN 2019040636 (ebook) |
    ISBN 9780520325784 (cloth) | ISBN 9780520325791 (paperback) |
    ISBN 9780520974272 (ebook)
Subjects: LCSH: Puerto Ricans—United States—-Migrations. | Puerto
    Ricans—United States—Social conditions. | Migrant labor—United
    States—Social conditions.
Classification: LCC E184.P85 G37 2020 (print) | LCC E184.P85 (ebook) |
    DDC 305.868/7295073—dc23
LC record available at https://lccn.loc.gov/2019040635
LC ebook record available at https://lccn.loc.gov/2019040636

Manufactured in the United States of America

28   27   26   25   24   23   22   21   20
10   9   8   7   6   5   4   3   2   1

*Para Ana, Emilio, Toti, y Margó*

# CONTENTS

# FIGURES AND TABLES

## FIGURES

# TABLES

## ACKNOWLEDGMENTS

Our journeys in life are sparked by people who offer their unconditional help and generously lift us to embark on unbelievable adventures. The long hours I spent doing research and writing were possible thanks to the assistance and enthusiasm of many institutions, colleagues, friends, and family in Puerto Rico and the United States. I express my gratitude to all the people in Cidra and small towns and camps throughout New Jersey and New York who opened their doors to me and offered countless conversations, especially those who are still migrating and working in the fields. Their struggles and successes inspired me to chronicle their experiences, after twenty-seven years away from my homeland.

I am deeply thankful to my late great-uncle, Tío Guelo, a migrant farmworker who left for Pennsylvania in the 1950s, for sharing his experiences with me. I learned about him and migrant farmworkers from my grandmother, Catalina, who was always wondering how he was doing and died without ever seeing him again. It is hard to imagine how, seventy years ago, migrant farmworkers left their relatives to work in the middle of nowhere without knowing either the language or a familiar face.

My former professors at the University of Connecticut are still there for me, providing advice and support during the different stages of my career. I am grateful to Samuel Martínez for his time, patience, and continual encouragement. I am also extremely indebted to professors Elizabeth Mahan and Blanca Silvestrini. Elizabeth challenged me and helped me to rethink and clarify many of the ideas presented in this book. Blanca has always found time to provide feedback and believes in my work.

Most of the research for this manuscript was funded by the City University of New York and the Centro de Estudios Puertorriqueños. Edwin Meléndez, *centro* director, as always, has generously provided access to resources for my research. Pedro Juan Hernández, Jorge Matos, and Félix Rivera, at the Library and Archives Unit, provided invaluable service. In addition, Don Robotham, at the CUNY Graduate Center's Advanced Research Collaborative, facilitated a distinguished CUNY fellowship that allowed me to write some chapters of this book.

The staff of several institutions also made this book possible. My sincere appreciation for their assistance goes to Marisol Ramos at the University of Connecticut; Magali Cintrón Butler at the Centro de Investigaciones Históricas in the University of Puerto Rico; Julio Quirós at the Archivo Luis Muñoz Marín; and José Flores, Hilda Chicón, and Pedro Roig at the Archivo General de Puerto Rico. The staff of the National Records Administration, the Puerto Rico Department of Labor, the Kheel Center and the Division of Rare and Manuscript Collections at Cornell University, and the University of Puerto Rico's Colección Puertorriqueña offered me excellent professional service. The staff of the Puerto Rican Civic Association of New Jersey, Jessica Culley and Nelson Carrasquillo at the Comité de Apoyo a los Trabajadores Agrícolas, and Pat Constantino, Robert Morales, Wilder Rodríguez, Angela Iocolano, and Jeffrey Lewis at Pathstone helped me locate labor camps with Puerto Rican migrant workers.

I also express my sincere appreciation to a group of friends and colleagues who collaborated by reading parts of the manuscript, offering their advice and leads, assisting in the research, and helping me maintain my health and sanity. Hoping that I do not miss anyone, they include Aldo Lauria, Leigh Binford, Carlos Vargas Ramos, Edgardo Meléndez, Juan J. Baldrich, Sonia Lee, Félix Matos Rodríguez, Isar Godreau, Hilda Lloréns, Gina Pérez, Marc Edelman, María Pérez y González, Margaret Gray, Suzanne Oboler, Jeff Maskovsky, Patricia Tovar, Jim O'Brien, Luis Martínez, Gerald Sider, Jorge Duany, Michael Lapp, Anthony de Jesús, Julie Skurski, Julio Hernández Delgado, Marco Martinelli, Johanna Dreby, M. Anne Visser, Max Pfeffer, Max Tomba, Yuri Kazepov, Sidney Mintz, Miguel Santos, Ricardo Pérez, César Ayala, Teresita Levy, Eileen Findlay, and the Moya family in upstate New York. Research assistants and students who have collaborated in this project are Guadalupe Martínez, Robert Unterman, Alex Avellán, Andrew Luecke, Kurt Birson, Lucas Pedraza, Pablo Benson, Zoenís López, Daitza Frydel, Agustín Bruno, Mahirym Holguín, Rafael Muñoz, Sarah Mobarak, Adriana González, Joyleen Albarracín, Nicholas Boyne, Ruth Hernández, Mike Fuller, Saulo Colón, Carlos Alicea, Oscar Beltrán, Marissa Beach,

Giselle Avilés, Sandra Quiñones, Aníbal Escobar, Sanu Thomas, and Kathleen Griesbach. At the College of Staten Island, many people provided invaluable support, including Alana Gaymon, Ananya Mukherjea, Angela Ramos, Dean Gerry Mulligan, Grace Cho, Jay Arena, and Saadia Toor. Loli, Juan, and Lori helped me keep my glucose levels in check.

My participation at several conferences and workshops contributed to strengthening the arguments of this book. I am indebted to Jorge Giovannetti for his invitation to present my project at the University of Puerto Rico, his always-enthusiastic attitude toward my research, and the leads he provided concerning the field notes of the People of Puerto Rico Project. Colleagues at the Seminar on Agrarian Labor Regimes, at the University of Syracuse, helped me improve my manuscript, particularly Don Mitchell, Emily Mitchell-Eaton, Jason Lee Newton, Fabiola Ortiz Valdez, Ileen A. Devault, and Verónica Martínez-Matsuda. Carmen Whalen, Andrés Torres, Emma Amador, Patricia Silver, Gilbert Marzán, Lorrin Thomas, Amilcar Tirado, Lilia Fernández, Luis Figueroa, and other participants at the Seminar on Puerto Rican Migration at Rutgers University contributed to clarifying many of the ideas in this book.

Sections of this book appeared previously in *Latino Studies Journal* 6 (3): 269–89; *American Ethnologist* 44 (3): 403–13; and *Centro Journal* 29 (2): 134–71 and 25 (2): 96–119. I am grateful to the publishers for their permission to include passages from these articles in this book.

I want to express my deepest gratitude for the hard work and patience of my editor Niels Hooper, Robin Manley, Kate Hoffman, Susan Silver, Victoria Baker, and the rest of the staff of University of California Press. They graciously facilitated a smooth publishing process. Two anonymous reviewers gave insightful suggestions for revisions.

This book has been possible because of the enormous support of my family. My sisters, Margie and Nelly, have always assisted with research and personal matters. My parents, Toti and Margó, gave me the encouragement to complete this project in the moments when I most needed it. My wife, Ana Bazán, and my son, Emilio, were my motivation in difficult times. I am extremely fortunate to have them in my life. Ana helps me find the passion to believe that a better world is possible. She, like many women of color, has made fighting for justice her life mission. These new leaders of the resistance will always inspire me to struggle against all forms of discrimination and inequality.

# ABBREVIATIONS

| | |
|---|---|
| ACLU-NJ | American Civil Liberties Union of New Jersey |
| AFL | American Federation of Labor |
| ATA | Agricultural Workers Association (Asociación de Trabajadores Agrícolas) |
| BEM | Bureau of Employment and Migration |
| BIA | Bureau of Insular Affairs |
| CAMP | Puerto Rican Migrant Support Committee (Comité de Apoyo al Migrante Puertorriqueño) |
| CATA | Agricultural Workers Support Committee (Comité de Apoyo a los Trabajadores Agrícolas) |
| CETA | Comprehensive Employment and Training Act |
| COTA | Agricultural Workers Organizing Committee (Comité Organizador de Trabajadores Agrícolas) |
| DPRCA | Department of Puerto Rican Community Affairs |
| DTIP | Division of Territories and Island Possessions |
| FGA | Farmers and Gardeners Association |
| FLEC | Farm Labor Executive Committee |
| FLP | Farm Labor Program |

| | |
|---|---|
| FLT | Free Federation of Labor (Federación Libre de Trabajadores) |
| FSA | Farm Security Administration |
| GSA | Glassboro Service Association |
| GSSCA | Garden State Service Cooperative Association |
| MD | Migration Division |
| META | Ecumenical Farmworkers Ministry (Ministerio Ecuménico de Trabajadores Agrícolas) |
| NAFTA | North American Free Trade Agreement |
| NEFWC | New England Farm Workers Council |
| NFSC | Northeast Farmworkers' Support Committee |
| NLRA | National Labor Relations Act |
| NYSCHR | New York State Commission on Human Rights |
| OSHA | Occupational Health and Safety Act |
| PIP | Puerto Rican Independence Party (Partido Independentista Puertorriqueño) |
| PNP | New Progressive Party (Partido Nuevo Progresista) |
| PPD | Popular Democratic Party (Partido Popular Democrático) |
| PRBES | Puerto Rico Bureau of Employment Security |
| PRDL | Puerto Rico Department of Labor |
| PRES | Puerto Rico Employment Service |
| PSP | Puerto Rican Socialist Party (Partido Socialista Puertorriqueño) |
| STGAA | Shade Tobacco Growers Agricultural Association |
| UFW | United Farm Workers |
| USBES | U.S. Bureau of Employment Security |
| USDA | U.S. Department of Agriculture |

| | |
|---|---|
| USDL | U.S. Department of Labor |
| USES | U.S. Employment Service |
| WEP | War Emergency Program |
| WFA | War Food Administration |
| WMC | War Manpower Commission |

# Introduction

THE PUERTO RICAN EXPERIENCE in farm-labor migration challenges our understanding of U.S. citizenship in relation to immigration policies. Seasonal farm-labor migration reveals how Puerto Ricans occupy a complicated status within the U.S. nation, regularly confronting questions about their citizenship in job interviews, government offices, and everyday encounters with North Americans and immigrants. Since 1898 Puerto Rico's incorporation as a U.S. colonial territory has complicated North Americans' perceptions of Puerto Ricans. Even after 1917, when the United States granted citizenship to the inhabitants of Puerto Rico, mainstream U.S. society has always suspected them of being "illegal aliens." Their designation as colonial subjects, mixed racial backgrounds, Latin American culture, and Spanish speaking marked them as different in a polity where being a white Anglo-Saxon embodied a dominant notion of citizenship.

Recent events illustrate the complexity of Puerto Ricans' role in farm labor in the United States. On January 5, 2015, Charlene Rachor, regional director of the Wage and Hour Division of the U.S. Department of Labor (USDL), announced charges against Cassaday Farms, in southern New Jersey, for unlawfully rejecting thirteen qualified Puerto Ricans who had applied for seasonal employment and hiring guest workers, in violation of the regulations of the H-2A visa program.[1] The owners agreed to pay $57,870 in civil penalties and $117,130 in back wages to settle the charges (Forand 2015). Because many agricultural employers view Puerto Ricans as undesirable owing to their U.S. citizenship, Cassaday Farms–type incidents have become more common, particularly as the current economic crisis in Puerto Rico impels migration to U.S. farms. Two cases illustrate how employers' ability to deport guest workers and undocumented workers shapes the agricultural-labor market. In 2016

LatinoJustice PRLDEF (Puerto Rican Legal Defense and Education Fund) filed a case before the U.S. Equal Opportunity Commission against a Michigan apple grower for discriminating against and unjustly firing a group of Puerto Rican workers (J. Delgado 2016; Llorente 2016). In January 2017 some dairy farmers in South Dakota expressed interest in hiring Puerto Ricans, but state officials and some farmers were skeptical, arguing that migrants could leave their jobs easily and return home because they do not depend on visas. One official added that U.S. workers "are not hungry enough" to remain in this type of job (Garcia Cano 2017).

Nowadays the majority of U.S. agricultural employers disdain Puerto Ricans, while guest workers and undocumented laborers have become what Cindy Hahamovitch (2003) calls "perfect immigrants" for a low-wage agrarian-labor regime that seeks a deportable, seasonal, and easily replaceable labor force. The undesirability of Puerto Rican migrant workers underscores the long history of contradictions in how farmers and government officials have acted to promote and control farm labor (see Duke 2011).

Since the late 1940s most Puerto Rican seasonal farmworkers have migrated to the northeastern United States, although many also went to Florida and Ohio and smaller numbers to Washington State, California, and Michigan. The center of Puerto Rican farm-labor migration was southern New Jersey, in and around Gloucester and Cumberland Counties, where workers harvested fruits and vegetables. Workers also migrated to Pennsylvania for the mushroom harvest in Chester County but also throughout the state, to Lancaster and Hamburg Counties and as far west as Lake Erie. Other migrants arrived in Maryland and Delaware, working on small farms that supplied the Green Giant Company. In New York the Buffalo and the Hudson Valley areas were the main destinations where migrants harvested vegetables and apples. The canneries around Rochester hired Puerto Ricans until 2017, housing hundreds of workers in labor camps. Workers also traveled to Long Island to harvest potatoes, and the tobacco fields of the Connecticut River Valley attracted migrants from tobacco-growing municipalities in Puerto Rico. Migrants also worked in the cranberry industry on Cape Cod and in apple orchards throughout New England.

In 2007 I began to document the experiences of farmworkers in the United States. My quest took me to southern New Jersey, where I expected to find elderly retirees who had migrated many years ago, so I was surprised to find several labor camps with Puerto Ricans. For more than sixty years, Puerto Ricans have ventured to U.S. farms in search of better opportunities, working in an industry that pays low wages and where immigrant labor predominates. Although the stream of migrant farmworkers has decreased, a couple thousand still travel seasonally to camps in New York and New Jersey. I met workers from different backgrounds, some as young as nineteen years old and as old as their late seventies. Some have been doing the same kind of work for more than fifty years, like Ramón, a seventy-eight-year-old who began to migrate seasonally in 1959. Some migrants become farmworkers because they like the work, but most indicate that they do it because of their family responsibilities. Grandparents send money to their children and grandchildren on the islands, and some young workers, among them many new fathers, work to support their families. Others have to pay rent in Puerto Rico or make car payments. Some had migrated to escape family problems and bad influences.

When I talk with other scholars about Puerto Rican farmworkers, some express surprise upon hearing that thousands of Puerto Ricans have migrated as seasonal farmworkers. Because of the long history of labor migration from Mexico, most North Americans think of migrant farmworkers as Mexicans—and undocumented. This perception corresponds to reality, since 75 percent of contemporary farmworkers are of Mexican origin, and 53 percent are undocumented (Pfeffer and Parra 2005, 4; 2006, 81; Gray 2010, 170; USDL 2005, ix; Alves Pena 2009, 856–57). Even so, Puerto Ricans, along with Filipinos, West Indians, African Americans, Chicanos, and Native Americans, are part of the history of U.S. farm labor. They were or still are the dominant labor force in some regions.

Few in number compared to Mexican migrant workers, Puerto Rican farmworkers nevertheless numbered more than 60,000 per year at the peak of their migration, during the late 1960s and early 1970s (Morales 1986). Today Puerto Ricans in agriculture-related activities in the United States number approximately 5,200, and most work on farms in Florida, Pennsylvania, Massachusetts, Connecticut, New Jersey, and New York (García-Colón and Meléndez 2013). Most of these seasonal migrants come as freelancers, but approximately 1,000 come on contracts through the Puerto Rico Department of Labor and in conjunction with the H-2A visa program (J. Delgado 2014, 4).

Puerto Rican migration to U.S. farms has grown and shrunk because of immigration policies and guest-worker programs. In 1948 Puerto Ricans began to migrate through contracts sponsored by the Puerto Rico Farm Labor Program (FLP) under the Puerto Rico Department of Labor, which oversaw

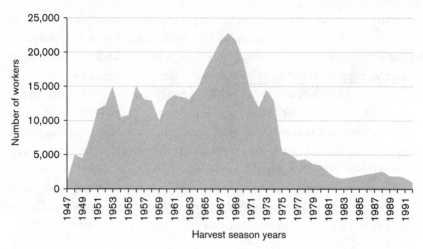

FIGURE 1. Number of Puerto Rican migrant contract workers on U.S. farms, 1947–92. OGPRUS (1953–92).

recruiting, arranged contracts, and transported workers to the continental United States (Lapp 1990; Meléndez 2017). By promoting migration and assisting workers, the government of Puerto Rico sought to eliminate unemployment on the islands while answering the postwar labor demands of U.S. employers. U.S. colonial status offered the government of Puerto Rico an important tool to shape both migratory flows and the formation of stateside communities (García-Colón 2008). Colonial officials, in effect, forced federal agencies and elected officials to pay attention to migrant farmworkers. In addition, the termination of the Bracero Program in 1964 and restrictions on H-2 workers increased the use of Puerto Rican farmworkers throughout the United States. During the mid-1970s, however, apple growers were successful in thwarting the preference for Puerto Rican workers over H-2 workers, contributing enormously to decrease the number of migrant contract farmworkers. Still, despite discrimination and shrinking numbers, contemporary Puerto Ricans continue their quest to earn a living by working in U.S. agriculture.

Labor migration from Puerto Rico to U.S. territories began as soon as the U.S. military invaded Puerto Rico in 1898, and U.S. elected officials immediately began to debate the place of their new colonial subjects in the nation. Between World Wars I and II, after Puerto Ricans were granted U.S. citizenship and the first Mexican braceros began to arrive, growers' preference for Puerto Ricans decreased. Farmers feared that Puerto Ricans would contest violations of their rights, become a burden for welfare agencies, and mix with whites, and, unlike Mexicans, they could not be deported. Puerto Ricans thus became part of a long history of how agricultural employers construct and maintain a labor force in part by elaborating and deploying racial myths about certain kinds of workers and their work ethic. Examining the processes of constructing labor forces exposes how employers use and dispose of women, children, immigrants, colonial subjects, and minorities (Griffith 1993).

Farmers' objections to Puerto Rican farmworkers went unchallenged until after World War II, when the Puerto Rican government established the Bureau of Employment and Migration (BEM) and its Migration Division (MD). Influenced by New Deal policies for managing labor markets and modeled after the U.S. Employment Service, the BEM devised a campaign to lobby federal officials and stateside farmers to employ contract workers, which resulted in the establishment of the FLP.

This book explores the long history of the administrative and legislative attempts to manage farm-labor migration and the experiences of migrant farmworkers to reveal how U.S. colonialism in Puerto Rico and the political economy of U.S. agriculture intersected with projects of citizenship and guest work. Citizenship and immigration discourses and practices reveal the connections of farm-labor migration to political and economic concerns within global processes of capitalism and states' attempts to manage migration (Grosfoguel 2003). My goal is to understand the social forces that shaped Puerto Rican migration to the United States and the impact of that migration on U.S. farm labor and, in doing so, broaden the discussion of farm-labor migration from its impact in Puerto Rico to its place in U.S. agriculture. Along the way I also want to illuminate the role of the FLP in U.S. farm labor.

Puerto Rican migrants were not passive objects of state projects. Their formation as farmworkers depended on their networks, perceptions of working and living conditions, and their own reproductive labor and that of their households and communities, as well as farmers' roles in recruitment and labor practices and the attitudes of rural communities toward migration. It also relied on the government of Puerto Rico's initiatives and those of local, state, and federal governments to manage labor (Binford 2009; Griffith 1993). Pioneer migrants in the Northeast transformed the racial, ethnic, and gender landscape of many towns and established an initial Puerto Rican foothold in some cities (Whalen and Vázquez-Hernández 2005).

Traditional paradigms of the Puerto Rican experience analyzed migration as part of capitalist development (History Task Force 1979; Padilla 1987). Newer studies have moved toward analysis of migration to large cities through the lenses of ethnic politics, citizenship, gender and domesticity, and transnationalism (Cruz 1998; Grosfoguel 2003; Whalen 2001; Ramos Zayas 2003; G. Pérez 2004). Meanwhile, studies of Puerto Rican farmworkers have centered on the problems encountered by migrants, unionization, contract labor, development, livelihood strategies, gendered labor, and transnationalism (Bonilla-Santiago 1986; Duany 2011; Duke 2011; Findlay 2014; Meléndez 2017; Nieves Falcón 1975; F. Rivera 1979; Stinson Fernández 1996; Valdés 1991). While these studies link migrant farm labor to the development strategies of the Popular Democratic Party (PPD; Partido Popular Democrático) government in Puerto Rico, what is missing from most is a sense of the formation of Puerto Rican farmworkers in relation to the overall history of U.S farm labor. To address this oversight, this book focuses on migration from rural areas in Puerto Rico to the rural United States. I outline the construction of the Puerto Rican labor force by considering its relationship to the formation of Puerto Ricans as a U.S. ethnic group, the political economy of farm labor, and processes of state formation in the United States and Puerto Rico.

In general, scholarship on Puerto Ricans in the United States focuses on the settlement and dynamics of urban communities, often ignoring the role of farmworkers in the construction of Puerto Rico as a modern colony and the development of U.S. immigration policies, although some newer work does address this gap. Edgardo Meléndez (2017), for example, explores the differences between Puerto Rican and other farmworkers as U.S. citizens, colonial subjects, and domestic workers as well as the relationship of the FLP to other U.S. farm-labor programs and the development of Puerto Rico's migration policy. In *Borderline Citizens,* Robert C. McGreevey (2018) focuses on how colonial policies, U.S. citizenship, the labor movement, and the settlement of migrants in New York City shaped Puerto Rican migration, and how, in turn, migrants pushed the limits of colonialism and blurred the boundaries of U.S. empire. Other studies have examined how the colonial relationship and citizenship of Puerto Ricans and the immigrant status of Mexicans shape their convergence in workplaces and neighborhoods. Lilia Fernández (2010) describes how Puerto Ricans' and Mexicans' common sense of exploitation and discrimination transcends their differences, despite their being pitted against each other. Nicholas De Genova and Ana Y. Ramos-Zayas (2003) explore how the unequal politics of citizenship results in different relations of Puerto Ricans and Mexicans to the U.S. state. Drawing on these contributions, I expand and explore the long history of

U.S. farm-labor policies and immigration laws affecting Puerto Rican migrant farmworkers.

The role of the Puerto Rican government in labor migration is central to the experiences of farmworkers. Michael Lapp's (1990) "Managing Migration," Meléndez's (2017) *Sponsored Migration,* and Gina Pérez (2004), in *The Near Northwest Side Story,* have documented the various roles played by the BEM and the MD. They argue that these migration offices worked as public-relations agencies to promote a positive image of Puerto Ricans, influencing private and public agencies' responses to their migration, facilitating their assimilation, and attempting to transform them into a constituency. My analysis takes these interpretations further and considers these agencies as tools of state formation in both Puerto Rico and the United States. By promoting migration and assisting Puerto Ricans, the BEM and the MD sought to eliminate unemployment in Puerto Rico, a critical problem for the emerging new colonial state during the 1950s. The colonial relationship of Puerto Rico to the United States offered a unique opportunity for the government of Puerto Rico to shape the formation of Puerto Rican communities throughout the Northeast. In stateside communities the MD acted, contradictorily, as a quasi–civil rights organization and labor union, fighting to protect the civil, labor, language, and cultural rights of Puerto Ricans as U.S. citizens while incorporating them into ethnic identity politics. Its presence distinguishes the history of stateside Puerto Rican communities from the histories of other ethnic groups.

Scholars have extensively documented how government policies in both the United States and migrants' countries of origin have sustained U.S. agriculture based on seasonal labor and inequality, concentrating on Mexicans and British West Indians (Daniel 1982; González 2006; Griffith 1993, 2006; Griffith and Kissam 1995; Hahamovitch 2011; A. López 2007; Plascencia 2018; Weber 1994). While scholarship on U.S. farm labor has often overlooked Puerto Ricans, the literature on Puerto Rican farmworkers has ignored their integration into a labor market shared by other minorities (D. Cohen 2011; Grosfoguel 2003; Hahamovitch 2011; Mitchell 2012; Molina 2014; Ngai 2004). Thus, although I draw on recent studies of Puerto Rican migrant workers as part of transnationalism and gendered history (Duany 2011; Findlay 2014), I believe that attention to social fields of power provides a more encompassing framework for the study of migrant farm labor. For Puerto Rican farmworkers, colonialism facilitated the insertion of Puerto Rican officials into the U.S. Department of Labor as well as the creation of the MD as an agency operating in the United States and lobbying congressional representatives and federal officials on behalf of Puerto Rico. My research focuses on the formation of Puerto Rican farmworkers within the complex fields of power in which U.S. colonialism made it possible to harness their labor (Mintz 1998; Narotzky and Smith 2006; Roseberry 1994, 2002; Wolf 2001).

One goal of this book is to expose how Puerto Ricans became part of the economic and political forces linked both to the demands of U.S. farming and to colonialism in Puerto Rico. Using historical anthropology rooted in the study of power and state formation, I trace the specific ways power has shaped the formation of Puerto Ricans as particular social subjects within U.S. farm labor. In analyzing how political and economic changes in Puerto Rico and the United States affected migrant farm labor and the development of the FLP, this case study illuminates the intersection and consequences of economic development and migration policies. The study of Puerto Rican farmworkers, especially how immigration policies, colonialism, and attempts to manage labor migration regimes shaped farm labor, offers a unique opportunity to understand the relationship of U.S. colonialism and citizenship to immigration and deportation policies, as well as to guest-worker programs.

### THEORIZING PUERTO RICAN FARM-LABOR MIGRATION

The intersection of the study of fields of power with the literature on colonialism and labor migration, citizenship, and immigration provides an important lens for analyzing Puerto Rican farm-labor migration that the dominant paradigms used to study Puerto Rican migration cannot provide. Therefore, this book privileges an anthropological political economy approach to the study of the history of migrant farmworkers to reveal how social forces shaped the options and action of farmers, officials, and migrant workers (Roseberry 2002; Wolf 2001; see also Foucault 1982; Narotzky and Smith 2006).

#### Colonialism and Labor Migration

In discussing colonialism I draw on Eric Wolf's concept of structural power, which "not only operates within settings or domains but . . . also organizes and orchestrates the settings themselves, and . . . specifies the distribution and direction of energy flows" (2001, 384). Specific U.S. colonial policies, legal decisions, and actions transformed migrants' field of action by incorporating them into the U.S. labor market. In turn, migration expanded the occupational, political, social, and educational opportunities for a population suffering economic distress. But, while the U.S. government developed public policies to manage the migration and employment of Puerto Rican agricultural workers by incorporating them into U.S. internal migration, and thereby into the U.S. labor market, agricultural employers preferred cheaper foreign labor (Pagán de Colón 1956a).

One of the pioneer works on Puerto Rican migration is *Labor Migration under Capitalism* (History Task Force 1979), a book that opened the door for political economy analyses of migration to the United States by discussing the role of colonialism and migration in the development of capitalism in Puerto Rico and the emergence of stateside communities. One of the limitations of this book, however, was its concentration on economic processes, which marginalized the place of state formation in Puerto Rico's development as a modern colony. This oversight is critical, because colonial migration and its role in the construction of a U.S farm labor force also emerged from processes of state formation.

In Puerto Rican studies, the work of José Cruz (1998) and Carmen Teresa Whalen (2001) proposes a similar approach but considers political economy within the study of colonialism and citizenship. As to why Puerto Ricans migrated to the States, Cruz argues,

> economic pull was matched not just by sources of information but by a favorable legal and political context created by the state. . . . Colonialism and capitalism and economics and politics provided the conditions that made migration possible, but individual Puerto Ricans, with help from institutional actors, such as Puerto Rico's Department of Labor, the U.S. Employment Service, and representatives of interested corporations, made the decisions to come. . . . All took the promise of American citizenship seriously, hoping that Americans on the mainland would welcome them as equals. (1998, 3–4)

While some scholars of Puerto Rican migration ignored Cruz's insightful analysis of the role of state institutions in migration, Whalen observed that federal and local policies shaped economic changes and promoted migration, intertwining the economic and political causes of migration, such that migrating in search of work became a survival strategy (2001, 4). Crucially, Whalen points not only to structural forces but to their interplay with migrants' agency (see also Grosfoguel 2003).

Understanding how Puerto Ricans migrated involves studying the role of government officials who sought to modernize the country. It also requires considering the role of several federal and Puerto Rican government agencies in contracting, transporting, and overseeing workers; negotiating with employers; and dealing with the diverse responses of local communities. The study of farmworkers thus demands examination of colonialism as a process for incorporating Puerto Ricans into the U.S. labor market and its implications for their fields of action.

### Constructing Puerto Rican Farmworkers

Although Puerto Ricans are U.S. citizens, like other colonial subjects they cross visible colonial, linguistic, ethnic, and cultural borders when migrating stateside (Duany 2002; Grosfoguel 2003; G. Pérez 2004). Migrants encountered these borders in a world that consisted mostly of labor camps, fields, and small towns. These new spaces contributed to classifying Puerto Ricans as desirable or undesirable subjects for U.S. farm labor. While noncontract workers could live in labor camps or rented rooms in towns surrounding the fields, contract workers were usually consigned to labor camps, which, for most, represented the center of their lives in the United States.

The formation of Puerto Rican farm labor depended on employers' control of production, state policing of borders, and regulation of recruitment, as well as workers' consciousness, common sense, ideologies, *habitus,* and culture, which together reproduce forms of control (Binford 2009). U.S farms that use migrant labor still rely on systems of recruitment for low-wage workers based on complex relationships of capital, the state, and migrants' households and communities (Griffith 1993). To understand these forces in the case of Puerto Ricans involves studying the processes and technologies devised by farmers, the government of Puerto Rico, and federal agencies to entice workers to migrate and then maintain them as an available labor force. Puerto Ricans experience, discuss, and act on their migration with reference to how they perceive their working and living conditions and wages abroad in relation to those at home (Binford 2009). Their home communities subsidize periods of unemployment and illness through wage or nonwage income activities, such as odd jobs, cultivation of crops, fishing, and small family enterprises. These activities relieve employers of paying living wages, sustain households during shorts periods of unemployment, and provide forms of health insurance and pension funds (Griffith 1993, 6, 43, 225), contributing to the construction of a domestic low-wage labor market for U.S. farms.

The status of Puerto Rico as a U.S. colonial territory also reveals how citizenship shapes the similarities and differences between the migration of Puerto Rican farmworkers and other migrants. With U.S. citizenship, migration became a viable alternative for Puerto Ricans to surmount their working and living conditions, while enabling U.S. employers to access and mobilize a labor force from other regions. In this regard, Puerto Ricans share experiences of struggle with other colonial migrant laborers who have endured policies of colonialism and imperialism while undergoing massive migration from their homelands to their metropolitan countries: Filipinos in the United States, Algerians in France, Koreans in Japan, and Caribbean colonial migrants in the United Kingdom, France, and the Netherlands (Bender and Lipman 2015; González 2006; Grosfoguel 2003; Guerin-Gonzales 1994; Hahamovitch 2011; Plascencia 2018; Mitchell 2012; Ngai 2004; Valdés 1991). Moving thousands of workers for temporary jobs, the United States and other imperial powers shaped a global economy connecting their possessions in the Caribbean, Africa, Asia, and the Pacific (see also Casey 2017; Giovannetti-Torres 2018). Nevertheless, migrant workers also defied colonial and imperialistic plans while managing to benefit from wages.

From the 1940s to the 1960s, Puerto Rican workers experienced an array of government policies that sought to plan and control their labor. In the late 1940s the government of Puerto Rico concocted a series of strategies designed to transform a mostly landless, rural, and agrarian population into urban workers for the manufacturing sector through land distribution and industrial manufacturing. Colonial officials were unable to provide enough employment, however, so they devised neo-Malthusian population-control policies—including migration—as the solution to underdevelopment and unemployment. One effect was the continuous migration of Puerto Ricans as farmworkers.

The colonial relationship of Puerto Rico to the United States facilitated the government of Puerto Rico's presence in stateside Puerto Rican communities. The BEM, and later the MD, administered the FLP, setting the tone for the elaboration of policies and the establishment of relationships among farmworkers, local officials, and residents of farm communities. The BEM, the MD and the FLP are examples of state institutions seeking to improve social and economic conditions among subalterns. Using Tania

Murray Li's (2005) concept of the will to improve, I consider the FLP as one of the state tools of development that launched processes unimagined by the officials involved in its creation. Puerto Rican migration to U.S. farms depended on political economic conditions in the United States and Puerto Rico, as well as the emergence of a new colonial state in Puerto Rico.

The creation of the FLP is part of the history of the formation of U.S. agrarian-labor regimes. Employment of Puerto Ricans in agriculture depended greatly on their citizenship status within the U.S. nation. From 1899 to 1917, as U.S. nationals but not citizens, Puerto Ricans migrated to other U.S. territories such as Hawaii and the Panama Canal Zone. The onset of naturalized U.S. citizenship in 1917 facilitated the recruitment of Puerto Ricans for work stateside but also began to mark their undesirability because they lacked deportability status. This issue still plagues Puerto Rican migrants.

### The Modern Colonial State

Between 1941 and 1952 Puerto Rico experienced a process of social, economic, and political transformation into a modern colony. World War II and the Cold War created a consensus among federal government agencies that sought to grant autonomy to the government of Puerto Rico while further incorporating Puerto Ricans into U.S. domestic and foreign policy (García-Colón 2009). By 1941 Puerto Ricans' status as "native-born" citizens intensified lobbying efforts by colonial-government officials for inclusion in the wartime effort to maintain agricultural production (Venator Santiago 2013). The new colonial government of Puerto Rico took advantage of this climate of labor demand. The PPD, with its populist and social democratic ideology, controlled the local legislature, while Roosevelt appointee Rexford G. Tugwell, one of the most radical New Dealers, led the executive branch. Working together, they began a project of modernization, government reform, and intense bureaucratic planning, focusing on child labor, minimum-wage laws, and the plight of poor rural laborers.

U.S. colonialism allowed Puerto Rican officials to directly lobby the federal government. When the federal government sought to bring Mexican, Canadian, Bahamian, and West Indian guest workers, North American governors in Puerto Rico, such as Tugwell (1941–46), sought to persuade the federal government to use Puerto Rican workers in other parts of the United States. Colonial officials collaborated with their federal counterparts by overseeing the hiring, transportation, and performance of migrant farmworkers.

The successful insertion of Puerto Rico's officials into the sphere of the federal government illustrates a distinctive feature of modern colonialism.

The reform trends in Puerto Rico were part of global changes in the western European and U.S. empires that led to modern colony formation. Colonial administrations organized or fostered the migration of colonial subjects, mostly unskilled workers from rural areas serving a labor market that offered them low-wage jobs at the core of the capitalist economies during the postwar economic boom. Modern colonies provide their citizens with democratic and civil rights, while the metropolitan governments provide large transfers of funds for welfare, loans, and credit. Modern colonial subjects usually earn higher wages than their counterparts in postcolonial countries, and, in addition to working under modern protective labor laws and regulations, they have easy access to mass consumption of manufactured goods (Grosfoguel 2003, 178, 180; Pierre-Charles 1979). Migrants from modern colonies share the citizenship of the metropolitan population and enjoy free mobility within their respective empires. Managing the migration of these subjects became an integral part of modern colonialism, and a constellation of policies and regulations aimed to organize the labor supply for employers claiming labor shortages.

At the end of World War II, as most colonial powers began to concede self-rule to their subjects, U.S. political reforms in Puerto Rico initiated an intense process of state formation that turned the colony into a laboratory for U.S. modernization policies. In 1946 the PPD gained control of the executive branch when President Harry S. Truman appointed Jesús T. Piñero as governor. In 1948 Puerto Ricans elected the PPD leader Luis Muñoz Marín as governor, and the U.S. Congress allowed the drafting of a constitution. During this period of intense colonial state formation, the PPD expanded its industrialization and land-reform programs and began to aggressively tackle population control, initiatives viewed as key to spurring development.

Facilitating farm-labor migration meant reducing the population and unemployment on the islands as well increasing the political power and influence of Puerto Rico's government officials in the States. The Mexican Bracero Program and the British West Indian Temporary Alien Program offered Puerto Rican officials excellent examples of labor migration, but they could also draw on their own history: Puerto Ricans had been moving to continental United States in increasing numbers since the 1930s.

In the postwar period, because Puerto Ricans were migrating in response to labor demands on the States, their recruitment by private and public agents gave government officials an ideal way to eliminate surplus population on the islands. But migration had unexpected consequences, as migrants encountered problematic work and living conditions. By 1946 negative news from migrants recruited for stateside farm labor prompted a visit to the camps that housed them by the Puerto Rican secretary of labor, who recommended that the government of Puerto Rico organize the recruitment of agricultural workers. In this context the government established the BEM, the MD, and the FLP, but discrimination against Puerto Rican migrants because of their "foreignness" continued, despite their U.S. "native-born" citizenship status.

The history of Puerto Rican farmworkers shows that U.S. agriculture has developed a labor regime in which the perfect worker is an immigrant whom authorities can deport. Puerto Rican farm laborers are thus imperfect for employers because their U.S. citizenship grants them rights. But one cannot explain fully how citizenship, race, and immigration policies shaped Puerto Rican farm-labor migration without understanding modern colonialism. Because of the colonial relationship, Puerto Rican officials could position the FLP within the implementation of U.S. labor and immigration laws. The eventual demise of the FLP, however, shows that Puerto Ricans, as distinctive U.S. citizens and colonial subjects, occupy a nebulous position between other U.S. minority workers and immigrants within the modern agrarian-labor regime.

## PICKING UP THE FRAGMENTS
### AT THE HEART OF EMPIRE

Researching the local history of western New York, I was frustrated about the invisibility of Puerto Ricans. I found only one reference to Puerto Rican farmworkers, in *History of Erie County, 1870–1970*, by Walter S. Dunn (1972). Dunn chronicles how immigrants and, later, Puerto Ricans solved the problems of labor shortage in the agricultural sector of Erie County, at the same time revealing his distaste for Puerto Ricans even while recognizing that other U.S. citizens did not want to accept farmwork.

For Dunn, Italian and Polish immigrants won their place in the community through their years of hard work. Their determination led them to ownership of their own farms and to membership in the community, while Puerto Ricans, in contrast, were the last and, it seems, least desirable resort for maintaining agricultural production. Dunn portrays farmers as benevolent employers who improved living conditions in the camps and complains about politicians' involvement in improving those conditions. His reference to Puerto Ricans offers a brief glimpse into how local communities rendered migrants as inconvenient necessities for the harvest (1972, 215).

*Colonial Migrants at the Heart of Empire* is part of my effort to document how government policies formed and transformed the lives of Puerto Rican agricultural workers in Puerto Rico as well as in the United States. This interest arises from my previous experience researching the impact of land reform in Puerto Rico on landless workers. Many of the interviewees for my first book, *Land Reform in Puerto Rico,* were former migrant farmworkers, which led me to analyze the impact of land distribution on migratory labor. My research has also been profoundly shaped by my experiences growing up in working-class rural Puerto Rico and by my relatives' experiences as migrant farmworkers.

Different from other studies on Puerto Rican farmworkers, this book uses ethnographic and extensive archival research to situate Puerto Ricans within global labor migration. I carried out interviews among former and current farmworkers and community organizers in New York, New Jersey, and Puerto Rico, some of whom began migrating as early as the late 1950s. My interviews document farmworkers' relationships with non–Puerto Ricans, incidents of unequal treatment, and the government's role in their migration. Conversations with farmers, supervisors, and officials illuminated labor practices, the history of agriculture, and attempts to manage labor migration.

The ethnographic research took place in Cidra, Puerto Rico, from 1993 to 1999 and in 2009 and in New Jersey and New York during the summers of 2007 and 2013. I interviewed current and former migrants and labor organizers. Research at the National Archives, the New York State Archives, the New Jersey State Archives, Cornell University, the Archivo General de Puerto Rico, Archivo Luis Muñoz Marín, the University of Puerto Rico, and the Center for Puerto Rican Studies yielded data about cooperation and conflicts between federal and state agencies and the Puerto Rican government from the 1940s to the 1990s and information on workers' claims, farmers' practices, disputes, changes in migration policies, and the formation of stateside communities. To my knowledge most scholars of Puerto Rican migration have not previously used a combination of these vast and rich sources.

*Colonial Migrants at the Heart of Empire* consists of two parts. In this introduction I lay out the conceptual framework of the book, which offers a way to understand modern colonialism as embodying state formation as well as the center-periphery, empire-colony kind of relationships that scholars generally think about. In introducing state formation in a colonial context, I am adding a new dimension to how scholars must think about colonialism in the present—and in the past. By drawing on the voices of government officials, part 1 explores this dimension in detail by explaining the administrative and legal processes and outcomes from 1898 through the 1940s that induced attempts to manage labor migration. Chapter 1 addresses the rise of guest work and colonial labor migration, U.S. colonialism, New Deal interventions in the labor market, and the emergence of contract migration. In chapter 2, I explore the emergence of the Puerto Rico Department of Labor, especially the BEM, the MD, and the FLP. Chapter 3 chronicles the implementation of the FLP in the 1950s, when the U.S. government incorporated Puerto Rico into the mandate of federal agencies. Colonial state formation entailed granting citizenship to Puerto Ricans while advancing efforts to address the social conditions in Puerto Rico, and it placed limits on how much those efforts could accomplish.

Migrant farmworkers came from a colonial society experiencing deep transformations that facilitated or disallowed certain relationships with U.S. officials, farmers, and the inhabitants of rural farming areas. Part 2 deals with the development of the FLP and the experiences of migrant workers. Based mostly on migrants' accounts, it explores how their experiences and the Puerto Rican government's attempts to manage those experiences reveal what is new about modern colonialism: that colonial entities have more agency than perhaps was previously assumed, even though that agency is limited by the unequal power relationship between metropolis and colony. Puerto Rican and colonial officials exercised remarkable agency, but in contradictory fields of power embedded in social, political, and economic assumptions about colonial peoples. Chapter 4 describes the process of migration and the labor conditions migrants encountered. Chapter 5 concerns workers' lives in the labor camps.

The end of the Bracero Program in 1964 and the vibrant civil rights movement drastically transformed Puerto Rican migration. Chapter 6 examines the settlement of farmworkers in towns and cities and the government of Puerto Rico's attempts to foster community participation during the tumultuous 1960s. Concentrating on the 1970s and 1980s, chapter 7 focuses on community leaders' attempts to organize farmworkers, apple growers' legal challenges to the preference for Puerto Rican workers, and the eventual demise of the FLP. Part 2 reveals not just the conditions that migrant workers faced but also how, from the late 1940s to the early 1990s, the Puerto Rican government maneuvered within the field of power it helped create to protect and advance workers' interests while having to accept the limitations imposed by colonialism. The epilogue concludes by analyzing migrants' current situation in relation to the long history of Puerto Rican labor migration.

This book documents an important aspect of the U.S. history of domestic farm-labor recruitment and its relationship to colonialism, citizenship, and immigration policies. My focus on the history of the FLP illustrates the challenges officials faced as they promoted migration within existing discourses of desirability and undesirability of specific workers within U.S. farm labor. The case of Puerto Ricans—distinctive U.S. citizens—is important because it exposes the effects of U.S. immigration policies and their relationship to colonial migration. This book also contributes to an understanding of Puerto Rican migration and the inequalities resulting from the intersection of the government of Puerto Rico's development policies with U.S. legal, sociocultural, and economic structures, the citizenship of Puerto Ricans notwithstanding.

# PART ONE

# The Formation of Agrarian Labor Regimes

# ONE

# The Making of
## Colonial Migrant Farmworkers

PUERTO RICAN FARMWORKERS are both expendable and disposable: expendable because they can be replaced with guest and undocumented workers and disposable because their U.S. citizenship does not protect them from discrimination in an industry that takes advantage of immigrants (Sider 2014). Some farmers still hire them because their precarious lives as migrants make them a legal, compliant, low-wage labor force, but many farmers resist hiring them because they refuse to perform tasks perceived by them as unfair or a form of extreme exploitation. This expendability and disposability are illustrated by the perceptions and feelings of a group of workers whom I met while identifying labor camps in the summer of 2010. Living in a small camp that housed no more than five migrants, these workers complained about feeling isolated and of their lack of access to health care in southern New Jersey and at home in Puerto Rico. While Mexican workers were visited by a local health clinic program in a nearby camp, they were denied services in the local hospital because they were not residents of New Jersey. One of them told us, "Even though we are citizens, they [government agencies and organizations] have abandoned us." Puerto Rican farmworkers still confront many obstacles to access basic government services.

Despite their U.S. citizenship, Puerto Ricans continue to be regarded by the mainstream society and even at times by federal and state officials as "alien citizens," or U.S.-born citizens who are somehow foreign (Ngai 2004, 2). Thus, their experience as migrant farmworkers has been much like that of Chicano, Filipino, Native American, and African American migrants whom local populations considered unassimilable foreigners, even if they were U.S. citizens or nationals. Their place in farm labor is the product of more than a century of forces shaping colonialism and U.S. agriculture.

To place Puerto Rican farm labor within the history of colonial labor migrations around the globe, this chapter examines the politics of empire and colonialism in the United States during the late nineteenth and early twentieth centuries. The Spanish-American War, World War I, immigration policies shaped by nativist fears, and the New Deal all fostered Puerto Rican migration to the United States. The U.S. federal government and the government of Puerto Rico elaborated programs and policies based on how officials understood why rural populations suffered poverty *and* what best served farmers' interests. Most studies of Puerto Rican migration mention these factors but do not explain how they encouraged farm-labor migration. I argue that imperialism and colonialism were and still are important forces shaping seasonal migration. They constructed a labor market that Puerto Ricans joined after the Spanish-American War as a result of U.S. economic and politicomilitary interests.

## THE RISE OF GUEST WORK
## AND COLONIAL MIGRATION

The origin of today's farm labor force lies in the emergence of contract farm labor during World War I, when U.S. colonial and neocolonial policies toward Mexico, the British Caribbean, the Philippines, and Puerto Rico facilitated the migration of thousands of workers. International convention required that U.S. officials admit colonial subjects into the country without restrictions (Baldoz 2011), but colonialist discourses shaped specific policies and practices, as did institutions, social actors, and interest groups with a stake in the implementation of new labor regimes. U.S. colonial policies, legal decisions, and actions transformed migrants' field of action by incorporating them into the U.S. labor market.

The United States gained prominence as an imperial world power with its victory in the Spanish-American War of 1898. As payment for the war, Spain ceded its jurisdiction over Cuba, the Philippines, Puerto Rico, and Guam to the United States. These new territories and the annexation of Hawaii incorporated millions of subjects into the new U.S. empire. Almost immediately, a public debate emerged about whether these new subjects should gain citizenship. According to Rick Baldoz, the acquisition of colonies "heightened anxieties about race and nationality" (2011, 11). In Congress some members, such as white supremacist Benjamin Tillman, cautioned that the influx of "inferior races" could dilute American Anglo-Saxon cultural and racial superiority (*Congressional Record* 1900, 3211). The U.S. Supreme Court, in *Downes v. Bidwell* (1901), decided that the status of colonial subjects and territories would be determined by Congress, which, from 1900 to 1948, debated several proposals and enacted legislation to this end (Baldoz 2011).[1]

Debates about new colonial subjects were also shaped by the regulation of contract-labor migration, which in turn reflected a climate of nativism and racism. The history of modern contract farm-labor migration began in the nineteenth century with the immigration of Asians and eastern Europeans to the United States, western European countries and their colonies, and Latin America after the abolition of the African slave trade forced plantation owners to find new sources of labor (Hahamovitch 2011; Jung 2006; Ngai 2004). Hiring immigrants allowed employers to control other workers, keep wages low, and lower the costs of social reproduction. Hence, the British imported indentured Indians for their sugar plantations in the Caribbean and mines in South Africa. The Spanish Caribbean and Latin American countries and the United States contracted Chinese workers. Puerto Ricans began migrating to the Dominican Republic, Venezuela, Panama, and Cuba in the 1870s, during the early postabolition years in the Caribbean, which were also the last decades of Spanish domination (History Task Force 1979).

During the transition from slavery to free labor, perceptions about immigrant labor transformed U.S. racial, class, and national identities (Jung 2006). Fear of "alien" races invading and changing the racial makeup of the United States influenced public opinion about labor migration. The Contract Labor Act of 1864 sought to facilitate immigration, but the Chinese Exclusion Act of 1882 and the Alien Contract Labor Law of 1885 repealed it and became obstacles to labor migration.[2] As a reaction to nativism and racism, both statutes restricted and regulated the hiring and transportation of foreign labor.

Between the 1870s and 1920s, an understanding of citizenship emerged based on the idea of membership in a nation-state that claimed an ethnically and racially homogenous population, and this in turn required the codification of immigration for temporary capitalist labor needs rather than permanent settlement. Western European countries and the United States began increasingly to define citizenship in terms of common descent. In the United States, being white, Anglo-Saxon, and Protestant encompassed the dominant definition of nationality and, hence, U.S. citizenship. In the early twentieth century, U.S. state and federal governments reinforced the legal requirement of whiteness as a precondition for naturalization. Immigrants considered white could presumably assimilate and become full and first-class U.S. citizens. Nonwhites, particularly Asians, were excluded from citizenship, while Mexicans and eastern and southern Europeans were regarded with suspicion but accepted. Between World Wars I and II, nativism and eugenics entrenched the notion of ethnic and racial citizenship in the United States and Germany, the only countries whose dominant definitions of citizenship and naturalization were based on whiteness (Fahrmeir 2007; Haney López 1996; R. Smith 1997). Under pressure from nativists and immigration restrictionists, governments began to devise guest-worker programs as an alternative to the permanent immigration of "undesirable subjects." Prussia, under the German Empire, recruited Poles; Australia imported Pacific Islanders; and the French contracted Algerians. South African mining companies began to hire seasonal workers from overseas and other African countries. Today's guest-worker programs and other forms of seasonal migrant farm labor persist between slavery and freedom in part because of these earlier restrictive immigration regimes (González 2006; Hahamovitch 2011, 14–17; Lee 2003; Martínez 1996).

The rise of ethnic and racial citizenship, together with nationalism, fostered new practices of state formation that shaped the development of domestic and migrant labor markets. The expansion of citizens' privileges, such as unemployment insurance and welfare benefits, coincided with the increased regulation of migrants, seen in the development of passports, work permits, birth certificates, visas, and other documents to prove eligibility to work in the United States.[3] These regulations, in effect, constituted the scientific management of migration to control racial purity, crime, and disease. Governments designed guest-worker programs that provided employers access to a seasonal, docile, and low-wage labor force underpinned by the threat of deportation (Burawoy 1985; Fahrmeir 2007; Hahamovitch 2011). As the category of illegal alien took center stage, guest-worker programs pretended to protect the privileges of ethnic and racial citizenship while serving employers' interests (De Genova and Peutz 2010; Ngai 2004).

In the early twentieth century, colonial governments began to transport and oversee the migration of their subjects to the metropolitan countries. For example, a 1915 law enacted by the government of the Philippines established a system to license labor brokers, requiring them to pay for an annual license and fees for each province where they recruited workers and to provide free return transportation at the end of a worker's contract or in case of physical incapacity.

The law also allowed the appointment of commissioners working outside the Philippines to ensure the enforcement of contracts and placed the supervision of contracts under the director of labor (Lasker 1969, 175, 207, 392–93).

Elsewhere, colonial powers directly carried out efforts to contract and transport workers. In 1916 the French deployed Algerian migrants through the Service for the Organization of Colonial Travelers (Service de l'Organisation des Travailleurs Coloniaux), under the Ministry of War, and guaranteed fair wages, housing, and working conditions for migrants. French officials in Algerian communes organized the recruitment and transportation of men to France, grouped into militarized labor units under the command of French army officers. After 1928 the Services of Surveillance, Protection, and Assistance to Indigenous North Africans (Services de Surveillance, Protection et Assistance des Indigènes Nord-Africains) was charged with overseeing colonial migrants in France (MacMaster 1997, 61–62, 153–69).

Colonial migration arose from the interests of imperialists but was also shaped by nativist and racist anxieties. Because of their condition and "privileges" as colonial subjects or outright second-class citizens, Puerto Rican and Filipino colonial migrants to the United States, together with U.S.-born African Americans, Native Americans, and Chicanos, came to occupy a marginal category in farm labor, excluded from or included in recruitment efforts depending on how agricultural interests could maneuver to maintain low labor costs. The temporary migration of U.S. colonial subjects thus became an alternative to foreign agricultural labor that nativists could not legally oppose. The rise of the modern nation-state, however, also led to gate-keeping or deportation regimes in the United States and western Europe that shaped the lives not only of immigrants and citizens but also of colonial subjects occupying an in-between space (Lee 2003; Torpey 2000). In this context Puerto Ricans laborers began to be viewed in the United States as "alien citizens" (Ngai 2004). Their right to stay rendered them undesirable to farmers who preferred deportable guest workers.

Labor organizing threatened agricultural interests. In 1913, after workers being organized by the International Workers of the World (IWW) complained about living conditions at the labor camp of the Durst Brothers Ranch in Wheatland, California, a riot erupted, leaving growers fearful of labor organizing among farmworkers, many of whom were immigrants. The protest spun out of control after Ralph Durst made a false complaint about rioting. Deputies arrived at the camp and found workers singing and their IWW leader, Richard "Blackie" Ford, making a speech. When one of the deputies fired a shot into the air, a worker described by authorities and the press as a "negro Porto Rican" grabbed his gun, killing him and the district attorney. The Puerto Rican and an English worker were both killed by deputies, and many others were injured in what became known as the Wheatland Hop Riot.

Despite the killing of workers and jailing of their leaders, the IWW increased its membership in California after the riots. The government and growers responded with both progressive and repressive measures to counteract labor organizing and, during World War I, confronted the militancy of IWW organized labor (Daniel 1982; McWilliams [1939] 1999; Mitchell 1996; Parker and Parker 1920, 192–93). The California Growers Exchange lobbied federal officials to relax immigration policy for foreign workers. Since nativist fears had defeated the possibilities of obtaining Chinese workers, some growers proposed hiring Mexicans and West Indians (Daniel 1982, 66–67; González 1994, 27–28; McWilliams [1939] 1999, 124–30; Scruggs 1960).

## THE CITIZENSHIP OF PUERTO RICANS

The formation of Puerto Rico as a U.S. colony fostered the integration of its peripheral labor market to the national labor market in ways that differed from the international norm of granting colonial subjects free movement within an empire's borders. U.S. colonial gatekeeping practices made possible  the construction of what Ramón Grosfoguel (2003) calls a "migratory field" between Puerto Rico and the United States, a colonial vestige that persists even in the so-called postcolonial world. Ingrained in global economic forces supported by the United States, colonial labor migration became an extension of Puerto Rico's economy.

Seeking to circumvent immigration policies, U.S. growers began to recruit colonial workers, as the British had done in the Caribbean and the French in Algeria. Indeed, Puerto Rican migration to the United States offers striking similarities to Algerian migration to France in the early twentieth century, but it also reveals that migration in the context of colonialism and imperialism is not simply the top-down process described by Gilbert González (2006; see also MacMaster 1997). In 1898 Puerto Ricans became U.S. nationals with limited rights and protections, and specific colonial policies, legal decisions, and actions elaborated by U.S. officials impacted their incorporation into the national labor market and transformed their field of action. As U.S. colonial domination opened the stateside labor market for workers to find jobs and for employers to access a cheap labor force, migration became a viable alternative for workers to surmount their working and living conditions.

In 1900 U.S. Congress passed the Foraker Act, providing a civil government to Puerto Rico. Although Senator Joseph B. Foraker included in his draft bill a provision granting U.S. citizenship to Puerto Ricans, and some U.S. officials supported U.S. citizenship for them, opposition was strong in Congress. Senator Foraker abandoned his efforts, bowing to the misgivings and racist and nativist views of other members of Congress who believed that the new colonial subjects were not fit for citizenship and feared extending it to people who might become migrant workers. The Foraker Act reaffirmed article 9 of the Treaty of Paris, which had settled the Spanish-American War, by establishing Puerto Rican—but not U.S.—citizenship. By creating a Puerto Rican citizenship, Congress created a colonial citizenship, as the Foraker Act did not clarify the status of Puerto Ricans who might migrate to the United States (Baldoz 2011; Burnett 2009; Trías Monge 1997; Venator Santiago 2013).[4]

That the colonialism embedded in the attitudes underpinning the Foraker Act confused many U.S. officials is illustrated by the case of Jorge Cruz, a twenty-five-year-old Puerto Rican who had been hired by the *New York Herald* newspaper and detained by immigration officials at Ellis Island in 1900. The secretary of the treasury, Lyman J. Gage, intervened, allowing Cruz to land, subject to deportation at any time within one year, but the commissioner of immigration, Thomas Fitchie, sued the *New York Herald* for $1,000 for violating labor contract laws. Being subject to U.S. jurisdiction, Cruz countersued the commissioner in the U.S. Circuit Court for imprisonment in violation of the Fifth Amendment to the U.S. Constitution, seeking damages of $50,000 (A. Johnson 1901, 260–63; *New York Times* 1900; U.S. Senate 1900a, 2; 1900b).

The Cruz case reveals the dilemma that the acquisition of new territories with nonwhite populations created for the U.S. government. Cruz arrived before the United States had passed the Foraker Act, and the U.S. administration handled his case as an isolated incident in which an employer violated alien-contract labor laws. Cruz also arrived before the first Puerto Rican resident commissioner, Federico Degetau, took office. Degetau, a Republican and supporter of statehood for Puerto Rico, had been involved in earlier cases brought before the U.S. Supreme Court that defined the status of the new U.S. colonial territories. Through what scholars refer to as the Insular Cases, the court defined the political relationship of Puerto Rico and Puerto Ricans to the United States. Thus, in *Downes v. Bidwell,* Puerto Rico became "foreign in the domestic sense," meaning that it was a nonincorporated territory treated as "not part" of the United States in terms of domestic policies and the application of the Constitution. U.S. laws did not automatically apply in Puerto Rico, opening a space for the exceptions in the interpretation of citizenship rights for colonial subjects. *Downes v. Bidwell* did not curtail the entry of Puerto Ricans to the United States. Rather, Puerto Ricans became "American aliens" who could apply individually for naturalization, which required, contradictorily, renunciation of allegiance to a sovereign, which in this case was the United States (Burnett 2009; Coudert 1903; Erman 2008, 2010, 2014; Meléndez 2013, 2017; Trías Monge 1997; Venator Santiago 2013).[5]

To confuse matters further, U.S. policy dictated that when outside the United States, colonial subjects would be considered U.S. citizens and carry U.S. passports (Schlimgen 2010). The ambiguous status of Puerto Ricans caused problems for federal officials and for Puerto Rican businessmen, who found it difficult to travel for commercial purposes. Responding to a Department of State request, in 1902 Congress passed the Insular Passport Act, which authorized the issuance of special passports to Puerto Rican citizens, recognizing their U.S. nationality without U.S. citizenship (Van Dyne 1904, 229; Venator Santiago 2013, 62–63).

The Insular Cases decision that would define the legal standing of Puerto Ricans for immigration purposes was *Gonzales v. Williams*.[6] Before 1902 the U.S. government attempted to control the entrance of Puerto Ricans and Filipinos by extending the 1891 immigration law barring "aliens by birth and race" (Meléndez 2017, 14–15). When Isabel González, a pregnant Puerto Rican woman, was denied entry and detained by immigration authorities in New York, Resident Commissioner Degetau filed a brief on her behalf, arguing that Puerto Ricans were already U.S. citizens:

> It is an accepted principle in international law that the nationality of a person follows the nationality of the territory in which such person is born; the word nationality from the Latin word *nascor* (to be born) being self-explanatory, . . . I cannot conceive how a native of a Territory of the United States because he is "a citizen" of said Territory and "as such (as such a citizen) is an American" can be at the same time "not a citizen of the United States." (Degetau y González 1903, 32–33)

Degetau sought to radically extend the intentions of the U.S. government by challenging the assumption that Puerto Ricans under U.S. sovereignty were aliens (Coudert 1903; Meléndez 2013). *Gonzales v. Williams* was a landmark case, establishing that colonial subjects from the new insular possessions were "American nationals" who could migrate freely within the U.S. states, territories, and colonial possessions. But the court's decision established that, while Puerto Ricans and other colonial migrants were not "aliens," they were also not U.S. citizens (Burnett 2008, 2009; Erman 2008). At the same time the U.S. government enacted laws restricting the entrance of foreigners into its colonial territories (Baldoz 2011).

In 1906, after Congress passed the Bureau of Immigration and Naturalization Act, Puerto Ricans could apply for naturalization after residing for two years in a state or U.S. incorporated territory (Venator Santiago 2013). In 1915 a federal judge ruled in *In Re Giralde* that the act of 1906 defined Puerto Rican citizens as white aliens able to naturalize.[7] By considering Puerto Ricans as U.S. nationals and allowing their individual naturalization, Congress facilitated their incorporation into the U.S. labor market. The status of U.S. nationals also underscored Puerto Ricans' lower position in the legal hierarchy of membership in the U.S. empire (Burnett 2009, 333; Venator Santiago 2017, 46).

In this legal context the emergence of the U.S. empire spurred the migration of colonial subjects within its territories. Better modes of transportation and new trade networks within the States and with its colonial possessions facilitated low-cost travel for peoples across the world. Filipinos and Puerto Ricans who migrated within the empire became part of a flexible labor force needed by U.S. agricultural interests in Hawaii, Cuba (at that time a U.S. protectorate), and the southwestern United States. Colonial labor migration began to replace other flows of migrant workers from Asia, creating an alternative, lower-cost labor force for U.S. agriculture (Baldoz 2011, 45).

The aftermath of the Spanish-American War left most of the population in dire poverty and starvation, as the closing of the Spanish market to Puerto Rico's coffee, U.S. tariffs on commodities, monetary devaluation, and the devastation caused by Hurricane San Ciriaco in 1899 weakened the territory's economy. Officials believed that migration could expand the occupational, political, social, and educational opportunities of a population suffering economic distress. U.S. occupation thus broadened opportunities for Puerto Ricans to integrate into a larger labor market.

Whatever benefits U.S. government officials believed would ensue from labor migration, the liberal press in Puerto Rico attacked the emigration of agricultural workers, and local planters protested it because they had to compete with the labor recruiters for workers. Still, Gov. Charles H. Allen stressed the need for emigration (History Task Force 1982; see also Rosario Natal 2001). Governor Allen, a Republican businessman and former assistant secretary of the navy, was the first North American civilian appointed as governor of Puerto Rico, on May 1, 1900 (Cabán 1999, 118–21, 154, 163). He was a controversial figure who sided with local Republicans and facilitated the penetration of American sugar corporations in Puerto Rico. His first annual report declared his support for emigration:

> It is the privilege of every person to emigrate if he chooses so to do, either with the hope of bettering his financial condition or finding a more agreeable residence. The humblest peon in the forests of El Yunque has the same right to expatriate himself if he chooses as does the millionaire. . . . If these native emigrants should not return when they are needed other persons will flock in to fill their places. They have not left the sheltering folds of our starry flag, and there are millions more beneath it who can give us all the assistance our circumstances may require now or hereafter. (History Task Force 1982, 15)

Governor Allen viewed the emigration of poor, working people as well as businessmen and professionals as beneficial. Puerto Rico had become part of a new colonial social field of power under—and symbolized by—the U.S. flag. The migration of farmworkers fulfilled the ideas of Manifest Destiny, as colonial and metropolitan frontiers blurred, creating a colonial workforce exported to the continental United States and among its colonial territories (Ngai 2004).

The first large effort to transport Puerto Ricans for farm labor overseas dates from 1900, when workers were contracted to work in the Hawaiian Islands (Beechert 1985; González 2006; Lasker 1969; Ngai 2004; Rosario Natal 2001). Between December 1900 and October 1901, recruiters for the Hawaiian Sugar Producers Association arranged for the migration of eleven different groups of contract workers, some with family members (History Task Force 1979). Accounts of migrants in Hawaii reveal the problems they confronted (Rosario Natal 2001). On December 27, 1901, the *Puerto Rico Herald* published the story of Juan Cancio Martínez, who had escaped from a Hawaiian sugar plantation. His experience in Hawaii was one of exploitation, hunger, and persecution by the police when workers assembled to discuss their problems (cited in History Task Force 1982, 48–50). Control and surveillance, three-year contracts, and plantation owners' refusal to accept workers who had previously worked for other employers limited Puerto

Ricans' mobility and challenged the practices of resistance to exploitation they had learned in Puerto Rico (García-Colón 2006a).

In 1902 a group of Puerto Ricans working on the Pa'auilo sugar plantation, on the island of Hawaii, complained to William H. Hunt, the North American governor of Puerto Rico, about mistreatment by their employers, alleging slave-like living and working conditions and asking for help in arranging their return home:

> We are more than slaves here and we cannot longer resist the savagery that is coming to every one of us Puerto Ricans; they are every day inflicting more barbarities on us. . . . The pay is small; it is not according to what was offered to us before we left Puerto Rico. . . . The store book stands us for half of our day's wage. (History Task Force 1982, 53)

These workers and their families had traveled by boat and train more than 5,700 miles across the Caribbean, continental United States, and the Pacific Ocean to escape unemployment and poor living conditions in Puerto Rico. This distance meant that few ever returned to Puerto Rico.

Migration to Hawaii was not an isolated outcome of U.S. policy. Puerto Ricans migrated in the larger context of the annexation of Hawaii by the United States in 1898 and the effects of the Chinese Exclusion Act of 1882, which included the recruitment of Japanese workers to work on Hawaiian sugarcane plantations. In 1898, however, Japanese workers were on strike during the critical planting and grinding seasons, therefore driving up the wages of field hands from sixty to seventy-six cents a day, a more than 25 percent increase. The arrival of Puerto Ricans reduced Japanese workers' bargaining power and increased the sugar corporations' leverage (Asher and Stephenson 1990; History Task Force 1982; Rosario Natal 2001). Puerto Ricans' in-between status as colonial subjects without U.S. citizenship fit the sugar growers' interests perfectly.

Although Puerto Rican labor migration was not the first of its kind, it was among the first of contracted colonial subjects from one U.S. territory to another. Migrants were also hired to work on the construction of the Panama Canal between 1910 and 1914, but because of the problems Puerto Ricans in Hawaii encountered, migrants to Panama were guaranteed return passage to Puerto Rico. During the first decade of the twentieth century, Puerto Ricans migrated to work in agriculture and mining in Cuba and the Dominican Republic, where there was great demand for workers and the wages paid were double the prevailing wage in Puerto Rico. A 1914 report by Puerto Rico's

Labor Bureau suggested that it was advisable to take small groups of workers to Cuba and Santo Domingo because Puerto Ricans adapted well and could compete with native workers. The report also stressed that workers needed to be protected by contracts to which the government of Puerto Rico could be a party (History Task Force 1979, 1982, 96; Paralitici 2006; Stinson Fernández 1996).

Transporting colonial subjects between the colonies and neighboring Latin American republics was completely different from sending them to the continental United States, if only because of the absence of language barriers and less hostility toward Puerto Rican migrants (Ngai 2004). The migration of contracted Puerto Rican laborers within the U.S. empire occurred because Puerto Ricans had been granted U.S. nationality. Motivated by the demands of World War I, the U.S. Congress had transformed the colonial government of Puerto Rico and modified the legal parameters of Puerto Rican migrants' entrance to the States. On March 2, 1917, Congress passed the Act to Provide a Civil Government for Porto Rico and for Other Purposes, best known as the Jones Act of 1917, which established two legislative bodies, a senate and a house of representatives, elected by residents of Puerto Rico, and gave them a bill of rights but left veto power in the hands of the U.S. president and the territory's governor. The Jones Act also granted naturalized U.S. citizenship to Puerto Ricans, encouraging their recruitment for the war effort, cementing their loyalty, and assuring the permanence of U.S. rule. At this time the U.S. government's fear of an enemy invasion outweighed its doubts about granting the benefits of citizenship to racially unfit colonial subjects (Franqui-Rivera 2013; Sparrow and Lamm 2017).

The U.S. Supreme Court had defined the U.S. citizenship of Puerto Ricans as a kind of second-class citizenship granted to culturally, racially, and linguistically different colonial subjects. But another important case, *Balzac v. People of Porto Rico*, also shaped labor migration by upholding Congress's intention that U.S. colonial subjects could move without any kind of restrictions within the empire's borders, including to the States (Meléndez 2013). U.S. Supreme Court justice William Howard Taft affirmed that the Jones Act of 1917 "enabled [Puerto Ricans] to move into the continental United States and [become] residents of any State [and] there to enjoy every right of any other citizen of the United States, civil, social, and political." He subsequently reiterated that the Jones Act gave Puerto Ricans "an opportunity, should they desire, to move into the United States proper, and there without naturalization to enjoy all political and other rights."[8]

Through the Jones Act the U.S. government imposed collective naturalization on Puerto Ricans with the expectation that they would receive it gratefully. But their U.S. citizenship was partial, because Puerto Rico remained an unincorporated territory of the United States, where U.S. laws did not automatically apply.[9] The U.S. citizenship of Puerto Ricans was thus a colonial one that reaffirmed the doctrines of alien exclusion (Franqui-Rivera 2013; Meléndez 2013; Trías Monge 1997). Moreover, collective naturalization transformed attitudes toward, and the legality of, hiring Puerto Rican workers as migrant laborers in the United States. In the 1920s U.S. citizenship greatly changed how growers' representatives considered Puerto Ricans for the stateside farm-labor market.

FROM WAR TO DEPRESSION

World War I fostered changes in U.S. immigration policies and contract-labor migration. Conscription, together with the decrease of European migration and the expansion of domestic industry as part of the war mobilization, created labor shortages. White and black rural migration from the South to the cities of the northern United States supplied some urban and industrial labor needs but at the expense of labor shortages in agriculture. The U.S. Department of Labor (USDL) responded to complaints about agricultural-labor shortages by creating an exchange system that assigned workers from surplus areas to places with labor scarcity. The USDL also recruited youth and women to alleviate the shortfall. When these measures failed to meet the needs of farmers, the USDL facilitated hiring workers from Mexico, Canada, the Philippines, Cape Verde, Puerto Rico, and the Bahamas and, notably, eased restrictions on Mexican immigration. In 1917 Mexican workers were exempted from the head tax-entry fee and literacy test required of immigrants; in 1924 they were exempted from national quotas. Southwestern employers' need for cheap labor took priority over the interests of nativist and labor groups hoping to restrict Mexican immigration (Falcón and Gilbarg 1994).

War, the shortage of cheap labor, and the U.S. government's gatekeeping practices (including deportation) gave rise to a bureaucracy to control immigrant farm labor and protect and regulate the employment opportunities of citizens. William M. Leserson, a USDL official, toured Europe to study other governments' policies and programs to curb unemployment, and the USDL created U.S. Employment Service (USES) in 1914 to manage labor shortages during World War I. For the first time, the U.S. federal government involved itself directly in creating a migrant-labor contract program. But the USES had a limited scope in setting contracts and planning migration. Private labor recruiters and agribusinesses remained preeminent in hiring and transporting Mexican braceros (Falcón and Gilbarg 1994, 59; Hahamovitch 2011, 19–20).

Viewing unemployment as a structural problem caused by the lack of government intervention in the labor market, USDL officials organized a free public-employment exchange with offices throughout the United States, and the USES's mission expanded to connect workers with jobs in a labor market plagued by a multitude of private employment offices (Breen 1997). These developments in turn influenced how Puerto Rican officials understood the problems of unemployment and poverty in their homeland.

Like his other North American predecessors, Puerto Rico's governor at the time, Arthur Yager, a professor of history and economics and a Democrat, believed that overpopulation was creating the poverty and hunger that had resulted in massive public protests and strikes among agricultural workers (Meléndez Badillo 2015). On October 22, 1915, he wrote that the remedy for these problems was emigration. Later, on April 17, 1917, Gen. Frank McIntyre, chief of the Bureau of Insular Affairs (BIA), indicated to the secretary of war that the permanent solution to the problem of overpopulation was the emigration of Puerto Ricans to the Dominican Republic and the temporary use of workers in agriculture and railroads in the continental United States. McIntyre believed that between fifty thousand and a hundred thousand workers could be transported to the United States. Governor Yager never implemented this plan, and other plans emerged to send workers to plantations in Cuba, while the Guánica Central, a sugar company in Puerto Rico, sent groups of workers to its partner plantation in La Romana, Dominican Republic (History Task Force 1979).

As part of the war effort and because of labor shortages, the U.S. Department of War and its BIA organized the recruitment of about thirteen thousand Puerto Ricans for jobs in the continental United States. This move represented a major shift of labor recruitment from peripheral areas of the empire to the metropolis (History Task Force 1979). In October 1917 the USDL began recruiting Puerto Ricans for war-related industries, assuring them protection and wages of $3.00 for an eight-hour work day, $4.50 for Saturdays, and $6.00 on Sundays. Workers dreamed of manufacturing jobs, but many ended up in agriculture, railroad labor, and military facilities. In

1918 the USES, with the help of local authorities, began to recruit workers from Puerto Rico and the U.S. Virgin Islands, proposing initially to contract and transport fifty thousand men for the war industries (Breen 1997; Marcus 1919; USES 1918b). Governor Yager, joined by some politicians, first opposed labor recruitment but later favored it because of poverty in Puerto Rico. The leadership of the Free Federation of Labor (FLT; Federación Libre de Trabajadores) also favored this initiative, seeing an opportunity to facilitate collective bargaining and jobs for its workers. The business sector, however, opposed emigration because a large labor pool allowed them to maintain low wages and a supply of strikebreakers, the same reasons why North American agricultural interests were seeking to hire migrant laborers. Nevertheless, by July 1918 more than eighteen thousand workers were participating in the program and, while the sometimes-deadly working and living conditions in the stateside labor camps led to problems and complaints, many workers continued in their jobs after the war, until 1919 (Marcus 1919; Marín Román 2009; Rojas, n.d.; USES 1918a, 1918b, 1918c, 1918d, 1918e).

Most workers were sent to the South, living in military camps in Louisiana, North and South Carolina, Arkansas, and Georgia, among other states, but this migration, like the previous ones to Hawaii, was a disaster. In Arkansas ninety-three migrant workers died between October 19, 1918, and February 1, 1919 (History Task Force 1982, 4–5; Rojas, n.d.). After workers complained about harsh living and working conditions, including inadequate food, medical care, housing, salaries, and clothing, the public demanded an investigation. Governor Yager, elected officials, politicians, and labor leaders doubted the success of the program and their decision to support it. When the USDL offered free transportation back to Puerto Rico, many workers returned, while others stayed in the South or migrated to cities, especially New York (Marchán 1918).

U.S. sugar corporations also used Puerto Rican labor in U.S. territories to expand their production and consolidate U.S. interests. After the annexation of the Virgin Islands in 1917, some workers were recruited for Saint Croix, and in 1919 hundreds of workers migrated to Cuba, Venezuela, and the United States. Another group went to Hawaii in 1921 (History Task Force 1979). In 1918 the War Trade Board, with the support of Puerto Rico's labor movement, proposed hiring workers for Cuban sugar mills. The U.S. occupation of Dominican Republic opened possibilities for workers, most of whom worked in food production under the U.S. occupation (History Task Force 1982; Marín Román 2009, 509–10).

In response to the problems that emerged with migrations to continental United States, Cuba, Mexico, and Hawaii, on May 29, 1919, the Puerto Rican legislature passed the Act to Regulate Emigration from Porto Rico, which authorized the commissioner of agriculture and labor to intervene in all aspects of the emigration of workers. Taking seriously petitions from migrant workers in Hawaii that called for protections, the act charged the commissioner with inquiring, inspecting, intervening, and regulating any organized emigration of workers; approving, overseeing, and enforcing labor-migration contracts; and overseeing the settlement or repatriation of workers. The act also prohibited the migration of minors under sixteen years of age, unless accompanied by their parents or legal guardians, and of people over seventy, unless they were traveling with their children or relatives. It also imposed a fine of $500 for violation of its terms (History Task Force 1982; S. Serrano 2017).

In the 1920s, as unemployment and underemployment continued to cause extreme poverty, a second wave of emigration from Puerto Rico began. By 1926, 30 percent of workers were unemployed, and only a third were employed during the *tiempo muerto* (after and before the harvest) in the sugar and tobacco industries. An intense debate developed, with officials and social scientists arguing that because Puerto Rico suffered from overpopulation, the practical solution was emigration. In contrast, labor leaders and workers' supporters insisted that the problem was employers who did not provide adequate wages and working conditions. Disagreement over the causes of poverty and unemployment notwithstanding, the flow of migrants to the States increased after World War I, as the United States experienced economic growth. Most migrants left for New York City, where a vibrant Puerto Rican community was emerging in several neighborhoods (Scarano 1993, 610–17).

After World War I government-sponsored guest-worker and colonial labor-contract programs were shelved, and migration resumed informally, without government intervention (Hahamovitch 2011). The USES's scope was reduced in the 1920s, until the New Deal revived it as a tool to alleviate unemployment and labor shortages during World War II (Breen 1997). During the early 1920s, although nativists and racist officials and growers in the States did not want Puerto Ricans, restrictive national immigration laws benefited their migration. The Johnson Act of 1921 and the Johnson-Reed Act of 1924 restricted immigration by setting quotas and barring Asians and some Europeans, creating more opportunities for Puerto Ricans to migrate. The Johnson-Reed Act specifically defined Puerto Rico as part of the United States, and colonial officials and members of the BIA lobbied officials in the

USDL and Congress to prefer Puerto Ricans over other guest workers and non-U.S. citizens (Baldoz 2011, 60, 253n1; Cruz 1998, 3).

In fiscal year 1926–27, net migration from Puerto Rico to the United States numbered 8,729 people, the largest cohort in the first forty years of U.S. occupation (Perloff 1950, cited in History Task Force 1982, 222). Migrants were establishing themselves in places like southern New Jersey, taking advantage of networks with friends and acquaintances from Puerto Rico and limitations on other migrant contract workers arriving during and after World War I (M. Pérez 1986; Aponte et al. 1994, 35–36).

In the 1920s Puerto Rican contract workers were again hired to work in agriculture in Arizona and Hawaii. A labor agent from Hawaii returned to Puerto Rico in 1922, recruiting 700 workers, who traveled through the Panama Canal to Hawaii. As increased enforcement of immigration laws limited the recruitment of Mexicans, the Arizona Cotton Growers Association sought to recruit Puerto Ricans, because other agricultural workers were leaving for work in cities. In 1926 cotton growers in Arizona organized two cohorts of workers, in family groups with children, altogether 1,061 migrants, to work in Arizona, but the experience was a disaster for both growers and workers. The conditions described by recruiters and the promises made by contractors did not match the reality the workers encountered (Maldonado 1979, 106; Senior 1947; U.S. House 1928, 187–90). Because migrants were not deportable, when their expectations were not met, they left their jobs and moved to nearby cities, often becoming indigent and sometimes engaging in crime. Migrations to Arizona and Hawaii also raised serious concerns among U.S. and Puerto Rican officials (*El Paso Herald* 1926; Lasker 1969; Rosario Natal 2001; U.S. Army 1930, 8).

Nativist concerns about Puerto Ricans as nondeportable laborers who could receive welfare assistance created a hostile climate for migrants. In response to a proposal to limit Mexican labor in favor of Filipinos, who were still American nationals, and Puerto Ricans, who were now citizens, growers' associations and government officials who favored Mexican workers launched a countercampaign (Beechert 1985; History Task Force 1982; Rosario Natal 2001; U.S. House 1928, 187–88; U.S. Senate 1928, 43). In 1927 the Convention of the Fruit Growers of California discussed the choice between encouraging the migration of Mexican versus Puerto Rican laborers. One of its officials, Dr. George P. Clements, head of the Los Angeles Chamber of Commerce's Agricultural Department, tried to deflect racism against Mexicans by highlighting their desirability as deportable labor, foregrounding Puerto Ricans' blackness and, in the chamber's view, inferiority as domestic labor (Molina 2014, 34–35):

> The Porto Rican negro is a thin lipped negro and is not so efficient as the Mexican ... [and] we cannot handle them like Mexicans. A Porto Rican has as much right to stay as we have. He cannot be deported as can a Mexican who becomes indigent.... The Mexicans can be deported if they become county charges, but the others are here to stay.... (Cited in N. Anderson 1940, 296)

Fearing that Puerto Ricans would contest violations of their rights or become dependent on welfare agencies, growers' associations and government officials opposed proposals that favored domestic workers over foreign labor, efforts underpinned by the racist fear of transplanting people with African heritage (Narváez 1977, 7).

Between 1927 and 1945 interest in hiring Puerto Rican labor decreased as stateside growers and farmers became dependent on Mexican braceros. But while growers in California, Arizona, and Texas did not want to hire Puerto Ricans and Filipinos, sugar producers in Hawaii were still hiring them (Beechert 1985; History Task Force 1982; Rosario Natal 2001; U.S. House 1928, 1930). Constructing, maintaining, and justifying a Mexican labor force required employers to elaborate myths about the work ethic of other migrants. They emphasized the racial hybridity of Puerto Ricans as a menace (Griffith 1993), rather than raising fears that citizen migrants would contest violations of their rights or fall back on public assistance.

While U.S. labor officials at the BIA and local colonial officials lobbied for hiring Puerto Ricans, many U.S. elected officials voiced fear and opposition to these citizen workers (Baldoz 2011; U.S. House 1928, 1930). From 1928 to 1930 Representatives John Box of Texas and William Harris of Georgia introduced several bills to include countries in the Western Hemisphere in immigration quotas. The initial impetus for these bills was the increase in Mexican migration and a desire to limit or halt it, but restricting Mexican migration meant that the only sources of labor outside the States would be the Philippines and Puerto Rico. In congressional hearings, growers, members of Congress, and Puerto Rico's resident commissioner debated for and against the use of Puerto Rican labor as a substitute for Mexican and Filipino workers. Those opposed to employing Puerto Ricans cited high transportation costs, racial inferiority, welfare dependence, and the failures of prior migrations to Hawaii and Arizona. In a 1930 House Committee on Immigration and Naturalization hearing, Fred J. Hart, a lettuce and seed grower in Salinas, California, and managing editor of *California Farm Bureau Monthly,* urged that "rather than exclude the Mexican you would shut the door to the Filipino and the Porto Rican first, and consider the Mexican last" (U.S. House 1930, 206–7). Committee chair Albert Johnson responded that Puerto Ricans were U.S. citizens and could not be excluded. Hart replied,

> Do you think that I should take this attitude from your statement, take back to my wife and family and my relatives that you say we are going to shut the Mexicans out because the Porto Rican is a citizen, and therefore he must come in, and knowing the Porto Rican as we know him, and knowing that class, that you are going to shut the Mexican out, so that if we are going to exist we must bring the Porto Rican in and put him alongside of our families, the thin lipped Porto Rican, an agitator, a trouble-maker, and a man that I don't want my family to have to associate with continuously?

Johnson answered, "Whether we like it or not, we have got a million and a half American citizens in Porto Rico" (U.S. House 1930, 207).

Although bills to favor Mexican workers failed in Congress, deportation, nativism, and proposals for immigration restriction increased after the onset of the Great Depression, but the U.S. citizenship and the political status of Puerto Rico deterred Congress from restricting the use of Puerto Rican labor. The U.S. government reduced the number of visas for Mexican workers, increased penalties for undocumented immigration, and reinforced border surveillance. As a result, neither large-scale state nor privately sponsored migration of Puerto Ricans would occur until World War II (Molina 2014, 58–59).

Nevertheless, Puerto Rican veterans, former contract workers, and adventurers found their way to destinations throughout the United States. The 1930 census recorded 52,774 island-born people living in the United States, up from 11,811 in 1920 (Senior and Watkins 1966, 701). By the late 1920s the Puerto Rico Bureau of Labor had recorded 7,000 Puerto Ricans leaving for New York City. In its 1930 annual report, the bureau exhorted the local legislative assembly to ask the U.S. Congress to facilitate emigration by allowing recent Puerto Rican graduates to travel by military transport to the States (History Task Force 1982, 206–10). Puerto Ricans were still present in the farm labor force despite growers' and their allies' resistance; in 1932 many participated in a spontaneous strike of pea pickers in central California (Bronfenbrenner 1990; Daniel 1982).

The Great Depression, with its massive unemployment and large number of destitute farmers, all but eliminated possibilities for farm-labor migration. Mexican workers were being deported and Filipinos were "repatriated" because high unemployment rendered migrant laborers unnecessary. Although Robert Hayes Gore, governor of Puerto Rico from 1933 to 1934, attempted to send farmworkers to Florida in the mid-1930s, the stateside economic situation was not favorable for contract-labor migration, and opportunities for workers disappeared (Baldoz 2011; Ngai 2004).

## THE NEW DEAL AND THE PRELUDE
## TO WORLD WAR II

After 1898 Puerto Rico became an important sugar and tobacco export-producer for U.S. markets. By the 1930s U.S. corporate interests were well established in Puerto Rico, where the colonial government had built roads, schools, hospitals, and irrigation systems. But economic, social, and political crises permeated all sectors of Puerto Rican society, and most of the population continued to be landless. From 1900 to 1910 the population of Puerto Rico grew by 17 percent, with sugarcane growing regions expanding as landless workers in the coffee and tobacco areas in the hinterland migrated there seeking work. A BIA report noted that, since 1914, 75 percent of the population, approximately eight hundred thousand inhabitants, had been landless. Between 1914 and 1930 nearly fifty-two thousand people (3.4 percent of the 1930 population) left the territory, and internal migration increased as workers tried to escape economic crises in the coffee, tobacco, and sugar regions (Dietz 1986, 130–32; History Task Force 1979, 110–11). Hurricane San Felipe struck Puerto Rico in 1928, exacerbating living conditions. By 1932 extreme poverty and persistent disease and malnutrition affected most of the Puerto Rican working class (Ayala and Bergad 2002; Cabán 1999, 247).

During the Great Depression, unemployment and underemployment substantially decreased incomes and increased the cost of living for working-class Puerto Ricans. By 1933 the economic downfall was clear, with a 30 percent decrease in average per capita income and skyrocketing food prices. The cost of rice increased from $2.40 per hundred pounds in December 1932 to $4.10 in December 1933, with similar increases for beans from $3.00 to $5.25 per hundred pounds, codfish from $19.00 to $28.00 per pound, and lard from $15.50 to $18.00 per hundred pounds. Milk increased from $0.05 to

$0.15 per quart; a pound of bread increased in cost from $0.04 to $0.10. At the same time thousands of jobs were disappearing. Only a third of the labor force had stable incomes (Dietz 1986, 139; Scarano 1993, 672–73). Wages in the sugar industry fell from $0.111 per hour in 1932 to $0.096 in 1933. The average income fell from $3.80 to $3.55 per week, while the number of work hours increased. Employers in the tobacco industry paid $0.043 per hour in 1933 to workers who toiled an average of 29.5 hours a week, for a total of $1.27 earned weekly. Income inequality for women, who earned less than men, exacerbated the living conditions of households. In the tobacco industry, women earned an average weekly wage of $0.97, while men earned $1.46. This was happening while nutritionists and physicians estimated that the cost of an adequate diet was $3.19 weekly per person. By the end of the 1930s, food prices remained 20 percent higher than prices in large North American cities. Unemployment in the sugar sector had risen to 33 percent, with a significant decrease of hours in the workday (Dietz 1986, 139–40; García-Colón 2009, 29–31; History Task Force 1979; Pons 1941).

Rural workers lived in small houses constructed of straw, pieces of castoff wood, metal from cans, galvanized iron, and cardboard. Visiting in the mid-1930s, future governor Rexford G. Tugwell described their houses as unsanitary, wretched, and overcrowded ([1945] 1975, 233). In 1932 Hurricane San Ciprián worsened the economic crisis by destroying crops, killing 225 people, and imposing losses amounting to $30 million. In 1935 life expectancy was 43.9 years. Low wages, malnutrition, and disease contributed to a death rate of 28 persons per 1,000 inhabitants, and infant mortality was 179 per 1,000 births, figures more than double those of the United States. Most people suffered from parasites, gastrointestinal diseases, and infectious illnesses (Crumbine 1930, 19, 37, 44, 57; García-Colón 2009, 29–31; Mejías 1946, 156–64).

The collapse of the economy and migration from rural to urban areas made calls for emigration and control of "overpopulation" more urgent, but from 1931 to 1934 the number of people leaving Puerto Rico decreased dramatically, with the total population gaining 8,694 inhabitants due to return migration (History Task Force 1979, 112; Perloff 1950, cited in History Task Force 1982, 222). Returning migrants found a country experiencing economic as well as social turmoil. Strikes were prevalent and, with the increasing militancy of the Puerto Rico Nationalist Party (Partido Nacionalista de Puerto Rico), getting the attention of officials in Puerto Rico and Washington, DC. In addition, dissent and irreparable divisions among the leaders of the principal Puerto Rican political parties led to the creation of new alliances and parties. A group of Republicans and Socialists, known locally as La Coalición (The Coalition), controlled the local government and opposed some New Deal measures on the islands. The Nationalist Party declared war against the United States. As the legitimacy of U.S. colonial rule was being questioned, colonial officials began taking measures to alleviate poverty.

On July 29, 1934, a presidential executive order established the Division of Territories and Island Possessions, assigning Puerto Rico to its jurisdiction (History Task Force 1979, 117). This gesture signaled a change in the federal government's attitude toward the administration of Puerto Rico, as governance and reform rather than geopolitical considerations took precedence. Officials in the Office of the Territories became important allies of the Puerto Rican government in its lobbying efforts for reforms and parity before Congress and President Franklin D. Roosevelt.

The New Deal laid the foundation for a scientifically planned migration of Puerto Ricans. In 1934 the Roosevelt administration created the Puerto Rico Policy Commission to study social and economic conditions in the colony and recommend solutions to problems. Dr. Carlos Chardón, president of the University of Puerto Rico and chair of the commission, submitted a report on those conditions to the U.S. Department of Interior (Stinson Fernández 1996, 121–23). Known as the Chardón Plan, the report became an important guide for Puerto Rican elites, proposing ideas, policies, and strategies to modernize and develop the country, in effect a New Deal plan for Puerto Rico that would include industrialization, land distribution, and migration (Dietz 1986). The report stated,

> Emigration . . . may eventually become imperative in any well-coordinated policy to improve economic conditions in Puerto Rico. Possibilities should be explored as to mass colonization projects in under-populated regions of tropical countries similar to Puerto Rico, not only in climate but also in language, religion, racial stock, traditions, and culture.
>
> These emigrants should go to settle in farm land, not to be exploited as wage laborers. . . . Santo Domingo, Cuba and Costa Rica are suggested as the neighboring countries which have under-populated regions and which afford conditions more closely approximate to those obtaining in Puerto Rico. Venezuela and Brazil may be tried also. (Puerto Rico Policy Commission 1934, 6–7)

The Chardón Plan put forth the same suggestions voiced in the early 1900s. Migration, land reform, construction of infrastructure, and expansion of government services became part of the plan for modernizing Puerto Rico.

But the Roosevelt administration found such proposals too radical and limited its response to the creation of federal relief programs, such as the Puerto Rico Emergency Relief Administration and the Puerto Rican Reconstruction Administration (Puerto Rico Policy Commission 1934; Santana Rabell 1984; Stinson Fernández 1996). Meanwhile, unorganized migration to the United States was resuming. From 1935 to 1940 the net loss of population from people leaving Puerto Rico was 17,737, compared to the gain of 8,694 return migrants from 1931 to 1934 (Perloff 1950, cited in History Task Force 1982, 222). Most of this migration was to major U.S. cities (see Senior and Watkins 1966).

To this point in the twentieth century, the U.S. farm labor force was composed largely of tenants, sharecroppers, and farmworkers, but mechanization and the decline of agricultural wages had been reducing the supply of year-round workers, transforming many farmworkers into low-wage seasonal migrants. The concentration of manufacturing in cities had eliminated several factories in small towns that had provided supplemental income to farmworkers during the agricultural off-seasons. To subsist, workers were obliged to take whatever seasonal agricultural jobs were available. Growers maintained low wages and cheap housing by keeping a surplus labor force, which deterred workers from moving from one place to another. In California the availability of a large pool of Mexican and Asian workers reduced wages (M. García 2002). Low-wage jobs in agriculture reinforced racism against "nonwhite" immigrants, a category that included Puerto Ricans despite their U.S. citizenship. Workers' opportunities for social and economic mobility in agriculture were few.

The number of U.S. farms operated by individual owners decreased from 1880 to 1930, but this trend began to be reversed in the 1930s, and in 1950 farm ownership surpassed the old numbers of the 1880s. Although individual farm ownership rose, tenants and sharecroppers increasingly became wage earners. The capital required to own land and equipment and to pay operating expenses curtailed the upward mobility of the farm labor force, and most of these workers began to abandon agricultural jobs as manufacturing expanded employment opportunities. From the late 1930s to around 1950, while the productivity of farmworkers increased, the size of the labor force decreased (Maier, Maitland, and Bowles 1960). In the northeastern United States, the farm labor force decreased from 40.6 percent of the population in 1940 to 34.5 percent in 1950. These changes point to transformations in the composition and conditions of the farm labor force, as well as to the mechanization of agriculture, but they did not diminish the significance of farmworkers.

In the 1930s workers began to move more frequently without being attached year-round to a particular farm. The economic crisis, combined with the extreme drought that created the so-called Dust Bowl, pushed thousands of farmers and agricultural workers away from the countryside. The mechanization of agricultural production increased the number of workers hired for short periods, and low wages became a common feature of farm labor. Unemployment soared, creating a cheap and highly mobile farm labor force (N. Anderson 1940; Folsom and Baker 1937; Galarza 1964; Ham 1940, 1941; Maier, Maitland, and Bowles 1960). Officials concerned about these trends offered the regulation of labor as the solution, thinking that a system of labor distribution would resolve the problems of overpopulation in urban areas and unemployment elsewhere in the country (Ham 1940). Large-scale agricultural operations among smaller and large growers widened the market for food products. Agricultural-sciences research helped increase crop yields, and farm mechanization allowed cultivation of large areas with a small labor force. Foods considered perishable in the early twentieth century were delivered quickly, thanks to refrigerated transportation. Agricultural production and food processing served national and international markets rather than just the local market. When this transition to intensive agricultural production created problems with the demand, supply, and distribution of labor, government initiatives smoothed the way (Berstein 1989; USES 1949).

New Deal policies and programs directly impacted the regulation of farm labor. During the 1920s, and markedly during the Depression, the federal and state governments passed child-labor laws, and state departments of labor began to oversee child labor on farms. New York State passed laws, in 1928, limiting the employment of minors on farms and regulating the employment of children fourteen years and older (Hurd 1953). The Fair Labor Standards Act of 1938 established the federal minimum age for employment and the number of hours children could work, rules that reduced the legal pool of available cheap labor in agriculture (Grossman 1978; Myers 2008).

As the Great Depression facilitated the implementation of labor-friendly government policies, the New Deal also began to transform agricultural-labor regimes. On June 6, 1933, Congress passed the Wagner-Peyser Act, establishing the basis for laws that would define farm labor to the present day. The act created a voluntary federal-state labor-exchange system to assist workers seeking opportunities in public works, relief projects, and areas with few workers.

The Wagner-Peyser Act also reorganized the USES, linking it to affiliated state offices funded through matching appropriations from the state and federal governments. The New Deal's USES sought to identify industries and geographic regions with labor shortages and surpluses to plan the efficient use and transportation, if necessary, of the domestic labor force and foreign workers. To this end the USES also certified the use of foreign labor and oversaw the Farm Placement Program, which between 1933 and 1942 provided services to growers, paid from taxes levied for unemployment insurance (Galarza 1977; O'Leary and Eberts 2008, 1–4). But the Wagner-Peyser Act did not create protections for farmworkers' wages, housing, or other needs, nor did federal officials extend the USES into Puerto Rico until the early 1940s, when relief efforts were carried out by the Civilian Conservation Corps, the Puerto Rico Emergency Relief Administration, the Puerto Rico Reconstruction Administration, and the Farm Security Administration (FSA) (Dietz 1986; Valdés Pizzini, González-Cruz, and Martínez-Reyes 2011).

In 1935 the federal government created the Resettlement Administration (RA), with then-U.S. undersecretary of agriculture Rexford G. Tugwell as director, to establish resettlement communities for agricultural workers and destitute farmers with the goal of providing stable living and workplaces for this highly mobile labor force. Facing criticism for poor management, the RA was merged into its successor, the FSA, under the U.S. Department of Agriculture, to provide assistance to small farmers, sharecroppers, and farmworkers. From 1935 to 1947 the RA and FSA administered the Migratory Labor Camp program for seasonal migrant workers. The FSA, together with the Bureau of Agricultural Economics and the USES, argued for the transfer of domestic workers from areas with a surplus of workers to areas of need (Baldwin 1968; Martínez Matsuda 2009; Mitchell 2012).

Other New Deal laws transformed the labor landscape in the United States and Puerto Rico. In 1935, with the support of the Roosevelt administration, Congress enacted the National Labor Relations Act (NLRA) and the Social Security Act, but these laws excluded farmworkers from regulations and organizing protections. Scholars argue that Southern Democrats pressured for the exclusion of farmworkers and domestic workers to curtail the rights of African Americans and women to the benefits and protections given to white men (Frymer 2008; Perea 2011). The NLRA, which created the National Labor Relations Board and protected the right of employees to collective bargaining, covered workers in food-processing factories but not the agricultural laborers who produced the food. It also guaranteed private employees' right to organize labor unions and to collective action, such as strikes. While provisions of Fair Labor Standards Act of 1938 covering a minimum wage, a forty-hour workweek, overtime pay, record-keeping requirements, and the prohibition of child labor were applicable in Puerto Rico from the outset, neither the NLRA nor the Social Security Act was formally extended to the territory until the 1940s and 1950s.

Except for the Wagner-Peyser Act, labor-market regulations for farm-workers were not at the core of New Deal policies. The lack of protections for farmworkers and their exclusion from federal labor legislation meant that the U.S. farm-labor movement's struggles focused on finding remedies to New Deal policies. In Puerto Rico the local government enacted its own version of the Wagner-Peyser Act, the Insular Labor Relations Act of 1945, modeled on the NLRA, but broader because it included agricultural workers (Daniel 1982, 258–85; Dietz 1986, 223).

Despite their limited reach in Puerto Rico, New Deal ideas of reform were taking hold among some sectors of the political class there. A realignment of political forces occurred at the end of the 1930s, as young radical and techno-cratic elements expelled from the Puerto Rican Liberal Party (Partido Liberal Puertorriqueño) established the Popular Democratic Party (PPD; Partido Popular Democrático) under the leadership of Luis Muñoz Marín. The PPD became an important partner of the federal government. Under the banner of "Bread, Land, and Liberty," the PPD gained control of the local legislature and most municipalities. After President Roosevelt appointed Tugwell as governor of Puerto Rico in 1941, pro-PPD and pro–New Deal political forces dreamed of a planned economy for Puerto Rico (Santana Rabell 1984). Like earlier colonial officials, New Deal politicians and technocrats continued to attribute Puerto Rico's poverty and unemployment to overpopulation. Managing labor migration became a priority.

By the late 1930s seasonal migration to U.S. farms was already an estab-lished trend. Farmworkers arrived from urban areas or traveled migratory routes from Florida and other states in the South, moving to New Jersey, Long Island, and, sometimes, to Maine. Italians from Camden and Philadelphia worked in southern New Jersey fields. Canadian workers from Quebec, Newfoundland, or Native American reservations migrated to bor-dering states in the Northeast, such as Connecticut and Massachusetts. The New Deal initiatives of the Wagner-Peyser Act, the RA, and the FSA attempted to manage the flow of these seasonal migrants and, in fact, increased the use of seasonal migrants in Northeast agriculture.

In Puerto Rico, land reform, industrialization, and population control through emigration and contraception became the pillars of the PPD's modernization project. In the following chapter, I explore how the drive for reform and planning, together with World War II–era guest-worker programs, led to the creation of the Puerto Rico Farm Labor Program, a key pillar of that project.

# TWO

# Establishing the Farm Labor Program

THE 1940S BROUGHT DRAMATIC CHANGES to the political landscape of Puerto Rico that directly affected U.S. agriculture. In the elections of 1940, the recently established Popular Democratic Party (PPD; Partido Popular Democrático), campaigning under a social-justice and reform platform, won majorities in the legislature and municipal governments, defeating a coalition of Republicans and Socialists. In 1941 President Franklin D. Roosevelt's appointment of the radical New Dealer Rexford G. Tugwell as governor signaled federal approval for drastic political reforms. The coalition formed by the PPD and Tugwell found common ground in the implementation of economic policies that required intensive government involvement. The colonial government was attempting to modernize the territory by fostering industrialization, agrarian reform, population control, and urbanization. Technocrats, intellectuals, and elected officials initially saw industrialization and land distribution as ways to address poverty (García-Colón 2006b). In Puerto Rico, however, because manufacturing jobs were scarce, migration to the States rather than from rural to urban areas became a key strategy for modernizing the country.

Technocrats and PPD elected officials nonetheless sought to tame the flows of labor migration, believing fervently that managed labor markets and migration should be part of a new modern colonial state. One of those officials, Antonio Fernós Isern, the PPD government's resident commissioner in Washington (1946–64), participated directly in the creation of the Farm Labor Program (FLP). In a March 12, 1947, letter he suggested that

> the migratory flow be directed to the northern and midwestern states, establishing a route by air, San Juan–Philadelphia, with a labor supply office in

Philadelphia. Thus, whichever office was responsible for running this program in Puerto Rico would also issue stipends and identification cards. There would also be a person in New York delegated to manage issues arising in New York City, where several people could be paid and be sent to the West, and a person in Philadelphia who would direct the flow of recent arrivals from Puerto Rico.[1] (1947d)

Fernós's ideas about channeling the migratory flow to the States illustrate how engaged PPD officials were in migration policy. Migration policy and the infrastructure created to facilitate it became state tools for reform and modernization. Contrary to established narratives, it was not the product of a single person but rather the collective product of North American and Puerto Rican officials, elected leaders, technocrats, and intellectuals—and the migrants themselves.

As the Roosevelt administration implemented important labor-market regulations that transformed labor migration, the government of Puerto Rico also began to implement reforms regulating its labor market and labor migration. Particularly noteworthy was the creation of the Bureau of Employment and Migration (BEM), which included the New York Office that would eventually become the Migration Division (MD), and the FLP. This chapter explores the establishment of the BEM from the middle 1940s to the early 1950s and traces the origins of the MD and the FLP in relation to the development of managed labor migration and the status of Puerto Ricans in U.S. farm labor during that decade. The migration of Puerto Ricans arose from the contradictions embedded in U.S. farm-labor policies, the legal definitions of Puerto Ricans' citizenship, and U.S. economic interests.

Drawing on the experience of the U.S. Employment Service (USES), the Farm Security Administration, and various New Deal policies, the colonial government designed a farm-labor program to help alleviate unemployment and poverty in Puerto Rico. The BEM, the MD, and the FLP are examples of state institutions driven by the will to improve social and economic conditions among subalterns. A close examination of the effects of the FLP on farmworkers reveals the contradictory and disorganized effects of development policies. It also uncovers how technocrats' and officials' *will to improve* unleashed conditions unprecedented at that time, which still linger (Li 2005, 2007). Migration to U.S. farms depended on political and economic conditions in the United States and Puerto Rico, as well as the emergence of a new colonial state in Puerto Rico. Examination of the emergence of the BEM, the

MD, and the FLP expands our understanding of how the government of Puerto Rico facilitated labor migration while attempting to establish a presence throughout the United States.

## THE WAR-EMERGENCY PROGRAMS

The conditions that fostered farm-labor migration arose from both external and internal factors. Federal policies for managing labor migration; the employment of agricultural workers; growers' preferences for cheap, deportable labor; economic conditions in Puerto Rico; and the integration of colonial territories into U.S. markets all structured the social fields of power that colonialism provided to Puerto Ricans. During the 1940s and 1950s, Puerto Ricans participated in a migration in which thousands of people moved to, within, and across the United States looking for employment, higher wages, and better living and working conditions (Pagán de Colón 1956a, 1–2). The outbreak of World War II allowed growers and small farmers to influence farm-labor policy by imposing their preference for guest workers over domestic workers. U.S. federal officials initially excluded Puerto Ricans from war-emergency programs because large stateside growers were reluctant to hire them, even though, ironically, the Nationality Act of 1940 declared that, beginning in 1941, all persons born in Puerto Rico would hold birthright citizenship, which made it difficult for growers to exclude Puerto Ricans. In 1948 Congress approved amendments to the Nationality Act of 1940 and the Jones Act, extending retroactively and without any residency requirements birthright citizenship to all persons born in Puerto Rico (Venator Santiago 2013, 70–71; 2017, 49–50). Affirmation of the U.S. citizenship of Puerto Ricans gave the local colonial administration and the U.S. Division of Territories and Island Possessions (DTIP) more leverage in lobbying for hiring Puerto Ricans during the war. Under the old banner of alleviating the substantial unemployment plaguing the territory, labor migration reappeared as a solution.

Since the early twentieth century, Puerto Rico had experienced a chronic "oversupply" of agricultural workers, even as agricultural-commodity production expanded, owing to large investments by North American corporations and the entrance of the territory into the U.S. tariff system. The value of tobacco exports increased from $376,000 (1901) to $20.6 million (1927); sugar exports increased from $5.8 million (1900) to $53.6 million (1930).

In contrast, coffee, the principal agricultural industry before 1898, declined by the 1930s from an export value of $1.6 million in 1901 to $207,739 in 1935 (Dietz 1986, 98–130). Large sugar-producing corporations controlled labor and agricultural production in the coastal regions and on the islands of Vieques and Culebra, while tobacco farms dominated in the east-central region of the territory, and farmers produced coffee in the west-central highlands.

The expansion of agrarian capitalism and the Great Depression worsened living conditions for working-class Puerto Ricans. In 1940 there were between 100,000 to 150,000 landless families (García-Colón 2009, 18–43). Workers with land could complement their earnings by growing their own gardens or earning artisanal wages, but the large number of unemployed workers seeking jobs allowed employers to offer low wages. The average daily wage of workers was $0.63 in 1917. A decade later, in 1928, 85 percent of workers in Puerto Rico earned less than $1.00 a day. In 1935 sugar workers earned $3.34 a week, of which they spent 94 percent on food (Dietz 1986, 111–12, 125).

Meanwhile, in U.S. agriculture the employment trends established between World I and World War II continued shaping a farm-labor market dependent on immigration. Chinese, Filipinos, Puerto Ricans, Mexicans, Europeans, Canadians, Native Americans, African Americans, and whites accounted for most of the pre–World War II farm labor force at different times and in different regions. All these groups included families and single workers, although transporting families and housing them in labor camps posed challenges. Gender ideas about the physical strength of men and their reliability for farmwork, the legacies of the slaveholding plantation society, and discourses of domesticity began to take hold in U.S. agricultural labor after World War I, and by the 1940s guest-worker programs in agriculture were hiring immigrant men only. Thus, men, particularly immigrants, became the preferred workers in the farm-labor market (Bowman 2002, 68; Dunn 1972, 215; Hahamovitch 1997, 89, 163, 200; Liss 1941; Morin 1952, 84–93; U.S. Extension Service 1947, 33–35).

The onset of World War II consolidated the interests of stateside growers and small farmers, who preferred male guest workers to Puerto Rican and other domestic workers. As food production became an internal security matter for the U.S. government, the growers' influence increased considerably, and they inserted themselves into both the determination of where labor shortages existed and the mobilization of the labor force. The War Manpower Commission (WMC), responsible for assessing and supplying labor needs, created local War Emergency Committees that grouped extension agents, employment-service officials, elected officials, and growers. In 1942, when growers complained about the possibility of losing their crops if a labor shortage occurred, they convinced the federal government to establish the Emergency Farm Labor Supply Program to contract guest workers from Mexico, the British West Indies, and Canada (Galarza 1964, 41–42).

Growers also influenced public policy by determining prevailing wages as part of wartime price- and wage-control measures. By 1938 U.S. farmworkers' wages had risen, which meant that they were becoming expensive for employers. Guest workers, in contrast, were willing to work for low wages, thereby reducing agricultural production costs and raising the value of farmland. Growers opposed migration and labor policies that raised wages, and some farmers and government officials worked to lower agricultural wages, which had been closing the gap with industrial wages during the 1930s (Galarza 1964, 42). Guest-worker programs and growers' influence overshadowed the dominant narrative of New Deal and World War II collectivism and labor organizing (Ham 1940, 914; Mills and Rockoff 1983; Rockoff 1984).

Between 1943 and 1945 the wartime draft reduced the number of farmworkers and increased demand for labor in the cities, both of which increased wages and justified growers seeking a larger labor pool (Galarza 1964, 41; Parsons 1952). In addition, the second generation of many immigrant families showed less interest in agriculture than had their parents, while higher prices for land restricted the social mobility of domestic farmworkers who aspired to become farm owners. As a result, migrants and guest workers became an important part of farm labor.

Unconvinced by growers' claims of labor shortages, federal officials began to investigate the need for immigrant labor. Farmers and officials who favored guest workers based their reports of labor shortages on the difficulty of hiring low-wage, underemployed U.S. workers because of the wartime draft (Martin 2002, 1128; see Vialet and McClure 1980, 16). In 1941 the U.S. Department of Agriculture (USDA) and the U.S. Department of Labor (USDL) created a coordinating committee to determine just how pressing the demand for farm labor was. Local USDA agents estimated farm-labor needs, while the USDL, through its local USES offices, estimated the labor supply. The committee concluded that growers had exaggerated their claims and observed that the growers complaining about labor shortages, particularly those in the South, paid the lowest wages. These growers had become accustomed to the oversupply of workers during the Great Depression and were unwilling to raise wages. In 1941 the

USDA and the USDL concluded that the problem was an ineffective distribution of labor, worsened by employers' reluctance to pay attractive wages. Federal officials argued that the unequal distribution of labor could be resolved by planning and scientifically managing labor demand and supply through better policy mechanisms and infrastructure (Hahamovitch 2011, 37–38).

Growers continued to prefer immigrants to citizens because they could send guest workers back to their home countries at the end of the harvest. In the words of tomato farmer and self-appointed lobbyist for Florida growers, Luther L. Chandler, writing to the U.S. secretary of agriculture in 1942,

> The vast difference between the Bahama Island labor and the domestic, including Puerto Rican, is that the labor transported from the Bahama Islands can be deported and sent home, if it does not work, which cannot be done in the instance of labor from domestic United States or Puerto Rico. (Rasmussen 1951, 234)

Any preference growers and farmers in the U.S. South might have had for Puerto Rican labor decreased almost as soon as Puerto Ricans obtained birthright citizenship and the first deportable Mexican braceros and Caribbean guest workers began to arrive in the United States. Further disincentivizing the hiring of domestic workers, the federal government covered transportation costs for braceros but denied the same benefits to Puerto Ricans and other U.S. citizens. Officials from the rural South predominated in the War Food Administration (WFA), where they exerted great influence in removing the Farm Placement Program from the Farm Security Administration (Hahamovitch 2011, 24, 42, 47). Immigrants were the perfect workers in the eyes of southern officials because they reduced the need to hire African Americans while also lowering labor costs (Galarza 1964, 41).

Between 1943 and 1947 the federal government enacted a number of laws that ensured the supply of guest workers and impeded the hiring of Puerto Ricans and other domestic workers (Kirstein 1977, 49). The USES collaborated with the War Emergency Program (WEP) and the USDA's Extension Service to recruit guest workers, while the WEP and the Immigration and Naturalization Service coordinated transportation. During the war the USES lost some influence as the result of the growers' increasing power. In January 1943 the WMC ordered the transfer of the Farm Placement Program, responsible for recruitment and placement of agricultural labor, to the Office of Agricultural Extension in the USDA, where it remained until December 1947. The federal government also took direct control of state employment offices (Fay and Lippoldt 1999, 31; Rushing 1948; Ruttenberg and Gutchess 1970, 4–5; USES 1949, 4).

In April 1943 the interests of growers' lobbies, such as the American Farm Bureau Federation and the Associated Famers, prevailed as Congress passed public law 45, under which the federal government allocated $13 million for the transportation and distribution of immigrant farmworkers (Hahamovitch 2011, 46). The law also barred federal officials from using the funds to improve the wages and working conditions of domestic farmworkers and forbade citizens from leaving one farm job for another or taking a job in manufacturing. Before quitting their jobs, domestic farmworkers needed the authorization of local extension agents, who usually had personal or kinship ties to local farmers. Under public law 45, federal officials lost the practical authority to move workers from areas of surplus labor to scarcity areas.

In this context the United States signed the famous agreement with Mexico that began the Bracero Program. The Immigration and Naturalization Service, together with the Departments of Justice, Labor, State, and Agriculture, and the WMC created the Special Committee on Importation of Mexican Labor and designed the Bracero Program (Calavita 1992, 19). The WEP began to transport migrant farmworkers, mostly from Mexico but also from the British Caribbean and Canada, while the Farm Placement Program mobilized local adults and youth, workers from urban areas, Italian and German prisoners of war, interned Japanese Americans, and soldiers and sailors. For example, between 1943 and 1947 New York State agriculture employed 167,000 local adults; 150,000 school youth; 9,000 people vacationing in New York City; 10,800 Jamaicans and Bahamians; 10,800 Germans and Italians; 5,600 soldiers and sailors from military camps and training centers; and 1,400 troops assigned by the Department of War in 1943 (NYSIC 1949). Mexican braceros dominated the immigrant labor force in the Southwest, and the Bracero Program sustained growers' wishes that Mexicans be the solution to alleged labor shortages (Rushing 1948).

The importation of workers from the Caribbean was also enabled by colonial policies and strategic military interests. Colonial powers saw unemployment as the real threat to their control of the region. Fear that unemployment and poverty in the Caribbean could lead to German occupation prompted the creation of the Anglo-American Caribbean Commission. The commission's plans for importing West Indians to the United States complemented its efforts to bring development and modernization to the British Caribbean (H. Johnson 1984, 185–89, 198).

Opponents of Puerto Rican farm-labor migration occupied important posts on the national and local boards of the WFA, but U.S. government officials and organized labor believed that a USES office in Puerto Rico would help provide additional workers for the war effort in the States. A. F. Whitney (1943), president of the Brotherhood of Railroad Trainmen, hoped that "the early establishment of a branch of the United States Employment Service on the territory will help relieve the serious unemployment situations existing there." In May 1943 the WMC established a USES office in Puerto Rico, under the direction of Winston Riley Jr., with a staff of twelve employees to help stateside manufacturers and farmers recruit workers who had vocational training and at least six months of work experience and could pay their own transportation costs. Attempting to manage the flow of workers from municipalities that had not played a major role in migration to the States, from May to December 1943 the USES facilitated the migration of 1,030 skilled workers who paid their own transportation and had a hundred dollars to cover living their expenses for two to three weeks (Maldonado 1979, 108; U.S. Senate 1941, 22).

The establishment of a USES office in Puerto Rico was the result of Governor Tugwell's work with the DTIP. In 1943 Tugwell met with Secretary of Interior Harold L. Ickes and representatives of the WMC and the WFA to lobby for hiring Puerto Ricans for the war effort and to work on U.S. farms. In response, Ickes wrote to U.S. secretary of agriculture Claude R. Wickards, asking for preferential treatment for Puerto Ricans over guest workers. The Senate Committee on Territories and Insular Affairs also attacked the use of West Indians instead of Puerto Ricans and issued a report that urged facilitating migration at government expense (*Atlanta Daily World* 1943; Maldonado 1979, 107–9). Nevertheless, stateside farmers still complained that they preferred West Indians to Spanish-speaking workers and that Puerto Ricans were lazy, undernourished, and could not be deported (Maldonado 1979, 110).

Although Tugwell's appeals to federal officials resulted in a limited number of workers being hired for agriculture, railroads, mining, and war-related manufacturing, by August 1943 the WMC was still recruiting West Indians and securing their transportation, even though some federal officials argued that one of the reasons for not hiring Puerto Ricans was the lack of passenger ships (*Atlanta Daily World* 1943). On December 21, 1942, Martin H. Miller, legislative representative of the Brotherhood of Railroad Trainmen, wrote to Santiago Iglesias Jr., Puerto Rico's acting commissioner of labor, informing him that he had asked the WMC to consider Puerto Ricans for the war effort. If federal and local officials could secure transportation for migrant workers, the WMC would consider them for agriculture in Florida (M. Miller 1942). In 1943, after Williard B. Kille, chair of the Farm Labor Committee of the Gloucester County Board of Agriculture, wrote to Tugwell and B. W. Thoron, director of the DTIP, requesting the importation of Puerto Ricans to southern New Jersey, the WMC sent migrant workers to the principal food-processing factories in the area (Killie 1943a, 1943b). In 1944 Seabrook Farms, Campbell Soup Company, and Hurff Soup Canning Company in New Jersey hired Puerto Ricans. Between 1944 and 1945 the Puerto Rico Department of Labor (PRDL) recruited 462 workers for the Utah Copper Mines and the Calco Chemical Company. Other companies, including the Lock Joint and Pipe Company, Bates Chevrolet, and the Long Island Fruit Company, asked for the PRDL's help in recruiting workers, but the government of Puerto Rico could not provide transportation, and the companies did not hire any workers (PRDL 1947, 33). These federal efforts notwithstanding, growers in the WEP continued to block attempts to bring large numbers of Puerto Ricans.

Another impediment to the migration of Puerto Ricans was that most employers wanted to hire workers only on a seasonal basis. Officials marginalized Puerto Ricans in farm-labor programs in part because they feared they would stay in the States after the war. The WMC encouraged Puerto Ricans and migrant workers from the U.S. South to return to their homes, and employers signed agreements promising to make an effort to return migrants to their homes and notify the WMC when workers quit or their employment ended. Nevertheless, many Puerto Ricans stayed after the war ended (U.S. House 1944, 33; Whalen 2009, 100–101).

By 1944 WMC funds for transportation had run out, and it became for difficult for Puerto Ricans to migrate stateside. The government of Puerto Rico found strong support in Congress for addressing this problem, in particular from Representative Fred L. Crawford and Senator Dennis Chávez. Crawford stated, "I would rather have Puerto Ricans here a million times over than Western Europeans and Southern Europeans, and, apparently, we're are going to have millions of people coming here from somewhere. Why do we not start with Puerto Ricans, with our own people, citizens of the United States?" (U.S. House 1944, 35).

During the war, even though Puerto Rico experienced high unemployment and food scarcity as German U-boats blockaded ships in the Caribbean,

U.S. emergency programs were not hiring a substantial number of Puerto Ricans and used guest workers instead. Finally, on May 27, 1944, Under-Secretary of Interior Abe Fortas, in charge of Puerto Rican affairs and lobbying on behalf of the Tugwell administration, wrote to Marvin Jones, War Food administrator, asking him to hire Puerto Ricans in the dairy industry. Fortas (1944) explained,

> I am informed by Insular authorities that Puerto Ricans resent the fact that they are denied the opportunity afforded to foreigners to fill the manpower shortage in the farms of this country. As one familiar with the conditions prevailing among these loyal people, who are suffering and have suffered from severe unemployment since we entered the war, I must say that their feeling of resentment is clearly understandable. I wish to urge that your Administration take steps for the utilization of Puerto Rican workers.

WFA officials in Washington, DC, also opposed the importation of Puerto Ricans for the dairy industry but approved hiring Basques and Portuguese, seemingly because they preferred white European workers to people of color. Officials defended their preference with references to Puerto Ricans' reputation as lazy and inefficient, reviving old criticisms of earlier migrants in the cotton industry of Arizona during the 1920s, but they also feared that some of the recruits might be black. Governor Tugwell believed that the main reason for the WFA's opposition was that Puerto Ricans could not be deported, though he also believed—and argued—that Puerto Ricans' deep attachment to their homeland would lure them back after the seasonal harvest. Nevertheless, in mid-1944 the WMC suspended hiring of Puerto Ricans because it was unable to enforce their return to the territory (Barr 1944c; G. Ramírez 1944; Thoron 1944a; Tugwell 1944b; *Washington Post* 1944).

Responding to growers' assertions about Puerto Rican workers, DTIP officials and the colonial government countered that hiring large groups of Puerto Ricans to work in agriculture in the States would not cause major problems, even though agricultural jobs were generally linked to social and racial discrimination. They also argued that problems of language and color could be resolved during the selection process, and that allegations of laziness and inefficiency were nonsense, noting that farmers said the same of Mexicans and Bahamians, in effect unmasking growers' primary concern that Puerto Ricans could not be forced to return home at the end of their contracts (Barr 1944b; History Task Force 1979, 124–25).

Some government officials in Puerto Rico also questioned the migration of workers to the States because of past experiences in Arizona and Hawaii (Avilés Lamberty 1974, 4–13; Manuel Pérez 1945b; Tugwell 1945). Writing in 1945, Manuel A. Pérez (1945a), commissioner of labor in Puerto Rico, observed, "Unless we plan these emigrations very carefully, making the proper selection of the workers according to their skill and that steps be taken to ensure that they would not have difficulties on account of the language, food, etc., I do not think that the government should encourage these emigrations." Lack of funds for, and access to, transportation also limited increased migration of Puerto Rican workers (Tugwell 1944a), and timely processing of remittances was a sticking point because the USES retained 25 percent of wages to send to workers' families. Despite ongoing irregularities in the payment of remittances to families, the Puerto Rican government supported the continuation of this practice, which workers greatly resented (Fernós Isern 1944).

During World War II farmers continued closing the U.S. farm-labor market to large numbers of Puerto Rican migrants, but the federal government did carry out small experiments that affected Puerto Ricans' postwar prospects. Although four hundred thousand Mexican and West Indian guest workers entered the United States between 1942 and 1945, the two thousand Puerto Ricans included in the labor-recruitment effort established small enclaves in southern New Jersey and Pennsylvania, and others dispersed to twenty of the forty-eight states, creating opportunities for seasonal migrants to obtain employment on farms when the WEP's emergency guest-worker programs ended (Henderson 1945; History Task Force 1979, 124–25; Senior 1947; Woytinsky 1946).

## EMPLOYING DOMESTIC WORKERS

After the war ended Puerto Rican farmworkers benefited from changes to the guest-worker programs. Even though immigration from Europe slowed and farmworkers moving to better-paid jobs in the cities created a scarcity of low-wage labor, the U.S. government continued to prioritize guest workers over domestic workers. New York farmers disagreed about the performance of West Indians but agreed that they were necessary for agriculture. Labor unions and the local press, however, blamed labor shortages on reliance on guest workers, former GIs' unwillingness to return to the fields, workers benefiting from unemployment insurance instead of accepting farm jobs, and the release of war prisoners who had been working in agriculture (Skeffington [1945–50?]a, [1945–50?]b).

Demobilization, the departure of women from war industries, the impending termination of guest-worker programs, and expectations of an expansion in production led government economists to anticipate labor shortages by 1950. Employers began to see Puerto Ricans as an excellent source of low-wage labor for agriculture and manufacturing, and Puerto Rican technocrats mobilized to claim a share of these new jobs (History Task Force 1979, 124–25; Kirstein 1977, 58). The government of Puerto Rico began to elaborate plans for its FLP, drawing on the experience of the Bracero Program (Cabranes 1949c).

As the possible cessation of the Bracero Program forced Mid-Atlantic farmers to search for new sources of labor, they rediscovered the efforts of colonial officials lobbying federal agencies to support hiring Puerto Rican migrant contract workers in agriculture. Farmers learned that their need for labor coincided with the end of the sugarcane harvest in Puerto Rico. Moreover, unlike farmers in the Midwest and Southwest, northeastern farmers did not consider Puerto Ricans to be a burden. As a result, private labor recruiters traveled to Puerto Rico seeking agricultural workers (Grosfoguel 2003, 180; Pagán de Colón 1956a, 5–6; Lapp 1990, 60).

From 1944 to 1949 the Puerto Rican Department of Labor (PRDL) turned its attention to migration to the United States and began discussions with various interested parties. In his annual report for 1945–46, the commissioner of labor recommended expansion of Puerto Rico's Employment Service to include emigration (Avilés Lamberty 1974, 4; PRDL 1947, 1948a, 9–10). The Puerto Rican government also used war-emergency funds to expand the PRDL, the Employment Service section, and later the BEM (PRDL 1947, 1948a, 1948b, 1949, 1950), in addition to taking another look at the federal government and Tugwell administration's ideas about sending migrants to the Dominican Republic, Venezuela, the Guyanas, Paraguay, the Panama Canal Zone, Colombia, and Brazil. Private proposals promoting migration to other countries continued until the 1950s. Puerto Rican and federal officials also discussed ways to transport workers and the feasibility of sending white workers to the U.S. South (Gautier 1948; Meléndez 2017, 61–64; Narváez 1977; Pagán de Colón 1948, 11).

In September 1946 another important development intensified attention to migration: President Harry S. Truman's appointment of Jesús T. Piñero, then the PPD's elected resident commissioner in the U.S. Congress, as governor of Puerto Rico. The replacement of Tugwell with the first Puerto Rican governor meant that the PPD had control of the local executive branch and was steps away from gaining the political autonomy it needed to implement local reforms and shape migration policy. The Piñero administration began to formulate policies to facilitate migration, overriding the hesitations and doubts expressed by Commissioner of Labor Manuel A. Pérez and some members of the Tugwell administration.

Meanwhile, private labor recruiters organized small groups of Puerto Ricans for agriculture, manufacturing, and domestic work in the United States. Initially, the PRDL collaborated with private contractors. Fred Dollenberg hired workers for New York, New Jersey, and Pennsylvania (Lapp 1990, 60; Pagán de Colón 1956a, 4–6), and Samuel Friedman was transporting workers to Glassboro, New Jersey, and Chalfont, Pennsylvania, and planning the transportation of 1,000 workers through contracts to be approved by the Puerto Rican commissioner of labor. Under act 19 of 1919 (amended by act 54 of 1936), the PRDL had the power to approve or disapprove contracts between recruitment agencies and workers. By 1946 Commissioner of Labor Pérez had approved contracts for 430 workers (*El Mundo* 1946a, 1946b, 1946c, 1946e, 1946g, 1946i; Pagán de Colón 1956a, 6; Sánchez Cappa 1946; Sierra Berdecía 1953, 1956a).

The selection and transportation of workers was the responsibility of the labor contractor. Dollenberg's United Labor Import Company had its own airplanes. Other labor brokers were owners or employees of private, fee-charging employment agencies and labor contractors. They used nonscheduled air carriers and local ticket agencies to transport workers. They also charged both the employer for recruiting workers and the workers for finding them jobs. Sometimes private agencies acted as travel agents and collected commissions from the airlines for tickets sold to migrants, making their businesses quite profitable (Castaño 1958, 31; Lapp 1990, 60; PRDL 1951, 56).

Since selling tickets was a lucrative business, labor contractors were recruiting more workers than there were jobs available. Immediately after the first workers hired by private contractors migrated to the States, reports of labor exploitation and inadequate working and living conditions reached Puerto Rico. Some migrants worked only a few weeks or a few hours per week and were not able to pay their living costs, and most of them confronted substandard wages, working conditions, and housing. Sometimes labor recruiters sold migrants old suitcases, winter jackets, and clothes at prices higher than those of new ones. The problem with private agencies and labor recruiters was that they found extreme ways to make a profit from migrants. Workers began to write to their relatives and the Puerto Rican government about their problems.

In the fall of 1946, some workers visited U.S. Congress representative Vito Marcantonio in East Harlem, complaining about low wages, poor housing conditions, and forced confinement in the Glassboro camp. Marcantonio attacked the Puerto Rican government for allowing contracted workers to live in concentration camp–like conditions, prompting an investigation by the Office of Puerto Rico, in Washington, and a visit from Commissioner of Labor Pérez. Their reports noted satisfactory conditions for most workers, though some problems with wages (*El Mundo* 1946b, 1946d, 1946f, 1946h; Lapp 1990, 60; Pagán de Colón 1956a, 5–13; S. Ortiz 1946; Senior 1965, 87).

In December 1946 Puerto Rican and progressive students from the University of Chicago issued a report criticizing the living and working conditions of three hundred women employed in domestic work and fifty men working at the Chicago Hardware Foundry Company who had been hired by the Castle, Barton, and Associates Employment Agency with contracts approved by the PRDL. Foundry workers paid $150 for a plane ticket, which usually cost $131.80, and a $60 fee to the agency. Their contract wages were $0.88 per hour, for a total of $35.40 for a forty-hour week. After deductions for taxes; payments for transportation and the agency fee; clothes, lodging, and board; and a payment of 25 percent of wages to their family in Puerto Rico, many workers received less than $1.00 in cash for a week's work. The report pointed out that this employment agency was violating PRDL regulations and that the Puerto Rican government did not inspect or supervise the conditions stipulated by the contract. They criticized Commissioner Pérez for witnessing the migrants' substandard living and working conditions without offering any solutions for their improvement. Pérez responded that these workers had left Puerto Rico voluntarily and that the government was not involved in transporting them. Elected officials in Puerto Rico called for an investigation. Carmen Isales, of the Division of Public Welfare, under Puerto Rico's Department of Health, found the same conditions exposed by the students. In January 1947, after investigating the situation in Chicago, Vicente Géigel Polanco, president of the Puerto Rican Senate Labor Committee and one of the architects of the PPD's social legislative agenda, proposed stricter regulations for the recruitment of contract-labor migrants. Conditions in Chicago reconfirmed the need for government intervention in the labor migration that elected officials, technocrats, and intellectuals had demanded to reduce unemployment (Alvarez et al. 1946; *El Imparcial* 1947a, 1947b, 1947c, 1947d, 1947e; *El Mundo* 1947a, 1947b, 1947c, 1947d; Lapp 1990, 61–62; Meléndez 2017, 53–56; Whalen 2001, 56; see also Amador 2015).

Even workers who had migrated to New York City fell prey to unscrupulous farm-labor recruiters. On March 6, 1947, the Puerto Rican *El Mundo* newspaper reported that six Puerto Rican workers, part of a group of twenty migrants, were lured to southern California from New York with false promises of employment in the fruit harvest. Ángel M. Cruz González, the leader of the group, indicated that labor agents offered them food, housing, and sixty cents per hour to move, but when they arrived they learned that they had to pay $125 for their bus transportation to California. Stanley Gue, California assistant commissioner of labor, said that farmers who were assigned the workers complained that they refused to work, giving "all kind of silly excuses" (*El Mundo* 1947d). These reports pressured the Puerto Rican government to act.

The problems with private labor recruitment motivated Governor Piñero, members of his administration, and elected officials to draft bills to organize farm-labor migration. In May 1947 Géigel Polanco's report led the legislature to pass and provide funding for public law 89, which replaced act 54 of 1936 and required the commissioner of labor to intervene in the migration of Puerto Ricans, monitor contracts, ensure the well-being of migrants, and coordinate any repatriation efforts. Through provisions of public law 89, the PRDL began to require employers recruiting in Puerto Rico to seek its approval. It imposed fines on violators and instructed the commissioner of labor to pursue legal actions in Puerto Rican courts. The government also enacted public law 417, regulating private employment agencies in Puerto Rico. In the summer of 1947, the first groups of contract workers sponsored by the PRDL arrived in the United States (*El Imparcial* 1947f; Lapp 1990, 173–74; Meléndez 2017, 55; Pagán de Colón 1948, 15, 17; PRDL 1949, 50).

Resident Commissioner Antonio Fernós Isern kept in close touch with Luis Muñoz Marín about the possibilities for managing the flow of migrants to the United States, including the establishment of an office in New York. Fernós Isern was not convinced that a New York office with the character of a consulate or with similar duties was needed or how it would operate. Instead, he proposed transforming Puerto Rico's Office of Information to serve Puerto Rican migrants. In a letter to Muñoz Marín, dated March 8, 1947, he stated that such an office should be supervised by the PRDL and take responsibility for the resettlement program requested by the Puerto Rican community of New York City (Fernós Isern 1947e; see also Fernós Isern 1947a, 1947b, 1947c, 1947d, 1947f). Leaders of the Puerto Rican community in New York City were pressuring Fernós Isern for the establishment of an office and had made a trip to Puerto Rico to meet with local officials and seek a legislative initiative about a migration office (Fernós Isern 1947d). Officials in the Piñero administration and the U.S. Department of Interior were drafting similar recommendations. Thus, private citizens, government employees, elected officials, intellectuals, and politicians were coming up with proposals for managing the flow of migrants. Fernós Isern's and Géigel Polanco's recommendations to Luis Muñoz Marín were among the ideas that set the stage for the Legislative Assembly to act.

In July 1947 Governor Piñero created a special advisory committee on migration, which included Luis Muñoz Marín, Teodoro Moscoso, Rafael Picó, Vicente Géigel Polanco, Fernando Sierra Berdecía, Ramón Colón Torres, Clarence Senior, Mariano Villaronga, Daisy D. Reck, and Paul Hatt, among others (Emigration Advisory Committee 1947; Maldonado Denis 1978, 110). The committee, with Sierra Berdecía presiding, held its first meeting on July 21, 1947, and discussed overpopulation and unemployment. Some members predicted that ongoing population growth would increase territory's population to around three million by 1960. Despite previous opposition, the committee considered various proposals for resettling Puerto Ricans in Latin America but ended up limiting its scope to the feasible option of organizing farm-labor migration (Barr 1946; Pons 1947).

Federal and local officials believed that Puerto Rican migration was similar to the migration from the U.S. South and that they could improve migrants' well-being through limited intervention. Managed migration also fit well with strategies for the economic development of Puerto Rico, and the United States was a feasible destination for migrants in terms of costs. Officials estimated that the cost per job would be around a hundred dollars or less per migrant. The initial suggestion was that the government of Puerto Rico would lend the money to migrants to subsidize their transportation expenses. In a memo to Governor Piñero, Donald J. O'Connor, an adviser to the government of Puerto Rico, asserted that ten thousand Puerto Ricans could likely find jobs for six months in the U.S. Northeast and Southwest and potentially earn more than seven million dollars, which would sustain a significant proportion of the Puerto Rican population directly—and also indirectly through remittances (1947, 1–8). O'Connor added,

Guided and encouraged removal and relocation mean not only jobs, particularly in the United States, which probably for years to come because of its immigration restrictions will offer an attractive market for employment of the unskilled "first generation," but also remittances to the "folks back home," an economic support which has potentialities of very great significance for the Island's people, and settlements on the mainland which, in the historic fashion of "immigrants," will send for their relatives and friends when "times are good." (11)

O'Connor anticipated political repercussions but argued that these were part of any significant migration scheme and that colonial officials should emphasize that Puerto Rican migration was part of the long history of U.S. internal migration. Nonetheless, fearing a backlash against all Puerto Ricans if migrants were relocated to New York City, O'Connor believed that the government should direct migration toward places such as Cleveland, Pittsburgh, Philadelphia-Camden, Detroit, the rural Southwest, and Colorado (1947, 1–8).

The government of Puerto Rico also took advantage of Congress's suspension of the Bracero Program for the harvest season of 1947. Mason Barr, director of DTIP, had written to Puerto Rican officials, expressing enthusiasm about the prospects for sending migrants to California (Barr 1947). In 1948 the DTIP intensified its commitment to bringing Puerto Ricans to the States, but Department of Interior officials wanted the government of Puerto Rico to hire a person to handle complaints from workers and another to deal with farmers to promote the use of migrant farmworkers, earmarking $10,000 for these efforts (O'Connor 1948).

In 1949 Alan Perl, legal adviser of BEM's New York Office, suggested that its director, Manuel Cabranes, visit the U.S. Department of State, in Washington, DC, with Commissioner Antonio Fernós Isern and Mason Barr to argue against granting work visas to Jamaicans (Cabranes 1949a, 1949b). Barr, who had been an assistant to Governor Tugwell in 1944, became director of the Interior Department's Caribbean Division in the late 1940s and defended the interests of the government of Puerto Rico in decertifying guest workers (Sierra Berdecía 1948d, 1948e). In this way the Caribbean Division played a part in the eventual creation of the FLP by providing language, precedents, and the infrastructure for visiting possible destinations of Puerto Rican migrants and by offering its offices as a place for Puerto Rican officials to meet with federal officials and interested growers.

The so-called Puerto Rican problem in New York City also influenced debates about migration. Tabloids published articles about the problems of overcrowded housing, unemployment, crime, illnesses, and lack of assimilation supposedly wrought by Puerto Ricans, criticizing the government of Puerto Rico for allowing massive migration to the city. Consequently, the government of Puerto Rico requested that Columbia University conduct a survey of Puerto Ricans in New York City, with recommendations for solving the problems the community confronted. The study, published in 1950 by C. Wright Mills, Rose Kohn Goldsen, and Clarence Senior as *The Puerto Rican Journey,* concluded that migrants went to the city searching for employment, not welfare, and that their socioeconomic characteristics were higher than the general standards in Puerto Rico. The study helped the government of Puerto Rico justify its migration policy and the establishment of the FLP (Avilés Lamberty 1974, 7; Meléndez 2017, 56–58).

In September 1947 Gov. Jesús T. Piñero assigned Fernando Sierra Berdecía, the new commissioner of labor, to study and make recommendations regarding migrant workers in the United States. Sierra Berdecía, who had been a conciliation commissioner of the Mediation and Conciliation Service of the Department of Labor, replaced Manuel A. Pérez, the commissioner who opposed migration during the war years (PRDL 1947). Sierra Berdecía visited workers, farmers, and federal, state, and local officials in the States as part of an investigation of labor-contracting practices. He found that recruiting agencies and labor contractors were making substantial profits at the expense of workers, who were paying inflated prices for transportation, clothing, and food. For their part, employers complained about workers who were not physically prepared to perform their jobs because of sickness or disabilities. In addition, stateside officials in schools and welfare agencies complained about challenges that Puerto Ricans were creating, citing classroom overcrowding, lack of English-language skills, health problems, and crime. Some men, unable to find jobs without institutional support, resorted to begging for help or turning to welfare programs (Castaño 1958, 31; Lapp 1990, 60, 63, 117–18; Pagán de Colón 1956a, 5–6).

## MIGRATION AGENCIES AND THE FARM LABOR PROGRAM

On November 17, 1947, Sierra Berdecía sent his report to the governor, recommending the reorganization of the Employment Office, the establishment of the BEM, and the creation of a farm-labor program to recruit migrant workers in Puerto Rico after the sugar harvest, when unemployment was highest. He also suggested contracting women as domestic employees. Sierra Berdecía envisioned the coordination of hiring, orientation, and transportation of migrants to New York, New Jersey, Pennsylvania, Delaware, Massachusetts, and Connecticut and their supervision by the staff of BEM branch offices. The Puerto Rican legislature followed these recommendations by approving public law 25 of 1947, creating the BEM (Pagán de Colón 1948, 3; 1956a, 6–8; Lapp 1990, 117–18; Sierra Berdecía 1947; Whalen 2001, 68). The government had concluded that a managed and planned migration program would benefit farmers, workers, host communities, and Puerto Rico (Castaño 1958, 31; Lapp 1990, 117–18; Whalen 2001, 68).

Using the experiences of the Bracero Program and of private labor recruitment, the government of Puerto Rico formalized the FLP in 1948 (Lapp 1990, 173–74). Sierra Berdecía stated that the services offered by the FLP established a precedent in the history of migration in the United States and perhaps in the world. Puerto Rico was using its own economic resources to cooperate with the local governments of the stateside communities where migrants worked and resided, with the goal of reducing problems of "adjustment" (Sierra Berdecía 1956a). The postwar period in Puerto Rico thus became the era of low-wage labor migration to the Northeast.

The end of World War II also brought changes to U.S. farm-labor programs and colonial policies in Puerto Rico. The BEM and the FLP were established as growers were losing their influence to shape internal labor policies, and the U.S. government was transforming its political relationship with Puerto Rico, allowing the drafting of a local constitution, which was ratified in 1952. These measures granted the political autonomy that paved the way for important reforms and policies sought by the PPD, whose technocrats and elected officials were turning to neo-Malthusian ideas about population growth and exploring scientific planning of the economy, the Mexican and West Indian guest-worker programs, and the creation of a bureaucracy that would provide technical knowledge on labor markets (Henderson 1945; Senior 1947; Woytinsky 1946).

The establishment of the BEM was part of the Puerto Rican government's effort to reform labor conditions, a process begun by Governor Tugwell and the PPD-led legislature. The postwar government continued this effort by passing labor legislation and establishing the bureaucracy to implement it. These laws included the regulation of minimum wages, hours, and employment conditions and the establishment of social security programs, such as workers compensation, and the Minimum Wage Board (Dietz 1986, 187; PRDL 1952b).

While local developments shaped many of the migration policies and actions of the Puerto Rican government, officials also drew from previous experiences with private labor recruitment. In drafting public laws 25 and 89, Puerto Rican officials considered the previous experiences of migrant workers in Hawaii and Arizona, as well as their own experiences of migration. For instance, Commissioner of Labor Fernando Sierra Berdecía had been a migrant living in Spanish Harlem in the 1920s. Another important development was the conversion of war airplanes for passenger transportation (Sierra Berdecía 1956a, 7–11), which resulted in Puerto Rican farm labor becoming part of one of the first large airborne migrations in world history.

Puerto Rican officials paid close attention to how federal agencies carried out programs for braceros during the war, and the FLP resembles the Bracero Program in its organization and attempts to micromanage the migration of farmworkers. The BEM's Alan Perl kept relevant examples of the contracts for the bracero and West Indian programs in a file in the New York Office, and Sierra Berdecía hired personnel with experience in the Bracero Program, such as William López, who had worked with Mexicans in Michigan before joining the FLP staff in New York (Consumers' League 1960; Goodwin 1951; Sierra Berdecía 1948c). Even Sierra Berdecía's (1949c) insistence that employers or the federal government pay for migrants' transportation was based on arrangements the U.S. government had made for Mexicans and West Indians.

One can better understand the FLP within the context of the 1933 Wagner-Peyser Act, whose passage reflected U.S. officials' belief that planned labor migration, under the federal government, would provide orderly recruitment and a guaranteed labor supply, set minimum wages, and return workers to their home countries (Breen 1997, xi–xiii; Galarza 1964, 44; 1977, 40–41; Goodwin 1948, 3). Wagner-Peyser had created a federal interstate labor exchange and placement system, under the aegis of the USES and the Farm Placement Service, to assist both job seekers and employers. Employers embraced the service because it did not concern itself with wages, housing, transportation, and other problems confronted by workers but rather assisted in the recruitment of workers for agribusinesses.

For USES and Farm Security Administration officials, managing labor migration was not always an efficient endeavor. In 1946 they estimated that nine thousand workers showed up for six thousand available jobs in North Carolina, resulting in overcrowded housing and poorly paid workers

(Pittman 1948, 13). That Jamaican workers were idle while farmers used soldiers to pack fruits and vegetables further indicated that a farm-placement program was needed to provide coordination and the efficient allocation of human and other resources (U.S. Senate 1946, 172).

The USES managed the recruitment of workers by channeling the migrants to areas with labor shortages (Mirengoff 1948, 7). According to USES director Robert C. Goodwin,

> To supply farmers, growers, and food processors with the labor they need, when they need it, calls for the most efficient use of all available supplies of this type of labor. It calls especially for wise, carefully planned utilization of migratory labor and labor that can be assisted in moving from one crop area to another as the need arises. The public Employment Service is planning intensive recruitment campaigns and community drives to rally all available labor resources in times of crop emergencies. The nation-wide pool of migratory labor will be utilized on a planned basis to meet the needs of individual employers and industries. (*Employment Service Review* 1948)

On January 1, 1948, the USES took charge of the Farm Placement Program and integrated the Farm Placement Service into its operations to create a unified national farm-labor market to ensure that enough workers would be available to produce, harvest, and process crops across the United States based on preseason estimates of crop yields and the labor supply.[2] The agricultural market served by the service was composed of a network of local and regional labor offices (Kirstein 1977; Rasmussen 1951; Spalding 1948). Puerto Rican officials lobbied federal officials to insert their programs into the USES.

State migration programs were another antecedent of the BEM. During World War II New Jersey and New York had central coordinating agencies and programs to oversee migrant labor camps, monitor the health of workers, and alleviate labor shortages (Scruggs 1988, 527; Vorse 1953). The New Jersey Department of Labor had a Migration Division (U.S. Extension Service 1947, 38), and New York State established the Interdepartmental Committee on Farm and Food Processing Labor, which also administered the Migrant Registration Law of 1946, child-labor laws from 1928, and wage-payment laws (Geach 1959, 35–42; Hurd 1953).

Puerto Rico's BEM followed the example of U.S. federal and state employment-services offices in designing its own FLP (Pagán de Colón 1948). From 1942 to 1946 the federal interstate exchange system to assist job seekers and employers established under the Wagner-Peyser Act included a new USES with affiliated state offices completely funded by the federal government. After the war, however, the state employment-service offices resumed their operations, with state and federal matching funds. By 1949 the U.S. government had eliminated matching monies and funded all state offices through the Federal Security Agency (Fay and Lippoldt 1999, 31–32; Ruttenberg and Gutchess 1970, 4–5). Each state designated an agency with the legal power to cooperate with the USES; in Puerto Rico the BEM functioned as one of those agencies (USES 1949, 4). But the role of the BEM and its MD mirrors that of the Farm Security Administration, state migration offices, European colonial agencies, and guest-worker programs. Managing labor migration required a bureaucracy for lobbying the federal government and transporting and overseeing workers.

In 1948 PPD government officials formally opened the BEM offices in Puerto Rico and New York City. The commissioner, and later secretary, of labor, Sierra Berdecía, began to shape the mission and structure of the BEM and the FLP. Another key technocrat in the development of the FLP was Petroamérica Pagán de Colón, who became director of the BEM in January 1948. Initially, BEM operations were small: Pagán de Colón began working from the commissioner of labor's conference room, and the budget for the first six months was only $101,025 (*El Mundo* 1947e; Pagán de Colón 1948, 4; 1955, 1; PRDL 1948b). Manuel Cabranes became the director of the BEM's New York Office, which was also under Fernando Sierra Berdecía's direct supervision. By 1950 the government of Puerto Rico ran BEM offices in New York and Ohio, in addition to its twenty-eight offices in Puerto Rico (PRDL 1951, 55–56; Sierra Berdecía 1948b, 1948f).

The emergence of a new colonial state based on self-government accelerated the transformations taking place in Puerto Rico in the 1940s. Modern colonialism devised tax exemptions for labor-intensive manufacturing, distributed small parcels of land to landless agricultural workers, and promoted population control through sterilization and migration. Puerto Rico itself became a social laboratory for U.S. policies in the Global South. Large-scale migration was a prominent feature of economic-development policies (see Lapp 1995, 181), and Puerto Ricans in the States became one the most important assets for the new colonial regime.

The FLP arose within a social and political climate that made Puerto Rico a showcase for development. From 1948 through 1968 its efforts to reach and oversee the circumstances of migrant workers also reflected the hegemony of the PPD. The FLP fostered the migration not only of workers from rural areas but also of poor Puerto Ricans who could not have imagined migrating because they lacked knowledge, networks, and financial assets. The exportation of excess labor was as crucial to Puerto Rico's impressive economic development as capital investments in the manufacturing sector. Migration was an escape valve that temporarily resolved the government's inability to provide working-class families with decent employment and incomes (Dietz 1986, 227–28).

While Puerto Rican farm-labor migration was increasing, the Truman administration sought to extend the New Deal by providing a safety net and more labor rights to farmworkers, protecting domestic workers, and regulating guest work (Robinson 2010). In 1950 the President's Commission on Migratory Labor in American Agriculture held hearings in which Clarence Senior represented the government of Puerto Rico. After the commission reported that guest-worker programs depressed the wages of domestic workers, USES officials accepted what growers paid in agricultural regions as "prevailing wages" for guest workers, even though these were not the result of collective bargaining (President's Commission 1951, 58–60).

The Korean War revived the fear of labor shortages, giving another triumph to growers. In July 1951 Congress passed U.S. public law 78, granting official status to the Bracero Program, without including any of the recommendations of the President's Commission on Migratory Labor—nor did the law define what a labor shortage was or how prevailing wages would be determined (Calavita 1992, 2, 44–45). The President's Commission had also pointed out the conflict between the USDL and states in protecting the interests of domestic farmworkers and administering the Bracero Program (125–26) and reiterated its preference for hiring Puerto Ricans rather than guest workers. In this context the Puerto Rican government enacted and applied its public laws 25 and 89. In the following chapter I discuss how the BEM and the MD devised strategies to implement the Farm Labor Program.

# THREE

## Implementing Contract Migration

IN THE LATE 1940S POSTWAR GEOPOLITICS impelled changes in U.S. government policies toward Puerto Rico. The Popular Democratic Party (PPD; Partido Popular Democrático) further consolidated its power through the election of the first native-born governor, in 1948, and expanded technocratic oversight of policy initiatives. Congressional approval of self-government, in 1952, removed Puerto Rico from the authority of the federal Division of Territories and Island Possessions. By granting self-rule, the federal government allowed the PPD to set domestic policies, and, in this climate of reform, the Puerto Rican government implemented its migration policies and accelerated many of the programs initiated by Governors Rexford G. Tugwell and Jesús T. Piñero, particularly industrialization, land distribution, and population control (Grosfoguel 2003, 180). Industrialization, under the so-called Operation Bootstrap, aimed to replace agricultural labor with manufacturing jobs, although officials understood that this would not provide enough employment. As intellectuals, elected officials, and technocrats linked the territory's high poverty level and social problems to overpopulation, migration and birth control were promoted to address economic and social ills. Women, who constituted the majority of the manufacturing labor force, became test subjects for birth-control pills and mass sterilization. Men were marketed as reliable workers for U.S. agriculture.

Discourses of "overpopulation" throughout the western European and U.S. colonies contained an ideological message that a Malthusian crisis had ruptured the balance between population growth and production, leading to unemployment.[1] By 1950, as unemployment in Puerto Rico hovered around

12.9 percent (Dietz 1986, 275; MacMaster 1997, 185; Meléndez 2017; Muñoz Marín 1946), colonial officials concocted policies and regulations to ensure careful planning of migration as a tool of population control and economic development. Officials in the Bureau of Employment and Migration (BEM) and the Migration Division (MD) made the PPD's reform and modernization mission manifest in the Farm Labor Program (FLP).

At the same time modern colonialism built a bureaucratic infrastructure capable of running the FLP, which took precedence over all other efforts to manage migration. As Petroamérica Pagán de Colón, a social worker and the director of the BEM, pointed out in the first annual report of the Puerto Rico Employment Service (PRES), in 1951,

> The largest number of opportunities for employment on the mainland for Puerto Rican workers at present are in agriculture. To take advantage of these opportunities the Puerto Rico Employment Service has devoted practically all its efforts toward the employment of our workers in this field. We estimate that the Island can supply around 50,000 workers for agricultural work on the mainland. We feel that this is the first step toward the final goal of getting jobs for Puerto Ricans in other fields of work. If they are accepted for agricultural employment, it will be the first step toward their employment in nonagricultural fields. (1951, 11)

For Pagán de Colón and other officials, the FLP was a tool to expand migration to other industries and facilitate the settlement of migrants. The policies of the PPD government of managing labor markets through migration reflect the important impact of the FLP and the New Deal policies in the history of Puerto Ricans in the United States.

This chapter explores how Puerto Rican government officials implemented the FLP in a context in which self-government, development, and modernization were goals to be achieved. The government of Puerto Rico inserted itself into the structure of managed labor at the federal level because self-government allowed PPD officials to directly lobby the U.S. Department of Labor, the U.S. Department of State, and other agencies responsible for farm-labor migration. By building a farm-labor migration infrastructure, the government ensured that poorly educated workers with few economic resources could migrate. New offices, leased airplanes, health certificates, and police records became part of official efforts to facilitate migration—a key strategy for developing and modernizing Puerto Rico.

Federal law stipulated that employers had to demonstrate a shortage of domestic workers before recruiting guest workers, but because not all employers considered Puerto Ricans to be domestic laborers, the Puerto Rico Department of Labor (PRDL) lobbied federal officials to recruit them for agricultural jobs. On February 10, 1949, Robert C. Goodwin, director of the U.S. Bureau of Employment Security, and Fernando Sierra Berdecía, the Puerto Rican commissioner of labor, signed a joint policy statement that recognized Puerto Rico as a source of domestic labor and extended the interstate clearance system to Puerto Rico.[2] Puerto Ricans thus gained precedence over guest workers when local labor was unavailable. The PRDL received funding from the U.S. Employment Service (USES) to recruit workers, initiating close cooperation between these organizations and affiliated state offices. The USES barred the entrance of guest workers, mostly West Indians, into states in the Northeast, such as New York, New Jersey, and Connecticut (Goott 1949, 45; Lapp 1990, 118–19, 174–76; *New York Times* 1950; Pagán de Colón 1956a, 13; USES 1949).

Puerto Rican officials intensified their lobbying in Washington (Sierra Berdecía and Descartes 1949), and on September 8, 1950, Congress extended the Wagner-Peyser Act of 1933 to Puerto Rico, reinforcing Goodwin and Sierra Berdecía's joint policy statement (USDL 1951) and making the BEM similar to the USES and state employment services. The extension of Wagner-Peyser also meant that the PRDL could access federal funding (Fay and Lippoldt 1999, 31–32; Ruttenberg and Gutchess 1970, 4–5). The Puerto Rican legislature established the PRES through passage of act 12 of December 20, 1950, which took effect on January 1, 1951, and extended the benefits of the USES to the territory (PRDL 1952b, 23). The BEM administered the PRES but was indistinguishable from it regarding use of federal funds under Wagner-Peyser, disseminating publicity and reporting its annual activities to federal agencies. The BEM director, Petroamérica Pagán de Colón, became the director of the PRES.[3] Like other state employment services, the PRES implemented the USES's program for job placement, counseling services to veterans, industrial services, labor-market information, and community participation (PRDL 1952a).

The BEM's New York Office began operations on June 30, 1948, and, until 1951, served as both a clearinghouse for all PRDL matters in the United States and an agency to aid migrants. This office did not place migrants directly in jobs but rather referred them to the USES, although farmers, agribusinesses, and other employers seeking to hire Puerto Ricans sometimes called the office. During the 1949–50 fiscal year, the BEM placed a total of 2,881 workers in this manner (PRDL 1951, 60–61).

In 1951 the PRDL reorganized its BEM offices in the United States, moving employment-service operations to the PRES, while migration activities came under a new national office called the Migration Division, which occupied the former BEM offices in Chicago and New York City (Segundo 1992, 759). Clarence Senior became the MD's first national director. Responsible for all activities in the continental United States, he established a close working relationship with several state employment services that were hiring Puerto Ricans. While the BEM had operated under the auspices of the PRES with federal funds, the MD operated exclusively with funds from the PRDL (PRDL 1952b, 25).

Incorporation into the interstate labor-exchange system created another controversial issue for the Puerto Rican government. Labor Commissioner Sierra Berdecía opposed Puerto Rico's inclusion in Region IV of the USES, whose offices were in Atlanta, Georgia, because of racial segregation in that region. As a result, Puerto Rico became part of Region II, with New York, New Jersey, and the Virgin Islands (Segundo 1992, 760). The MD, as the representative of the PRDL in the United States, gained more power in developing and administering the FLP by working closely with federal, state, and local governments and negotiating contracts with farmers (Lapp 1990, 175). The new agency collaborated with the New York City Farm Unit, which referred city residents to employment on farms. During the 1950s most farmworkers referred to the New York City Farm Unit by the New York State Employment Service were Puerto Ricans (NYSDL 1957, 7).

On February 1, 1951, the PRES began to operate officially as a USES affiliate, merging the activities of the BEM and the Veteran's Employment Service. Between February 1 and June 30, 1951, the PRES received $205,897 from federal appropriations, of which $125,125 went to personnel expenses and $80,771 for general expenses. That the PRES was under the USES's regional office in New York highlighted the growing importance of the MD's New York Office (Castaño 1958, 32; PRDL 1952b, 23–24).

PRES's affiliation with the USES enhanced the PRDL's mission to promote employment opportunities inside and outside Puerto Rico. Immediately after the extension of Wagner-Peyser, the USES national office in Washington and the MD began a public-relations campaign throughout the United

States, announcing the establishment of the PRES and urging state employment offices to use Puerto Rican workers in areas of labor shortage in agriculture and other industries. The PRES received applications for employment from workers and increasing numbers of requests for workers from employers, matching job orders to registered applicants and vice versa (School of Public Administration 1951, 6).

Between 1948 and 1956 the BEM grew considerably. It had begun operations with a budget of $22,000 and 19 employees. During its first six months, it placed 11,128 persons in jobs inside and outside Puerto Rico, compared with 6,037 placements the previous year by the former Employment Service of the PRDL. Throughout 1948 the BEM recruited 4,906 migrant farmworkers, and its New York Office served 800 persons per month seeking employment or social services. The following year the BEM received a total of $418,979 for its operations, of which $29,737 were allocated to the FLP. Its staff eventually increased to 131 employees, not counting around 40 members of the MD staff (Sierra Berdecía 1949e, 13–15).[4]

On February 10, 1956, the Puerto Rican legislature approved public law 2, increasing the MD's budget by $75,000, and the agency increased its personnel to 96. The number of offices increased to thirteen, as eight new field offices overseeing the FLP opened in Hartford, Connecticut; Boston, Massachusetts; Keyport and Camden, New Jersey; Rochester, Middletown, and Riverhead, New York; and Hamburg, Pennsylvania. (The MD already had offices in New York City, Chicago, San Juan, and Cleveland, in addition to its national office.) By 1956 the BEM had a budget of $971,413, with 317 employees, while the MD had a budget of $647,117 and 106 employees (Migration Division 1954, 13; 1956a, 4–5, 25, 29; 1957, 19; Pagán de Colón 1955; PRDL 1952b, 21–25; 1957, 5–6). By 1958 the MD had placed 85,000 workers in farms, hotels, restaurants, and factories throughout the United States, including 13,067 migrant farmworkers (PRDL 1958).

For Commissioner Sierra Berdecía, the extension of Wagner-Peyser was the most important factor in the existence of the BEM (Meléndez 2017, 80). BEM director Pagán de Colón characterized the extension as a "big deal" for Puerto Rico, believing it comparable in significance to the Puerto Rico Nationalist Party (Partido Nacionalista de Puerto Rico) revolt that occurred in October 1950 (Pagán de Colón 1950b). By the end of the 1950s, their assessments proved correct, with a massive migration of Puerto Ricans and the continuous extension of employment services and benefits, facilitated by the creation of the Puerto Rico Bureau of Employment Security (PRBES).

The legal changes to, and perceptions of, the U.S. citizenship of Puerto Ricans impacted the success of Puerto Rican and U.S. officials' lobbying efforts and the insertion of Puerto Rican agencies into the labor-management apparatus of the federal government. Some U.S. elected officials and policy makers proposed the permanent resettlement of migrants in the United States in addition to their migration as seasonal farmworkers. Michigan Congress representative Fred Crawford argued,

> We have 2,300,000 people in Puerto Rico. They are citizens of the United States.... If you could put 50,000 in the United States annually as permanent citizens, you would do more than all of the efforts that have been done in the last 50 years for Puerto Rico or that you can do in the next 50. (U.S. House 1951a, 160–61)

Despite the USES's efforts, Puerto Rican officials confronted opposition and competition from guest-worker programs. In 1949 a bilateral agreement granted undocumented Mexicans bracero status over new recruits, effectively eroding the gains made by the BEM (Calavita 1992, 28). The Puerto Rican government was able, however, to persuade stateside labor unions and community organizations to support its efforts to protect the rights of migrant workers. Clarence Senior (1952a) wrote to U.S. labor movement leaders for help in identifying violations of wage and labor standards experienced by workers, arguing,

> We are heavily dependent on the various state employment services to avoid sending men to areas where labor standards might be threatened. Therefore, we appeal to organized labor to help us in this respect. We would greatly appreciate notices of any violations of prevailing wage rates and of any other low labor standards involving Puerto Rican workers.

H. L. Mitchell, president of the Southern Tenant Farmers' Union, an affiliate of the American Federation of Labor, became an enthusiastic supporter of FLP, praising its contract as the best benefit offer for farmworkers (Sierra Berdecía 1952a, 36–37, 43–44).

Clarification of the U.S. citizenship of Puerto Ricans shaped the relationship of the FLP to other guest-worker programs. U.S. public law 45 of 1943, which sanctioned the Mexican Bracero Program, expired in 1947, but the program continued informally and without official oversight by the USES, the Immigration and Naturalization Service, or growers. The lack of oversight fostered an increase in undocumented labor that, along with investigations by the President's Commission on Migratory Labor and the claims of labor shortages resulting from the Korean War, led Congress, in 1951, to approve U.S. public law 78, which amended the Agricultural Act of 1949 to include agricultural labor and reinstitute the Bracero Program (Briggs 2004).[5] Public law 78 denied Mexicans the right to strike or renegotiate their wages, but it also prohibited employers from using Mexicans as strikebreakers.

The enactment of public law 78 represented a challenge for Puerto Rican officials who were promoting farm-labor migration. Violations of regulations to protect domestic workers were common, and U.S. Department of Labor officials, working with growers, were shaping labor policies by allowing braceros and rejecting domestic workers (Briggs 2004; Galarza 1977, 83–87, 215–21, 223; Pollitt 1960; U.S. Senate 1962a). MD director Senior made clear in congressional hearings on public law 78 that a new Bracero Program meant that guest workers would take jobs with low wages and substandard conditions:

> As phrased, the bill would permit the importation of foreign laborers upon the sole showing that domestic workers would not take employment at such inhuman terms. . . . The criterion should be that no foreign workers may be imported at wage standards or under working conditions lower than those for which continental workers will work. (1952c, 8)

In its opposition to public law 78, the MD insisted that the government's goal was not to depress wages but rather to send workers to areas where farmers needed them (Senior 1952c, 8–11).

Initial reluctance by USES officials to promote the hiring of Puerto Ricans arose because Congress had signaled a preference for guest workers over domestic workers during World War II. At that time Congress favored a temporary labor force that could be regulated through immigration law rather than domestic migrant workers who could become a burden on farming communities. In effect, U.S. citizenship was a handicap for Puerto Rican migrants seeking work in the States. Stella Draper, a Puerto Rican official working for the MD, reported to Manuel Cabranes, director of the New York Office,

> I got the definite impression from everyone I have talked to in USES that they are scared to death of Congress, if they help Puerto Rican laborers. Apparently, the Appropriations Committee has a long memory, and during

the war that committee expressed preference for Mexican labor so it could be returned when the jobs were over, and not Puerto Ricans, who might become a problem. (Draper 1948b)

To change the minds of federal officials and members of Congress who opposed hiring Puerto Ricans, colonial officials reassured the USES that they would continue to encourage workers to return home after the harvest. U.S. Bureau of Employment Security director Robert Goodwin reaffirmed that "arrangements have been made with Puerto Rico, and we have a provision for the return of those brought in on farm work. . . . Puerto Rican officials have been extremely cooperative in working out an arrangement" (U.S. House 1949b, 14).

Although the government of Puerto Rico justified migration to the United States, officials did not see themselves as part of a transnational state fostering international migration (see Duany 2011; Findlay 2014). In publications and official speeches, the MD emphasized that Puerto Rican migration was part of U.S. internal migratory patterns, arguing that five million workers in the United States moved from one state to another, and, as with Puerto Rican migrants, their main motivation was better job opportunities. Puerto Rican migration varied according to the job opportunities in the United States, and this had an impact at home. Between 1952 and 1953 the estimated negative population growth in Puerto Rico was -0.3 and -0.6, respectively. The short recession of 1954 resulted in a 69 percent decrease in the number of migrants, and the same occurred in the latter part of 1957 and in 1958, with 28 and 26 percent drops, respectively (Migration Division 1959, 2, 8, 15).

Another impediment to the migration plan was the cost of transporting workers stateside. In the initial negotiations Sierra Berdecía insisted that employers pay for transportation, but employers wanted workers to contribute at least thirty-five dollars each. Discussions in Congress regarding the reauthorization of the Mexican Bracero Program revealed that it cost more to transport Puerto Ricans than Mexicans. (In the 1950s the transportation cost for Puerto Ricans was thirty-eight dollars per trip, but only twenty dollars for Mexicans.) Congress had paid to transport Mexican workers in the 1940s, but it remained reluctant to pay for Puerto Ricans. After the reauthorization of the Bracero Program in 1951, the federal government spent $2 million to transport braceros but nothing on domestic workers. The federal government also became the guarantor of the contracts for Mexican workers (Briggs 2004; Goott 1949; Kassner 1954; U.S. House 1951a, 174–77). Although Sierra

Berdecía (1949d) argued that most Puerto Rican migrant farmworkers could not afford to migrate, his efforts proved unsuccessful, and they had to pay for their own tickets.

Puerto Rican officials continued to confront the perception of employers; local, state, and federal officials; and even some journalists that the mostly monolingual Spanish-speaking Puerto Ricans were foreigners who would displace local workers (Duany 2011, 90; Pagán de Colón 1956a, 13), although some growers also opposed hiring Puerto Ricans because they were citizens who could not be deported. For example, in a 1950 congressional hearing on farm labor, Keith Mets, president of the Imperial Valley Farmers' Association, stated,

> In our area we feel that Puerto Rican labor would not be practical. We like Mexican laborers better. They have always done our work, understand the work, are suited for the labor, and are familiar with it. . . . During the hot months is when we have our peak labor season, and when it is over they go back home, to Mexico, [and] don't furnish a social problem of relief. If we bring Puerto Ricans in, and they stay, there might be a social problem. (U.S. House 1951b, 175)

From 1949 to 1951 Puerto Rican officials pressed the USES to authorize Puerto Ricans as substitutes for Mexicans. California growers and officials pushed back, indicating that it was more feasible to transport and return Mexicans. Unwilling to accept the terms of Puerto Rico's labor contract, growers, some labor unions, and government officials blocked the use of Puerto Ricans. At that time the USES was approving Bahamians to work in New York State, so MD director Manuel Cabranes visited Washington to lobby U.S. Department of State officials to deny visas for West Indians (Cabranes 1949a, 1949b). Eventually, PRDL commissioner Sierra Berdecía decided that it would be better to promote labor migration to the U.S. Northeast. He explicitly told MD staffers Manuel Cabranes, Stella Draper, and Alan Perl,

> We do not want Puerto Ricans to contribute to the lowering of labor standards in any part of the United States. . . . We don't want to place them against the open hostility of local government officials. We do not want to send them to the South. That was stated very clearly by former Governor Piñero and the present Governor Muñoz Marín.

Sierra Berdecía nonetheless pressed federal officials to limit West Indians and Bahamians, and MD officials monitored the hiring of West Indians by reviewing reports from the USES and state employment-service offices (1949b; Latourette 1951; Monserrat 1957, 5–7).

The Puerto Rican government, aided by labor organizations and activists, continued to lobby the federal government to recruit contract workers. In the 1951 hearings for the Federal Security Agency appropriation, New Mexico senator Dennis Chávez scolded U.S. secretary of labor Maurice J. Tobin for not fostering the use of Puerto Ricans:

> We have conferences here on pan-Americanism, and on this and that; but we neglect to do anything about giving work to our own Puerto Rican citizens who are willing to die and some do die for their country, just because we may want to import some workers from Jamaica or Mexico or elsewhere. It is a little beyond my comprehension. (U.S. Senate 1951b, 21)

In the same hearing Puerto Rico's resident commissioner Fernós Isern argued in favor of Puerto Rican farm-labor migration, and H. L. Mitchell, chair of the National Legislative Board of the American Federation of Labor, insisted that Puerto Ricans were available. Meanwhile, William G. Latourette, general manager of the Garden State Service Cooperative Association (GSSCA), indicated that there were not enough Puerto Ricans to meet the demand for agricultural labor. Other members of Congress, such as Senator Herbert H. Lehman of New York, expressed their support for Puerto Ricans. The discussion turned on the question of providing funds to transport migrants, although colonial officials also took pains to reassure farmers, elected officials, and the USES that Puerto Ricans would return home after the harvest. The same debate took place in the 1952 congressional hearing for migratory farm labor, when senators advocated strongly for Puerto Rican workers (U.S. Senate 1951a, 7, 135, 146–47; 1952a, 1952b).

In New Jersey the prospects for contract farmworkers were more favorable because state officials, farmers, and community organizations perceived the FLP as beneficial to agriculture; labor unions agreed that seasonal migration could help resolve problems caused by unemployment in Puerto Rico, the immigration of workers from other countries, and farmers' exploitation of migrant workers. New Jersey farmers traveled to Puerto Rico in 1948, looking for a reliable supply of workers for the summer harvest because they were experiencing a severe labor shortage (Bonilla-Santiago 1986, 76–78; U.S. Senate 1951a, 1951b).

As early as 1948, New York State officials in the Department of Social Welfare worried that Puerto Rican migrant workers would become welfare charges and bring disease to farming communities. They wanted reassurance that they would depart after the harvest, and the government of Puerto Rico and New York State Employment Service assured them that most would return to their homes (NYSIC 1948a, 1948b, 1953; Siciliano 1956). But by 1953 New York State officials were warning about the creation of upstate Puerto Rican settlements as a result of farm-labor migration. One official stated, "We read about it in New York City and it is quite possible that in 10 or 15 years we may have what is called a Puerto Rican problem all over the State, which we may not be prepared for unless someone starts preparing the public for it before it happens" (NYSIC 1953). The "Puerto Rican problem" elaborated by some press reports about migrants in New York City was affecting others seeking jobs in agriculture (see Meléndez 2017).

While some New York farmers expressed satisfaction with their contract workers, others expressed negative views. Many argued that the main problem was the language barrier, but one farmer indicated that the unwelcoming attitude of some farmers was to blame. He had made the effort to learn Spanish so he could communicate with his workers. Complaints about language were partly due to some farmers' preference for West Indians, who had arrived during the war, and southern African Americans. Political pressure had led USES officials to stop certifying guest workers, but in 1951 it again allowed employers to bring Jamaican and Bahamian workers because of an anticipated labor shortage due to the draft for the Korean War (Clinton Migrant Committee 1953; Consumers' League 1957, 21; n.d.; Cornell University 1948).

To justify hiring West Indian or Bahamian workers, some farmers racialized Puerto Ricans, claiming their body build was inferior. Other employers even argued that the BEM had negotiated an eight-hour workday because Puerto Ricans were too weak for hard work (Mann 1949). MD official Stella Draper reported that a farmer, whom the New York State Employment Service allowed to hire Bahamians, asserted that Puerto Ricans were not strong enough to carry bags of onions weighing seventy-five pounds. Writing to Pagán de Colón, she urged Sierra Berdecía to pressure USES director Goodwin about hiring Puerto Ricans. The BEM even recorded the weights of migrant workers to show that they were prepared for heavy work (Draper 1950).

In Michigan employers argued that they wanted West Indians because they were unfamiliar with Puerto Ricans. Harold Mann, the BEM representative in the Midwest during the late 1940s, pointed out, "Employers do ... place weight on the fact that Jamaican workers are bound to them both by their contract and by the regulations of immigration service," adding that they would rather hire local workers or Tejanos (Mexican Americans from Texas) than Puerto Ricans (Mann 1949). Sierra Berdecía (1949a) commiserated, noting that the Jamaican contract also gave maximum advantages to employers and no protection to workers and that transportation costs for Jamaicans were often less than the FLP's costs. Connecticut farmers also complained about hiring contract workers. In the opinion of the director of the Shade Tobacco Company, Puerto Ricans were being brought in at the request of the federal government, while West Indians provided growers with a workforce that could be supervised and bound by immigration regulation, so any person causing trouble could be deported and barred from reentry (*Hartford Courant* 1952).

At the same time many employers and officials treated Puerto Ricans as deportable immigrants. For example, in 1952 a district attorney in Gettysburg, Pennsylvania, complained to government officials that migrants remained in towns and cities after the harvest, and he wanted the government to send them back to Puerto Rico. MD director Senior had to intervene to clarify the U.S. citizenship of Puerto Rican farmworkers (Senior 1952b). In one case Gustavo Pérez, a migrant, wrote to the governor of Puerto Rico, asking for help in obtaining his birth certificate because he had been detained in the States, suspected of being an undocumented immigrant. He urged the Puerto Rican government to contact the Immigration and Naturalization Service so he could be set free (Pérez Perález 1952).

In 1952, because of Puerto Ricans' growing importance in farm labor, the USES commissioned surveys of their work conditions in the Mid-Atlantic states and Florida. Both surveys were designed to describe and evaluate the migration and employment patterns of farmworkers to identify problems associated with their hiring from both the workers' and employers' points of view. The surveys revealed that 15,500 Puerto Ricans were employed in seasonal farm jobs in the Mid-Atlantic states and 3,000 in Florida. The Mid-Atlantic report characterized Puerto Ricans as newcomers to U.S. agriculture, although for some time they had composed a large proportion of the seasonal migrants for farms in New Jersey, New York, and Pennsylvania, particularly in August and September, and farmers praised the quality and quantity of their work. In fact, both reports emphasized the positive aspects of hiring Puerto Ricans (Mirengoff 1954, 1; USBES 1955, 1, 5).

U.S. citizenship remained an obstacle for the expansion of the FLP. Puerto Rican officials fought in Congress, in the fields, and in meetings with federal agencies against immigration policies promoting guest work, but deporting guest workers was a powerful tool that employers were unwilling to discard.

Despite these obstacles, federal agencies became more open to hiring Puerto Ricans, and the integration of Puerto Rico's government agencies with federal and state agencies allowed the FLP to prosper. The government of Puerto Rico became more than a mere intermediary between workers and growers. Educating the public, officials, and growers about Puerto Ricans became part of its core mission in the United States.

## PROMOTING THE CONTRACT

For growers, hiring contract workers through the USES was not as simple as hiring stateside workers. The government of Puerto Rico did not allow recruitment of Puerto Ricans unless employers accepted its FLP contract, and growers' requests for workers still had to be handled according to USES clearing procedures. Employers submitted job orders to the USES that specified position descriptions, wages, and employment conditions. When these reached the PRDL, officials recruited, interviewed, and selected workers, including some for supervisor jobs, as growers were also looking for experienced personnel to better manage their migrant farmworkers (E. Torres 1956). The FLP also opened possibilities for workers with formal education credentials and administrative experience to take jobs in U.S. agriculture. For example, in 1956 Bob Miller, of Seabrook Farms, visited Puerto Rico, inquiring about the possibility of developing a summer program for Puerto Rican students attending agricultural schools (Migration Division 1956b).

To ensure that labor shortages would not disrupt the harvest, the USES collected an array of data, including preseason estimates of labor needs from large employers, the number of workers hired in previous years in specific counties, reports from state and federal statisticians, and placement records. These data helped state employment agencies, among them the PRBES, prepare recruitment plans and campaigns in the States and in Puerto Rican municipalities. The USES assigned farm-placement representatives to branch offices, and county agricultural-extension agents informed employment-service offices in the South and Puerto Rico about crop cultivation and labor needs in their local areas. The USES also operated information stations for migrants in Florida, North Carolina, Virginia, and Maryland, and PRES operated one at the airport in San Juan (USES 1949, 5, 13).

The Puerto Rican government established relationships with large associations, such as GSSCA and Shade Tobacco Company, among others, to negotiate contracts for migrant workers. These associations emerged from growers' need to maintain a migrant-labor pool and promote labor conditions favorable to themselves. Because all growers confronted the same challenges with respect to wages, management, control of workers, and crop prices, farm bureaus worked with their members to set picking rates and wages, which eventually became the USES prevailing wages (Galarza 1964, 35–38). In the 1950s the GSSCA's services and membership also extended to farmers in Maryland, Pennsylvania, and New York (Coll 1963), which sometimes created problems between the association and the MD because workers were not supposed to be transferred freely between states, as the number of workers hired was supposed to conform to the specific labor needs of a particular region.

The BEM participated in the annual contract negotiations with individual farmers and growers' associations in the States, finding that farmers in the Northeast preferred Puerto Ricans because they were available, had experience, worked for lower wages, and could be hired without the visas and alien registration required for Mexicans and West Indians (Morales 1986, 79). This preference may also have been shaped by the limitation the USES imposed on farmers and associations that wanted to request guest workers. Some farmers realized that the FLP contract and the activities of the MD improved the relationship between workers, farmers, and the community. The MD also presented itself as interested in helping employers, not just the workers (Castaño 1958, 32). The FLP offered two contracts: one for independent farmers and another for associations. Both were written in Spanish and English but difficult to read, literally, because of the fine print. Reporting on the 1959 postseason meeting with farmers and associations, Guadalupe Ruiz acknowledged that the contract "in its present form it makes for difficult reading: 'small print' and that is probably why employers apparently never bother to read it." Similarly, because most workers were either illiterate or had limited schooling, addressing their confusion and misunderstandings about their contracts was part of MD officials' daily business (Ruiz 1959b).

Puerto Rican officials modeled their migrant-labor contract primarily on those of the Mexican and West Indian guest-worker programs, but they also drew on the contracts of private labor recruiters. They understood that Puerto Rican workers were in a tenuous position because farmers, labor contractors, and stateside officials could not coerce them into complying with the terms of their contracts. Sierra Berdecía (1948a) recognized that this potential weakness in the relationship established through the contract resulted from Puerto Ricans' citizenship rights, but he believed this problem could be addressed by fostering compliance with the contract:

> This contract represents the best terms we could get after considerable bargaining which actually verged on haggling. We had a sample of the contract used in the case of the Mexican workers, which had been approved by the USES. However, I would like to point out that our contract is of necessity a unilateral contract. We must keep in mind the fact that Puerto Ricans, unlike the Mexicans, cannot be forced to live up to their contracts. We must solve this problem through guidance by attempting to induce the workers to live up to their contracts even when they are unwilling to do so. Coercion being impossible, we must rely on appeals to their honor or their patriotism. The farmers are well aware of this. Consequently, that is a very weak point in our bargaining position. However, we would welcome any suggestions for a standard contract, and we will use such a standard contract as much as possible.

The government of Puerto Rico issued contracts that set wages at a minimum determined by PRDL or the USES prevailing wage, if it were higher.[6] But the USES's procedure for establishing prevailing wages was often flawed. Extension agents collected data on wages being paid by farmers, but interviewers who did not speak Spanish overlooked Spanish-speaking workers (NYSDL 1959, 19–23). Moreover, because local USES officials ran the program as a supplier of farm labor, they often acceded to prevailing wages set by growers' associations (Calavita 1992, 117–18). For example, in California, after the passage of public law 78, the USES-affiliated Farm Placement Office in Imperial County approved a reduction of the prevailing wage from $1.00 to $0.70 an hour for domestic workers (Galarza 1977, 40–42). Thus, while USES did not intend to adversely affect the wages of local domestic workers, in practice wages were determined by the farmers, and although the USES could modify wages, it rarely did.

In the early 1950s the President's Commission on Migratory Labor noted a correlation between farm wages and the concentration of braceros, finding that guest workers depressed wages (Calavita 1992, 30–31). Since the government of Puerto Rico followed the USES guidelines on prevailing wages, contract workers also contributed to depressing the wages of local and domestic migrant workers in many regions. In 1948 the lowest that a contract offered workers was forty-five cents per hour, in contrast to the Southwest, where farmers paid sixty cents a day without board or housing. As late as 1954, undocumented workers worked for forty cents an hour in California's

Imperial Valley (Galarza 1964, 30; Mitchell and Harrington 1979, 279). Farm wages increased by 14 percent from 1953 to 1959 but remained stagnant in the regions hiring braceros (Calavita 1992, 70–71). In the 1951 congressional hearings on farm labor, Philip Robb, representing the Consumers League of New Jersey, indicated that while Puerto Ricans got fifty-five cents per hour, southern African Americans could get up to seventy-five cents an hour, but without the benefits and protections of a contract (U.S. Senate 1951a, 168–73). By 1959, when New Jersey governor Robert B. Meyer testified before the U.S. Senate Subcommittee on Migrant Labor, he stated that the recruitment of local labor, the use of southern migrants, and the contracts with the government of Puerto Rico tended to improve wage levels on New Jersey farms (1959, 3).

The FLP contract intended to raise workers' standard of living as well as wages. Associations and farmers could charge workers for airfares, local transportation to the camps, and food, deducting these costs from paychecks, but they were also required to provide three hot meals a day, with meat at both lunch and dinner. The contract also stipulated that adequate, hygienic, and rent-free housing be provided to workers and that employers guarantee 160 hours of work over each four-week period. The Puerto Rican government offered workers' compensation insurance through the Agricultural Insurance Fund and authorized the secretary of labor to intervene in cases of contract workers injured in their workplaces (J. López 1993; V. Serrano 1991). Puerto Rico's public law 77 of 1958 authorized the Puerto Rico State Insurance Fund to cover medical and hospital services for contract workers injured in the United States (Migration Division 1958a, 7–8; Segundo 1992, 762).[7]

In 1954 health insurance, financed by workers' contributions, also became a feature of the FLP contract. By 1959 it had become a comprehensive health-insurance plan for migrant workers covered by the contract (Morales 1986, 85). In 1966 employers were also required to contribute to the health-insurance fund. In addition to protecting workers, offering health insurance avoided problems in local communities that feared migrants would become a burden on their hospitals and welfare agencies. Consequently, workers with contracts were more likely to receive medical treatment (Castaño 1958, 32; Lapp 1990, 178–81; Nieves Falcón 1975, 134; Pagán de Colón 1956a, 9).

The PRDL also instituted a bonding protocol to ensure that employers would comply with the contract and protect workers. Between 1949 and 1950 the commissioner of labor set ten dollars in cash, per worker, as the minimum bond to be posted by employers with a government-approved insurance company in Puerto Rico (PRDL 1951, 56). On April 24, 1951, the Puerto Rican legislature enacted public law 111 to institutionalize these bonding provisions (Segundo 1992, 761). PRDL regulations also required employment agencies to post a $1,000 bond to operate in Puerto Rico, prohibited charges to brokers, and reduced the costs of transportation, food, and medical care (Pagán de Colón 1956a, 9).

Many employers, particularly at the beginning of the FLP, objected to the PRDL's regulations. Some farmers argued that since Puerto Ricans were U.S. citizens, they did not need such protections. Others accepted, or eventually came to accept, the conditions for employing Puerto Ricans. The contract agreements and regulations helped manage problems, and complaints from workers and farmers decreased from 3,900 in 1952 to 1,890 in 1957. By the end of the 1950s, the FLP also found favor because of PRDL officials' cooperation with federal and local agencies and increasing public support for better working and living conditions for farmworkers (Castaño 1958, 32). The contract became a symbol that Puerto Rican officials used to entice workers and farmers to participate in the FLP.

## RECRUITING CONTRACT FARMWORKERS

Convincing men to become migrant farmworkers depended on the PRDL's recruitment strategies as well as the contract. In 1949 the BEM carried out a public orientation campaign across the territory, and in 1951 the PRDL created an Orientation and Information Section, with offices in San Juan, Caguas, Humacao, Guayama, Ponce, Mayagüez, Aguadilla, and Bayamón, to inform potential workers via radio programs and announcements, newspaper articles and ads, posters, pamphlets, handbills, and letters to municipal mayors. Some leaflets contained information about preparing for employment or how to look for a job; others advised workers about weather in the States and the kinds and colors of clothing to wear. Trucks with loudspeakers traveled throughout the countryside, announcing the availability of jobs. Local PPD political bosses often recommended party members for jobs as migrant farmworkers. The BEM also worked with local Protestant churches and Catholic parishes and created municipal committees to offer guidance to migrants. In 1956 the committees had representation from mayors, labor unions, and 350 designated storekeepers in barrios. Whenever recruitment lagged, officials mobilized these networks. Sierra Berdecía informed area

FIGURE 2. Farmworkers being recruited by an official of the Puerto Rico Department of Labor, circa 1950s. Courtesy of the Records of the Migration Division, Archives of the Puerto Rican Diaspora, Centro de Estudios Puertorriqueños, Hunter College, City University of New York.

administrators of the Puerto Rico Bureau of Labor Standards, which maintained offices in all municipalities, to work with mayors so that migrants could access orientation materials and reconsider their plans if they were thinking to leave for U.S. farms without contracts (Holman 1957, 2–3; Senior 1957d).

The BEM's regional offices in Puerto Rico posted job announcements and interviewed and hired laborers. Artemio, a former contract worker, recalled his excitement when he traveled to the BEM office in Mayagüez. Arriving early in the morning, he found a long line of people looking for placements in farmwork. He received a contract that took him to Erie County, New York, where he had a friend. Artemio wrote to his friend for assistance and lived with him after finishing his contract.

The BEM perceived its recruitment mission as extending to workers, employers, and the host communities. As part of the interview and application process, BEM officials informed potential migrants of job vacancies in different areas and of the various job orders received, with descriptions of their requirements and expectations. BEM officials also provided information about wages, workers' responsibilities, and living and working conditions. Workers then chose their employer and place of work (Castaño 1958, 33).

The BEM orientation program familiarized migrants with the living and working conditions in stateside labor camps and farms, emphasizing the differences in housing, dress, and food; requirements for employment; and opportunities of work outside New York City. The BEM used radio, distribution of literature, personal contacts with migrants and potential migrants, and press releases to answer the general population's many questions and doubts about migration. Radio station WEVM transmitted the program *Guía del viajero* (Traveler's Guide) throughout the territory every Thursday from 9:15 to 9:30 A.M. From March to September 1953, the program discussed airlines, customs, jobs in the United States, appropriate clothes for travel, labor rights, housing, military service, the U.S. educational system, income taxes, cities with Puerto Rican communities, gangs, and crime. Other state offices and community organizations also distributed literature explaining life in the United States (Human Relations Council [1959?], 2–8; Migration Division, n.d.).

As officials believed that farms employing English-speaking workers would enjoy better employer-worker relations, the Puerto Rico Department of Education expanded and intensified the teaching of English among prospective migrants. On June 25, 1958, the legislature passed public law 108, authorizing the secretary of labor and the secretary of education to open local English programs for adult men referred for work in stateside farms who would also be living in labor camps. The MD offered classes at the Perkins de Wilde Camp in New Jersey (Meléndez 2017; Migration Division 1958a, 7–8; 1962, 177–78; Segundo 1992, 762).

The BEM also distributed flyers and pamphlets to promote learning English (PRES 1953). One pamphlet, *Usted en los Estados Unidos: La oportunidad de Pedro y Ramón* (You are in the United States: The opportunity of Pedro and Ramón), advised potential migrants, "The best thing is that you don't have to forget your Spanish, and you can handle things better by learning English." The pamphlet told the story of workers who had learned English, which led the farmer to raise their wages and help them bring their families. The pamphlet romanticized the relationship between workers and farmers, stating that both the workers' and farmers' families seemed to compose one family "united by friendship and honorable understanding" (Migration Division [1963?]).

FIGURE 3. Teacher Richard Cartright and migrant workers in an English class in a camp, circa 1950s. Courtesy of the Records of the Migration Division, Archives of the Puerto Rican Diaspora, Centro de Estudios Puertorriqueños, Hunter College, City University of New York.

Another publication, *Un mensaje del comisionado del trabajo a los obreros que desean ir a trabajar en fincas de los Estados Unidos* (A message from the commissioner of labor to workers who want to work on U.S. farms), emphasized that because workers had voluntarily chosen to migrate, they had to take responsibility for themselves:

> If you are going to the United States to work, always take into consideration the following: You are going because you wish to. You are going because of own will. You are going because you want to earn money for you and your family. The government is not sending you. The commissioner of labor is not sending you. You are sending yourself as the free citizen you are. You assume that responsibility by yourself, as the free citizen you are. (Sierra Berdecía 1950b, 1)

This publication also insisted that those who had not worked in agriculture should not migrate as farmworkers because work conditions were hard, and living conditions in the camps and farms were like those in Puerto Rico, with people living without electricity or running water. Moreover, food and clothes in the States were different, so if migrants did not like the descriptions of what they would encounter, they should not leave Puerto Rico (Sierra Berdecía 1950b). In fiscal year 1949–50, MD officials distributed twenty thousand copies of the pamphlet to prospective farmworkers. The government's goal was to advise workers about the nature of the jobs offered, emphasizing that they should migrate only if they were willing to accept the conditions of employment (PRDL 1951, 64).

Not all prospective migrants heeded this advice. In 1957 farmers in Harvey, Illinois, informed the MD that Puerto Ricans they hired were not farmers but rather city people unfamiliar with agriculture. One such worker, Avelino, recalled that officials in Puerto Rico told him that he would be building irrigation systems, not working in farming. Upon arriving, however, he was placed in a labor camp and expected to work in the fields, bending down all day tending asparagus. These employers had wanted experienced workers, but Clarence Senior doubted that Puerto Rican farmers would choose to be temporary farmworkers in the States (Senior 1957a, 4).

The MD also made a substantial effort to improve labor-management relations by providing farmers and communities interpretative information about Puerto Rican customs, behavior, and way of life (Low and Monserrat 1959, 29–37; Migration Division 1956b, 1958a, 8; Pagán de Colón 1956b). Publications targeting growers, food-processing establishments, hotels, restaurants, and manufacturers portrayed Puerto Rican workers as capable and readily available (Economic Development Administration [1950?]; Migration Division, n.d.). Puerto Rican officials also attended relevant U.S. national meetings. In 1950, for example, Labor Commissioner Sierra Berdecía attended the National Labor Conference, where he met with Max Henderson, director of the Worker Program for the Michigan Field Crops Association, which had hired and worked satisfactorily with a small group of Puerto Ricans in 1949. They discussed recruiting a large number of Puerto Ricans, and Alan F. Perl was charged with drafting the contract. Henderson estimated that five thousand workers could be employed in Michigan (Sierra Berdecía 1950a). The government of Puerto Rico also showcased migration as a development strategy before employers and state placement representatives at the Annual Farm Placement Conference in San Juan and arranged several official tours of farms and offices in the States to assess the situation of workers. Stateside officials also visited the PRDL, touring the BEM's facilities and learning about the migration program (PRDL 1953a, 1954c). The conferences and the tours provided firsthand knowledge of the requirements of farmwork and workers' characteristics, with the goal of improving the recruitment and placement of migrants (Castaño 1958, 33).

The BEM initially established MD offices in principal U.S. cities receiving migrants and then throughout Puerto Rico. These offices oversaw the various activities of the FLP, such as recruitment in Puerto Rico, transportation, contract negotiations, and problems of housing, employment, and health, establishing a vast network that grouped workers, farmers, associations, and local and state government officials in the U.S. Northeast and Midwest. Some of the regional offices resulted from community demands and the need for FLP staff to oversee immense territories. In the process field agents became public-relations officials, arbiters of disputes, social workers, and community organizers. The MD hired Antonio Del Río in 1956 to establish a regional office in Massachusetts. Del Río, who had worked with Puerto Rican farmworkers since 1954 as a translator for the Massachusetts Employment Service's farm-labor program, now oversaw the FLP and negotiations with farmers and the service (Morales 1986, 82–84).

Because MD field representatives were essential to implementing the FLP contract, the PRDL sought to hire personnel with experience in U.S. farm labor as well as in other guest-worker programs. Harold M. Mann, who had worked with braceros in the Midwest, assumed responsibility for recruiting Puerto Rican workers for the fields of Michigan and Illinois (Mann 1950). William D. López, after working for different guest-worker programs, became a field representative in New York.

The MD's regional offices were staffed with migration specialists whose job was to implement the FLP, find jobs for nonagricultural laborers, work with local community organization and agencies, facilitate the settlement of Puerto Rican workers and their families, collaborate with the USES and state employment-service offices, and avoid the duplication of efforts among the various local, state, and federal agencies (Castaño 1958, 33). In the larger associations' camps, the regional field staff were present when employers picked workers up so they could provide orientation to both workers and employers (Senior 1957d). One MD official requested that field personnel own cars so they could provide good service to the program (T. Zeno 1958a, 2).

MD officials also coordinated with local lawyers and state agencies to handle personal-injury cases through Puerto Rico's Industrial Commission, so injured workers returning to Puerto Rico did not have to attend to case hearings in the States (E. Torres 1960a).

MD officials pursued claims not only from workers against farmers but also the other way around. In a letter to a farmworker from Vega Baja, Puerto Rico, Migration Specialist Guadalupe Ruiz asks a worker to pay a bill for $6.71 that he owed to a merchant. Because his employer, a farmer, had actually paid the bill, Ruiz was asking the worker to forward the money to the farmer. Ruiz wrote, very diplomatically, "We will appreciate it greatly if you can pay your debt so you don't damage your credit and the good name of the Puerto Rican workers because we are certain that this was an oversight on your part" (Ruiz 1957b). Making sure that workers fulfilled their obligations to avoid tarnishing the image of Puerto Rican workers was an ever-present concern of MD officials.

The BEM granted the first licenses to recruit and transport workers to the private labor contractors Samuel Friedman and Fred P. Dollenberg. In New York Dollenberg's United Labor Import Company handled the transportation of 1,500 workers in 1948 (Consumers' League 1960; NYSDL 1949, 39–41). The problems caused by private labor-recruitment companies, however, led the Puerto Rican government to take full charge of the program. Private companies often sent workers to locations where there was no real need for them, leaving them without stable jobs and creating more problems for the BEM and MD. In the early spring of 1948, the MD decided to handle transportation itself (Draper 1948b). Friedman then tried to become an employer so he could subcontract workers to employers, a move the PRDL completely opposed. Petroamérica Pagán de Colón believed the FLP was created to fix the problems caused by labor contractors like Friedman:

> Mr. Alvarez from Friedman's agency . . . wants us to consider Friedman as the Employer which we cannot do, as you know. He raised hell about this and wanted us to make exceptions for Friedman, who he says is the man who has contributed most to establishing of this program.
>
> Sometimes I think he is right because the program was established to correct *malpractice* in labor contracting by some unscrupulous labor contractors. Only that he and I have a different view of what each means by contributing to the establishment of the program.
>
> He was somewhat insolent and made the Commissioner very mad—If you read the clippings, I am sending Cabranes you will get the whole story. (Pagán de Colón 1949)

Despite Friedman's protests, by 1950 most of the contract workers were being hired and transported for the GSSCA by the FLP (Consumers' League 1957, 20–21).

The initial agreement between the government of Puerto Rico and the USES provided for the orderly recruitment of Puerto Ricans to prevent an influx of workers without jobs in specific regions. In 1948 around 5,000 farmworkers migrated to the United States: 2,600 who traveled before the federal and Puerto Rican governments signed the agreement and 2,400 after it went into effect. The prospect of work on U.S. farms was so enticing that the BEM received 9,064 applications from potential migrants for the 1949–50 fiscal year, from which officials made 8,846 placements (Mirengoff 1954, 1; Sierra Berdecía 1949e, 13–15; PRDL 1951, 60; USES 1949, 28). While noncontract workers had to raise their own money to migrate, which they often received or borrowed from families or friends, in most cases farmers paid for contract workers' trips to the continental United States as an advance on their wages. Migrants' transportation cost obligations were usually completely met by the time they fulfilled their contracts, and most were reimbursed for their round-trip tickets after the harvest.

After the war, as military aviation was reoriented to civilian purposes, cheaper, faster air transportation began to fuel the migration of workers, enabling small groups of workers to be distributed in a large geographic area. Migration increased from two thousand in 1940 to twenty-three thousand in 1946. The Puerto Rican government, recognizing that migration fulfilled the demand for workers in the United States while also addressing local unemployment (U.S. Office of Territories [1952?]), leased airplanes from shipping carriers and lobbied airlines to lower transportation costs. The local aviation industry experienced rapid growth, and travel-agency offices opened throughout the territory. The PRDL requested and obtained from the Legislative Assembly a law giving the Public Service Commission power to regulate the sale of tickets for air and water transportation (Sierra Berdecía 1949e, 15).

Even before the establishment of the FLP, the PRDL intervened with airlines transporting noncontract workers for private recruiters in Puerto Rico, seeking permission to inspect airplanes. Pagán de Colón explained,

> The first time that representatives of the Employment Service entered one of those airplanes, their impression was one of revulsion and terror. The airplanes used to transport workers were the same cargo planes used to bring cattle or meat from the United States. They did not have seats and only had two bucket seats . . . during the nine hours that took to travel from San Juan to the airports of New Jersey and Pennsylvania.

FIGURE 4. Chartered flight with Puerto Rican migrant farmworkers, circa 1948. Courtesy of the Records of the Migration Division, Archives of the Puerto Rican Diaspora, Centro de Estudios Puertorriqueños, Hunter College, City University of New York.

The PRDL forced the airlines to keep airplanes clean and provide food for the travelers (Pagán de Colón 1956a, 11).

To facilitate general migration and the FLP, in 1948 the government of Puerto Rico also pushed the U.S. Civil Aeronautics Board to break Pan American Airlines' monopoly, which kept fares high and limited the number of flights. Puerto Rican officials' complaints resulted in an immediate reduction of fares by Pan Am. By the late 1950s airlines were offering tickets to migrants for forty-five dollars, a thirty-dollar reduction from the early 1950s (Eastern Airlines 1956; Gillespie 1956; Meléndez 2017, 108–11; Morrisette 1956; Sierra Berdecía 1956b; Stinson Fernández 1996, 124). The government of Puerto Rico also lobbied the board to act against private contractors who were transporting noncontract workers and operating as ticketing agencies (Fortas 1948a, 1948b; Robertson 1948; Whitcomb 1947).

The air transportation of workers did not proceed without problems. In the early 1950s several airplanes transporting migrants crashed, leading the Puerto Rican government to increase its inspections of airlines. On June 5, 1950, a Westair Corporation airplane carrying sixty-two migrants crashed in the Atlantic, and twenty-eight workers lost their lives. In an interview with a survivor, Luis Asencio Camacho captured the agony of the experience: "There were no friends there. There was no 'I know you' or 'I met you at the airport'; no, that had no meaning there. We fought for our lives, punching and biting. If we had to crawl over you and drown you in the process, just to get out of the plane, we did" (2013, 128). Sierra Berdecía visited the survivors in South Carolina and arranged transportation for thirty to Michigan and four back to Puerto Rico. Governor Muñoz Marín, in turn, banned transportation of workers on nonscheduled airplanes, replacing them with Pan American and Eastern Airlines flights (PRDL 1951, 57–58).

One of the transportation program's main problems was cost. Before 1952 workers were often rejected after they arrived at the airport with their luggage because they could not afford the thirty dollars required by employers for their transportation to the States. Other workers did not have their health certificates ready by the time of departure. Workers were also leaving on their own initiative to work with farmers for whom they had previously worked. In 1952 the PRDL attempted to address these problems by decentralizing recruitment from San Juan to FLP offices throughout Puerto Rico (PRES 1952, 3, 9). Decentralization resulted in the hiring of an additional 10,000 workers a year and lowered costs.

An important incident that shaped the FLP was the 1950 airlift of 5,314 migrants to work in the sugar-beet harvest in Michigan (Findlay 2014; Meléndez 2017; Valdés 1991), the result of negotiations between the PRDL and sugar-beet growers, aided by Michigan Congress representative Fred Crawford. Operation Farmlift was one of the largest airlifts of people in history. Some 3,550 workers were transported in only seven days, with 728 workers traveling on one day alone. Pan American and Eastern Airlines used eleven planes for this operation (PRDL 1951, 57–58). But the MD office in Michigan lacked the infrastructure for such a large operation, and myriad problems arose (Valdés 1991, 121). After arrival workers were not given enough hours of work, and some workers in the labor camps had to turn their wages over to persons who had provided them with advances. These conditions led to protests and the departure of some workers (PRES 1952, 10). In a letter to his wife, a worker explains the situation and the feeling of being misled by false promises:

> We are crazy for work until today Monday we have not worked as soon as I work I will help you all. Take a credit in the store of Luis Quiñones. I am not willing to go back to Puerto Rico until I fulfill my duty with all of those who have served me.... Here the nights are hours only.... At 10 in the night and at 4:30 in the morning it gets light at 5. On Saturday we were in the town of San Johns that it is like 16 miles far away we went walking and we walk there for three hours and half and three hours back we got lost and we woke up with swollen feet on Sunday. Conchita you do not know what we are going through at last in the world we had to curse at the Americans at the Mexicans. As for Joni we were going to beat him he had to lock himself in a building because he lied to us in Puerto Rico because the kitchen does not have meat, potatoes, sauce, milk, eggs, coffee, the lard is spoiled, the rice is long grain and codfish and Saturday we did not eat and Sunday we did not have lunch until Joni arrived and he got frightened. I do not want mom to know we are willing to die or win or we are all going to jail and if she knows, she would die of suffering. (F. Zeno 1952)

Michigan migrant workers were so desperate that they began to contact their relatives and elected officials. Many referred to political loyalties and claimed their rights as citizens in their appeals to Puerto Rican elected officials. One worker wrote to the governor,

> I want you to pay attention to this letter as a good Puerto Rican American citizen and *popular* [PPD member]. I answer for myself as a migrant in Michigan. We left to work on May 13th to our work in Michigan. There are 16 days that I am in Michigan. And I have only been able to work for 9 hours. Until now there has not been any correspondence about money. I ask you to provide me with work. Although we are all in the same situation. But I only speak for myself. Because I do not know the rights of other people. I only know my rights. (M. G. 1952).

Workers reminded PPD officials that their hegemony depended on political support. They learned about their electoral power from Governor Muñoz

Marín's famous political speeches and the PPD's populist political practices (Findlay 2014, 143–46).

In addition to writing letters, many workers resisted poor living and working conditions in the beet fields with their feet, deserting their jobs for other areas in the United States or returning to Puerto Rico. Many settled in New York, Chicago, and Detroit (Valdés 1991, 132), although some remained in Michigan to work in agriculture or in manufacturing, for example, with the Ford Motor Company (Social Services Section 1951g). Facing this situation, the government of Puerto Rico authorized payment for return trips for Michigan workers who were sick and paid others' transportation to different jobs stateside (*La Prensa* 1950).

Harold M. Mann, the BEM representative in the Midwest region, had warned high-level officials in the PRDL that placing workers in the beet industry was problematic for Michigan growers, who had been negative about hiring Puerto Ricans and accepting the 1949 contract. After fifteen years of placing beet workers, he knew that growers preferred Tejano families. Nonetheless, the Puerto Rican government went ahead with a contract that stipulated that beet workers would be paid at the end of the season, ignoring that they would need to money to feed themselves in the labor camps and their families in Puerto Rico (PRDL 1951, 57–58; Findlay 2014; Meléndez 2017; Valdés 1991). The impact of the turmoil in Michigan after the 1950 harvest was evident in several hearings before Congress and the President's Commission on Migratory Labor and contributed to the official inclusion of Puerto Rico in the USES. The BEM then transformed the FLP by allocating more resources, hiring additional field officials, and expanding its infrastructure.

The MD's charge was to mediate between workers and employers over problems like unpaid wages, insufficient hours of work, injuries and disease, transportation, and workers who left before the contract ended. During the 1959 season Guadalupe Ruiz assessed the problems arising from several provisions of the contract negotiated with the GSSCA. Some farmers felt that providing health insurance was a waste of money, but workers protested when they had to pay for medicines and visits to doctors. Growers complained that workers left their jobs before the expiration of the contract, even though they were still needed and there were no replacements available. The number of migrants leaving their jobs reached 405 by November 1959. Growers also complained about workers reneging on their transportation debts after 22 left, owing $677.77. (A similar amount, $683.87, was owed in

1958.) The MD was also vexed because the Glassboro Service Association, an affiliate of the GSSCA, continued hiring Puerto Ricans without government-sanctioned contracts. In 1959 about 500 workers were living in the Glassboro camp, most of them Puerto Ricans, of whom only 30 had been referred by the MD (Ruiz 1959b).

Enforcing the contract was also a challenge. In 1959 John Tilelli, labor-camp manager for the Farmers and Gardeners Association, an affiliate of the GSSCA, instructed farmers to withhold one week's pay from each worker for the duration of their employment, but most farmers ignored these instructions and paid their workers properly, understanding that the instructions conflicted with the contract clause authorizing withholding only of money owed to the GSSCA. The MD also encountered difficulty getting copies of payrolls, which were usually incomplete or submitted late, in violation of the contract. In 1958 the MD received no payrolls at all from growers, and only ninety signed copies of grower agreements were on file, even though an additional forty-one growers were using contract workers. Tilelli refused to provide information on forty-five contract workers, asserting that if there were a problem at a farm, he would be notified, after which he and MD official Guadalupe Ruiz could visit the farm together. Tilelli also did not provide written termination letters to any workers at this camp, although he had fired several (Ruiz 1959b).

Although the BEM and its successor, the PRBES, sought to manage the flow of migrant farmworkers, U.S. citizenship allowed Puerto Ricans to move freely, resulting in informal and illegal hiring practices. In the early 1950s, for example, Evaristo, in his twenties, left Puerto Rico with a group of neighbors who were migrating with contracts. He worked in Massachusetts and New Jersey for a couple of years and later moved to Lancaster, Pennsylvania, where he became a crew leader. He brought his wife with him, and together they cooked and washed clothes for contract workers. Evaristo also rented land from farmers to cultivate tomatoes and vegetables to supply to large food processors in Pennsylvania, eventually hiring noncontract workers to help him. This practice of informal hiring facilitated the establishment of migration networks between workers in Puerto Rico and farmers— nor could the FLP prevent U.S. farmers from sending workers to Puerto Rico as recruiters or providing former employees with tickets and letters promising jobs. In 1962, however, Puerto Rico's public law 87 amended public law 89 of 1947 and imposed penalties on any person or entity recruiting workers without notification to and authorization from the Puerto Rico secretary of labor (Segundo 1992, 762).

Most workers dreamed of returning to Puerto Rico, but many were determined to stay in the continental United States. Aided by families and friends living in the United States, migrants ventured to work on farms as a springboard to better employment opportunities. Rafael, who came to the States without a contract, described his initial experience:

> I ended up in Florida by way of a relative who had come here before me. He promised to send me the money for an airline ticket. So, two or three months later, he sent me a letter with the money, and I traveled to Florida myself. I came alone. I didn't know any English. Later, we came ... we were taken to a camp that they call here a "labor camp" of workers, and that's where we stayed.

Noncontract farmworkers were generally paid less than contract workers, and their work and living conditions were similar to what other noncitizen migrants and African Americans experienced (Galarza 1964). Their problems often led to intervention by the Puerto Rican government. An excellent example of this paternalism is how workers approached government agencies for help. Petroamérica Pagán de Colón, in a letter to Alan F. Perl, the MD's labor-relations lawyer, mentions a problem between migrants and locals in Pompano, Florida. Migrants complained that police and the public mistreated them, but Pagán de Colón criticized them, noting, "Every time they get in trouble, they call and 'papa' [the Puerto Rican government] will send somebody to pat them on the shoulders." At the same time she acknowledged that the migrants' attitude reflected confidence that the government would help them (Pagán de Colón 1950a).

BEM and, later, PRBES officials identified recruiters and crew leaders who might help stop illegal hiring. In addition to visiting neighborhoods in Puerto Rico and U.S. farms that hired noncontract workers, these agencies had a counter at the San Juan Airport where officials attempted to stop workers without contracts from migrating, while offering information about opportunities for "legal" contract migration. The government also prosecuted illegal recruiters. In 1958 Telesforo Carrasco was sentenced to five months in prison for recruiting workers in Maunabo and Patillas, Puerto Rico, with promises of jobs in Florida with a full week's work, good salaries, and excellent working conditions, none of which was true (PRDL 1958).

Government officials envisioned planned migration and settlement, but, as with so many state strategies for development, managing migration remained more a goal than an achievement. The BEM and the MD received reports of significant numbers of workers recruited by unauthorized agents in the U.S. Northeast via radio programs and advertisements that seemed to make false claims about job opportunities and of ticket agencies representing nonscheduled airlines that transported noncontract workers. The PRDL notified the Public Service Commission and the Puerto Rico Transportation Authority of agencies and airlines operating without authorization. This problem received the attention of Puerto Rico's attorney general when one airplane was stopped from leaving the Isla Grande Airport (PRDL 1951). The BEM and the PRBES also worked with municipal police throughout Puerto Rico to stop illegal recruitment by more stringently overseeing local authorities' issuance of health and good-conduct certificates to potential migrant farmworkers. Only after workers received their certificates and had been fingerprinted would they receive official identification cards (Arroyo 1950).

The PRDL tried as well to limit migration to the U.S. South because of Jim Crow laws, having dealt with past incidents of discrimination and being mindful of the experience of West Indians in Florida. During World War II the Jamaican government disallowed work assignments south of the Mason-Dixon Line. In contrast, Oliver Stanley, the British colonial secretary, permitted Bahamians to work in the South because, he averred, they were experienced with Jim Crow since the Bahamas had similar restrictions for blacks in hotels, restaurants, and cinemas. PRDL officials, on the other hand, did not want Puerto Ricans to suffer any kind of discrimination that would jeopardize the FLP and create unnecessary problems (Hahamovitch 2011, 50, 61). In the 1950s, however, PRDL officials began to consider sending migrants to certain areas of the South (Senior 1957b), perhaps recognizing that discrimination and segregation were more general problems, as, in the Northeast and Midwest, Puerto Ricans experienced and fought against racism alongside Mexicans and Jamaicans (see Barr 1944a; Hahamovitch 2011, 64–65).

Sierra Berdecía, Pagán de Colón, Clarence Senior, and other Puerto Rican officials built a massive infrastructure for migration composed of offices, procedures, personnel, public-relations campaigns, and educational materials, all of which shaped the migratory field. The personnel in offices charged with developing and overseeing the migration program worked diligently, believing in the principles of social justice emphasized by PPD government. Field agents showed an impressive work ethic by traveling long distances and writing extensive reports on their work. Their political commitments—and the economic interests of farmers—were also evident in the development of the FLP, which experienced enormous growth, but not without challenges and obstacles.

The government's success was limited, however, since unemployment rates in Puerto Rico remained high, at around 15 percent of the labor force. In the 1950s 450,000 migrants left for the United States, and, by the end of the decade, the MD estimated that some 30,000 migrant farmworkers traveled to the United States each year (FLP 1960). Despite the migration of thousands of farmworkers, employment in manufacturing and services could not compensate for the jobs being lost in agriculture to mechanization and the decline of the plantation economy. The agricultural labor force decreased from 203,000 workers in 1950 to 124,000 in 1960, while jobs in manufacturing increased only from 55,000 to 82,000 (Ayala 1996, 75). Migration became an escape valve that kept unemployment steady.

During the 1950s and 1960s, the unexpected consequences of labor migration began to appear in such diverse communities as Vineland, New Jersey; Springfield, Massachusetts; and North Collins, New York. As they became a visible part of the farm and industrial labor force in the rural Northeast, migrant farmworkers began to encounter the myths, images, and racism leveled against Puerto Ricans in urban areas (NYSIC 1948a, 1953; Siciliano 1956), and the Puerto Rican government, the State of New York, and the USES tried to redirect the migration away from New York City. The next part of the book explores the process of migration, migrants' experiences in the fields and the rural United States, and the protests and labor organizing of migrants.

# PART TWO

*Managing Hope, Despair, and Dissent*

# FOUR

# Pa'lla Afuera and the Life Experiences of Migrants

SCHOLARS HAVE OFTEN CAST PUERTO RICANS as "weak citizens," lacking agency, although it took initiative and courage to migrate (Thomas 2010, 166–67). While I share conviction that Puerto Ricans and farmworkers were not victims, it is romantic to propose that migrants' encounters with domination and subordination are unaffected by power (D. J. Austin 1983, 229, in Wolf 2001, 358). As well as improving their economic lives, migrant workers constructed meanings through their engagement with social forces at home and stateside (Wolf 2001, 368–67). Most farmworkers I interviewed migrated because they were *"buscando ambiente,"* looking for better economic conditions (García-Colón 2006b). Juan, a sixty-eight-year-old working on a farm in southern New Jersey, whom I interviewed in 2007 and who made his first trip in 1958, recalled, "I migrated because I hoped to earn a living in a better way, get married, have a family, and improve my life." After almost fifty years Juan was still migrating to southern New Jersey, picking peaches and fumigating the trees. Like Juan, most migrants worked to save money and send remittances to their families. Others dreamed of marrying or living with their families in the United States. Feelings of powerlessness and hope shaped their consciousness and their engagement in social relations (Simpson 1995, 41–42; Williams 1977, 128–35). Migration became a social field where they could venture to the United States to realize their hope of earning a decent living, and in the process they became part of the formation of Puerto Ricans as an ethnic group in the United States.

Puerto Rican government officials understood that hope drove workers' aspirations for better conditions. Idalie Morales de Cuevas (1954), an official with the Puerto Rico Department of Labor's (PRDL) Division of Employment Placement, wrote,

We find again and again that the mental state of the migrant is the basic factor to be taken into consideration when we interview him and [it] is dominated by two opposed feelings: the hope of finding the desired job [and] the suspicion that the interviewer is unwilling to appreciate his qualities. . . . This distrust compels him to exaggerate and perhaps lie, in his anxiety to make the best impression.

Fear of not being selected impelled potential migrants to impress their interviewers, whose evaluation, disapproving some while approving others, was integral to the government's migration policies.

The massive migration of Puerto Ricans to stateside farm labor in the late 1940s and 1950s stemmed from a well-orchestrated public campaign in Puerto Rico—and the migratory experience itself, which transformed life in Puerto Rico as migrants returned home. The formation of the Puerto Rican migrant labor force also depended on the efforts of farmers; their associations, churches, and community organizations; and federal, state, and local governments to entice workers to keep working in agriculture. Enticement, not coercion, shaped farmworkers' feelings about migration. Eagerness to find a better deal and a sense of adventure drove them to accept low wages and the harsh working and living conditions of farm labor (Griffith 2006, 9; see also Hahamovitch 1997).

Michael Burawoy argues that enticement shapes maintenance and renewal, the dual processes that reproduce the migrant labor force:

The organization of migrant labor not only makes the distinction apparent but is even defined by the separation of the processes of maintenance from those of renewal. . . . The two processes take place in geographically separate locations. . . . They remain, however, indissolubly interdependent, as reflected in the oscillatory movement of migrants between work and home. (1976, 1052)

Workers decide how and when to migrate by evaluating conditions at home and abroad, weighing the financial and emotional costs and benefits of staying or going. The social construction of workplace and home in two different geographic locations created myths, ideas, and practices that guided migrants to *pa'lla afuera,* the continental United States. *La isla,* Puerto Rico, was home.

Pa'lla afuera (*para allá afuera* in its standard Spanish form), translated as "outside over there," implies traveling or living outside the country and suggests how Puerto Ricans constructed place as part of their experiences of migration. Although the dichotomy between the homeland and the host society is obvious, by itself it does not explain how Puerto Ricans experienced migration. In this chapter I explore how migration unfolded for the workers themselves: how they decided to migrate, how they talked about migrating and migration, and how they negotiated the complicated government policies that promoted and managed migration.

Although Puerto Ricans are U.S. citizens, when they migrate to any stateside agricultural area, they cross visible colonial, linguistic, ethnic, and cultural borders (Meléndez 2017; G. Pérez 2004, 15–16), entering a new world consisting mostly of labor camps, fields, and small towns. These spaces contributed to the construction of Puerto Ricans as desirable or undesirable subjects for U.S. farm labor. Steve Striffler (2007) explores how migrants' understandings and memories and the physicality of places are produced in tension with one another in an ongoing movement between different and distant geographic places (678). Pa'lla afuera, where workers migrate to work, is produced in tension with *la isla*, their homeland. Gastón Gordillo's observation clarifies the contradictions within the Puerto Rican migrant experience: "The study of these contradictions is crucial to dismantle the appearance of places as well-bounded entities, for it reveals, first, the fractures and struggles that make them ongoing, unstable, and unfinished historical processes, and, second, the relations that integrate them with other geographies" (2004, 5). Pa'lla afuera simultaneously expresses migrants' estrangement and sense of belonging. That sense of belonging remains anchored in Puerto Rico (Striffler 2007, 678), even when migrants established lives in the States. Some workers I interviewed still construct their understandings and memories of pa'lla afuera and *la isla* through their experience of labor migration.

## FROM WORKERS TO PUERTO RICANS

Farm-labor migration emerged from the economic and social conditions in Puerto Rico and the development of labor migration in U.S. agriculture. Growers initially wanted to hire migrant families, which they believed would help maintain a tractable, available labor force, so officials struggled but failed to design a plan for bringing entire families (Mitchell 2012, 24, 68–69, 116). Efforts to bring women also failed (Carlo [1957?]). Following the example of the Mexican and West Indian programs, the PRDL transported only men to stateside farms.

To manage migration the PRDL tracked migrants' demographics. An April 1952 survey of farmworkers, mostly from Arecibo, Humacao, and Caguas, indicated that 703 of the 1,141 migrants interviewed were employed when they migrated; of these, fewer than half were working in agriculture, although most had worked in agriculture for more than two years and considered farming their occupation, including many who were landless workers or small farmers living on sugar, coffee, and tobacco plantations. Of the 565 workers offered work stateside, 537 were placed in unskilled agricultural jobs. A full 99 percent of the workers were older than fourteen years, while 892 were between twenty and thirty-nine years old. A total of 69 percent of migrants lived in rural areas, and 69 percent were traveling for the first time, principally to New York, New Jersey, and Pennsylvania. The survey also demonstrated the importance of the Puerto Rico Employment Service, because 33.2 percent of all travelers from April 21 to 27, 1952, were migrating through referrals and contracts issued by the service (Oficina del Gobernador 1952). Two years later a U.S. Employment Service (USES) survey reported similar findings. The main reasons for migrating were almost exclusively economic, due to unemployment and poor living conditions in Puerto Rico, although sometimes these motivations combined with personal problems and political persecution. Of the workers surveyed 31 percent intended to settle in the United States, while half planned to go home and then return to the States for agricultural work. Those who stayed after the harvest season usually worked in one or two jobs in manufacturing, food processing, or construction (Mirengoff 1954, 2, 4–5).

After World War II, economic changes were transforming the Puerto Rican labor force. Industrial manufacturing policies and land-reform programs had decimated the sugarcane industry, leaving thousands of workers jobless (Ayala 1996). Whereas in 1910 more than 60 percent of the labor force worked in agriculture and 40 percent in nonagricultural activities, by 1950 more than 63 percent held nonagricultural jobs, while 37 percent worked in agriculture (PRDL 1952b). Government policies had increased public-sector and manufacturing jobs, but these were insufficient to meet the demand for good jobs. In addition, because these programs created low-wage and gender-specific jobs, more women were hired than men, who remained unemployed or underemployed, performing seasonal and occasional jobs in the service and agricultural sectors.

Despite the government's efforts to pass minimum-wage and work-hour laws, for workers the *tiempo muerto* (dead time) between the end of the harvest and the beginning of a new season meant underemployment, idleness, and hunger.[1] Therefore, many residing near sugar-producing areas at the time were "fleeing the cane" (G. Pérez 2004, 52–53). Bending to harvest asparagus and other vegetables in the States was backbreaking work but not comparable to swinging a machete under the sun on a tropical island (Shotwell 1958–59, 6).

As Rafael, a former migrant worker, told me, there was no work and no path to progress in Puerto Rico. The economic situation in his household and his eagerness to find a job led him to seek help from a relative working as a farm laborer in Florida. An orphan who lived with his grandparents, Rafael saw migration as an opportunity to improve his living conditions and to evade the negative repercussions of his political activities. He explained,

> The thing that motivated me to come to the United States was the economic situation. In those years, [specifically] in 1954, there was too much poverty, need, and unemployment in Puerto Rico. . . . Before I came here, I went to Ponce and stayed in the house of some relatives to see if I could find . . . work. I was . . . from the countryside, but I was savvy. However, I was never able to find a job because people had seen me [participating] in prohomeland [political] activities. . . . I didn't have any other option than to come to Florida and start working on tomato and vegetable farms.

Avelino, a World War II veteran and member of the Puerto Rican Independence Party (PIP; Partido Independentista Puertorriqueño) in the 1950s, left Puerto Rico after political persecution denied him a government job. Many migrants were veterans lacking social mobility in Puerto Rico whose knowledge of English allowed them to become leaders of groups traveling to the United States. Many saved enough money to buy land, open businesses, and further their children's education or their own (see González 2006, 99). Avelino, for example, saved enough money to return to Puerto Rico and open a store.

The PRDL designed the Farm Labor Program (FLP), cognizant that the Puerto Rican and northeastern U.S. harvest seasons were complementary. In Puerto Rico sugarcane was harvested from January through July, employing around 158,000 workers. The citrus season was similar, but it employed fewer workers. The tobacco harvest occurred from October through April, while coffee picking started in September and ended in March. From July through December, unemployment was high among agricultural and food-processing workers, which offered them an incentive to search for seasonal jobs in the U.S. Northeast (Mirengoff 1954, 3).

Migration separated and ruptured families. Migrant men depended on their relatives and friends to monitor their wives, but husbands and wives sometimes abandoned each other and their children. In 1948 anthropologist Sidney Mintz commented on an informant's attitude toward separation from his wife:

> It seemed that he thought it somehow undignified for man and wife to be apart.... How much importance this dignity may have is not clear, but it may be a factor which could permanently decrease familial solidarity, after emigration. Some men may emigrate at a considerable cost psychologically, dependent on their families and friends to guard the fidelity of their wives.[2]

Women expected their men to remain faithful. In 1957 a pregnant wife went to the Migration Division (MD) offices in Puerto Rico because her husband, who lived in a labor camp, did not answer her letters. An official talked to the husband, who showed the letters in which his wife accused him of running with other women. He said that he didn't write back because he was working constantly, and he chided the official, who he thought should know there was no time for parties when working on the farms (Ruiz 1957d).

Wives' fears were nevertheless often realized. After their contracts ended many men would settle in surrounding towns and cities, engaging in common-law marriages and sexual relationships. Some established a new stateside family. One of my interviewees separated from her migrant husband for several years, moving to Philadelphia with her children to live with relatives, after he cheated on her. One interviewee who migrated in the early 1950s told me that his wife abandoned him when he left Puerto Rico. He eventually married another woman in the United States. Other workers eloped, married, or cohabited with local residents and farmworkers. In an upstate New York camp in 1957, researchers found married Puerto Ricans cohabiting and sometimes having children with southern African American women (Larson 1957).

Workers often struggled with family problems, the need to send money to their families, and the constant search for better job opportunities. Forty-year-old Sergio, who migrated in 1949, went to the New York MD office after receiving a letter from the Public Welfare Unit of Puerto Rico regarding financial support of his children. Before he left Puerto Rico, he sold a house for $250 and built another for $125 for his wife and children, using the remaining money to travel as a contract worker to Buffalo for five months. After his contract terminated, he spent three months in New York City, unemployed and supported by members of his church until he got a job at the Waldorf Astoria Hotel as a busboy, with a weekly salary of $39 and $159 in monthly expenses. Sergio told the MD that his expenses did not allow him to send more than $12 every two weeks to his family. He tried to convince his wife to move to New York City, but she refused. She had sold their house to pay for medicine for one of the children. She wanted a divorce and to send their oldest son, who was misbehaving, to live with his father (Social Services Section 1951f).

Many workers did send money to Puerto Rico. The Puerto Rico Planning Board estimated that remittances reached $1,326,000 in fiscal year 1951; $1,279,000 in 1952; $2,384,000 in 1953; and $2,783,000 in 1954, for a total of $7,772,000. Workers brought back to Puerto Rico an additional $10,760,000, for a grand total of $18,532,000 over a four-year period. The benefits of remittances led MD officials to facilitate the purchase of money orders in the labor camps. The money migrants sent was used mostly for living expenses but also for building houses, establishing businesses, and educating their children and relatives (PRES 1954, 12).

More workers wanted to migrate than there were positions available through the FLP. In fact, eagerness to migrate with a contract was so great that officials rejected many applications. As of July 30, 1958, the FLP had registered 15,884 people, of whom 9,676 were referred for work and 4,973 were ready to migrate (Migration Division 1958b). The main destinations of contract migrant workers were New Jersey, New York, Connecticut, Massachusetts, Illinois, Pennsylvania, and Ohio, although Delaware, Florida, Maryland, Michigan, and Washington also received workers (Stinson Fernández 1996, 135), as did other states and territories (PRDL 1951, 58; Sierra Berdecía 1952b). Noncontract workers also had a significant presence in Florida.

Government officials met arriving workers at the airports, after which they usually were taken to farms. When Artemio arrived at Buffalo's airport in 1952, the men were lined up by government officials and chosen by farmers. By the late 1950s the placement protocol had evolved, and passenger manifests indicated which farms migrants were headed to. Farmers sometimes rejected workers after they arrived at the labor camps because of their physical appearance and health. A Glassboro representative rejected a worker because he suffered from blurred vision in one eye, even though he had been issued both health and good-conduct certificates in Puerto Rico. This same worker had experience working as a noncontract migrant in Florida (Monroy 1956).

FIGURE 5. Puerto Rican migrant farmworkers disembarking in Buffalo, New York, circa 1948. Courtesy of the Records of the Migration Division, Archives of the Puerto Rican Diaspora, Centro de Estudios Puertorriqueños, Hunter College, City University of New York.

While the magnitude of migration was due to the FLP, workers also shaped and transformed the flows and contours of their own journeys. For many workers life in the U.S. agricultural-labor industry was their first experience of pa'lla afuera. As workers fled economic, personal, and political problems, farm-labor migration opened a space of opportunity in which they

FIGURE 6. PRDL official Eulalio Torres greeting migrant farmworkers arriving in the United States, circa 1948. Courtesy of the Records of the Migration Division, Archives of the Puerto Rican Diaspora, Centro de Estudios Puertorriqueños, Hunter College, City University of New York.

gained experience they could deploy whenever conditions in either Puerto Rico or the United States were not conducive to maintaining an adequate standard of living.

## MIGRATING AS A NONCONTRACT WORKER

The practice of informal hiring did not stop with the establishment of the FLP. On the contrary, contract migration facilitated the establishment of informal networks between Puerto Ricans and U.S. farmers. In some cases whole families migrated without contracts. Women worked on farms as well as in canneries, in domestic service for farmers, and in the camps, cleaning and cooking. Some noncontract women ended up in the fields, after being told they would be cooking for workers (Migration Division 1963–69). Other workers joined the migratory stream to the East Coast by themselves, working and moving from Florida to the Northeast as the harvest progressed.

U.S. citizenship, which permitted all Puerto Ricans to migrate freely, impeded the efforts of the PRDL to manage farm-labor migration. In effect, the migration of contract workers opened opportunities for noncontract workers. By 1956 many farmers who initially worked with the FLP were recruiting migrant workers directly and illegally (U.S. House 1955, 236), and the number of contract workers dropped from 15,000 in 1953 to 11,000 in 1955 (Migration Division 1953, 1955). For the 1957 season MD officials reported between 350 to 400 noncontract workers arriving weekly in the United States for referral to jobs through the New York State Employment Service (Senior 1957d).

The FLP could not prevent farmers from sending recruiters to Puerto Rico or providing former employees with plane tickets and letters promising jobs. Indeed, such practices increased with the establishment of the FLP because farmers gained knowledge of workers' networks they could use for recruitment. Hence, in 1966 Francisco, from Guayama, recruited workers in Puerto Rico to work in Florida, moving them to New York after the harvest season ended (E. Torres 1966b). Most of those workers hoped to return to Puerto Rico, but some with family problems were determined to stay and establish themselves in the United States.

MD officials designated recruiters and crew leaders in an effort to stop illegal hiring, while working with farmers' associations to curb illegal recruitment. In 1961 the Garden State Service Cooperative Association was recruiting workers for New Jersey nurseries at a salary of $0.90 per hour, in contrast to the FLP contract rate of $1.00 per hour. The Puerto Rican secretary of labor accused the association of violating federal procedures for hiring migrants, and authorities in Puerto Rico arrested José Torres and Diego Ortiz, two association agents, for illegal recruitment (Migration Division 1961).

The MD engaged in a public-relations campaign against noncontract migration, providing workers with information about the benefits of the contract and the problems that noncontract workers faced. In 1959 officials compiled a list of fifty-eight employers, mostly in Massachusetts but also a few in Rhode Island and New Hampshire, who were bringing noncontract workers through local travel agencies and Eastern Airlines' offices in Puerto Rico (Del Río 1959b). Illegal recruitment concerned officials, who did not want workers to migrate to Jim Crow states, where they would likely encounter racial conflicts, but many workers traveled to Florida regardless of the orientation and advice given to them.

Puerto Ricans began migrating to Florida in large numbers at the end of World War II. In 1951 the Travelers Aid Society of Miami informed Puerto Rican officials of a large contingent of Puerto Ricans in the city without food, shelter, or employment, which supposedly posed a problem for local social-welfare agencies. The officials responded that Puerto Rico, like other states, could not assume responsibility for migrants who were no longer under its jurisdiction. Nevertheless, PRDL officials assisted Florida's welfare agencies, and some of the migrants obtained jobs on farms. Others were jailed for violating vagrancy laws but released and provided with food, housing, and jobs. The Puerto Rican government publicized this situation to discourage workers from migrating to Florida without contracts (PRDL 1951), and the secretary of labor issued press releases and gave interviews, asking workers not to migrate to Florida (Sierra Berdecía [1952–53?]). Still, migration to Florida remained a constant problem for the PRDL, which, between 1952 and 1953, investigated workers' complaints about discrimination, police brutality, and lost wages.

By 1953 a sizable group of Puerto Ricans was part of the seasonal labor force in the southeastern coastal area of Florida, where the vegetable harvest provided continuous employment from December through March. Approximately three thousand migrants, one-fourth of employed seasonal farm laborers, were working in the area. Most came from rural areas in Puerto Rico, and most intended to stay in the United States, working in agriculture and moving between Florida and the Mid-Atlantic states (see Mirengoff 1954; USBES 1955).

The agricultural skills workers had acquired in Puerto Rico facilitated their adjustment to U.S. farms despite language problems. In reports to the government of Puerto Rico, some Florida farmers praised the migrants (PRDL 1951), calling them "industrious and resourceful" and expressing a desire to employ more to compensate for the loss of local workers (USBES 1955, 1). Among the farmers' comments on Puerto Ricans:

Puerto Ricans are a godsend to the farmer of Florida. Puerto Ricans want to work and get ahead and save money and send it home.

Quicker thinkers, faster workers, more eager to work.

Good workers, ambitious, thrifty, dependable.

Like to work—make money to send home. Follow instructions, don't have to stand over them to get them to work.

Steady with work. Good workers after they learn what you want. Show interest in their work. (USBES 1955, 5)

Despite employers' testimonials, however, the government of Puerto Rico remained unconvinced of the wisdom of sending contract workers to Florida, maintaining its ban on the South until 1969, when contract workers were hired in South Carolina.

Although migrating was hard for many workers, relationships between some farmers and workers created friendships that endured for decades. Some farmers even vacationed in Puerto Rico. Their visits were social, but they offered opportunities to recruit additional workers and to ensure that already-hired workers would return to their farms for the harvest (Morales 1986, 80). In 2010 I encountered a group of workers in Vineland, New Jersey, who, when I asked why they came to this particular farm, replied that their parents had worked there decades before, for the farmer's father. Nearby I met older workers who had been migrating to the farm since the 1960s and now were bringing their children and younger workers from their neighborhood. They were very eager to tell me how friendly "their" farmer was, that he knew Spanish and used to send his children to Puerto Rico during the summer to stay in their households and spend time with their children. Nevertheless, some of these relationships were paternalistic and served to maintain the flow of workers to the farms (Griffith 1993, 7–8, 43). Whatever personal bonds developed, farmers still need to ensure their sources of labor.

U.S. citizenship allowed noncontract workers to move from one farm to another where farmers better met their expectations. In effect, citizenship allowed them to violate the regulations the FLP imposed on contract workers. Noncontract workers were often abused, working and living in substandard conditions even as their jobs afforded them mobility and flexibility to find other jobs. Noncontract workers sought to establish bonds with farmers and the community, deeming these to be preferable to the impersonal environment created by large labor camps and the farm-management associations.

EARNING A WAGE

The most obvious reasons for migrating were un- and underemployment in Puerto Rico and the promise of higher wages in the States. From 1946 to 1947 the average daily wage of agricultural workers in Caguas, Puerto Rico, was $1.67. Sugarcane workers earned a better daily salary of $2.67. Dairies paid $1.80 per day. Coffee farms paid the least, $1.20 per day (PPRP 1946–47). In tobacco, between November 1952 and February 1953, the average wage per hour was $0.166. In general, workers toiled an average of 30.6 hours per week for a salary of around $5.05 (PRDL 1954e). The hourly wage for cane workers increased from $0.34 in 1949 to $0.43 in 1953, and the average wage for cultivating pineapple was $0.29 per hour, suggesting that the FLP had little impact on local wages (1953b, 1953c). In contrast, between 1952 and 1956 contract migrant workers could earn $0.65 per hour and work more than 40 hours per week (Migration Division 1953, 1957), which made jobs in the United States attractive.

In 1953 the average salary of migrants, who worked varying hours and days, from four to forty-four or more weeks during the year, was $531. An average of $460 was reported by the largest group of migrants, who stayed from twelve to fifteen weeks. The second-largest group comprised workers staying from four to seven weeks, with average earnings of $168. Workers who stayed for the whole six-month season earned $1,488. These earnings helped maintain a steady flow of contract and noncontract migrants to farms where most were employed in stoop-labor crops: asparagus, beans, tomatoes, and the fruit harvest. Their daily wages averaged $6.15 in New York, $6.62 in New Jersey, and $7.31 in Pennsylvania (Mirengoff 1954, 5–6).

The PRDL regularly battled with farmers and associations over wages. Eulalio Torres, director of FLP Field Operations, argued that farmers did not offer high enough wages, or they offered hourly rates when workers could earn more by working at piece rates, thereby creating an artificial shortage of workers because most potential workers would not work for low wages (Montero 1960). In New York State, wages for migrant workers were one-third lower in 1951 than in 1944, despite a 48 percent increase in the cost of living. This amounted to a one-third cut in real wages. Piece rates did not change much, with berries being paid at seven cents per quart in 1944 and seven to eight cents a quart in 1951 (Crosby 1952, 7). From 1947 to 1957 the hourly wages of farmworkers increased by 33 percent, while their output increased 125 percent, representing a decline in the agricultural wage bill from 18 percent of total production costs in 1945 to 9 percent in 1959 (Jorgenson, Williams, and Burma 1961, 2–4). For comparison, wages in the manufacturing sector were higher, averaging around fifty-five cents an hour in mid-1954, while the typical workweek ranged from 33.7 hours in April to 35.9 hours in June (PRDL 1954d).

MD officials also tried to protect the Puerto Rican government's interests vis-à-vis farmers and guest workers. In a letter to Petroamérica Pagán de Colón, dated August 23, 1960, Eulalio Torres reports that an employer in Woodcliff

Lake, New Jersey, wants to hire ten workers, but he suggests that the job order be rejected because this employer had pending a claim of $390 from workers. He further recommends that the Puerto Rico Bureau of Employment Security ask the New Jersey Employment Service not to help recruit workers for this employer in the United States or abroad because he had violated the Puerto Rican contract. Torres even asked Fred Watts, director of New Jersey Farm Placement Bureau, to reject this employer's certification for importing Jamaican workers instead of Puerto Ricans (E. Torres 1960b).

By the mid-1950s competition between U.S. and Puerto Rican farmers for workers began to improve local wages and working conditions. The Puerto Rico Employment Service reported that a coffee grower offered housing with beds and free transportation during the weekends and charged only $3.00 per week for three meals a day. He also provided a free can of powdered milk and seven pounds of sugar to workers with more than one child, if they agreed to remain on his farm, and sold workers bananas at a discount. These offers resulted in thirty-six workers being hired for the season, including nine families. Other growers offered free meals, higher wages, and housing with electricity (PRDL 1954a, 2).

Although the PRDL attempted to resolve problems, migrant workers continued to protest low wages and poor working and living conditions. In 1956 the San Juan newspaper *El Mundo* reported that migrants in New Jersey were striking against a farmer, claiming mistreatment, insults, and low wages. The New Jersey Farmers Workers Association, which represented Puerto Ricans and was led by Casimiro González Correa, intervened, achieving a wage increase from $0.65 to $0.75 per hour and improved treatment (Padros Herrero 1956). A year later the Catholic Association of Unionized Workers intervened in favor of Puerto Ricans in Glassboro (Lumen Román 1957a).

In 1959 another group of contract and noncontract workers, led by a walk-in Puerto Rican from New York City, protested for better wages from an Oswego, New York, farmer, demanding $1.00 an hour.[3] An MD official mediated the situation, siding with the farmer, arguing that the prevailing wage in the area was $0.80 but that if a wage survey found an increase in the prevailing wage, the workers would be paid the difference. Workers expressed appreciation for the MD's interest in their situation (Vilar 1959).

Migrants often blamed Governor Muñoz Marín for their hardships, and journalists regularly reported their anger with the Popular Democratic Party (Partido Popular Democrático). In 1957 a worker in Glassboro complained,

"The Popular government is at fault . . . because it does not protect us against exploiters" (Lumen Román 1957b). A group of workers wrote to Gilberto Concepción de Gracia, leader of the Puerto Rican Independence Party, indicating that they had no money and did not want to return to Puerto Rico because they wanted to work and had been waiting for three weeks for jobs in food processing (Concepción de Gracia 1958). Other workers wrote directly to Governor Muñoz Marín asking for help (Mendoza 1959a; Ruiz Gutiérrez 1959). Although workers criticized the Puerto Rican government, MD officials often intervened on their behalf, sometimes creating problems between local officials and employers. In January 1965 an MD official in the Delaware Valley Office reported eighteen wage-related claims, mostly allegations of unpaid wages, compared to only five for workers' compensation. He also reported forty-four wage claims versus twenty-eight cases for workers' compensation, from 1960 to 1965 (P. Rivera 1965a).

Employers often resented the FLP contract and inspections by Puerto Rican officials, and state employment-service offices frequently sided with farmers when MD representatives showed up unannounced to inspect farms (Coll 1963). Conflicts between MD officials and association managers arose over workers' claims, as when dissatisfied workers filed false claims to leave their jobs, a situation that growers and managers used to justify their illtreatment of workers. In a letter to the MD, John Tilelli, manager of the Farmers and Gardeners Association's labor camp, wrote,

> Please don't waste my time and yours processing such stupid claims as submitted by this man. As you know the policy of this organization is to take care of the men and find work for them. Correa was returned to camp as an unsatisfactory worker on September 19. Correa did leave camp on his own on Sept. 19. The statement he made that he was forced to leave camp on November 3, because the cook did not like to feed one man is a lie. (Cited in P. Rivera 1965a)

Farmers and managers regularly forced workers out by claiming they had voluntarily left their jobs (P. Rivera 1965a); some summarily fired workers who got sick. In 1948 an employer fired a young worker who had arrived in New Jersey under contract and was sent to Goshen, New York. After about five weeks he could no longer work because his abdomen and legs were swollen. The farmer put him on a train to New York City and told him to go wherever he liked. The worker asked for help from the New York City Department of Welfare, which referred him to the MD, which, in turn, asked the man's official employer, the United Labor Import Company, to return him to Puerto Rico (Draper 1948a; Gomez 1948).

As early as 1948 New York farmers were complaining that 15 to 30 percent of Puerto Ricans were leaving work before the end of their contracts, although some evidence suggests they did so because of dissatisfaction with their limited hours of work and other labor conditions (NYSDL 1949, 39–40). The problem of workers leaving before the harvest ended, however, continued. A farmer in Hadley, Massachusetts, complained to the MD,

> This note is to let you know that three of my Puerto Ricans have left today. They told me this morning that they were leaving at six o'clock the next morning. This is a bad time for me, as I am right in the middle of cutting my ensilage corn. I have all my potatoes to dig and also take down my tobacco. Their contract with me doesn't expire until November 15th. When you hire Puerto Ricans and sign a contract you expect them to stay. They have broken their contract with me and left me right in the middle of a lot of work. There are times when I had to find work for them because I wanted to give them hours. That's what they like. I don't think this was the right thing to do. (Zgodnik 1966)

It was common for workers to leave the farms for New York City, where government agencies sometimes covered their travel expenses to new farm jobs. The New York State Employment Service referred Miguel, who had a brother in Brant, New York, to a farm job. The supervisor of social services gave him $4.00 from a private fund, and Miguel promised to return the money as soon as he got paid. Other workers left their jobs because of mental-health problems and for personal reasons, often creating anxiety among their families at home. The father of a worker hospitalized in a mental-health institution in Marlboro, New Jersey, contacted the MD seeking information about his son because nobody from the government or the hospital had contacted him. The sister of a worker also asked the MD for help finding her brother, who had arrived in New Jersey to work on the farms. Her brother, who suffered from mental illness, had left for New York City, where a Protestant church was helping him. In another case Marcelino complained of neck pain after four days of work, but the Glassboro dispensary did not treat him, so he left for New York City. A driver took him to El Barrio, where, because he had no money or relatives in the city, he slept on the streets. MD officials gave him the choice of returning to Glassboro or going to the municipal shelter. Another Puerto Rican who was visiting the MD office at the time gave Marcelino $3.00 for his return fare to Glassboro. MD personnel accompanied him to the Greyhound terminal (Social Services Section 1951a, 1951b, 1951c, 1951d, 1951e).

Some migrant workers sent most of the money they earned to their families, so when they quit their jobs, they found themselves destitute and asking for help. When Antonio arrived in Glassboro in 1951, he was forty-seven years old, with a wife and children living in a public-housing project in Lares, Puerto Rico. Antonio worked ten and a half weeks as farmworker, earning $135.78 after deductions of $65.00 for food and transportation, and sent $83.25 to his wife and children. Because he left his job before the end of his contract, however, MD officials could not provide him with money to travel back to Puerto Rico (Social Services Section 1951g).

Workers often complained about being overcharged by farmers for food or housing expenses. They also protested the failure to keep the promise of at least 160 hours of work for the duration of the contract. In a letter to the MD office, Miguel wrote,

> It seems that the general belief of Americans is that the worker in the camp is their own toy, which they can play with at their will, making false promises, having them waste their time; others like me have seen them, and I can say that has happened, take a Puerto Rican by the neck and shake him and later, with the help of the police, throw him and his luggage outside without cause.
> Are the governments of Puerto Rico and the United States paying employees to sit in an office and do nothing for the worker?
> Is it just that the Puerto Rican is useful only when there is a problem, be that a war or the possibility of losing the harvest?
> It should not be like this because we are as much citizens as those born here; well, they were born here in American territory, and we under the American flag.
> There are many abuses committed against Puerto Rican citizens in the camps; there are so many that one of these days we will have to protest. (Casiano 1958)

Camp managers and farmers sometimes became violent and verbally abused workers, occasionally calling the police to evict them (García La Torre 1956). A worker asked the MD for help after the manager of a New Jersey camp threatened him with physical harm. The worker still owed the farmer for his transportation expenses but wanted to be transferred to another employer, though he promised to pay his debt. In North Collins, New York, a farmer fired workers after they protested his lowering the wage for picking beans from five to two cents per pound. When workers became unruly, employers called the police, who remained in the camp after workers left (*El Imparcial* 1958; Stone 1958; Venegas [1958?]; Vilar 1958).

Workers' agency helped shape how federal, state, and Puerto Rican governments extended benefits, rights, and duties under the farm-labor contract. Amendments to the Social Security law, in 1955, included Puerto Rico in the Social Security system and extended coverage to farmworkers (PRDL 1954f). By 1960 Illinois, New York, Montana, Oklahoma, and Nebraska cooperated with Puerto Rico regarding unemployment benefits; in the summer of 1961, the USES lobbied for all state employment offices to extend interstate unemployment benefit payments to Puerto Rico (Zorrilla 1962, 1). Additional changes during the 1960s provided more benefits for workers and flexibility for employers, including unemployment benefits for migrant agricultural workers.

In the 1960s changes to the FLP allowed contract workers to move to new jobs after their contracts expired, at which point the MD considered them to be noncontract workers. But workers who left their jobs before the termination of the contract and were rehired by their employers were still covered by the contract. Another contract change covered industries, such as dairy and food processing, that needed year-round workers and had requested permission to make migrant employees full-time, permanent workers. In response MD officials encouraged workers to stay after the harvest, providing them with placement services (Gomez 1966b; Stinson Fernández 1996, 126).

The wages and benefits earned as farmworkers were part of the migrants' dream of social mobility. But higher wages alone did not impel migration. Workers also considered long work hours and days, personal relationships with employers, and cost of living as they assessed the possibilities migration offered or if, after they migrated, their experience had paid off. Migrants protested whenever employers and government officials did not meet their expectations or failed to carry out their promises. In these ways the FLP fostered circular migration between Puerto Rico and the United States, transforming the lives of migrants and the people at home.


RETURNING HOME


By the end of the 1950s, the economic, social, and political forces transforming Puerto Rico were unstoppable. The workforce was older, and older men bore the brunt of unemployment. As agriculture and home needlework declined, jobs in the U.S. Northeast and the San Juan metropolitan area attracted many working-class families, the unemployed, the young, and anyone looking for new and better opportunities. Between 1950 and 1953, 46 percent of new manufacturing jobs were in San Juan, and they employed 23 percent of the population. At the same time, while agricultural jobs decreased for men, manufacturing jobs for women increased. These developments, together with stagnant unemployment and underemployment, spurred farm-labor migration (PRDL 1954b; Whalen 2001, 25–31), and each new wave of migrants created a new wave of return migrants.

Workers returned to Puerto Rico or stopped working without finishing their contracts for many reasons. In a 1958 memorandum MD official Matilde Fernández detailed that one worker refused treatment at the Glassboro camp infirmary and decided to return to Puerto Rico. Two workers returned to pick coffee on their farms in Mayagüez. Another worker drank too much and decided to go home. In a bizarre incident a worker had a nightmare and jumped out of a second-floor window; a doctor indicated that he was drunk when he jumped. Another worker left because his wife was sick (M. Fernández 1958a). Clearly, seasonal farm-labor migration was difficult for workers far away from their families. Most workers migrated to support their families, and they worried constantly about their well-being.

For some migrant workers, ties to Puerto Rico were so strong that they continued to engage in electoral politics. In October 1960 a worker wrote to the MD asking for funds to travel to Puerto Rico for the November elections. Without an absentee-ballot law at the time, the MD responded that they did not have funds, but they would ask his employer to end his contract so he could return to Puerto Rico to vote (E. Torres 1960c). Eventually, the government introduced a program for absentee voting that included migrant farmworkers.

Once home return migrants often exaggerated the wonders of their work in the States, remaining silent about the hardships so as not to impugn their honor and status in their home communities (see MacMaster 1997, 69–70). For example, when one worker in Michigan got sick, he asked his wife to sell their house and send him the money for ticket back to Puerto Rico. He stressed that she should be discreet so that others would not know how bad his situation was (Serrano Molina 1952). Some migrants, out of concern for their families or to cover their disappointment, pretended that they liked their work situation and were fine.[4]

Gossip, letters, news, and firsthand experiences, part of what Roger David Waldinger and Michael Ira Lichter call a "dual frame of reference" (2003, 9,

40–41), contributed to decisions to migrate and to return to Puerto Rico. Both experienced and first-time migrants assessed wages and working conditions on U.S. farms in relation to those in Puerto Rico (Binford 2009, 505; Waldinger and Lichter 2003, 9, 40–41). Thus, for example, in 1958 fewer workers applied to the MD to migrate because they were receiving news from other migrants that the economic situation in the United States was bad (T. Zeno 1958b).

When migrants returned to Puerto Rico, there was plenty of conversation about their experience as farmworkers. Mintz recorded details about return migrants in his field notes for the People of Puerto Rico Project, describing how they talked extensively about working and living conditions after returning from *el Norte* (the North, i.e., the continental United States) (see García-Colón 2017a). Some complained about being mistreated and exploited by employers; others acknowledged that they earned more but had to spend more in the United States; and many expressed extreme displeasure at the cold weather. They complained that meals were sparse and that men had to cook their own food.[5]

Mintz's field notes on a worker I call Yayo reveal migrant workers' ambivalence. Yayo was one of the first to migrate under the Puerto Rican contract in 1948. He had been working on a sugar plantation as a *palero,* or ditch digger, and living with Paola, his common-law wife, and their five children. He migrated with three other men and spent three months working on a Long Island potato farm. Paola missed him and was anxious for him to return. Although his fellow workers were receiving $6.00 per ten-hour day, Yayo was not offered as many hours and had to save for his trip back home. He got along with his foreman but had fights with some whites because he didn't understand enough English to know when he was being insulted. Yayo wrote that he wanted to return to Puerto Rico and preferred to earn less money as a *palero* and be near his family.[6]

After just five weeks in Puerto Rico, Yayo was unhappy. Working as a *palero* was hard; he said he was getting old and complained about aches all over his body after a day's work, but he was only twenty-nine years old. He began talking about returning to the States during the summer of 1949, saying that he liked the weather on Long Island, even after complaining about the terrible cold. Yayo said that he would return to the States because, in Puerto Rico, he worked seven hours a day for only $2.82. Explaining his changed attitude, Yayo said that he was burdened by having so many children and by his wife's relatives' intrusion into their marital problems. He also saw migration as a way to deter his only son from becoming a sugarcane worker.[7]

Workers often used the FLP as a springboard to establish their families in the United States. Yayo wanted to sell his cow, calf, and cart to get money to migrate, leaving half the proceeds behind for his family's expenses. He thought he should keep his house in case they had to return to Puerto Rico. His wife preferred to stay in Puerto Rico, but she was willing to migrate if her husband decided to go, seeing getting away from the dirt, heat, and mosquitoes in their neighborhood as one advantage of living in New York, even though she disliked cities.[8]

Migrants' dreams were shaped by the prospect of breaking out of poverty, a possibility that arose in part from the hegemony of the Popular Democratic Party, which had transformed the Puerto Rico of the 1950s into a country looking toward modernization and development. Migrants, their families, and neighbors hoped to achieve progress within the new consumption-based lifestyle of the "middle class" in the United States.

## FARM LABOR IN THE U.S. NORTHEAST

When Puerto Ricans began to migrate in the late 1940s, agriculture in the U.S. Northeast was still a large and important sector of the economy. During the 1950s, however, unprecedented economic activity increased employment in the service and manufacturing sectors, leading to increases in income and the gross national product and to a general decline in size of the farm labor force despite increasing agricultural productivity. The disparity between farm and nonfarm wages lured workers from farms to the cities (Goodwin 1958, 3). As demand for agricultural products grew, farmers responded by increasing production even as the number of acres under cultivation and the number of farms and farmworkers decreased (Mirengoff and Bail 1958).

In the United States 4.2 million workers earned wages in agriculture during the late 1950s and early 1960s. Of these workers only 1.6 percent worked seasonally, from 25 to 150 days each year, earning an average of $0.73 per hour, compared to the $1.09 earned by laundry workers, $1.65 in retail, $2.07 in manufacturing, and $2.96 in construction (Jorgenson, Williams, and Burma 1961, 1–2).

The number of Puerto Rican migrants who stayed stateside increased from 28,031 in 1947–48 to 41,920 in 1950–51 (PRDL 1952b, 25). In 1948 farmers in New York State hired 1,051 workers from Puerto Rico, and there were also Puerto Ricans among 700 New York City farmworkers. The PRDL estimated that 30,000 contract and noncontract workers were employed in the harvests during the late 1950s, a number that grew to 60,000 by the early 1960s, including 15,000 contract workers (Hurd 1953; Jorgenson, Williams, and Burma 1961, 9).

Agricultural cooperatives tended to hire offshore workers such as Puerto Ricans, Canadians, and Jamaicans, while small farmers preferred local workers and southern African Americans. As a result, the number of FLP contract workers varied from year to year. In 1954 five growers' cooperatives and nine individual growers requested only 1,173 workers, compared to 3,802 in 1953, and approximately 2,600 contract workers were employed on farms and in food-processing plants. Both contract and noncontract workers numbered around 5,000 in 1954, compared to more than 6,000 in 1953. Noncontract workers numbered 2,300 in 1954, compared to 2,650 in 1952. In 1954, out of three growers' cooperatives in Ulster County, New York, only one employed Puerto Ricans to harvest vegetables, while the other two employed guest workers for harvesting and packing fruit (NYSDL 1955, 9–10).

In 1955 five growers' cooperatives and five individual farmers requested 2,646 contract workers, of which an estimated 2,250 were hired on farms and in food-processing facilities. By the mid-1950s the downward trend in hiring contract workers in New York State was reflected in a pronounced decrease in requests for certification of need for temporary workers. At the same time twelve different growers hired guest workers, including nine who hired West Indians and three who opted for Canadians (NYSDL 1956, 9). The New York City Farm Unit, working with the MD's New York Office, helped placed noncontract workers residing in New York City. Overall, while the number of contract workers dwindled in the state, noncontract workers increased from 3,100 in 1956 to 3,900 in 1957 (NYSDL 1958, 7).

Although mechanization and an increase in walk-ins had reduced the number of contract workers (NYSDL 1951, 1958, 7, 11; 1959, 11), in the late 1950s the New York State Joint Legislative Committee on Migrant Labor feared that the southern U.S. agricultural-labor pool was disappearing because workers were choosing to work in other industries. Nonetheless, unemployment fed the southern migrant pool in New York State, a situation that also facilitated the entrance of more Puerto Ricans and West Indians into the state (NYSJLC 1957, 10). Farmers and large growers hired Puerto Ricans primarily for food-processing industries (1958, 16) but complained that those based in New York City were less reliable than insular Puerto Ricans. New York Puerto Ricans left their jobs as soon as they could find better opportunities in factories and were also less compliant than the islanders (Morales 1986, 79; NYSDL 1951, 6).

In the mid-1950s the field-crop sector of the New York State agricultural economy was generating an annual value of more than $124 million, while orchard crops exceeded $48 million (NYSJLC 1957, 11). Migrant labor was critical to maintain those earnings, but the Joint Legislative Committee on Migrant Labor reported a decrease in contract and noncontract workers in 1958 because of the increased use of mechanical bean pickers and the availability of local labor. The number of contract workers in western New York's Erie and Chautauqua Counties declined steeply, with only 279 Puerto Ricans hired in these counties compared to 1,000 or more in previous years. Farmers argued that it was cheaper to hire noncontract workers, when they could entice them to migrate. Even so, the hiring of noncontract workers, concentrated in Long Island and in Wayne, Ulster, and Orange Counties, also declined. In 1958 farmers hired only 3,600 noncontract Puerto Ricans, compared to 3,900 in 1957. New York State also experienced a 56 percent reduction in guest workers (NYSDL 1959, 11–12; NYSJLC 1959, 16).

Farmers in the Hudson Valley and Long Island who depended on noncontract New York City Puerto Ricans saw a considerable decrease in their availability from mid-August through the fall due perhaps to reports of substandard housing and working conditions. In western New York, food processors hired more Puerto Ricans to replenish the declining supply of local workers. Puerto Ricans seemed to prefer jobs in food processing, and employers found them willing to work. This created a problem for farmers, however, because many of these workers had begun by working on farms, and they had left farmers with a reduced and inadequate labor force for the harvest (NYSDL 1958, 11).

The USES continued pressuring growers to hire Puerto Ricans instead of West Indians. In 1958 USES acting director E. L. Keegan wrote to George S. Pfaus, deputy commissioner of the New Jersey Department of Labor, explaining his decision to certify domestic workers instead of West Indians for the Bergen-Rockland Association, even though the USES believed that guest workers were needed to avoid crop loss. The association was willing to employ Puerto Ricans but would not pay more than one-way transportation for seasonal workers (Keegan 1958). For the harvest of 1957, Glassboro hired West Indians for the first time. The following year some MD officials believed that the Garden State Service Cooperative Association was slowing the recruitment of Puerto Ricans to justify hiring West Indians after some of its members complained to USES director Robert Goodwin about Puerto Ricans and the FLP (Perl and Torres 1958). At the same time noncontract Puerto Ricans were being hired at the association's camps for the 1957 harvest, and the USES was canceling job orders from employers such as Shade Tobacco, in Connecticut, because of the influx of walk-in workers. José Villegas, the MD representative attached to the Travelers Aid Society at Idlewild Airport in New York, reported an increased number of migrants arriving without definite job offers, and farmers in New York were hiring walk-in migrants who had left their contract jobs in New Jersey (Senior 1957c, 4–5).

Farmers' perceptions of Puerto Ricans varied throughout the Northeast. In 1956 *Rural New Yorkers* published an article by an eastern Pennsylvania farmer praising Puerto Ricans. R. C. Walker described how, during the previous year, the death of one of his expert local pruners, the advanced age of another, and the unreliability of another left him with unfinished work and little or no profit. Puerto Ricans completed his harvest, increasing his profit. He stated,

> Our American citizens from the Caribbean are admirably refilling the steadily decreasing supply of local farm labor. Besides financial benefits, they have brought cultural gains to me. I know from working with them that they are warm, friendly and happy people. Furthermore, they helped me learn to speak Spanish. . . . The minimum agricultural wage in America is 35 cents an hour higher than that in Puerto Rico. At the end of our harvest season the Puerto Ricans return to their homes with hundreds of dollars in their pockets.

Walker had a small farm of twenty-eight acres, of which fifteen were dedicated to fruit, seven to a woodlot, one to a pond for irrigation, and the rest to a truck patch and buildings. He also managed five acres of fruit for a neighbor. The farm, located well away from any sizable town, had 1,200 peach trees; 4,000 strawberry plants; 100 blueberry bushes; and 20 apple, plum, cherry, and pear trees. While children in farming areas often worked on their parents' farms, local high school students did not wish to do so because they found work in factories and stores. As a result, Walker turned to Puerto Ricans, whom the community accepted out of respect for him.

Walker had begun employing Puerto Ricans when, one night at ten o'clock, four Puerto Ricans knocked on his door. They were standing on his porch with luggage. One of the men who spoke a little English explained that they were unhappy and poorly treated by their boss and had left his farm and hoped to work for Walker. He initially refused to take workers from another farmer, but they refused to return to their employer. Walker relented and they stayed, sometimes working until one in the morning. Eventually Walker provided lodging: a small house for the workers and a separate one for a worker and his wife. When work on his farm was down, he referred them to a waiting list of neighbors needing workers. Walker also learned Spanish by using a book, records, and taking classes. Paying $0.75 per hour, he was producing a half bushel of peaches for $1.00 and averaging a selling price of $1.25 (Walker 1956). Walker's story could have been a paid advertisement for the government of Puerto Rico's contract-labor program, but, in fact, his story resembles that of many farmers in the Northeast who were hiring Puerto Ricans.

The importance of agriculture in the Northeast, together with the decreased availability of local workers and most employers' desires for a cheap, deportable labor force, shaped migration pa'lla afuera. Some employers found hiring Puerto Ricans to be beneficial to their interests. Other employers looked for any opportunity to bring in guest workers under the H-2A program. Employers hired or rejected Puerto Ricans according to labor costs and the availability of other workers.

Although the Puerto Rican government was the force behind migration, migrants played an active role in shaping policies through their willingness to live estranged from home, working for days and months under often difficult conditions. Federal policies supported by the government of Puerto Rico also facilitated the hiring of migrants, but workers fit the opportunity to migrate to their own ends and desires. The Puerto Rican government's attempts to manage farm-labor migration and migrants' struggle to earn a living shaped the contours of the migratory field. As farmwork is, in general, unpleasant and often abandoned by workers because of hardship, injury, or the arrival of better opportunities, constructing a migrant labor force required constant enticement and control by both farmers and government officials. Their strategies helped shape migrants' understandings of life in the United States—their pa'lla afuera. Many migrants used the FLP to gain a foothold, but many did not participate, preferring to migrate without contracts or remaining at home. Overall, the FLP fostered migration in unprecedented numbers and thus shaped the shared framework that migrants used to live through, talk about, and act on their circumstances—opportunities as well as challenges. Employers and government officials constructed migrants into a labor force composed mostly of men in their most productive years, many of whom were married. Their hopes and drive formed how they imagined, experienced, and idealized (or complained about) the United States.

U.S. citizenship allowed contracted workers to leave their jobs and become noncontract workers without the protection of the government of Puerto Rico, subject to their own will but also to the will of employers. Workers and their families calculated the economic and social costs of migrating. Returning to their communities, seasonal workers carried knowledge, contacts, and money that expanded the migratory field. In chapter 5, I explore the role of labor camps in Puerto Rican farm-labor migration. The fields, the labor camps, and new Puerto Rican communities played a major role in how migrants imagined the United States and, in the process, gave rise to many Puerto Rican dreams.

# FIVE

## *Labor Camps as Prisons in the Fields*

*EL CAMPAMENTO,* THE LABOR CAMP, was the social arena where migrant workers learned about work and life in the United States. New migrants arrived with hopes, dreams, and fears about the future. Their experiences of joy, estrangement, adventure, and powerlessness in the labor camps developed a framework that they reproduced in conversations and letters to their families and friends, many of whom succumbed to "migration fever" (G. Pérez 2004). In this chapter I look at the labor-camp experience and how the camps served to discipline and control migrants.

In talking to migrant workers, I was struck by how often they compared living in labor camps to being in prison. Juan, a sixty-eight-year-old farmworker I met during the summer of 2007 in Swedesboro, New Jersey, remembered clearly his first trip to the States, in 1958. He left behind his entire family and a girlfriend and, like many other workers, experienced sadness and depression during the first weeks. He could barely eat, and he wanted to return to Puerto Rico. Living in a labor camp magnified his homesickness. He had to get used to new food, new people, new labor conditions, and the strange life of the camps. After several weeks he became accustomed to long work hours, reminding himself that migration offered him a chance to improve his life. After almost fifty years, Juan was still migrating to southern New Jersey because factory jobs in Puerto Rico and the United States never offered him stability.

Most first-time seasonal migrants living in camps share Juan's feelings of separation and imprisonment. Their memories are fundamentally of places and people, and encounters and struggles in the camps, and from these they constructed the meaning of their experience as migrant workers, an experience shaped by the contradictory feelings of estrangement and hope. Their estrangement results from migration itself and their experience of economic exploitation as well as their social position as an undervalued ethnic group incorporated into a U.S. labor regime where they have little power (Gordillo 2004, 4, 137, 257). Their hope resides in a belief that, through their labor, they can secure a better future for themselves and their families.

In *A Harvest of Loneliness,* Henry P. Anderson (1964), a fervent critic of the Bracero Program, captures the essence of migrants' estrangement:

> It is saddening that other men, from another country, to whom pride and dignity are very important—these, really, are all that they have left—should permit themselves to fall into thrall to a system which humiliates them mercilessly. It is saddening that men, caught in the toils of such a system, are estranged from all those things which ought to give their lives sense and dimension. Within the bracero system, men are estranged from their families, their homeland, their culture; they are estranged from their fellow workers on the land, from the land itself, and the harvests which grow upon it. Above all, the men are estranged from themselves, from what they would like to be, and from what they are capable of becoming. (1964, 12)

Estrangement is key to understanding the thoughts, aspirations, and fields of power in which workers maneuver. Hope alone does not drive them to migrate. Quite the opposite, hope and estrangement go hand in hand, accompanying workers on their journey to the United States. The labor regime on the farms—in the fields and camps—was unbearable for some workers accustomed to the protection of labor unions, political bosses, and the paternalism of landowners. Others, like Juan, adjusted.

When the Puerto Rican government enacted the public law 25 of 1947, creating the Bureau of Employment and Migration, the Migration Division (MD), and the Farm Labor Program (FLP), it recognized the feelings of estrangement workers confronted (Lapp 1990, 173–74). The preamble to public law stated,

> The Government of Puerto Rico neither encourages nor discourages the migration of Puerto Rican workmen [sic] to the United States or any foreign country; but considers it its duty ... to provide the proper guidance with respect to opportunities for employment and the problems of adjustment usually encountered in environments which are ethnologically alien. (Sierra Berdecía 1953, 3)

This recognition of the States as an alien place resulted from migrants' complaints during previous attempts to employ Puerto Ricans in U.S. agriculture. Therefore, in addition to monitoring conditions in the labor camps, the Puerto Rican officials held orientations for U.S. farmers and managers to foster their understanding of workers. In a conference for farmers, Carlos Martínez, director of the MD's Camden Office explained,

> Our men respond to good treatment.... I am not here to make excuses for shirkers, but I say that if they are treated right, these are as good as any other workers.... Community problems occur ... when these men are brought here to strange surroundings, and they must be solved in the community.... These men do not know the customs of this country and their ways often seem strange in the new land.... You farmers must realize that many times these men are flown up here to a strange land in the dark night and by morning are in the farmer's fields ready for work. There is no time for any sort of adjustment. The Puerto Rican is plunged into a strange environment with not even the advantage of a common language among these strangers. (NJDLI 1957, 4–5)

Perceptions of impersonal relationships with managers, farmers, and locals increased feeling of estrangement among workers. Dolores Rivera Hernández, a Puerto Rico Department of Labor (PRDL) official from Puerto Rico, observed after visiting the camps,

> Many of our workers, when they tell us that they couldn't stand the cold and wanted to go back and leave there, were not referring to the cold caused by a change of season but to the internal cold produced when, for one reason or another, ... [they were] thoughtlessly ignored, never receiving a word of encouragement. (1956, 6–7)

Because farmers' cooperation in ameliorating feelings of estrangement was important to enticing workers to migrate and thereby ensure a constant flow of new workers, the MD established a bond with farmers and farm associations that, in effect, made it a partner in maintaining order in the labor camps.

The literature about migrant workers underscores the perception of the camp as a prison. In *They Saved the Crops,* Don Mitchell mentions that Puerto Rican workers in Santa Barbara County, California, reported little contact outside the camp. Forbidden to leave the premises at night, they commented that living in the camp was "like being in prison" (2012, 366). Diane Austin reports that migrant workers in the U.S. shipping industry likened the camps to "a prison [and] we are like prisoners." Residents of surrounding communities also believed that migrant workers were treated like slaves, locked up in large, fortresslike camps (2014, 129). Workers' sense of imprisonment was also shaped by how some farmers treated them. In 1957 a migrant complained to Gov. Luis Muñoz Marín,

> I am sure that when we left Puerto Rico, we were not animals. My opinion is that migrants have rights and that we have the right that the government defend us like any U.S. citizens. You know that we left Puerto Rico as friends and not as enemies.... Many crimes in the fields and workers' rebelliousness [occur] because the farmers think that we are obligated to be prisoners. (Ramos 1957)

The labor camp has always evoked images of destitution, poverty, and despair (Hahamovitch 2011, 34–35). The Puerto Rican press in New York City, in particular, portrayed labor camps as prisons or concentration camps. In 1961 Jesús Colón, a Puerto Rican writer and political activist, denounced these conditions:

> An increasing number of Puerto Ricans are coming ... [to New York City] ... not from Chicago or Philadelphia but from one of those concentration camps in which the Puerto Rican seasonal workers are kept, for all intents and purposes, in practical slavery, under the worst living conditions possible, getting beatings and very little pay when the "deductions" are made against the pennies per hour they receive as wages. (1993, 96)

The image of the camp as a prison embodies the social relations of power on the farms and how the agrarian-labor regime structured workers' experiences. Labor camps "are historically made and unmade through practice, fields of power and struggle, and networks of social relations" (Gordillo 2004, 4, 137, 257; see also Mitchell 1996). As films, photographs, journalism, and literature portrayed the dire conditions in the camps, the image of destitute and oppressed migrant workers became dominant in debates about farm labor.

Farm labor is constructed through a series of processes that shape workers' subjectivities. "The agricultural labor supply ... has been manipulated by government agencies working in concert with private growers and labor contractors, using housing in particular as a tool to attract, retain, and control workers" (Griffith 2006, 9). In this sense the formation of a Puerto Rican farm labor force stemmed largely from *el campamento,* the labor camp. Life in a camp requires adjustment to demanding conditions: unfamiliar work rhythms, bosses' expectations, changes in traditional gender roles, a different climate and landscape, absence of immediate relatives, and little privacy.

The labor camp reveals how the state and employers plan and enact measures to regulate the everyday life of workers (Binford 2009). It becomes the principal tool for monitoring workers' schedules and spaces, central to constructing a compliant labor force. Following Erving Goffman (1961), I regard the labor camp as a total institution, a place that, like a prison, must be equipped with everything needed for survival, where workers can live for months without ever having to leave. Total institutions are, in effect, apparatuses for enacting top-down strategies of domination that attempt to obliterate and destroy workers' agency. Labor camps are thus fields of power in which social actors and state institutions struggle to subordinate migrant labor and make it tractable (Binford 2009, 505; Bourdieu and Wacquant 1992, 102; De Genova 2010, 57; Goffman 1961; Griffith 1993, 43; 2006, 9–10). The labor camp became the center of migrants' lives stateside, facilitating federal, state, and the Puerto Rican governments' intrusion into their lives under the banner of free enterprise, job creation, and community service.

Although the physical structure of camps evolved during the second half of the twentieth century, life in them did not change very much for workers. In the following sections I explore the labor camp in the context of migration: the MD's oversight of the camps, perceptions of the camps in relation to the outside world and the fields, and the interaction of workers with farmers and government officials.

### THE RISE OF THE MODERN LABOR CAMP

Slaves and indentured servants on plantations and farms were often housed in barracks, and contemporary labor camps in many ways reproduce this mode of housing. The use of modern labor camps in U.S. agriculture coincides with employers' need to attract and maintain a seasonal migrant labor force. Modern camps allow workers to reduce their expenses and thus reproduce their labor power more cheaply through social networks. For example, in small camps workers can generate nonwage income through such activities as raising chickens and maintaining a garden. Workers also lend and borrow money. Their activities center on reducing their consumer needs for food or clothing, but these survival strategies also subsidize their employers' farms (Griffith 1993, 43; 2006, 9–10; Hahamovitch 1997).

In the 1930s state and federal agencies began to standardize and institutionalize labor camps. State governments regulated the building of housing facilities and established health codes and operational licensing requirements. In 1935 the federal government's Resettlement Administration built the first migrant labor camps in regions of high demand for seasonal workers, using funds provided by the U.S. Congress. Within months of the German invasion of Poland, farm wages fell, increasing homelessness among workers. In response, the Farm Security Administration established new permanent and mobile labor camps for migratory workers (Galarza 1977, 129–32; Mitchell 1996, 156–97; Martínez Matsuda 2009, 5–9; U.S. House 1949a, 32; 1949c).

Reformism through state interventions in the labor market was a dominant theme in the country and a force in the labor camps. In 1940 the Farm Security Administration built the first labor camp in Belle Glade, Florida, where its social workers taught canning, sewing, and literacy to migrant families. By 1943 it was operating 89 labor camps around the country and considering the establishment of 140 new sites. Working with the U.S. Employment Service, the Farm Security Administration recruited farmworkers to areas with labor shortages, and German and Japanese prisoners in U.S. internment camps were mobilized for work in agriculture (Rasmussen 1951, 96–99). In the late 1940s the camps were sold to farmers' associations (Galarza 1977, 129–32; Hurd 1953; U.S. House 1949a). By fostering the use of camps and linking them to associations, the federal government sought to modernize the supply of farmworkers. The federal government had become the crew leader of the nation, and Puerto Rican officials took note (Hahamovitch 2011, 38).

During World War II the Emergency Farm Labor Supply Program housed contract Mexicans, Bahamians, Jamaicans, Barbadians, and Canadians in camps (Rasmussen 1951, 199–287). In New York the number of camps housing more than ten workers increased from 287 in 1943 to 451 in 1948. From 1943 to 1945 the New York Extension Service operated 150 labor camps that housed twenty-five thousand workers, part of a concerted effort that included thirty cooperative associations of farmers and thirteen associations of farmers and food processors. State and federal officials were also active in improving the living and working conditions in the camps. The New York Extension Service provided a camp construction specialist to assist farmers in siting and repairing camps and camp-management specialists who helped employers find, train, and assist managers (Galarza 1977, 129–32; Hurd 1953; U.S. House 1949a).

Puerto Ricans lived in a variety of labor camps throughout the Northeast, among them camps operated by associations and large growers, camps

FIGURE 7. Glassboro labor camp in New Jersey, circa 1957. Courtesy of the Records of the Migration Division, Archives of the Puerto Rican Diaspora, Centro de Estudios Puertorriqueños, Hunter College, City University of New York.

housing farmworkers' families, and small former chicken coops converted into worker housing (H. Anderson 1976, 66–69). Most of the large labor camps were operated by associations. The Glassboro Service Association (GSA) in southern New Jersey, the Farmers and Gardeners Association (FGA) in northern New Jersey, and the Shade Tobacco Growers Agricultural Association in Connecticut ran the largest camps housing Puerto Ricans. Camp Windsor, in Connecticut, could house eight hundred workers— Jamaicans as well as Puerto Ricans (Bonilla-Santiago 1986, 95). The Glassboro camp had been used by participants in the Civilian Conservation Corps and later for German prisoners of war. In 1947 the GSA acquired the Swedesboro camp, which had operated previously as an information and placement center for migrant workers. After the war both camps housed Puerto Ricans. The Puerto Rico Economic Development Bank provided funds to improve the infrastructure of the Glassboro camp throughout the years that the association and the government of Puerto Rico maintained agreements to hire contract workers (Stinson Fernández 1996, 135).

FIGURE 8. Puerto Rican farmworkers' barracks, circa 1948. Courtesy of the Records of the Migration Division, Archives of the Puerto Rican Diaspora, Centro de Estudios Puertorriqueños, Hunter College, City University of New York.

During the 1950s the agreement with the Puerto Rican government helped the GSA spread its influence into Pennsylvania and New York. Seeking representation in the annual contract negotiations with the government of Puerto Rico, local farmers' associations joined the Garden State Service Cooperative Association, which grouped affiliates such as GSA and FGA. Growers and counties operated large camps for migratory workers (U.S. Farm Labor Service 1957), and smaller associations also had camps, such as the Brant Labor Camp in western New York, property of the Brant Labor Cooperative.

The spatial arrangements of the camps contributed to reproducing the encamped labor force. Larger camps had an administrative office, recreation facilities, a dining hall, and a health clinic, which sometimes operated out of separate buildings. Glassboro's housing consisted of wooden barracks a hundred feet long, with galvanized aluminum roofs. Each barrack was divided into six-by-eight-foot rooms and housed six to eight people (Stinson Fernández 1996, 136). The FGA camp consisted of three twenty-six-by-forty-four-foot dormitory buildings with rooms for showers and laundry. There was also a thirty-one-by-sixty-six-foot building with a kitchen, dining room, and recreational facilities. Both camps had management offices (NJDLI 1957, 4–5).

The New Jersey State Migration Division inspected the housing, health, and living conditions of seasonal workers in the camps, but the Puerto Rican government also made sure that conditions met federal and state guidelines (U.S. Extension Service 1947, 37–38). Notwithstanding, conditions in the camps were difficult for workers. Luis first migrated to work in the 1970s, when he was in his early twenties. He remembered Glassboro as a hostile environment where it was difficult to sleep. Workers were afraid of being robbed, and loud noise and fights were routine.

In the Northeast most workers lived in small camps, in groups of four to fifteen. Because most came for the harvest and returned to Puerto Rico after it ended, they usually lived in camps specifically designated for them, apart from African American and West Indian migrants (Nelkin 1970, 2–3). In some rural areas, however, residents refused to rent to Puerto Ricans, forcing workers and their families to stay in camps, some of which were former barns or chicken coops (*CALC Report/TWC Bulletin* 1984, 8). Artemio recalled staying in a small camp in western New York, in the early 1950s. A strong smell of manure interfered with his sleep for a couple of days until he got used to it. In 1957 a group of workers in a Pennsylvania camp complained to a journalist for *El Diario* that "a total of 24 workers had to live there in a dog house under very bad hygienic conditions" (*El Diario* [1957?]).

Camps were also sites for social research and engineering. In 1944 the U.S. Department of Interior explored the possibility of studying food habits among Puerto Rican workers to better plan how workers living in camps could sustain their productivity and avoid conflicts (Thoron 1944b). The Glassboro camp broadcast a radio program in its camps to orient workers (Cunningham 1957). During the 1950s and 1960s, to mitigate problems in the camps, the MD created an English-language program for farmworkers and offered programs to teach farmers Spanish (Jorge Colón 1966d).

As Puerto Rican officials, camp managers, and the leaders of Puerto Rican communities in the United States fostered the interactions between workers and Puerto Ricans settled in nearby towns and cities, the GSA and FGA camps became activity centers. In 1957 the MD coordinated a meeting of Puerto Rican organizations in northern New Jersey at the FGA camp, which was conveniently located and had adequate facilities for meetings. Puerto Rican communities organized events for camp-dwelling workers, which

FIGURE 9. Sleeping quarters for Puerto Rican workers, circa 1948. Courtesy of the Records of the Migration Division, Archives of the Puerto Rican Diaspora, Centro de Estudios Puertorriqueños, Hunter College, City University of New York.

helped create networks between migrants and local residents and eased life in the camps. The Puerto Rican government also used these events for publicity, particularly when problems arose over workers' treatment and living conditions (Ruiz 1957a).

The GSA camp was a center for religious ministry. Protestant and Catholic clergy visited this and other camps, offering English classes, movies, and religious services. The Reverend Charles S. Bean worked as a chaplain at Glassboro and regularly helped migrants because he knew Spanish and understood their customs; in early 1967, during an unusually cold spell, he

FIGURE 10. Jaime Quiñones, working for the Council of Churches, distributes letters to workers in the Rath Camp, circa 1950s. Courtesy of the Records of the Migration Division, Archives of the Puerto Rican Diaspora, Centro de Estudios Puertorriqueños, Hunter College, City University of New York.

organized a community clothing drive for migrant workers so they could stay warm (Vargas 2010). Throughout the Northeast, religious groups visited workers in the camps and assisted them with personal problems.

While images of prison-like conditions in labor camps gave rise to comparisons between migrant farmworkers and slaves (see Hahamovitch 2015), contemporary labor camps differ markedly from nineteenth-century slave quarters and early twentieth-century workers' barracks in part because of New Deal reforms (even if many farmers took a long time to accept them). Some of the camps I visited have electricity, air-conditioning, adequate plumbing, and even cable TV. On the outside, however, most still resemble the structures built in the mid-twentieth century. In the Northeast, labor camps are readily visible among the different farm buildings. Most are large rectangular structures, painted either red clay or white, or small rectangular gray houses. Conditions inside the sleeping quarters vary. I have seen camps with old iron-frame beds, rough cement floors, and no heat. Not by chance, farmers with the best facilities have been very welcoming when I inquired about their workers, while farmers hostile to my presence had the worst facilities, reminiscent of photos of labor camps in the 1940s and 1950s, which speaks to the limited changes in the U.S. agrarian-labor regime even into the twentieth-first century.

## STRUCTURAL VIOLENCE

A central, persistent feature of the political economy of U.S. agriculture is inadequate living conditions in most agricultural-labor camps. A 1980 survey found that 62 percent of camps were overcrowded (exceeding their legal capacity to house workers), and 80 percent lacked laundry facilities. A 1997 survey by the nonprofit Housing Assistance Council in Washington, DC, documented that almost 85 percent of camp housing was overcrowded (Holden 2002, 169–70, 172; Housing Assistance Council 1997, 16). Conditions in the camps illustrate what Peter Benson calls the structural violence and faciality of camps. Benson argues that U.S. farmworkers face structural violence through nonliving wages, poverty, discrimination and racism, occupational health and safety hazards, lack of adequate health care, and deportation. Faciality refers to the ethnographic and phenomenological narratives workers construct to explain these relations of inequality: how they experience and express estrangement and familiarity and react to suffering (2008, 591, 594; see also Farmer 2002). The faciality of power manifests itself in the everyday life of the camps and the coercive practices of those managing them.

In the early twentieth century, reports from Hawaii and the U.S. Southwest highlighted the difficult living conditions of Puerto Ricans in labor camps. Therefore, the MD devoted significant resources and energy to inspecting camps, since negative reports from workers migrating to the farms could threaten the entire FLP. Petroamérica Pagán de Colón, the first director of the Bureau of Employment and Migration, reflected on her camp visits in May 1948:

> The dormitories assigned to the workers were old wooden ranches without paint, poorly maintained, dirty and surrounded by wired fences that looked like prisons or concentration camps.
> There were no toilets and showers in many of them. Men had to shower outdoors. The bedrooms were equipped with bunk beds with straw mats covered in dark color, no pillows and only a military fleece as covering. They

FIGURE 11. Gov. Luis Muñoz Marín playing baseball with migrant workers, circa 1956. Courtesy of the Records of the Migration Division, Archives of the Puerto Rican Diaspora, Centro de Estudios Puertorriqueños, Hunter College, City University of New York.

had no sheets or blankets; they lacked a suitable place to store their clothes or their luggage; there was no suitable room where the men could gather and they were not provided with recreational facilities.

Some of these conditions still prevail in some camps. Most camps have been improved. All camps have adequate recreation and sanitary facilities with good showers. As for the beds, many camps still retain the system of mattresses and blankets without sheets and without pillows. Cleaning in general has improved, although the men themselves could do more in this regard. (1956a, 11–12)

Recognizing the deplorable conditions, Puerto Rican officials pressured farmers and their associations for improved food, sheets, pillows, and entertainment to keep workers happy.

A decade after the first contract migrants arrived, problems in the camps persisted. In New Jersey, during fiscal year 1955–56, inspections found that half of the 2,668 labor camps violated state and federal regulations

(Cunningham 1957, 6). Ten years later MD officials Jorge Colón and Carlos Gómez visited a camp in North Collins, New York, and reported,

> This is one of the worst camps. It has a raw sewage of 2 inches from the top of the [toilet] seat. A well was constructed next to the kitchen floor, the shower is on the same side but inside the kitchen with a drain, the water runs under the kitchen wich [sic] in turn, part of it runs into the well and is pumped back to the house for further use. The inside walls of the entire old dwelling home were covered with newspapers, mats and cardboards. This camp was found without a health permit and is not registered with the Health Department. (Jorge Colón 1966c)

> [Other workers] were paying $15 weekly for lodging in a "shack" structure camp built in the back yard of one of the homes in North Collins. (1966e)

> In other camps the conditions were deplorable; open sewage, no bathroom, fire hazards, sewage running into open fields, no screens on windows and doors. In general, the situation was unsafe and unsanitary. None of the workers at these camps were under contract. (1966f)

After visiting several appalling camps, Colón met with the health commissioner, who complained about his budget and personnel, saying that his biggest concerns were dairies, restaurants, and hotels and that some residents in the area lived in worse conditions than the migrant workers. Colón's perception was that Puerto Ricans were not important for local officials (1966c).

The emergence of the camp as a tool to maintain a labor force was also shaped by New Deal interventions in hygiene and health. Usually, state departments of labor would oversee and inspect migrant-camp accommodations, while departments of health inspected hygiene and the water supply. Camps were supposed to follow building and health codes, but inspectors were often political appointees and very close to farmers, which prejudiced their evaluation of camps.

In the early 1950s lack of coordination impeded adequate inspection of labor camps. In some states several agencies duplicated work or failed to carry out inspections because of confusing regulations and jurisdictions. Farmers could often play agencies against one another, making them lose track of original violations (H. Anderson 1976, 72–73). In 1954 investigators in one Pennsylvania county found that inspectors were unaware of many labor camps in their territory. Their supervisors had not insisted on the importance of inspecting camps, and some believed that camp inspections fell outside their duties (Blair et. al 1954, 6–8, 29).

Workers regularly contacted Puerto Rican officials to protest conditions in the camps and demand changes in their housing conditions. In 1957 a migrant complained to the director of the MD,

> I have the opportunity to write to you only to see if you can investigate this house where we are living, seven workers as if we were animals. The beds don't work nor the mattresses.... We cannot open our eyes with the dust. Here nobody comes to investigate.... We don't even have anywhere to take a bath.... My belief is that we Puerto Ricans are willing to come to this country to work, but we are not willing to live like pigs.... We expect your cooperation. (Figueroa 1957)

Workers knew that writing letters would trigger the MD to intervene.

The Puerto Rican government also received complaints from workers in areas where the MD did not send contract workers. In 1957, after Governor Muñoz Marín heard from a group of Puerto Ricans in Florida about the conditions in their camp, the MD asked Ralph Moss, chief of the U.S. Employment Service's Farm Placement Office in Tallahassee, to investigate. The workers interviewed did not voice any complaints and rated the conditions in the camp as excellent. Perhaps they were hesitant to talk to a North American or Moss was overstating excellent conditions of the camp (Arnold 1958; Moss 1958). Be that as it may, from the 1940s through the 1980s, the MD received many complaints from contract and noncontract workers about conditions in labor camps.

Because the MD did not have the personnel to reach all areas where Puerto Ricans worked, it collaborated, if not always harmoniously, with state agencies. In Maryland, in 1963, friction arose with the state farm-placement supervisor after MD officials visited some camps without prior notice. The state official also complained about the FLP contract, calling it one-sided in favor of workers and complaining that because new contracts were not delivered on time, farmers had to sign old contracts that had to be resigned when the new version arrived (Coll 1963).

Close living quarters bred conflict among seasonal migrant workers, sometimes leading to physical fights. To avoid conflicts, farmers and managers at the Glassboro and Shade Tobacco Growers Agricultural Association's camps, and in some smaller camps, tried to keep workers separated by national origin and ethnicity (Nelkin 1970, 3). Nevertheless, conflict arose. In 1958 two workers were viciously attacked by southern white workers at the Glassboro camp, one of whom cut a Puerto Rican worker's throat, beat him up, and stole thirty dollars (M. Fernández 1958b). The most common fights, however, were among Puerto Ricans themselves. In 1958 MD officials discussed the case of Jesús, a migrant in southern New Jersey, who had been jailed for fighting with another worker who, he alleged, was drunk, asked him for money to buy alcohol, and insulted him when he refused to give it. Jesús attacked the worker with a guitar and was charged with creating a false alarm and sentenced to six months in prison. Amazingly, the worker who actually started the fight was not arrested and served as Jesús's interpreter in court. Even more incredible was the arrest of Jesús's friend, Ovidio, who argued that he was not part of the fight and had left the labor camp when everything started and gone to sleep with friends elsewhere. When he arrived at the farm the next day with Jesús, he was arrested and sentenced to a month in jail for disorderly conduct. Also strange about this case is that Ovidio's identification in jail read, "Ovidio aka Rubén," which was name of the worker who was allegedly drunk and began the fight. Clearly, the police and the courts were not always fair to Puerto Ricans, most of whom could not speak English (M. Fernández 1958c).

The depression and disorientation of first-time migrants also led to fights and tension among workers. In 1959 José, a twenty-three-year-old first-time migrant, who was married and had two children back in Puerto Rico, arrived at a camp in Maryland. His coworkers indicated that, from the day after he arrived, José wished he had the money to return home. He complained that he did not like living at the farm and often sat by himself, refusing to talk to the other workers. One night, while workers were in bed and the lights were out, he threatened to cut the throat of a man sitting next to him and the lips of another. Saying, "tonight I don't go to bed without drinking blood," he became violent, frightening his coworkers. MD officials arranged for his return to Puerto Rico, asking local officials not to refer him to the program again (Plá 1959).

Alcohol has always been a problem in labor camps, implicated in fights among workers but also creating serious health problems. The excruciating conditions of farmwork led many workers to self-medicate with alcohol. In many camps I observed the use of beer as the principal drink for relieving thirst. Juan remembered a crew leader who provided workers with beer only, not water, during the day in the fields. I have also observed workers with heart problems and diabetes who drink constantly. Many workers, after a long day of work, begin drinking immediately, to the point of dropping, drunk, into their beds and falling asleep. Among the workers who abandoned the Glassboro camp in 1958 was another named Juan, who, under the influence of alcohol, had a nightmare and jumped from the second floor, hurting himself

(M. Fernández 1958a). Another worker, Pedro, got drunk, became violent, and was arrested. MD officials tried to counsel him, but he kept on drinking and getting arrested. At the end of the report on this incident, the MD official asked, "What else can we do with this individual?" (1958c).

The labor-camp experience was very isolating, not only due to living conditions but also because most camps were located far from towns. Moreover, some migrants feared to interact with the outside community, so most social activities, which included eating, drinking, gambling, and listening to music, occurred within the camp (Nelkin 1970, 34–35, 53). In western New York Puerto Rican pastor Jaime Quiñones visited the camps every Sunday, providing dominoes, writing letters to workers' relatives, and sharing Puerto Rican culture through music, poetry, and storytelling (*Christian Science Monitor*, n.d.). Even now there are Puerto Rican peddlers who visit the camps, selling clothing and food to workers. Some crew leaders, farmers, and businesses also provide workers with food, alcohol, and even sex workers and drugs.

There is also a sexual economy in labor camps housing Puerto Ricans in the Northeast (see Norris and Worby 2012). On paydays men might leave the camps to visit bars and sex workers, or women will visit the camps (Torres Penchi 1996, 41–42). I suspect that homosexual relations also occur in the camps, but the taboos associated with this topic make it difficult to investigate and offer evidence. Documented cases of unreciprocated sexual advances do surface, however, as in a labor camp in Wareham, Massachusetts, where a fight broke out after a Puerto Rican accused another worker of making sexual advances and derogatory remarks about him while he was in the shower. He attacked him with a knife, inflicting a deep wound above the elbow of his right arm. Both workers were drinking at the time of the incident (Migration Division 1972).

Although the labor camp was an alienating experience for workers, many got so used to working and living in them that they continued migrating for decades. Other workers looked for better opportunities as soon as they could. Overall, the labor camp was a social arena where workers struggled to reproduce the world they knew and understood. They were not so accepting of the living conditions, however, that they considered labor camps satisfactory.

## THE FIELDS

Agricultural fields are central to the experience of migration and a central feature of the landscape of social relations migrants had to navigate. In the fields migrants learned the rhythms and dangers of their jobs; they cooperated and competed to become reliable workers and negotiated compliance with productivity expectations. The fields provided a venue for socializing workers into the disciplinary tactics and expectations of time and work enforced by farmers, managers, and crew leaders. As they toiled in the fields, Puerto Ricans also interacted with farmworkers of different nationalities, ethnicities, and races.

Workers woke up between four and six in the morning to be ready to leave for the fields, which, for those living in the larger camps, could be quite a distance away. In one instance workers complained that it took two hours to get from the camp to an apple orchard. They also complained about having to work from Mondays through Saturdays, which left them without access to the post office or stores on Sundays for mailing letters and buying groceries. After intervention by an MD official, the farmer agreed to pay workers on Friday and give them Saturdays as a rest day. The official also found that workers had exaggerated the travel time, but long travel times were nonetheless quite common for many workers (Muñiz 1965).

Accidents during transportation to the fields were common and always taken seriously by MD officials, particularly when they resulted in death. MD officials visited injured workers, obtained death certificates, contracted attorneys, and met with farmers and community organizers. The MD also investigated mishaps among illegally recruited noncontract workers, as in a fatal 1966 accident in Florida, involving a train and a car transporting workers. The dead and injured workers had come from New Jersey. MD officials visited the hospital to make sure that attorneys and insurance adjusters did not take advantage of them (Gomez 1966a) and coordinated with their lawyers in personal-injury cases by facilitating communication and translation. The MD took pains to ensure that the workers' cases would be adjudicated promptly and that the risks and opportunities offered in the settlement were explained in detail.

Farmers, managers, and crew leaders oversaw the performance of contract and noncontract migrants in the fields as well as in daily life in the camps. Most crew leaders tended to be Puerto Ricans who had been contract workers themselves. For example, Evaristo, who migrated for the first time under a government contract in the 1950s, eventually became a crew leader, cooking for and transporting noncontract workers and leasing land from large farmers. Crew leaders were sometimes labor recruiters, including Evaristo, who recruited undocumented workers in the early 1980s. Because crew leaders served as intermediaries and supervisors, they could exercise considerable power over workers, so in the 1940s states began to regulate their activities. In New York crew leaders had to be registered with the New York Department of Labor, and growers could not hire unregistered crew leaders (NYSIC 1961, 16). When I interviewed Evaristo, he showed me his crew leader's identification card, which had been issued by the Commonwealth of Pennsylvania.

Unlike the camps, which most of the time were segregated, the fields were where workers of different ethnicities learned to interact. One migrant worker got to know Charlie, an African American farmworker from Long Island, whom he considered to be an American regardless of his race. The migrant wanted and even asked if he could visit Charlie's family. Charlie said yes, but the worker decided not to go because he feared his speaking only Spanish might offend Charlie's parents. Having heard that Americans discriminate and have prejudices, he still thought he could win people over and improve his job prospects by working hard and being good, honest, and friendly.[1]

Competition to be the hardest working and most productive structured relations among workers in the fields. They expressed their machismo by degrading those who could not endure farmwork and praising those who could withstand its rigors. For example, harvesting tomatoes is backbreaking work that must be done fast, under the sun, with mosquitoes biting. When work is paid by the piece, competition among workers is particularly fierce. Julio Morales (1986) mentions a farm where the count per bushel of tomatoes was posted above the refrigerator as a weekly record of each worker's wages. While spurring workers to compete and compare their earnings, these records also limited the bonds that formed among workers.

Workers pushed one another to work for long hours through bullying, jokes, and teasing (Morales 1986, 80), and groups of workers often bullied and harassed others. An MD official described tense situations he witnessed in a camp he was visiting. Someone had burned another worker's pillow; another wanted to work by himself due to harassment by a group of workers (M. Fernández 1958c). In other instances workers bullied coworkers because of their supposed unmanliness. A worker in New York complained to MD officials that English-speaking supervisors constantly accused him of being effeminate. The MD official believed that the worker, a humble person, suffered from depression; the worker eventually left the farm for Puerto Rico (Machado 1963).

Some farmers pushed workers to the edge of their endurance, sparking confrontations or complaints to the Bureau of Employment and Migration,

FIGURE 12. Migrants working in the fields, circa 1948. Courtesy of the Records of the Migration Division, Archives of the Puerto Rican Diaspora, Centro de Estudios Puertorriqueños, Hunter College, City University of New York.

as in 1952, when a small group of workers in Pennsylvania asked for help after a farmer forced them to work long hours without rest or time to eat or prepare their meals. This farmer also took them to work on other farms when he did not have enough work on his own farm. The workers threatened to leave their jobs, but they pleaded with the bureau not to consider them as abandoning their work without cause and asked for immediate assistance (Soto et al. 1952). MD officials intervened in another case of workers who wanted to take leave from the camps on Saturdays and Sundays but faced resistance from farmers who needed them to complete the harvest (North Jersey Office 1959a; Reoyo 1963). When such situations arose, some workers wrote to the government for help in resolving their problems and for money to return to Puerto Rico (Cardona 1957).

Puerto Ricans accommodated, resisted, and transformed their lives in relation to the rhythm of work in the fields. Farmers, crew leaders, and farm managers also shaped the fields, since they commanded the workers in these spaces. In the fields, where workers interacted closely with those of other ethnicities, Puerto Ricans became just another group of toiling migrants. To prevent desertion farmers deployed both enticement and coercion, but because of their U.S. citizenship, Puerto Ricans were not bound to the wishes of farmers, crew leaders, and managers.

## THE POLITICS OF FOOD

Rice and beans, codfish, and coffee were central to Puerto Ricans' diet and had been since the nineteenth century, when sugarcane plantations imported rice to feed their slaves and workers (Ortíz Cuadra 2013). Migrants assumed they would continue eating the foods they had eaten at home while working on stateside farms, foods they associated with manhood and the strength needed for heavy lifting and agricultural work. Greens and meat were usually out of reach for most agricultural workers, but they were proud of their capacity to work, even when they were aware of the deficiency of their diet.[2]

Puerto Rican food was a signifier of difference and identity for migrant workers. Ji-Yeon Yuh argues that, in the United States, food "is a terrain where ethnicity is contested, denigrated, and affirmed. It is an arena of struggle between Americanization and adherence to native cultural ways, where the demands are often either-or, but the lives lived are more often constructed from pieces of both" (2002, 126). Food in the camps thus became an object of struggle for Puerto Rican identity, manliness, and happiness. Workers' craving for Puerto Rican food was accompanied by homesickness, loneliness, and, sometimes, depression (130). Not consuming Puerto Rican food took a toll on workers who had to confront demanding working conditions. Those who didn't like the food provided in the camps often lost weight.

Migrants' complaints about meals are widespread in Puerto Rican government records from the 1920s through the early 1990s.[3] As workers expected to be served big, delicious Puerto Rican–style meals after working for long hours in the fields, most of their complaints reveal how types of food and cooking techniques differed among Puerto Ricans, farmers, and other workers. Puerto Ricans' idea of lunch and dinner also differed from farmers', but for most workers either or both meals had to include rice and beans. They expected to be fed properly, according to their tastes.

Anthropologist Eduardo Seda Bonilla narrates the story of Filomeno Santos, also known as Chico, who was a cook in one of the Stoolewell Company's camps in the late 1950s and early 1960s. He cooked for 350 men, of whom 45 were southern "Americans" who ate the Puerto Rican–style food he prepared without complaint, though they did not always like it (1973, 20–23). Filomeno reflected on how workers' lives—and tolerance for unusual food—changed after the implementation of the FLP. He considered his coworkers' complaints about food to be reflections of their ingratitude for their improved conditions, stating,

> The Puerto Rican is the most ungrateful fellow alive. I went to work at a place, and I boarded with the "boss." They served canned soup with corn kernels in it. I could starve to death before I would eat that! I asked for a sandwich and a glass of milk, and I left that very day. If the Puerto Rican doesn't like something, he just won't eat it. (21)

Filomeno recalled that during the 1930s and early 1940s, when agricultural workers led rough lives, exacerbated by inadequate access to food, they would have been unlikely to refuse the canned soup and other "American" food he and his coworkers now disdained.

In 1948 Puerto Rican officials also found the food served in labor camps and company towns unacceptable. Pagán de Colón reported,

> The kitchens, although some had refrigerators, were not equipped with the necessary facilities for the number of people who had to be cooked for. The food consisted invariably of soggy oatmeal for breakfast and a cup of coffee; American coffee made in the worst way. The lunch consisted of two sand-wiches and a quart of milk. The dinner was soggy white rice, the worst kind of codfish, boiled served with tomato sauce, and scraggly, unsalted beans. . . . Workers paid $1.50 daily for this kind of meal. (1956a, 12)

In the small camps workers had to cook their own meals, while in the larger camps employers paid cooks and charged fees for the meals. Either way workers complained about the quality and quantity of food served to them. Both North Americans and West Indians cooked and seasoned the food following their own habits, eliciting a bad reaction from Puerto Ricans (Guerra-Mondragón 1944). Farmers who did not consider the ethnic and national differences among farmworkers soon encountered problems with workers because of the food they provided.

Having analyzed the principal complaints of workers who migrated before 1948, Puerto Rican government officials included language in the FLP con-tract they hoped would resolve the problem with food. The contract stipulated that workers receive at least three hot meals a day, at reduced cost, but the

FIGURE 13. Gov. Luis Muñoz Marín with officials inspecting food at a labor camp, circa 1956. Courtesy of the Records of the Migration Division, Archives of the Puerto Rican Diaspora, Centro de Estudios Puertorriqueños, Hunter College, City University of New York.

complaints persisted. In many instances farmers overcharged workers or did not provide adequate—or hot—meals. A group of workers from the municipality of Utuado complained that after protesting to the farmer that they were being overcharged for food, he told them to eat it or leave. Workers also indicated that when a PRDL official came to inspect a camp, the cooks made a feast so that the official did not believe their complaints (*El Imparcial* 1949).

In the 1950s the MD continued to inspect the camps' cooking facilities and what workers ate, because farmers did not always comply with their contractual obligations. At the PRDL's Post-Harvest Season Meeting of 1959, MD official Guadalupe Ruiz (1959a) reported on complaints at the FGA labor camp in Holmdel, New Jersey:

> We had many complaints on food at the Camp this year. Rice and beans every day were protested by every group of men; but when they were told that there was no charge for food when they were not working and only 50¢ a day when working day-haul, they did not insist on their complaint.

FIGURE 14. Puerto Rican officials with farmworkers in a dining hall of a labor camp, 1956. *Left to right (standing):* PRDL secretary Fernando Sierra Berdecía, Gov. Luis Muñoz Marín, MD director Joseph Monserrat, and PRDL official Eulalio Torres. Courtesy of the Records of the Migration Division, Archives of the Puerto Rican Diaspora, Centro de Estudios Puertorriqueños, Hunter College, City University of New York.

Regarding this charge of only 50¢ a day for day-haul workers, Mr. Tilelli has managed it by charging the farmer one extra dollar a day for each worker and applying this extra pay toward the cost of food. This, in fact, means an increase in pay for the man on day-haul, with the only disadvantage that he has no control over that dollar himself and therefore cannot demand better food for the 50¢ a day that comes out of his pay envelope.

When high-ranking Puerto Rican officials visited the United States, they toured the camps and ate with farmworkers. In 1956, when Fernando Sierra Berdecía, Luis Muñoz Marín, Joseph Monserrat, and Eulalio Torres visited the labor camps, the MD took photographs of them having meals with the workers in the Glassboro labor camp (NJDLI 1956). In 1966, during a visit to a Florida camp to investigate an accident that killed twenty noncontract workers and left many others injured, MD officials also inspected and tasted the food served to workers. In 1971 Gilberto Camacho, an MD official with the Hartford Office, visited the camp of Adams Nurseries, in Massachusetts, where workers were complaining about food. Camacho suggested that the owner hire a worker to cook for the others and serve as a supervisor. MD officials had learned from their experiences with the FLP that camps housing more than ten workers needed a cook-manager. To facilitate understanding between workers and employers, MD officials proposed hiring or designating a supervisor or crew leader who could cook, clean, enforce the rules in the camp, and provide advice to workers.

Satisfying Puerto Ricans' hunger proved to be a sensitive but critical affair, key to maintaining an available labor force. As mundane as they may seem, complaints, particularly about food, are important to understanding the migrant experience. They clarify how officials and employers transformed their tactics to entice workers to migrate. The improvement of working conditions in the labor camps, which included serving Puerto Rican–style food and paying higher wages than could be earned in Puerto Rico, attracted new migrant workers.

### SURVEILLANCE, DISCIPLINE, AND COERCION

Labor camps constituted total institutions because of the disciplinary and coercive strategies imposed by growers, supervisors, crew leaders, and camp managers to control access to farms (Stinson Fernández 1996, 135–36). Beginning in the 1940s, local police were recruited to oversee workers (Dyckman 1944). In the GSA camp armed surveillance was intended to intimidate workers and keep them within the confines of the camp. A former migrant informed me that a farmer in North Collins, New York, on horseback and with a rifle, watched workers. Also, because farmers generally could not speak Spanish, workers felt imprisoned by the regulations and life within the camp. In some camps they had to wear identification badges in the fields and on farmers' properties or risk being fired. In 1966 in one Florida camp complaints erupted because the company did not allow workers to shop outside the compound and imposed barriers to collecting their end-of-harvest bonuses. Police visited the camp, searching for nonexistent gambling, and four workers were arrested and charged with vagrancy. No first aid was available, and workers falling sick in the field had to wait until they returned to the camp at the end of the day for possible treatment. If the foreman determined that workers had not behaved well, he forced them to walk ten miles back to the camp at the end of the day (Gomez 1966a).[4]

Some farmers would not allow state or MD officials to enter their properties without prior notice, perceiving any attempt to talk to their workers as a
menace to their business. Indeed, some large labor camps, among them
Glassboro, were "closed camps," fenced with barbed wire and "No
Trespassing" signs. These camps had padlocked gates, limited-access roads,
and armed guards, and they denied entry to any visitors without the consent
of management. They were self-contained worlds, where management dis-
couraged outside interactions by providing work, food, lodging, entertainment, and even stores, although some states, including New York, required
camp store operators to obtain a permit out of a concern that company stores
tied workers to a system of debt (NYSIC 1961, 16). Labor organizers and
community organizations had to struggle in the courts to gain access to labor
camps until the 1970s, when the federal and state courts officially opened
access (DuFresne and McDonnell 1971, 284–86).

In 1970 a public-health worker and an attorney for Camden Regional
Legal Services entered a camp to assist farmworkers in southern New Jersey.
The grower insisted that the visit take place under his direct supervision, a
stipulation unacceptable to the visitors, who refused to leave. The grower
called the police, who arrested them, and they were subsequently convicted
of criminal trespass. In 1971 the New Jersey Supreme Court reversed the
decision on the grounds that ownership of a labor camp does not include the
right to limit migrant workers' access to government services. The court
established that government officials, charitable agencies, migrants' visitors,
members of the press (with the consent of workers), and peddlers who provide necessary items for workers must be allowed access to the labor camps
(DuFresne and McDonnell 1971, 300–301). Nonetheless, some farmers continued to require visitors to give advance notice and called the police to
report community organizers for trespassing.

The situation was the same in the 1980s. Ángel Domínguez, director of
the Farmworkers Support Committee (El Comité de Apoyo a los
Trabajadores Agrícolas), reported being refused entry to camps on farms and
to the GSA camp. James R. Zazzali, New Jersey attorney general, notified the
police in 1982 that farmers could not deny visitors entry to migrant camps.
Arthur Read, acting director of the Farmworker Division of Camden
Regional Legal Services, argued that a minority of farmers had a "feudal
mentality" that resulted in restricted access to their camps. In 1979 Read
himself was injured by a knife-wielding farm foreman during a visit to discuss workers' pay (Janson 1982).

The location of most camps far from major cities and towns isolated workers from the rest of society. Crew leaders, most of them Puerto Ricans, and farmers reinforced this isolation. In fact, for farmers, crew leaders were essential to reproduce a labor force through recruitment and surveillance. Crew leaders had access to social and family networks in neighborhoods in Puerto Rico, so friendships and family relationships tied workers and crew leaders together. Inside the labor camps, crew leaders had so much power that their control over workers seemed absolute. Many farmers negotiated and paid the crew leader by the piece of fruits or vegetables harvested by workers under his supervision, creating an incentive for exploitation. Workers sometimes had to buy food and clothes from crew leaders. Juan recalled that a crew leader did not bring water to the field because he sold the workers beer. Nevertheless, despite the crew leader's threats, workers contacted the MD office in New York City, which sent a representative to investigate. In general, however, the lack of English-language skills impeded direct communication of problems to employers. Some migrants did not know they had the legal right to leave a camp or to remain in the United States after the harvest. Crew leaders might threaten workers with physical harm if they denounced their conditions to government officials and community organizers (Nelkin 1970, 11–12, 20, 55–56).

Conditions in some camps were tolerable. The MD saw well-maintained labor camps as a tool to discourage noncontract migration and as a kind of advertisement for the FLP program that would simultaneously enhance the reputation of the government of Puerto Rico. Therefore, the MD regularly inspected camps in regions with high concentrations of contract workers or when incidents happened that threatened the reputation of the FLP. Thus, in 1966 the MD sent Eulalio Torres to inspect the Red Wind Company's labor camp in New York. Torres praised the camp as a model for the FLP:

> I want to point out that in the area where this tour was conducted, the Red Wind Company is going to operate a labor camp for about 55 Puerto Rican contract migrant workers which is considered the best labor camp in the region, and I am very hopeful that this will set a good example to other growers who are contemplating utilizing contract workers if their supply of "walk-ins" is restrained in Puerto Rico. (E. Torres 1966b)

In other regions the MD did not have resources necessary to maintain an inspection regime that ensured proper maintenance of camps, and problems persisted.

Despite the attempts of many farmers and crew leaders to keep workers content and isolated, migrants found ways to leave the camps. For some workers the pressure of living in the camps was unbearable; some even suffered sudden death after migrating for farmwork. This was the case of Domingo, who left the FGA camp in Keyport, New Jersey, on the night of August 1, 1957, and headed toward a highway. The camp's cook tried but failed to stop him, and the next day Domingo was found dead of natural causes. He had taken off his shoes and hat and put them by his side and lain down to sleep or rest in the woods. Perhaps he hoped to reach relatives in Paterson, New Jersey, who promised to send the details of his death to his family in Puerto Rico. An MD official obtained official copies of his death certificate to process his family's claim for Social Security benefits (North Jersey Office 1957a).

In other cases depression and homesickness resulted in suicide. Jaime, a nineteen-year-old migrant, shot himself in the head with a revolver. The police reported that he was homesick. The farmer and his coworkers stated that although he "was a very good worker . . ., lately he had seemed worried about some personal problems involving his wife and a 'girlfriend' he supposedly had in Puerto Rico" (Muñiz 1964). Other workers went to psychiatric institutions, but many self-medicated by drinking heavily.

Some workers left a camp after finding the living routines and behavior of other workers unbearable. Valeriano, a forty-four-year-old worker, returned to Puerto Rico after failing to live harmoniously with coworkers on several farms. An MD official suggested that his problems were related to his manliness:

> He is a man of weak structure, thin voice and mannerisms that show that he suffers from biological disorders. He cooks, washes, irons, cleans, and has been a domestic worker in family homes. Valeriano is aware of his tendency and wrote to Governor Muñoz for help in curing himself. The Glassboro Association recommends that he not be sent again because of his disgraceful condition. They recommend this for his own well-being as he is subjected to the mockery and derision of other workers. (M. Fernández 1958c)

Proximity to other workers and living among men could be suffocating for people who did not conform to dominant expectations of gender roles and sexual identities. Bullying and teasing were part of the cruel rituals performed by workers in the camps, and, in many instances, MD officials blamed the victims of harassment instead of the instigators for "maladaptation" to life in a camp.

Many workers fled the camps because of bad living and working conditions or because their ultimate goal was to settle in the cities. In 1959 a recent arrival at the Glassboro camp began to look for trouble immediately, and the night he left the camp he told other workers, "I just came for the ride; they [Glassboro] deserve to get stuck with my fare [$51.65] because they are a bunch of crooks" (North Jersey Office 1959a).

One of the most important reasons for the leaving the camps, however, was wages. When workers felt cheated or underpaid, they abandoned the camps. In April 1957 an MD official visited a farm with a small camp to inquire why three workers had been returned to the GSA camp. He found the small camp to be in generally good condition. The real reason the men had left was to go to a farm where they could do piecework and earn more money (North Jersey Office 1957b). MD officials expressed their intention to follow up on such cases and obtain reimbursement from workers for the airfare they owed to farmers (1960).

Migrants often dreamed of buying cars to travel to cities and towns outside the camps (Haddad 1982). Some bought used cars and left them in the camps to use when they returned for the next harvest. Others drove without licenses or even without knowing how to drive a car. MD officials often complained about workers being arrested for driving without a license. For their part farmers complained that workers liked the nomad life without acknowledging the reasons why workers might wish to escape the camps (PRES 1956, 2, 7).

Workers lived in the camps but were keenly aware of their surroundings and the wider world. The writer and political activist Jesús Colón wrote in the *Worker* (June 6, 1961) that migrant workers were leaving labor camps in New Jersey. Some arrived in New York City after hitchhiking day and night, crossing the George Washington Bridge to enter the city (cited in 1993, 96–97); others arrived through the Holland Tunnel after hitchhiking for days. In 1966 the MD officials Jorge Colón and Carlos Gómez reported that out of sixteen workers assigned to a farm in Oswego, New York, only twelve remained. Two had deserted as soon as they arrived at Kennedy Airport, and two more left the night before MD officials visited their camp (Jorge Colón 1966h). It is rumored that, in the late 1960s and early 1970s, some members of the Young Lords, the Puerto Rican youth political organization, visited the camps, urging workers to leave.

Workers also left the camps to escape violence perpetrated by employers. In the fall of 1960, fourteen workers recruited illegally in Puerto Rico arrived at a farm in Patterson, New York, where they were told that the employer had threatened and severely beaten some workers. Fearing the same treatment, the newcomers left and headed for the Patterson railroad station so they could get to New York City. The farmer and his son intercepted them and used force to make them stay. On the order of a local justice, police intervened in favor of the farmer, throwing the workers into jail and charging them with vagrancy. A MD official was sent immediately to investigate and provide assistance to the workers, four of whom wanted to file charges against the farmer for assault and battery. Local authorities did not take any action (U.S. House 1961, 304, 353).

Outside the camps a different world awaited workers. Some establishments did not serve Puerto Ricans or segregated them from the white public. Dark-skinned Puerto Ricans experienced even more prejudice. Rafael, a migrant farmworker during the 1950s, told me of an incident in Delaware when he and other workers stopped to rest on a trip from Florida to New Jersey:

> We went into a small cafeteria. There was a black guy from Vieques with us. When we sat down, the waitress said, "that guy has to go sit with the other blacks, over there." . . . But there was a guy sitting in the corner who . . . spoke Spanish. And he directed the waitress to "serve these five guys here." . . . And he said that if she didn't, he'd "shut down the restaurant." She asked him, "and who are you?" He said, "I was the sergeant of a Korean War camp and the platoon leader of men like these guys. While you were back here selling your food and enjoying democracy, these guys were offering their lives for you. So you better serve them or I'll shut down this restaurant." She shut up and served us.

Incidents like these did not stop some workers from venturing outside the camps, but they also led others to remain in the camps or look for shelter in the Puerto Rican neighborhoods of nearby cities or with relatives and friends residing stateside. Workers without any kind of network were easily at the mercy of employers, camp managers, and crew leaders.

Some farmers and camp managers treated disgruntled Puerto Ricans like guest workers who could be deported. In a letter to FGA manager John Tilelli, dated August 13, 1957, MD migration specialist Guadalupe Ruiz intercedes on behalf of a worker who, because of "very bad treatment from his farmer Cialone Bros.," asked to be reassigned to another farm. Tilelli forced the worker to pay seven dollars and leave the camp immediately (Ruiz 1957c). Often migrant farmworkers appeared at the MD offices or community organizations after being evicted by camp managers. Evicting workers from the camps was a way to enforce discipline and control workers, but it also reproduced the deportation regime. Labor camps, as total institutions, reinforced migrants' isolation, as many employers and officials treated them as deportable immigrants.

The rise of large labor camps administered by farmers' and growers' associations facilitated the massive use of workers from Puerto Rico. For farmers and growers camps were important tools for harnessing and allocating labor. For workers labor camps represented a chance to continue searching for better economic opportunities and a first step to adventure in the United States. For the MD the camps were an arena for managing migration by mediating conflicts among farmers, managers, and workers.

Camps became a key element of workers' constructed meanings about their migratory experiences. From the 1940s to the 1960s, the government of Puerto Rico's migration policies and the FLP shaped the perceptions, dreams, and ways of life of many families in rural Puerto Rico, but the camps became a point of reference even for workers who did not know places beyond their neighborhoods and small towns. Workers returned to Puerto Rico, talking about their adventures pa'lla afuera and their lives in the camps. While government agencies and religious organizations worked hard to ameliorate conditions in the camps and keep workers happy, overall, the coercive strategies that farmers and managers staged in the camps reinforced their feelings of estrangement, leading many to protest and sometimes flee unbearable situations. Camps also functioned to keep an unwanted population invisible to most other U.S. citizens. They were essential to the enforcement of immigration policies, both gatekeeping and deportation, and for calming fears of increasing the welfare rolls.

Constructing labor camps as total institutions was a constant struggle for farmers, crew leaders, and government officials. For the workers who yearned for the outside world, the camps and fields were socially constructed in relation to a particular realm: Puerto Rico and the cities and towns of the United States to which migrants living in labor camps had restricted access. Policing farmworkers was an everyday challenge for farmers concerned with having enough workers to harvest their crops. As a result, the courts, police, government agencies, and even the MD registered, inspected, and monitored the behavior of farmworkers within their reach, but using force never was a completely effective tool. These prisoners dreamed to be free, and at the first opportunity many escaped.

The U.S. citizenship of Puerto Ricans was an obstacle to the wishes of many government officials, farmers, and people living in small towns and cities where migrants decided to establish homes. In chapter 6, I explore the settlement of migrant workers in rural communities throughout the United States. The hope and estrangement of the migrants in the fields and labor camps faded away in their new homes, while they confronted and struggled against discrimination in the States.

# SIX

# Puerto Ricans in the Rural United States

IN THE 1960S, AS PUERTO RICAN OFFICIALS encouraged migration to rural areas of the United States, the effects of the Farm Labor Program (FLP) were unprecedented. The 1960 U.S. Census recorded 30,464 Puerto Ricans living in rural nonfarm areas and 2,802 in rural farm areas. Most were men (62 percent in rural areas, compared to 49.6 percent in cities), with a median age of 20.9 in rural nonfarm areas and 24.8 in rural farm areas. Of the total male Puerto Rican rural nonfarm and farm population, 55 percent worked as farmworkers and foremen (U.S. Census 1963, 2, 63). In some small rural communities, migrants composed a substantial part of the population, transforming the ethnic, racial, and gender landscape and presenting new challenges for local authorities and residents. No longer confined to labor camps, some migrants decided to settle and bring or establish families.

Although net migration to the United States decreased from 460,826 in the 1950s to 145,010 in the 1960s, the yearly population movement between Puerto Rico and the States increased dramatically. From 307,299 passengers leaving Puerto Rico in 1950, it increased to 1,309,770 in 1960 and 4,217,481 in 1970. Many of these travelers were seasonal migrants. The stateside Puerto Rican population also grew considerably from 1940 to 1970, from 69,967 to 783,358 people born in Puerto Rico and an increase in people of Puerto Rican parentage from 75,265 in 1950 to 646,038 in 1970 (Dietz 1986, 284–85; Wagenheim 1975, 71, 78).

The Migration Division's (MD) success in promoting the FLP as a strategy to settle Puerto Ricans outside New York City is evident (Whalen 2005, 30). Those living in the city composed 87.6 percent of the stateside Puerto Rican population in 1940 but only 61 percent in 1970 (Jesús Colón 1993; Wagenheim 1975, 71; Whalen and Vázquez-Hernández 2005). Connecticut, Delaware,

Florida, Illinois, Maryland, Massachusetts, Michigan, New Jersey, New York, Ohio, and Pennsylvania, states consistently hiring contract and non-contract workers, all experienced considerable Puerto Rican population growth from 1960 to 1970 (Wagenheim 1975, 73).

Despite the growth of Puerto Rican communities throughout the Northeast, New York City continued to be a main destination. Pablo, born in Juana Díaz, graduated from the Ponce Vocational High School in 1954, where he studied welding. In 1961 he visited the MD offices in New York City seeking a job, having worked during the previous year as a farmworker in Florida and Delaware. Although he was literate in Spanish and could read English, he spoke only a little English (Employment Section 1963). Migrants like Pablo wanted service and manufacturing jobs in the cities but were usually willing to take any stable job in or outside the city and to work night shifts, if necessary, so they could settle and establish families.

With the expansion of manufacturing jobs, migrants joined existing communities in northern cities, such as Buffalo, Rochester, Syracuse, Hartford, Camden, Philadelphia, Springfield (Massachusetts), and Boston. Farmworkers also became the nucleus of small communities in towns such as North Collins, New York; Lancaster, Pennsylvania; Holyoke, Massachusetts; and Vineland, New Jersey. This chapter explores the power relations between Puerto Ricans and white residents in rural stateside communities. I attempt to grasp the processes of ethnic formation that resulted from labor migration as responses to the historically unfolding dynamics of labor mobilization and domination (Wolf 2001, 368–67). I highlight an instance of social protest in North Collins, a western New York farm community, in July 1966, when farmworkers gathered in the center of the village demanding justice and protesting police brutality, segregation, and discrimination.

The North Collins incident offers an opportunity to analyze how power relations between Puerto Ricans and their Anglo neighbors played out in migrant labor policies in a rural setting. It illustrates points of rupture where consent cannot be achieved and where alternative understandings emerge (Crehan 2016; Roseberry 1989, 27, 47–48; 1996, 82–83), and demonstrates how Puerto Ricans have actively opposed the institutions that define them as inferior colonial subjects (L. Ortiz 1998, 5, 101–10). My main goal in this chapter is to document the intersection of objective political economy conditions and power relations with the subjective context of workers' attempts to transform their life conditions (Torres and Katsiaficas 1999, 5). Solidarity increased among Puerto Ricans "in the context of a migration that [was] disenfranchising and [which had] imposed a de-facto second-class status on a colonial people" (Benmayor, Torruellas, and Juarbe 1997, 202). In North Collins Puerto Ricans carved a place in civil society and claimed their U.S. citizenship.

## SETTLERS, NOT FARMERS

The settlement of Puerto Ricans around northeastern farming communities stemmed from the U.S. agricultural-labor regime, which in the 1940s became dependent on migrant laborers rather than local workers. By the 1960s northeastern agriculture had passed through several phases of ethnic succession that consolidated the use of Puerto Rican and southern African American migrants who, along with West Indians, replaced southern whites and Italian and Polish farmworkers.

Puerto Rican farmworkers usually traveled with contracts sponsored by the FLP, some to the same farms for a couple of years, establishing relationships with farmers or other workers residing in the community and then moving from farms to factories or the service sector. While some eventually owned restaurants, houses, and land, few became farmers. MD officials reported that Félix Rodríguez Sampayo, who had previously migrated to Utah, established a restaurant in Landisville, New Jersey; Blas Meléndez owned a farm and several trucks; and some Campbell Soup Company workers also owned farms and houses in southern New Jersey (Frías de Hempel 1956, 6).

In the 1960s community organizations and urban Puerto Ricans became aware of the strategies and tools necessary to struggle for their civil rights and began to listen, watch, and act on the claims of rural migrant workers. In southern New Jersey Protestant and Catholic churches arranged activities for farmworkers at the Glassboro camp. In Connecticut, in the late 1960s, the Episcopal Church helped organize workers. In Buffalo a Catholic Spanish-speaking ministry initially affiliated with a Hungarian Catholic church was active among Puerto Ricans—the only church to minister to them as a community in the city (Olmo and Valderruten 1988, 2). The Fair Lawn Bible Church in New Jersey joined with several local churches and major Bible societies to visit and evangelize farmworkers, in Spanish, on the farms. The Reverend Miguel Mena, pastor of Iglesia Cristiana Pentecostal, and the Reverend Blas Silva, pastor of Iglesia Discípulos de Cristo, worked together through this program in Passaic County (Wesler 1959). In Massachusetts the Catholic Church was a strong ally of the government of Puerto Rico (see Morales 1986, 85). The Holy See even appointed a director of Puerto Rican migration in the United States and opened an office at Idlewild Airport, staffed by a trained Puerto Rican social worker (Senior 1957d). In southern New Jersey, around Camden, Father Charles S. Bean, who was fluent in Spanish, served as the Catholic chaplain for the Glassboro camp (Vargas 2010).

The demographics of Puerto Ricans migrating to agricultural jobs were also changing. In 1960 the MD official Eulalio Torres reported,

> We have always thought of Puerto Rican agricultural workers as single males. A look into the Eastern Seaboard migrant stream has revealed thirteen Puerto Rican families with 22 children arriving in the State of New Jersey as part of that migrant stream.
>
> These Puerto Rican families, who have joined the Migrant stream from Florida, received some intense attention during the week from Delaware Valley office staff, which worked closely with the State Department of Education and the Migrant Bureau. These thirteen Puerto Rican families were visited at different farms and the 22 children recruited for Migrant Children Schools. The fact that complete Puerto Rican families are joining the migrant stream presents a new dimension to the work of the office in the sense that stabilization of these families is a necessary part in our activities, possibly to be accomplished by finding them permanent employment.[1] (1960d, 1–2)

The integration of families into the eastern migratory farm-labor flow brought new challenges to the MD and local communities. Families were less mobile than single men, and their health and housing problems were more complex. In October 1959 Erasmo, his wife, and their six children (ranging in age from two to eleven years) arrived in New Jersey with a migrant crew from Florida to work on a potato farm. The crew leader left the farm over a disagreement with the employer, but Erasmo stayed because his wife was in the hospital, having another baby. After the farmer evicted them from the labor camp, church leaders convinced him to let them use one of his houses until Erasmo's wife could leave the hospital and authorities could find somewhere for them to live. Erasmo offered to continue to work to repay any money they had to borrow while church leaders tried to raise money for transportation (North Jersey Office 1959c, 1–2).

Other cases were more unfortunate. Rufino lost three children in a fire on the farm where he and his family lived and worked in Toms River, New Jersey (North Jersey Office 1959b). On another New Jersey farm, two migrant girls were poisoned and a third died after ingesting insecticide (Vega 1967). In a 1968 car accident, nineteen members of a large family from Barrio Los Angeles in Utuado, Puerto Rico, were killed making their trek from Florida to the Northeast (Muñiz 1968).

Responding to the migrant workforce's needs, the Federal Migrant Health Act of 1962 provided grants to pay for clinics and other projects to improve health conditions and services for domestic migrants and their families. In 1964 the MD established a pilot project for migrant families under the direction of Dr. Ruben Nazario, from the University of Puerto Rico School of Medicine (E. Torres 1964a). Although their impact was limited, clinics improved migrant families' access to health services.

The presence of families was a sign that Puerto Ricans in the northeastern migratory stream were becoming a desirable option for farmers as the overall size of the migrant workforce was declining. For example, in New York State the number of migrant farmworkers declined from 27,600 in 1960 to 14,400 in 1968 (Nelkin 1970, 3). Northeastern farmers had to compete with local restaurants and hotels for noncontract workers. Migrants, as well as Puerto Ricans living close to farms that hired seasonal workers, would often take farm jobs and then move to factory or service jobs when the first opportunity arose. Some farmers provided housing and found jobs for their workers during winter to entice them return to the fields. Virgilio, who migrated from Cidra to a farm in the 1960s, worked during the winter as a janitor in a nearby hotel but continued to live in the labor camp, getting rides to his job from the farmer and his family. Other workers returned to the fields in the summer when factories would close or reduce their personnel. The MD estimated that 25,000 Puerto Ricans living in large cities benefited from farmwork during the summer months (FLP 1960, 3).

In 1965 the government of Puerto Rico attempted to increase farmworkers' wages in New Jersey to the federal minimum, but Gov. Richard Hughes and farmers opposed the change. Responding to U.S. labor secretary Willard Wirtz's directive requiring that guest workers be paid the $1.30 federal minimum wage, Hughes argued that farmers paid the highest property taxes in the United States and that any increase in labor costs would negatively affect their businesses. He supported the $1.00 minimum wage then in effect (P. Rivera 1965b). The Puerto Rican government prevailed, and between 1965 and 1970 Puerto Rico's contract wage fluctuated from $1.25 to $1.65 per hour, depending on the type of crop, surpassing New Jersey's minimum agricultural wage.

Nonetheless, wages remained a bone of contention. Individual growers and associations often violated the FLP contract, cheating workers out of their pay. On a farm in Mohnton, Pennsylvania, a farmer offered workers, whom he had hired illegally, $0.90 per hour and then reduced their pay to $0.85 an hour and withheld a promised bonus when they decided to return to Puerto Rico. MD official Roberto Mendoza visited the workers to investigate their claims and called the police after the farm manager subjected him to threats, insults, and obscene language. The manager paid the workers before the police arrived (1959b).

In a 1964 internal memorandum, MD officials discussed the problem of wages, noting that the Glassboro Service Association was violating the FLP contract by refusing to provide wage records. Glassboro administrators said they couldn't provide the records because it was impossible to keep track of hours worked when pay was based on a piece rate. When workers filed claims, however, the administrators managed to produce paperwork to disprove their claims (E. Torres 1964b).

The 1960s brought important legal and policy changes that affected all migrant farmworkers. *Harvest of Shame,* a CBS documentary, aired weeks after the election of President John F. Kennedy in November 1960 and showed the difficult living and working conditions of migrant farmworkers (Murrow 1960). The groundwork for the controversy surrounding *Harvest of Shame* had been laid in a 1959 U.S. Department of Labor report showing that competition from the Mexican braceros kept the wages of domestic farmworkers low and limited their employment opportunities (USDL [1959] 1961).

To maintain the migratory stream and minimize, if not end, violations by employers and labor recruiters, in 1962 the Puerto Rican legislature enacted public law 87, expanding the provisions of the 1947 public law 89, which regulated the recruitment of migrant workers. The new law granted the secretary of labor the power to establish requirements for employers, including a guaranteed minimum income, insurance coverage, record keeping, and freedom from discrimination and reprisals for forming, joining, or helping a labor organization. Contracts had to conform to other standards established by the Puerto Rico secretary of labor, including approval of housing by a local board of health, prepayment of transportation costs, payment of return-trip costs by the employer if the worker completed his contract, posting of a performance bond by the employer, workers' compensation coverage, and payment of a minimum wage. The law gave the secretary of labor authority over all recruitment efforts within the Commonwealth of Puerto Rico and the sole power to approve contract services for migrant workers (DeWind, Seidl, and Shenk 1977, 22; Young 1975, 16–17).

During the 1960s other important developments improved conditions for migrants. The MD strengthened the Agricultural Group Insurance program for contract workers, which in 1963 provided migrant workers with a $2,000 life-insurance policy and benefits for accidents or sickness. The weekly premium was a dollar, of which workers and employers each paid half (FLP 1964). An important federal development to promote and protect migrant Puerto Rican and other U.S. domestic workers was the National Farm Labor Stabilization Act, sponsored by New Jersey senator Harrison A. Williams, chair of the Subcommittee on Farm Labor. This bill aimed to improve working and living conditions for domestic workers and included some provisions of the FLP contract, for example, the guarantee of 160 hours of work during the contract period. Many farmers objected to this guarantee, which some members of Congress called the "Puerto Rican provision," arguing that it would be difficult to fulfill. The Puerto Rican government and several members of Congress noted that many farmers were already meeting this provision of FLP contract. Puerto Rican officials favored the bill because it covered all domestic workers and would therefore also improve the working and living conditions of noncontract farmworkers (U.S. Senate 1962b, 463, 525, 546). Although Congress did not pass most of the protections proposed in this bill, it did extend the Fair Labor Standards Act to farmworkers, providing them a minimum wage of $1.60 per hour on farms employing the equivalent of at least seven full-time workers during the entire harvest season (Lianos and Cauchois 1972; WHD, n.d.).

The most important development that impacted the FLP was the fate of guest-worker programs, which became the subject of intense debate after the airing of *Harvest of Shame* (Murrow 1960). Many people, including Secretary of Labor James Mitchell, who were concerned about how employers determined wages sought to extend the same benefits guaranteed to braceros, such as a minimum wage, free meals, and paid transportation, to domestic workers (Vialet and McClure 1980, 45, 47). Growing opposition from labor, civil rights, and social-welfare organizations; the mechanization of the harvest; the rise of the United Farm Workers of America; and new, stricter regulations introduced by the U.S. Department of Labor led, in 1964, to the termination of public law 78, ending the Bracero Program and transforming Puerto Rican farm labor (46; Martin 2003, 50–52). As the number of guest workers declined, the number of Puerto Rican contract workers increased (see tables 1 and 2).

TABLE I Number of Puerto Rican contract workers and guest workers, 1947–1964

| Year | Mexicans | Puerto Ricans | British West Indians | Bahamians | Canadians | Others[1] | Total |
|------|----------|---------------|----------------------|-----------|-----------|-----------|-------|
| 1947 | 19,632 | 1,241 | 1,017 | 2,705 | 7,421 | — | 32,016 |
| 1948 | 35,345 | 4,906 | 2,421 | 1,250 | 5,900 | — | 49,822 |
| 1949 | 107,000 | 4,598 | 1,715 | 1,050 | 3,000 | — | 117,363 |
| 1950 | 67,500 | 7,602 | 4,425 | 1,800 | 2,800 | — | 84,127 |
| 1951 | 192,000 | 11,747 | 6,540 | 2,500 | 2,600 | — | 215,387 |
| 1952 | 197,100 | 12,277 | 4,410 | 3,500 | 5,200 | — | 222,487 |
| 1953 | 201,380 | 14,930 | 4,802 | 2,939 | 6,200 | — | 230,251 |
| 1954 | 309,033 | 10,637 | 2,159 | 2,545 | 7,000 | — | 331,374 |
| 1955 | 398,850 | 10,876 | 3,651 | 2,965 | 6,700 | — | 423,042 |
| 1956 | 445,197 | 14,969 | 4,369 | 3,194 | 6,700 | 390 | 474,819 |
| 1957 | 436,049 | 13,214 | 5,707 | 2,464 | 7,300 | 685 | 465,419 |
| 1958 | 432,857 | 13,067 | 5,204 | 2,237 | 6,900 | 315 | 460,580 |
| 1959 | 437,643 | 10,012 | 6,622 | 2,150 | 8,600 | 405 | 465,432 |
| 1960 | 315,846 | 12,986 | 8,150 | 1,670 | 8,200 | 863 | 347,715 |
| 1961 | 291,420 | 13,765 | 8,875 | 1,440 | 8,600 | 40 | 324,140 |
| 1962 | 194,978 | 13,526 | 11,729 | 1,199 | 8,700 | 404 | 230,536 |
| 1963 | 186,865 | 13,116 | 11,856 | 1,074 | 8,500 | 923 | 222,334 |
| 1964 | 177,736 | 14,628 | 14,361[2] | | 7,900 | 25 | 214,650 |

SOURCE: Vialet and McClure (1980, 36); OGPRUS (1953–92).
1. This column includes Japanese and Filipino workers.
2. This figure represents both British West Indians and Bahamians.

After the termination of the Bracero Program, some agricultural associations in affected states showed interest in hiring Puerto Rican farmworkers (NYSJLC 1964, 21). Consequently, the 1964 season was the first time since the beginning of the FLP that the Puerto Rico Department of Labor officials referred migrants to farms in Washington and California and the first time, since 1956, that the FLP recruited more than 14,000 workers (Farm Placement Division 1964, 11). FLP director Eulalio Torres visited Arizona and California to gauge farmers' interest in hiring Puerto Rican migrants, expecting an increase because the Bracero Program had ended (1964c). The press also predicted an increase in demand for Puerto Rican and other domestic workers in California. On January 13, 1965, *New York Amsterdam News* warned that Suffolk County farmers faced a possible decrease in migrant labor because of the end of the Bracero Program, increasing competi-

TABLE 2  Workers placed in U.S. farms by
Puerto Rico's Farm Labor Program, 1960–1969

| Year | Number of workers |
| --- | --- |
| 1960 | 12,986 |
| 1961 | 13,765 |
| 1962 | 13,526 |
| 1963 | 13,116 |
| 1964 | 14,628 |
| 1965 | 17,385 |
| 1966 | 19,537 |
| 1967 | 21,654 |
| 1968 | 22,902 |
| 1969 | 21,864 |

*SOURCE:* OGPRUS (1953–92).

tion for domestic workers from California growers. The predictions proved wrong, however, since California growers hired relatively few Puerto Rican contract workers: 102 in 1964 and 877 in 1965 (Migration Division 1964, 1966a).

Although MD officials had limited success in establishing a steady stream of migrants contracted to California growers, this was not the case for non-contract workers, who had been migrating to California since the early twentieth century. In 1968 Richard A. Fineberg, working for the United Church of Christ, recorded 20 percent of the workers in the San Joaquin Valley as being Puerto Ricans and "Arabian" (U.S. Senate 1969, 2729). Northeastern farms hired more Puerto Ricans after the termination of the Bracero Program, and the flow of migrants to small northeastern towns increased after passage of the Immigration and Naturalization Act of 1965, which restricted the use of noncitizen guest workers for temporary farm labor (Morales 1986, 80; see also table 2). For African Americans in the Northeast, increased demand for domestic migrant labor meant that state legislatures in New York and New Jersey paid attention to their situation, as many activists and elected officials demanded the same guarantees offered to Puerto Ricans (Consumers' League 1960; *New York Times* 1967).

The elimination of the Bracero Program and limits imposed on guest workers by the U.S. Department of Labor increased job opportunities for migrant workers all over the United States (see table 3). The impact was so

TABLE 3 Number of guest workers versus Puerto Rican
contract migrant workers, 1963

| Nationality/ethnicity | Number | Percent |
| --- | --- | --- |
| Mexican | 186,865 | 84 |
| Puerto Rican | 13,116 | 6 |
| West Indians and Bahamians | 12,930 | 6 |
| Canadian | 8,500 | 4 |
| Total | 221,411 | 100 |

SOURCE: McElroy and Gavett (1965, 12); OGPRUS (1953–92).

strong on Puerto Rican contract farm-labor migration that the number of
workers hired by the end of the 1960s doubled, although Mexicans remained
a significant part of the farm labor force in the Southwest and Michigan. In
the East, while growers continued to hire British West Indians, Bahamians,
and Canadians, the number of Puerto Rican contract workers increased
from 13,116 in 1963 to a peak of 22,902 in 1968. In Michigan, where growers
competed with Texas and California for labor, Puerto Ricans increased from
1.3 percent of the total interstate seasonal farmworkers in 1964 to 2.7 percent
in 1965 (USDA 1967, 35). The U.S. Department of Agriculture, through the
Farmers Home Administration, planned to expand housing for domestic
workers who would fill the void left by braceros (McElroy and Gavett 1965,
2). With the repeal of public law 78, growers had to use the H-2 visa program
to import British West Indian and Canadian workers, but after Secretary
Wirtz opposed expanding this program, there was an 83 percent reduction in
the use of guest workers in 1965 compared to 1964 (Vialet and McClure 1980,
62–67; Martin 2003, 50–51).

Demand for agricultural workers declined as mechanization of agriculture increased, so jobs remained seasonal and wages stagnated. Confined to
low-wage jobs, few seasonal farmworkers could establish networks in their
host communities and, especially important, buy land and open businesses—
nor did the cities afford migrants many opportunities to achieve social
mobility.

The dominance of seasonal labor in U.S. agriculture in the 1960s belied
migrants' social mobility. Low wages in agriculture and competition gener-
ated by farmers' use of guest workers and undocumented workers became
obstacles to earning wages sufficient to aspire to farm ownership. By the end
of the 1960s, migrant farmworkers had the lowest annual income of all U.S.

workers. In 1968 the annual income of all migrant workers, including women and children, averaged $1,562. In the same year 57 percent of all migrant workers who did only farmwork earned $1,018. In the Northeast the median daily earnings in 1968 were $9.05 (Nelkin 1970, 5).

The value of land and buildings as part of total farm assets increased from 62 percent in 1950 to 72 percent in 1990, moving farm ownership further out of migrants' reach. Farm mechanization and technological changes also drove the substitution of capital for labor, transforming farms into capital-intensive units needing large amounts of credit. Success in farming required technological expertise and access to credit and financing. Migrants without local connections could not marshal the necessary networks or resources to purchase farms (Cochrane 1993, 203–5).

## MIGRATION TO WESTERN NEW YORK

Since the late nineteenth century, New York State farmers have cultivated small fruits and vegetables, such as raspberries, grapes, strawberries, potatoes, onions, and tomatoes, that were processed by private and cooperative canneries and sold in New York City and Canada. In the late 1890s agriculture created a demand for workers that fostered the immigration of Italians and later, after World War II, the use of African American, West Indian, Mexican, and Puerto Rican labor (Bowman 2002, 7–8, 14, 68; NYSIC 1963, 1; Weller 1941, 7–11, 34–41). By 1963 New York was the third largest producer of vegetables for processing and one of the largest for several fruits. By the end of the 1960s, the agricultural economy was controlled by a mix of Quaker, German, and Italian descendants who also dominated the political landscape.

The scarcity of workers after World War II led western New York farmers and cooperatives to contact the Puerto Rican government to initiate official recruitment. Men traveling without their families were flown to Buffalo to work in 1948, although by some accounts they had been arriving in this region since 1946. African Americans came later, some of them with their wives and children. The towns of Hamburg, Silver Creek, Gowanda, North Collins, Brant, and Eden formed one of the centers of agricultural production in the region during the 1960s, housing approximately a thousand migrants (*Buffalo Courier-Express* 1948; Catholic and Protestant Clergy 1966; Hepler 1966). Puerto Ricans, at the bottom of this microcosm with other nonwhite workers, constituted most of the migrant labor force in the area.

In the early 1950s farmers in North Collins, a small town located thirty miles south of Buffalo in Erie County, established the Brant Cooperative to arrange contracts through the MD to hire, transport, and house migrant workers. By the end of the 1950s, however, many northeastern growers had stopped participating in the FLP because they found it easier and cheaper to hire noncontract workers (Del Río 1959a). By the mid-1960s most of the Puerto Rican migrants in Erie County were working without government-sponsored contracts.

The migrants of the 1950s became the veterans who paved the way for many others in western New York, most of whom worked without contracts in the 1960s. They came directly from Puerto Rico and New York City, recruited by employment agencies and farmers, or they approached farmers directly. Anthony Vega, an MD official who met with some of these noncontract workers, observed, "All of them told me they come to the area because there was no work for them in Puerto Rico. The majority were sugar-cane cutters. A great many of them were very young (18–19–20 years old). . . . They were all paid less than the going contract rate at this time (except the packing house workers)" (Vega 1966). New York farmers also hired some three thousand Puerto Ricans from Florida who traveled north in the spring, at the end of the southern harvests (Jorge Colón 1966b).

By the early 1960s New York State was hiring the largest number of domestic seasonal migrants on the Eastern Seaboard. In 1962 the New York Employment Service filled 1,800 seasonal job openings with Puerto Rican contract workers and 12,500 with other domestic migrant workers (NYSIC 1963, 1, 11). By this time families of Puerto Rican origin were well enough established in the migration stream that the MD began to use funds for education programs for their children (USDA 1967, 25).

Small western New York farming towns such as Erie, Westfield, and Dunkirk became transitional places for Puerto Rican workers hoping to move to factory jobs in Buffalo that required few or no skills or knowledge of English. During the harvest they spent their days in the fields, and some moved during the late afternoons and evenings to the canneries. After the harvest many continued working in nurseries and canning factories (Jorge Colón 1966b; Vega 1966), but several who settled in Buffalo and nearby towns worked in the steel-manufacturing plants that dominated the region at that time (Olmo and Valderruten 1988, 2). In 1960 Puerto Ricans in Buffalo numbered 2,176, increasing by 1970 to 6,090 (Wagenheim 1975, 74; Whalen 2005, 33). Factory jobs were so plentiful that, on some Buffalo streets, job recruiters would pick up workers who could change jobs the next day, if they wished, by going back to meet other recruiters on the streets. The economic rewards were extraordinary, lessening the problems of inadequate housing, unpleasant working conditions, isolation, lack of English-language skills, and the violence of employers and other employees (Olmo and Valderruten 1988, 1–2).

In 1966 farmers in Erie County paid most noncontract workers $1.00 an hour, sometimes deducting $0.10 per hour to be repaid if the worker stayed until the end of the season. In contrast, FLP contract workers usually earned between $0.20 to $0.40 more per hour than the average paid to noncontract workers, and some farmers offered a bonus per hour, to be paid at the end of the harvest (Vega 1966). Most noncontract workers received no overtime pay and were not covered by workers' compensation (Geo H. Angle's Sons 1966). Because of their high mobility and seasonal migration, however, it is difficult to estimate how many Puerto Ricans migrated as farmworkers to Erie County; the statistics available account only for contract farmworkers. For example, in 1966 the MD facilitated the migration of 19,537 contract workers to the States, and, of that total, 2,301 migrated to New York (Bonilla-Santiago 1986, 77; *Buffalo Courier-Express* 1969; OGPRUS 1953–92; Ruiz 1966; Vega 1966).

By 1966 Puerto Ricans had at least an eighteen-year presence as farmworkers in western New York. Interactions with the local population led many to marry or cohabitate with women of other ethnicities. Around Buffalo, in Chautauqua and Erie Counties, men married or lived with Native American women, unions that helped build bridges between migrants and locals. For example, a Native American woman married to a Puerto Rican became a translator for the Community Action Organization, a multiservice community organization in Erie County. Young Native American women who befriended Puerto Ricans came from a Seneca reservation four miles from North Collins (Vega 1966). A clinic for migrant workers and Native Americans was established at Thomas Indian School on the reservation (Migration Division 1968).

## SPEAKING PUERTO RICAN

"This is America, and they don't speak American. So they get nothing to drink," the owner of Roeller's Grill, a local bar in Eden, told Paul L.

Montgomery, a *New York Times* reporter, in July 1966. Like many stores in Erie County, Roeller's Grill did not serve Puerto Ricans, creating conflicts that exploded in North Collins that summer.[2] A July 17, 1966, *New York Times* article, titled "Puerto Rican Migrants Upset Upstate Town," described a crowd armed with bats, bricks, and Molotov cocktails, ready to burn down the village of North Collins in protest over unfair treatment at the hands of local police (Montgomery 1966).

The population of the village of North Collins was 1,000, and the township consisted of 3,000 to 4,000 people. It had a permanent police force of 3 men, in addition to 2 temporary officers during the summer. A total of 60 Puerto Ricans resided permanently in the village, and about forty nearby camps housed as many as 1,200 Puerto Rican and southern African American migrants (Hepler 1966; Vega 1966).

A fight involving a Puerto Rican resident named Carlos, the chief of police, and Anthony, son of the village clerk, precipitated the protest. On July 3 the chief had stopped, beaten, and detained a Puerto Rican named Pablo because of a traffic violation. After Carlos inquired about bail for his friend and was denied information by the local judge, he made some remarks to the court and left the courtroom. On instructions from the judge, the police chief chased him and, from fifty feet away, told him to stop. When Carlos did not stop, the chief reportedly drew his gun and gave chase, hitting him on the head and taking him into custody. Anthony got involved, but it is not clear if he helped detain Carlos and José, another Puerto Rican who was also arrested. José testified that Anthony stopped him at gunpoint, saying, "Don't move or I'll shoot you."

In response to accusations against the police arising from Carlos's and José's arrests, the police chief and Anthony were arraigned on felony charges in a preliminary hearing on July 7, 1966. Carlos signed the warrant against the chief, and José signed one against Anthony (Vega 1966). The chief and Anthony were charged with second-degree assault, but both were found innocent by a judge from the nearby town of Hamburg, who also asked the District Attorney's Office to investigate whether a grand jury should be summoned to determine if Puerto Ricans had been trying to incite a riot in North Collins (*Buffalo Courier-Express* 1966). Local authorities and residents of North Collins blamed the unrest on outside agitators (Jorge Colón 1966a, 3; *El Tiempo* 1966a, 1966c).

On July 5 the North Collins local authorities and community leaders from Buffalo informed the MD regional office in the Rochester area that a group of Puerto Ricans had almost rioted against the local police and the town authorities (Jorge Colón 1966a; Migration Division 1966b). This incident of social unrest and its probable repercussions raised fears of a backlash against Puerto Rican communities and the MD's efforts to encourage migration. In response, the MD assumed the role of mediator and sent Jorge Colón to assess the circumstances and ease tensions.

At one o'clock on July 6, Colón visited Mike's Rustic Bar, one of the few businesses that served Puerto Ricans in an area that included the towns of Eden, North Collins, and Brant. He encountered about fifty Puerto Ricans "talking about the most effective way to burn" town buildings, police cars, and commercial establishments that refused to serve them. One among the group stated that he had twenty cars from the nearby camps and cities "loaded with bricks, bottles of gasoline, bats, and stones for the event." Another, nicknamed Superman, indicated that they had twenty guns and pistols. Colón persuaded the group to channel their grievances formally. They agreed, on the condition that authorities would arrest some of the individuals involved in the mistreatment of Puerto Ricans (Jorge Colón 1966a; Migration Division 1966b).

On the same day, at about four thirty, carloads of farmworkers began arriving in North Collins, met by the police chief, who was dispersing people with a police dog. Colón convinced the police to remove the dog and let him handle the situation. By six o'clock an estimated three hundred workers had gathered on Main Street. Colón contacted the mayor of North Collins, who provided a hall for a mass meeting and asked town officials to let people express their grievances. To maintain order Colón asked the town judge to remain quiet at the meeting. The protesters listed fifteen questions and concerns for the local authorities, mostly dealing with accusations of police harassment. Town officials insisted they had no knowledge of any of the problems raised but said they would investigate. After the meeting Colón convinced those attending "to walk home in silence," easing some tensions among workers (Jorge Colón 1966a; Migration Division 1966b).

On July 8 Colón attended a meeting at the local firehouse, where officials were planning to use fire hoses to disperse workers if they gathered again in the center of North Collins. Colón asked the officials to be patient and try to resolve the conflict peacefully, adding that "they were better off chasing hoodlums and the teenagers who came around calling the P.R. dirty names that might lead to problems" (Jorge Colón 1966a). During the months of July and August, following meetings among Puerto Ricans, government officials, and representatives of churches and community organizations, peace prevailed.

This confrontation was not the workers' first with the police (Jorge Colón 1966a; Migration Division 1966d, 3; Montgomery 1966, 60; Vazquez Malavez 1966). Puerto Ricans suspected and mistrusted the local police and complained to the MD about the chief's arbitrary mistreatment. Bernabé, a resident of North Collins since 1951, who served as interpreter between the police and detained Puerto Ricans, declared that the police chief would ask them how much money they had in their pockets, fine them accordingly, take their money, and release them without providing any receipt for the fine (B. Rivera 1966). Other Puerto Ricans reported that the chief had ordered them not to congregate in front of their houses between five in the morning and seven thirty at night (Mendez 1966; R. Torres 1966). The protest that exploded in North Collins in July 1966 was not an isolated and impulsive incident but rather the culmination of many grievances that Puerto Ricans held against the local police, government, businesses, and employers.

## THE SOCIAL FIELD

The *New York Times* article on the protest in North Collins opened the public debate on the situation in Erie County, revealing how the seasonal migration of mostly men affected residents' perceptions. While some white residents talked about "the trouble we're having" with Puerto Ricans, the farmworkers' protest surprised local officials, who thought that migrants were well treated. The mayor observed, "They walk by here on the road and I wave at them and they laugh and smile. One time I was going to throw away an old bed—it was my mother's I guess—and I offered it to them. You should have seen them, carrying it down the road on their heads. Real happy, you know!" (Montgomery 1966, 60). Because many residents thought that farmworkers lived under appropriate conditions and believed that they experienced less discrimination in North Collins than in nearby towns, the mayor and police chief blamed the protest on outsiders (Crafts 1966). The mayor did acknowledge that residents had not paid attention to the migrant workers' living conditions, but he argued that the protest was the first time he had heard about them. Residents believed that the spotlight had been turned unjustly on their village (Catholic and Protestant Clergy 1966).

As in many communities that hosted migrant workers, some North Collins residents attributed the problems to Puerto Ricans' culture and lack of English-language skills, believing that they did not need the same amenities as white residents to live well (Nelkin 1970, 56; Nieves Falcón 1975, 60–78, 92). The police chief's wife claimed, "The [camp] is a paradise compared to what they're used to living in. . . . Of course you or I wouldn't want to live like that, but I believe they like it fine" (Montgomery 1966, 60). As the July 1966 incident showed, however, farmworkers did not like their living and social conditions or the segregation and discrimination they encountered from the local population.

Farmworkers were also denied due process if they got into trouble with authorities in rural and small towns. Lack of English hindered their access to adequate and fair representation during arrests or in court and even led to conflicts. In southern New Jersey a fight among workers resulted in some being arrested and sent to prison. In court one of the workers who was jailed didn't know why he was there and didn't have an interpreter (M. Fernández 1958c; Nieves Falcón 1975, 43–59, 60–78, 92, 96; see also Urciuoli 1996).

Incidents complicated by language barriers between North Collins town officials, farmers, the police, and Puerto Ricans had been occurring since the early 1950s (*Chronicle Express* 1952). Some of the town officials in 1966 were former members of the Brant Cooperative, which closed in 1960 because running a regulated camp that provided optimal living conditions was too expensive. They complained that workers too often deserted their contracts after arriving at the airport, or else they left the labor camps before the work was completed. Farmers also complained of problems collecting the money they had lent workers for travel, putting the MD in an embarrassing position (Jorge Colón 1966c).

In the North Collins area, farmers paid lower wages to workers who walked in or whom they hired illegally in Puerto Rico, violating Puerto Rican law by sending workers airplane tickets and flouting both state and federal laws by offering five cents to recruiters for every dollar earned by each worker (*El Diario* 1966). The consequence for noncontract workers was that farmers paid them less and they lacked the protection of workers' compensation insurance (Vega 1966). In 1966 only one farmer was paying the basic minimum wage; other farmers called him a fool because he was trying to pay a decent living wage (Migration Division 1966b, 1966d).

Most Puerto Ricans complained about places where they interacted with the local community, underscoring Félix Padilla's observation that most ethnic conflicts occur not at work but in sites of social reproduction, such as bars, stores, and camps (1987, 11). In these places the local population perceived Puerto Ricans' need for housing, education, recreation, and health care as a threat. When Jorge Colón visited several white residents and business owners without identifying himself, he heard constant criticism of Puerto Ricans (Jorge Colón 1966a). In a meeting with Catholic and Protestant clergy, Father Bernard Weiss of North Collins Church of the Holy Spirit criticized the workers' behavior: "Too many complaints related to bars; not enough [related] to knocking on the doors of the churches" (Catholic and Protestant Clergy 1966). But Puerto Ricans did not feel welcome in most places, including churches, and not all visited bars just to drink. In addition to being places of recreation, bars were often the only establishments where they could eat. Puerto Ricans and the local population interacted in bars and stores, so it is no surprise that the North Collins protest happened within the town and not on the farms and camps, where most Puerto Ricans worked and slept.

Puerto Ricans claimed that the police, courts, government officials, and businesses treated them unfairly, for example, by imposing a curfew and not allowing them to walk freely on the sidewalks and streets and by denying them due process in court proceedings. Local officials often barred them from establishing businesses and voting in elections, and some school officials refused to register migrant children because they did not speak English. Problems also arose because workers were mostly single men and a few of them dated local white and Native American women (Vega 1966). One complaint against the North Collins police chief was that he told white women not to go out with Puerto Ricans. Similar incidents happened in other states. In Glassboro, New Jersey, the police did not let workers visit the town after five in the afternoon, and they constantly watched migrants (Nieves Falcón 1975, 43–59, 60–78, 92, 96).

Local authorities considered the needs (to say nothing of the rights) of Puerto Ricans to access government services to be a burden on the community. Some physicians refused to treat migrants, and some farmers were careless about providing health coverage for injuries. In one case a woman worked for six months with an untreated broken arm. After the North Collins incident, however, the MD and the New York State Department of Health began inspecting the camps, finding violations in twenty-three of the thirty-three camps visited. Some camps lacked health certificates and were crowded and dirty, without bathrooms, potable water, and mattresses. Other camps operated with fire hazards and open sewage. In one workers had to bathe in a creek and sleep on rags (Jorge Colón 1966a, 1966f, 1966h; Mendoza 1966a; Montgomery 1966). Some workers in North Collins were paying $15.00

weekly for lodging in a shack built in the backyard of a home (Jorge Colón 1966e).

Because of the poor conditions in most camps, workers sought to rent rooms, apartments, or houses in the local community, but landlords usually refused to rent to Puerto Ricans. One migrant stated that while he earned $80.00 a week and had plenty of money in his pockets, he had to sleep in a car because no one would rent him a room (Ruiz 1966). Housing discrimination forced workers to stay in the camps, move to the cities, or return to Puerto Rico when the farm season ended.

Low salaries were another matter of concern. A worker who had picked six hundred flats of strawberries in a week received $63.00, but the deductions for food and transportation reduced his pay to $25.20. Workers also had to pay when they went into town to eat (Bowles [1966?]). Some workers hired by employment agencies in New York City complained about the lack of work after they arrived at the camps (Jorge Colón 1966a, 1966b), but keeping a large pool of workers secured a cheap labor force for the farmers (F. Rivera 1979, 242).

Emboldened by publicity given to the North Collins protests, Puerto Ricans living and working in other towns began to reveal their perilous living and working conditions. In Dunkirk, New York, community leaders acknowledged that there were 98 families, a total of 368 residents, and 400 agricultural workers "sleeping on dirty floors, chicken coops and pig pens." They declared, nonetheless, that while discrimination against Puerto Ricans was a problem, they had often succeeded in avoiding public protests (Ruiz 1966).

Farmers, crew leaders, local officials, and the police formed the power structure that attempted to reinforce inequality and segregation to ensure the availability of a disciplined labor force. But Puerto Ricans were not passive subjects. They challenged the existing power relations and material conditions, and many escaped the camps. After all, they had arrived looking for better living conditions, and this implied continually moving until they found proper working and living conditions.

## STATE AND CIVIL SOCIETY INTERVENTIONS

The North Collins incident raised awareness of farmworkers' living and working conditions in western New York. In response, the federal, state, and Puerto Rican governments all asserted their presence in the region, seeking to decrease tensions by establishing communication between workers and residents. Community leaders, politicians, and government officials held meetings and hearings and toured the region during the summer of 1966 (E. Torres 1966a). Government officials aimed to foster civil society through the creation of community organizations that would incorporate Puerto Ricans. The lieutenant governor of New York, the New York State Commission on Human Rights (NYSCHR), the New York State Assembly, the MD, and the office of U.S. senator Robert F. Kennedy all got involved in the investigation of the North Collins protest and its aftermath.

On July 26, 1966, federal, state, and MD officials and local community organizations met in North Collins and drafted several proposals, one of which was to obtain loans for farmers to improve migrants' housing. The Erie County health commissioner expressed his desire to work with the Community Action Organization of Erie County, an antipoverty program, by providing workers with medical aid and transportation. When the town supervisor stated that the local government lacked the resources to implement programs for migrants, the officials responded that federal and state government subsidies were available for housing, health facilities, sanitation, and children's day care. This meeting revealed that local government officials and some residents did not wish to accept any responsibility for the workers' protest and that they seemed unwilling to fulfill their obligations to farmworkers. U.S. congressional hearings at the end of the decade confirmed that local government officials showed little commitment to assisting migrant farmworkers and enforcing the law in their favor (Jorge Colón 1966c; U.S. Senate 1970, 1928–30).

Some residents of North Collins obstructed the efforts of community organizations that offered solutions to farmworkers' problems. Thomas A. Penna, a representative of the Community Action Organization, faced opposition from white residents to creating programs for farmworkers and even to renting space for a community center because it would be used as a meeting place for Puerto Ricans. Local authorities and residents "[hoped] to run all Puerto Ricans out of North Collins in due time" (E. Torres 1966a, 4–5). By October 1966, however, the organization had established the North Collins Migrant Center, which offered adult education, recreational activities, and assistance to migrants with social and economic problems. (Jorge Colón 1967a, 1967b). The Spanish American Organization was also operating as a support group for residents and migrants in the area (Vasquez 1969).

After the July protests New York lieutenant governor Malcolm Wilson ordered the NYSCHR to investigate the situation of Puerto Ricans in North

Collins. The resulting report found no reasons for alarm and defended the measures taken by the town government, employers, and store owners, asserting that the challenge was to establish programs that would be fair to both migrants and farmers. The report also alleged that discriminatory practices in establishments that previously refused to serve Puerto Ricans had ceased, except for one business in the town of Eden, concluding that discrimination was no longer evident and that farmers operated the migrant camps in accordance with the law. The report, however, relied simply on the word of store owners (E. Cohen 1967, 3–5). The absence of serious consideration of the farmworkers' accusations suggests that the investigation was mainly intended to dissipate tensions in the area.

In fact, the report assigned a large part of the blame to the farmworkers, attributing the conflict to lack of communication between workers and residents (E. Cohen 1967, 3). While acknowledging that the socioeconomic inequalities implicit in farm labor were one cause of conflict, it denied that specific situations of segregation and discrimination existed (*El Tiempo* 1966b). Likewise, the report argued that the protest arose because of the lack of recreational facilities and the resulting "congregation of numbers of persons on the streets, many of whom might prefer to spend their time in athletic and educational activities" (E. Cohen 1967, 3), but it failed to offer recommendations for addressing the problems identified. The NYSCHR merely hoped that churches and community organizations would improve the channels of communication between workers, farmers, residents, and officials.

The NYSCHR report contradicted the findings of the New York State Legislature. On August 21, 1966, members of the Joint Legislative Committee on Migrant Labor of the New York Assembly toured some of the migrant workers' camps in Erie and Chautauqua Counties and Long Island (E. Torres 1966b, 1). New York State assembly member Arthur Hardwick Jr. of Erie County, an African American legislator, characterized the farmworkers' working and living conditions as shameful and outrageous (1966a, 3). The Joint Legislative Committee noted that local county health officers did not enforce the sanitary code effectively because many inspectors were friends and neighbors of farmers (Nelkin 1970, 56–57).

The North Collins incident expanded the visibility of the MD in western New York. Local activists urged Puerto Ricans to register with the FLP and to migrate from Puerto Rico only under official contracts (Catholic and Protestant Clergy 1966). The MD also began educating new contract workers in Erie County about their rights and responsibilities. The officials thought it was essential that workers understand their duties and learn English to ensure the success of the FLP (Mendoza 1966a, 1966b). Working with local government, canning factories, and farmers, the MD began to offer English classes to workers. In Buffalo the MD and representatives of the Puerto Rican Social Club, the Council of Christian Organizations, the Mutual Aid Organization, and the Latin American Democratic Club met to organize a federation to offer support services for migrant workers (Jorge Colón 1966g, 1966b).

Another of the immediate solutions offered by the MD was to remove dissatisfied migrants from the area. The Travelers Aid Society offered to help those who wanted to leave (Jorge Colón 1966a), but most workers declined because farmers owed them wages and bonuses and because farmers, in response to the findings of investigations following the North Collins protests, were changing conditions in the camps by providing new mattresses and repairing the premises (Migration Division 1966c). The MD also intensified its efforts to encourage farmers to hire contract workers. Most farmers and association representatives questioned and challenged the MD programs, but some decided to participate in the FLP (Jorge Colón 1967b). By promoting the establishment of contract-labor camps in Erie County and restricting the movement of noncontract workers from Puerto Rico, the MD hoped to set an example for farmers still relying on walk-ins (E. Torres 1966b, 1–3).

Responding to the MD's concerns, the Erie County Health Department closed four of the forty-two camps in the county, one of which had eleven shacks occupied by more than forty people. The shacks were old, full of holes, small—fifteen by ten feet and seven feet high—made of wood and cardboard, and without running water. But many of the camps not closed were similar to those condemned by the Health Department (Montgomery 1966, 60). Notwithstanding, the problems migrants faced in North Collins and nearby towns continued. In 1969 the Spanish American Organization called a meeting to discuss alleged housing discrimination against families in Durkin, New York. The organization's representative and migrants also complained that the Migrant Center was ineffective and asked for removal of its director (Alicea 1969; E. Rivera 1969, 1–2).

Migrant workers' problems continued because farmers, politicians, and government officials generally believed that seasonal migrants in the Northeast would disappear as the mechanization of agriculture eliminated the need for this labor force (Nelkin 1970, 70). But migrants who settled in western New York were not about to go away, as their continuing advocacy for better treatment made clear. After 1966 they counted on institutions like the Spanish American Organization to organize more formal challenges to unacceptable political, social, and economic conditions.

Another recourse against the poor living conditions, discrimination, and segregation was to move to nearby small cities. Puerto Ricans who took this path expanded and established many urban communities, for example in Buffalo and Rochester, New York; Dover and Vineland, New Jersey; Allentown and Bethlehem, Pennsylvania; Lorain, Ohio; Gary, Indiana; and Waltham, Massachusetts, and further entrenched themselves in Chicago, New York City, Hartford, Springfield, and Boston. These migrants fostered and maintained networks between stateside and insular communities, and this facilitated finding employment and housing—and migrating (Whalen 2005, 31–34).

The expansion of Puerto Rican communities created social problems for the migrants and the small towns and cities housing them. In August 1966 MD officials Jorge Colón and Carlos M. Gómez traveled to Westfield, New York, in Chautauqua County, where they were joined by community leaders from Buffalo to investigate area residents' complaints. Rafael Rivera, the father of five, complained of deplorable housing and that his children were being bullied in the Westfield neighborhood where they had lived for five years. Rivera was blind and receiving Social Security and public assistance totaling $266 a month. Confesor Cruz, a social worker from the Erie County Department of Welfare, advised him about moving to Buffalo, promising to help him find suitable housing by contacting the Chautauqua County Public Assistance Department (Jorge Colón 1966c).

Although they recognized the discrimination migrants and residents faced, MD officials also blamed their troubles on their supposed moral failings, especially the persistence of common-law unions. Welfare assistance was often denied to families with unemployed fathers because they were not in legally recognized marriages. The MD official assigned to one such case reported, "I have advised them to get married at once. This family may not be very bright, but I have no doubt that they have been despicably abused, and they need all the help they can get" (Rodríguez 1964). Some MD officials upheld conservative family values and perceived not being married as detrimental to the reputation of the Puerto Rican community in general.

Some migrants left the labor camps to establish residence and find better jobs in the steel and automobile industry in Erie County, New York, although some workers combined agriculture and manufacturing. Few, however, became homeowners. Artemio, a former farmworker, was an exception, working days at General Electric and on nearby farms during the evenings and weekends. His wife also worked, and they raised two daughters together. They bought a house by saving what they earned from their extra weekend and evening work. Artemio's was among the first Puerto Rican families to move into their neighborhood in a small city in western New York. His wife recalled that one of their neighbors began to tell other neighbors that they planned to move because Puerto Ricans had bought a house in the neighborhood.

In the late 1960s the image of farmworkers in the United States was changing. Surveys of farmers and articles in farmers' magazines and newspapers in the 1950s had praised Puerto Rico migrant farmworkers, and William L. Batt Jr., Pennsylvania's secretary of labor, stated at the 1960 National Conference to Stabilize Migrant Labor that the FLP's achievements inspired him to improve farmworkers' living and working conditions (FLP 1960, 1–2). Even so, migrants still had the lowest wage income in the United States, and unemployment was prevalent. Moreover, Puerto Ricans were becoming disposable subjects, considered by many farmers to be lazy and unreliable. As they had done previously to Chinese, Japanese, Filipino, and Mexican migrant workers, farmers and officials applied negative stereotypes to Puerto Ricans because they demanded higher wages or picketed farms, defining them as unsuitable whenever a cheaper source of labor became available (see Galarza 1977, 30).

Officials and scholars continued to regard the "Puerto Rican contract" as securing better conditions than those offered to other domestic workers. Max H. Rothman, director of the Farm Workers Division of Camden Regional Legal Services, recommended that "the State law . . . be amended to be at least as strong for all workers as it is for Puerto Rican contract workers. . . . The protection should include wage guarantee, hospitalization, group health insurance and having someone represent the worker in enforcing the contract" (U.S. Senate 1970, 1928). Scholars Jeffrey Hoffman and Richard Seltzer argued for a New York state law that would go further than Puerto Rico's contract, which at the time covered only 5 percent of the farmworker population (1735, 1746).

CONTENTIOUS CITIZENS

While U.S. citizenship enabled Puerto Ricans to migrate to agricultural jobs in the United States, it could not shield them from the exploitation and poor labor and living conditions faced by all farmworkers. The MD, acting as a labor organization but also hindering independent labor-organizing efforts, encouraged Puerto Ricans to take advantage of their U.S. citizenship. While the FLP was successful in mobilizing the unemployed from one geographic region to another (Fuller 1967, 107), the MD could not resolve all the complaints of migrant workers. As it attempted to control migration to the States, the MD left many workers stuck in untenable situations, as the North Collins case illustrates (F. Rivera 1979). The MD aimed at developing loyal and politically strong Puerto Rican communities in the United States, a strategy that replicated Puerto Rico's domestic social and economic policies and complemented U.S. labor policies and the demands of agricultural interests for cheap labor (Torres and Katsiaficas 1999, 8). But the citizenship claims of migrant workers in North Collins and elsewhere in the United States underpinned their struggle to improve their working and living conditions and shaped the constitution of their ethnicity and their engagement in the political process (G. Smith 1999, 198–99).

The North Collins incident exposes how white residents' prejudice against migrant workers shaped the political economy of farm labor and state agriculture policies. The problems in North Collins did not emerge solely from cultural misunderstandings among residents, authorities, and Puerto Ricans but also from the struggle to impose and maintain certain power relations. The farmworkers demonstrated the weakness of such power relations. The attitudes and actions of local authorities and residents—and those of Puerto Ricans—remind us that power relations, economic conditions, and discourses are linked to processes of state formation and that social justice and labor rights are ways to confront exploitation (Roseberry 1996; G. Smith 1999).

In western New York farmworkers experienced discrimination and police brutality, but the North Collins fiasco also shows how they resisted through protest and claimed their rights as U.S. citizens. In addition, the government of Puerto Rico, through its MD, played an important role in mobilizing workers as well as promoting their insertion into ethnic-identity politics and cheap labor. Ironically, in the 1960s Puerto Ricans' advantages as citizens who could receive food stamps and public housing reinforced their negative image. The unequal exchanges of labor, goods, and technologies between the United States and Puerto Rico and the perceptions of white residents pushed Puerto Ricans to the urban ghettos, where they continue to be second-class citizens. They could escape the farms and become visible in the cities, but what most of them could not escape was inequality and poverty.

The North Collins case shows how common narratives and power relations have moments of rupture in which people openly resist oppressive conditions. When these ruptures occur, government agencies sometimes mobilize to convince people to take their grievances through institutional channels, fostering civil society by encouraging the creation of community organizations to promote political and social participation. These actions are responses to initiatives taken against disadvantaged groups, but Puerto Ricans were not mere recipients of government designs. In western New York and elsewhere, they struggled to improve their living conditions and establish their presence.

The North Collins protest shares the same history of tensions and inequality with other past and present Latinx populations in rural and urban areas. The negative images of workers, the lack of appropriate housing, exploitation, nonpayment of wages, retaliation, violence, threats, and dangerous and unsanitary conditions with little access to medical care—these are the same problems confronting present-day farmworkers and day laborers. The 1970s and 1980s brought winds of labor militancy against these conditions in confrontation with the reactionary forces of farmers and their allies in the federal, state, and local governments.

# SEVEN

# Labor Organizing and the End of an Era

EVEN AS MIGRATION BECAME A VIABLE STRATEGY for Puerto Ricans seeking better opportunities, their search for work did not mean abdicating their rights and aspirations. Migrant workers were and are not passive victims of government officials and farmers. Using the language of citizenship and knowing their labor rights, they participated in the struggle to improve their living and working conditions on stateside farms. Maneuvering in a field of power where citizenship defined their status, migrants resisted accommodation to unjust and poor conditions in the fields and camps because they did not fear deportation. They recognized that their citizenship opened other possibilities, among them labor organizing. Farmers' opposition to labor was also strong, landing a blow from which the Farm Labor Program (FLP) never recovered.

This chapter explores the most important historical developments for Puerto Rican farmworkers from the 1970s to the early 1990s: tobacco workers' protests in Connecticut, the first important attempts at labor organizing, apple growers' refusal to hire Puerto Ricans, and the creation of the Agricultural Workers Support Committee (CATA; Comité de Apoyo a los Trabajadores Agrícolas). These developments open a window onto the growers' role in shaping the political economy of farm labor and how labor organizations, legal-advocacy groups, workers, and government officials responded.

## CRISIS AT HOME AND ABROAD

The civil rights movement left an imprint on politics that transformed farm labor and the hiring of Puerto Ricans in the 1970s. The United Farm Workers

FIGURE 15. Workers harvesting peaches, 1991. Photo by Doel Vázquez. Courtesy of the Records of the Department of Puerto Rican Community Affairs, Archives of the Puerto Rican Diaspora, Centro de Estudios Puertorriqueños, Hunter College, City University of New York.

(UFW) of America, through its boycotts of California growers, was establishing both its influence and union shops beyond California (Hahamovitch 2011, 172–73). Legal-services organizations expanded their defense of farmworkers. The political activism of Chicanos and Puerto Ricans in the inner cities was at its highest. In the United States the Young Lords and U.S. chapters of the Puerto Rican Socialist Party (PSP; Partido Socialista Puertorriqueño) were influencing the activism and organizing of Puerto Ricans in communities and workplaces, and farm labor took center stage.

The political and social climate for farmworkers was changing. In 1960 both the Republican and Democratic Parties included statements on migrant workers in their platforms. The Democrats pledged to expand welfare services, while the Republicans argued for improving job opportunities and working conditions. Federal assistance programs commissioned several surveys of migrant farmworkers (Martin 1988, 6–8), and the NAACP sued the U.S. Department of Labor (USDL), alleging that African American workers were only referred to agricultural jobs rather than placed in specific job openings.[1]

During the 1970s big corporations continued to buy large tracts of land, invest in farm equipment, operate food-processing factories, and own food stores, a trend that decreased the number of farms owned by individuals and increased the size of farms. Nationwide, the number of farms declined from 6,350,000 in 1940 to 2,662,000 in 1970, while average farm size increased from 167 acres in 1940 to 387 acres in 1970 (Thomas-Lycklama à Nijeholt 1980, 12–13). In Massachusetts the number of farms declined from 9,400 in 1964 to 5,700 in 1973. Farms hiring farmworkers also declined from 3,534 in 1964 to 2,632 in 1969. Agricultural acreage decreased by 50 percent from the late 1950s to the early 1970s, although the average size of a Massachusetts farm increased from 60 acres in 1950 to 126 acres in 1973. In the apple industry thirteen growers owned 38 percent of apple trees in 1970, up from nine who owned 29 percent in 1965. The number of Massachusetts' orchards also decreased from 227 in 1965 to 197 in 1970 (Nash 1973, 2). The rise of large agribusinesses meant less political power and job security for farmworkers.

Inflation, recession, and unemployment ensuing from energy shortages during the 1973 oil embargo also changed the labor force. As inflation doubled from 5.4 percent in 1969 to 11 percent in 1974, participation in the labor force increased from 59.7 percent to 61.9 percent, but unemployment also increased from 3.3 percent in 1968 to 7.9 percent in 1976. Many U.S. workers sought work as agricultural laborers. In Puerto Rico an economic crisis also increased the number of people unemployed as well as the number of return migrants, reducing the FLP from 12,700 workers in 1974 to 5,600 in 1975 (see García-Colón 2017b, 171; OGPRUS 1953–92). A general decrease in the demand for stateside farmworkers created a dire situation for migrants seeking farm-labor jobs (Dunbar and Kravitz 1976, 50).

In the 1960s the federal government created and expanded training programs to broaden the labor market as part of its so-called manpower policies and to decentralize the work of the U.S. Manpower Administration (Weir 1993, 11, 103–5). Rising inflation and international economic competition drove the federal government to promote employment through skill training. In 1969 the U.S. Bureau of Employment Security was dissolved and folded into a new federal agency, the U.S. Training and Employment Service, which began to shape programs targeting and coordinating employment services with other training programs. The USDL also enhanced the power of regional administrators, a move that President Richard Nixon hoped would advance his political influence (108–9). Decentralization brought new relations between the Puerto Rico Department of Labor (PRDL), the Migration Division (MD), and its regional directors.

Unemployment led the Nixon administration to create new federal training programs. In December 1973 Congress passed the Comprehensive Employment and Training Act, perhaps the most important employment program since the New Deal. Using CETA funds, state governments expanded existing programs and created new ones, some targeting migrant workers. In January 1976 Congress raised the minimum wage to $2.30 per hour, covering more than 1.5 million nonfarmworkers. In 1978 the Carter administration expanded and revised CETA to bolster public-service and other employment programs. The government also raised the minimum wage from $2.30 to $3.35 per hour on January 1, 1981, including farmworkers for the first time (MacLaury 1988a, 1988b; USDL 1977, 1–4). Federal and state governments continued developing programs for migrant workers while implementing new strategies for fulfilling the employment needs of the rural population (Marshall 1981, 1–2).

In Puerto Rico proposals to hire guest workers for an invigorated agricultural sector began to circulate as a political split within the Popular Democratic Party (PPD; Partido Popular Democrático) brought the New Progressive Party (PNP; Partido Nuevo Progresista) to the governorship. In 1969 Luis A. Ferré became the first governor who was a member of both the prostatehood PNP and the U.S. Republican Party, and he opposed a plan articulated by Oreste Ramos, the president of the Puerto Rico Farmers Association (Asociación de Agricultores de Puerto Rico), to bring twenty-five thousand migrants from Haiti, the Dominican Republic, and other islands for the sugar harvest. Ferré countered that what was needed were higher wages and better working conditions in the agricultural sector, so that Puerto Ricans—at home and in the States—could be persuaded to work in the fields (*El Diario* [1969?]). Under a market-oriented banner geared toward privatization, the Ferré administration began to dismantle New Deal programs. The effects on the FLP were disastrous (Segundo 1992, 762–63).

Managerial changes under the Ferré administration reduced the effectiveness of the FLP, as new and inexperienced personnel were hired, and communication between the new administrators and old personnel became testy. Ferré's secretary of labor, Julia Rivera de Vicenti, acknowledged that MD officials were not following the proper procedures regarding agricultural job orders issued by the USDL:

The Regional Offices of Boston and New York did not extend orders to Puerto Rico as they did not have in their possession the current terms and conditions of the 1971 agricultural contract. Clearance orders continued to be received late throughout most of the season. The delay in extending the orders on time caused several drawbacks and extra workload to the staff. This was especially true in the case of independent employers who requested a small number of workers. The problem worsened when employers requesting predesignated workers gave short notice and pressured for their referral. It was necessary to explain on several occasions our difficulties and the expenses involved in contacting these particular workers and of the importance of fulfilling all requirements on time, in order to alleviate the problem. (1971, 7–8)

The PRDL was also hostile to community organizations that served farmworkers and often sided with growers (Young 1975, 103). Exacerbating this situation was the Nixon administration's insistence that the USDL's Region II Office, serving New York and New Jersey, send agricultural job orders to Puerto Rico only after circulating them in the States. This policy change gave priority to workers in the States, while the previous policy had applied equally to workers in Puerto Rico (Rivera de Vicenti 1971, 7–8).

The MD also faced inadequate resources in some of its regional offices. In the mid-1970s the Hartford Office had only one field supervisor and a secretary to oversee more than six thousand farmworkers in the Connecticut River Valley, in addition to providing other general services to the Puerto Rican community in the area (Young 1975, 51). The field supervisor functioned primarily as a "grievance officer," administering the implementation of the FLP contract and helping workers charged with violations. Migrants did not always contact the field supervisors, however, although they still complained that the representative did not effectively address their grievances and that the regional office was sympathetic to the growers (Nash 1973, 11).

The impact of the macroeconomic changes occurring in the early 1970s was obvious, as referrals to U.S. farm jobs dropped to a thirteen-year low of 11,900 in 1972. The PRDL referred and recruited more than 11,000 fewer workers between 1968 and 1972, a drop of 48 percent (Segundo 1992, 762). Despite this decrease, Puerto Rican government officials estimated that the total number of migrant farmworkers ranged from 60,000 to 200,000 (Morales 1986, 77–78). In 1973 approximately one-third of the migrants in Massachusetts were noncontract workers, although the number of contract versus noncontract workers varied from industry to industry. Most tobacco workers worked under contract, while noncontract workers were largely employed in nurseries and cranberry and vegetable farms. Farmers and growers argued that workers were better off without FLP contracts, but the increasing number of noncontract workers really reflected farmers' reluctance to accept the higher wages and costly obligations required by the contract (Nash 1973, 13–14; Bonilla-Santiago 1986, 82).

In New Jersey the number of contract workers decreased from 9,463 in 1969 to 2,020 in 1977, owing to legal actions against growers in the late 1960s and early 1970s. Notwithstanding, the Puerto Rican migrant labor force remained attractive for vegetable farmers, particularly in New Jersey, although noncontract laborers began to replace contract workers. In 1977 between 8,000 and 10,000 Puerto Ricans without contracts traveled to New Jersey, and farmers employed 10,000 to 12,000 day laborers, mostly from Philadelphia and Camden (Bonilla-Santiago 1986, 78–80). Some of these workers had been migrating for more than twenty years, and most of them intended to return to Puerto Rico to work in factories (31 percent) or on farms (30 percent) (Nash 1973, 10; Young 1975, 66).

In the Northeast the average Puerto Rican farmworker was thirty years old. Married workers composed 39 percent of the total. Their household size averaged four members, illustrating the effects of population-control policies on younger households. Most workers had no more than six years of formal education. A third were homeowners, but in Massachusetts and Connecticut 49.1 percent of tobacco workers owned homes because that industry paid higher wages (Young 1975, 55).

More than twenty years after the creation of the FLP, conditions in the labor camps, fields, and surrounding farming communities were relatively unchanged, but farmwork offered opportunities unavailable in Puerto Rico. Andrés, who arrived in New Jersey in the mid-1950s, had earned $0.33 an hour in Puerto Rico as a sugarcane worker. He earned double that as asparagus picker in New Jersey. In 1974 he felt fortunate when he could earn $1.20 an hour in a Connecticut tobacco factory. Other workers in Connecticut earned less than $1.00 an hour, working nine hours a day, seven days a week. Andrés thought that workers were now eating "beefsteak" compared to when he first arrived. Eventually, he took a job with the New England Farm Workers Council (NEFWC), a social-service organization serving mostly migrant workers, because he didn't want his compatriots to "suffer the bitterness" he experienced as migrant (Papirno 1974b).

In 1970 the median yearly earnings of a male farmworker age sixteen or older were $2,597 compared to $4,647 for nonfarmworkers (Thomas-Lycklama à Nijeholt 1980, 15). The average annual income for a migrant worker was $2,600, with 68 percent, or $1,768, earned as a farmworker and the rest earned in other jobs after the harvest. Migrant workers netted approximately $75 per week after deductions for food, airplane tickets, group insurance coverage, Social Security, and other expenditures (Young 1975, 60–62). MD officials heard the same complaints about wages and benefits year after year. Some men claimed they had been promised $2.00 per hour, while the rate was only $1.55, and some contract workers refused to work for an employer after he paid for their trip. Other migrants never intended to work, arriving without any luggage and insisting that they would work only for $2.00 an hour (Migration Division 1973).

Inefficient management within the MD was also becoming a problem. In 1969 Antonio Del Río, the MD field representative in Boston, complained to his superior that the lists of contract workers being sent to Massachusetts farms often overstated how many workers would arrive to begin work. Occasionally, when he showed up at the airport to meet the indicated number of workers, fewer—or none—were there. He stated,

> This is a problem that we have never had before and I hope that we will not have much of this again. The few men who arrived were interviewed and given a very short orientation talk. No one in the group actually knew what happened to the rest of the men. We were told, however, that half of the men did not report to the airport because of the cold weather. I can understand this, but it is most difficult to explain to the employers.

Clearly, the infrastructure of the FLP was being affected by the political changes in Puerto Rico.

The composition of the Puerto Rican farm labor force was also changing. In the 1950s a third of migrant workers came from the agricultural sector, but by the 1970s urban workers in a declining economy dominated by service, construction, and manufacturing were turning to seasonal migration. Only 11 percent of men were employed in agriculture in Puerto Rico, compared to 1.7 percent stateside (M. Rivera [1968?], 47; USDL 1975, 18, 25). Although the official pool of farmworkers had shrunk from 250,000 workers in 1948 to 36,000 workers in the early 1970s (Loperena 1973a, 21; Morales 1986, 77–78), Puerto Ricans faced increased competition for jobs in the Northeast as employers began to recruit documented and undocumented Mexican workers. On a farm in Avondale, Pennsylvania, a worker wrote to the MD complaining about the farmer's preference for Mexicans (Rios 1971). Yet Puerto Rico, along with California, Texas, and Florida, continued to send workers into the migratory labor stream (Dunbar and Kravitz 1976, 4).

In qualitative terms the Puerto Rican labor force was also changing from a rural to an urban one, and the number of experienced agricultural workers was decreasing. Farmers and older workers alike criticized new migrant workers. On one farm an older worker complained about the new migrants' youthful games (Camacho 1969), and using, buying, and planting marijuana were added to the old list of complaints about alcoholism, gambling, soliciting prostitutes, fights, and robberies (H. Pérez 1975).

In 1972 Rafael Hernández Colón, the new leader of the PPD, became governor, ending the first four years of the PNP and Republican-oriented policies. The new administration actively sought the support of stateside communities, cultivating a prolabor and promigrant farm-labor image. In a speech in New York City, Hernández Colón stated,

> Puerto Rico's major interest is to be concerned and look actively after the welfare of our people while they reside in the United States. Puerto Rico cannot maintain an indifferent position toward the problems of our compatriots who reside here. The social, economic, cultural, and political cost would be very high—so high in relation to the personal lives of hundreds of thousands of these Puerto Ricans as well as the collective life of Puerto Rico. (1973, 7)

Marco Rigau, a young prolabor lawyer, became director of the MD in March 1973 (PRDL 1973b, 1). In 1975, as unemployment worsened in Puerto Rico, the Hernández Colón administration increased the FLP's funding, allocating an additional $62,546 from January 1 through June 30, 1975, to hire more migration specialists (Silva Recio 1975). The economic recession had diminished tax revenue in Puerto Rico, however, and the FLP received minimal funds in fiscal year 1975–76 (Esquilín 1975). The MD's annual budget at this time was about $1.1 million, a sum inadequate to administer programs catering to more than one million stateside Puerto Ricans, including fifty thousand migrant workers. The reduction of the FLP under the PNP administration (1969–72) and the failure to increase the MD's budget as stateside communities grew and farm-labor migration increased crippled the PPD government's efforts to assist migrants (Young 1975, 51). Even so, as Puerto Rican communities in the States grew, so too did the activism of their members. Farmworkers' resistance to new challenges from employers marked the administration of the FLP and the reproduction of the Puerto Rican farm labor force in the 1970s. Organizing efforts among farmworkers in the Northeast revealed the increasing political power of stateside communities and heightened the visibility of the farm-labor movement within the struggle for civil rights.

The Ferré administration had fought the establishment of antipoverty agencies in Puerto Rico and allied with agribusiness in the States to defund programs for migrant workers. After its defeat by the PPD in 1972, the Ferré administration's efforts did not, however, impede the establishment of non-profit organizations and legal-services programs that supported farmworkers. In August 1973 the U.S. Office of Economic Opportunity funded Puerto Rico Legal Services, which became such a strong defender of migrant workers that employers had to retain attorneys in Puerto Rico. New organizations such as the NEFWC and the Farmworkers' Corporation of New Jersey also extended legal services to Puerto Ricans on the East Coast (Llamas 1977, 30–31, 35; Young 1975).

Despite sporadic efforts to organize farmworkers in the 1950s, it was not until the 1960s that concerted efforts to do so were made in the Northeast. The UFW Organizing Committee of the American Federation of Labor and Congress of Industrial Organizations (AFL-CIO) sent Paul Sanchez and Joseph Garcia to set up pickets at labor camps and assist workers with disputes and claims against farmers in upstate New York (Ruffini 2003, 119; Sanchez 1967; *Times Union* 1968). In 1969 the most important attempts at labor organizing occurred in New Jersey and Connecticut, as religious organizations responded to press reports about the living and working conditions of Puerto Rican farmworkers. A group of clergy, labor organizers, community activists, and militant members of the PSP and the Puerto Rican Independence Party gained the sponsorship of the prolabor Industrial Mission of Puerto Rico (Misión Industrial de Puerto Rico) and the Episcopal Church and began to organize workers to defend their rights. They created the Puerto Rican Migrant Support Committee (CAMP; Comité de Apoyo al Migrante Puertorriqueño) to organize migrants and inform the public about their situation (Bonilla-Santiago 1986, 109–13; Llamas 1977, 30–31).

While UFW action in the Northeast faded as its focus shifted to the western United States, its militancy spurred action at the federal level that shaped the issues advocates used to organize Puerto Rican migrants. The Occupational Health and Safety Act (OSHA) of 1970 set a legal framework for appropriate working and housing conditions for farmworkers and empowered the U.S. secretary of labor to establish work and living standards for workers in manufacturing and agriculture, including arrangements for sleeping, dining, and lavatory facilities. But routine oversight of these

regulations fell to the states and their local boards of health, and local officials were often hesitant to fine employers for OSHA violations (Young 1975,
20). Inadequate enforcement of health and safety regulations and related
clauses in the FLP contract became the legal and organizing pillars of
churches, labor groups, and workers who sought to defend farmworkers'
rights.

Religious organizations were at the forefront of the farmworkers' struggle.
As part of CAMP, the National Migrant Ministry hired the Reverend
Wilmer R. Silva as director of the Puerto Rican Farmworkers Ministry in
Vineland, New Jersey. In 1970 CAMP organizers visited several municipali-
ties in Puerto Rico, and Juan Reyes Soto, a member of the PSP and the
CAMP coordinator in Puerto Rico, visited New Jersey, Connecticut, and
Massachusetts to investigate workers' situation and plan the formation of a
migrant workers' organization (Bonilla-Santiago 1986, 109–13; *CALC
Report/TWC Bulletin* 1984, 9–10; Llamas 1977, 30–31).

This first effort by CAMP led to the creation, in 1972, of the Ecumenical
Farmworkers Ministry (META; Ministerio Ecuménico de Trabajadores
Agrícolas), with offices in Puerto Rico, Connecticut, and New Jersey. META
received funding from the Episcopal Church, the Catholic Church, the
Disciples of Christ, and the Joint Strategy Action Committee of the U.S.
Christian Churches (*Hartford Courant* 1973a). Its staff visited camps, distributed literature, exposed the conditions on farms and in the camps, and met
with workers to discuss their problems. META also established connections
with organizations like the UFW and national labor organizations, fostered
leadership development among workers, and participated in legal challenges
to the FLP over inadequate enforcement of the contract's requirement that
workers received three hot meals per day (Bonilla-Santiago 1986, 113–16).
Aided by META, during the summer of 1972, workers in Connecticut struck
against the Shade Tobacco Growers Agricultural Association (STGAA)
because of contract violations. In a class-action suit, they alleged violation of
the food clause, but the court dismissed the suit (Janson 1973, 1974).[2]

In 1972 the Puerto Rican Legal Defense and Education Fund sued the
governments of Puerto Rico and New Jersey for violating federal, state, and
Puerto Rican laws regarding the working and living conditions of migrant
farmworkers.[3] The Puerto Rican government and the state of New Jersey
accepted the claims and negotiated with lawyers to fix the problems. Puerto
Rican Legal Defense and Education Fund lawyers also urged that farmworker organizations identify leaders to represent workers in contract talks

and facilitate communication with the government (Bonilla-Santiago 1986, 117–19; Lillesand 1973; Perales 1973; *Revista Avance* 1973; J. Rivera 1973; Sheehan 1974). This case was beneficial for META because it publicized the workers' plight.

Connecticut became the center of labor organizing among tobacco workers. The strong ties between the Connecticut River Valley and the tobacco region in eastern Puerto Rico dated to the 1940s. During World War II the first migrants arrived to work in the Hartford area tobacco fields, spreading north into western Massachusetts. In the 1950s the Massachusetts State Division of Employment Security began recruiting Puerto Ricans from New York City, and the Puerto Rican government, aided by the U.S. Employment Service, pressured the STGAA to hire contract migrant workers (Carvalho 2015, 51).

The Connecticut River Valley, famous for shade tobacco production, a labor-intensive process that had little room for mechanization, was an ideal area for organizing farmworkers (Bonilla-Santiago 1986, 95, 122; see also DeWind, Seidl, and Shenk 1977, 25). Around seventeen corporate and family-owned growers belonged to the STGAA, a nonprofit corporation located in Windsor, Connecticut, whose role was public relations and to recruit and manage seasonal farm labor. The two main corporate members were the Consolidated Cigar Division of Gulf and Western Industries and the Culbro Tobacco Division of the General Cigar Company, each of which planted from 1,000 to 2,000 acres of shade tobacco yearly. Five small family farms planted between 300 and 500 acres a year, and ten small farmers planted between 50 and 150 acres of shade and broadleaf tobacco. Most of the members of the STGAA sold their tobacco to Consolidated and Culbro (Carvalho 2015, 49; Young 1975, xvii, 9–10).

By 1971 the industry had declined from 9,000 acres cultivated with shade tobacco and 20,000 with broadleaf to 4,700 acres and 1,610, respectively. Of the three hundred tobacco farmers after World War II, only fifty remained, but tobacco cultivation still required 150 percent more workers than other crops and 275 percent more seasonal migrant workers. In 1973 Connecticut tobacco growers reported a gross return of $20 million on a $30 million investment (Carvalho 2015, 49; Young 1975, xvii, 3–12).

The General Cigar Company, the Consolidated Cigar Corporation, and Meyer and Mendelsohn, all members of the STGAA, had subsidiaries in Puerto Rico. Attracted by lower minimum wages, tax exemptions, and the availability of skilled workers, these companies employed thousands of workers in the central eastern highlands of Puerto Rico, the traditional region of tobacco cultivation (Carvalho 2015, 49; Young 1975, xvii, 9, 10). Many tobacco workers from this region became migrant farmworkers, often for the same employers in the States, such as one migrant from the municipality of Cidra, who told me, "When I left the island I had been working in tobacco, and [I] came here to work in tobacco." By the early 1970s, out of a total labor force of 17,500 workers, the STGAA was employing 5,000 Puerto Rican seasonal contract workers annually, most of whom prepared tobacco plants for harvest. Of the migrants employed by the STGAA, 31 percent returned home before completing their contracts, while small farms retained most of their labor force until the end of the contract (Nash 1973, 14; Young 1975, 3–12).

The strong ties between tobacco companies and Puerto Rico began to splinter in April 1973, when 30 workers, accompanied by META organizers, demonstrated at Camp Windsor to protest violation of the contract's requirement that employers provide three hot meals daily. Workers complained of inedible meals and showed a reporter a dish with several human hairs in it (Schiffman 1973). The growers' response was swift. The STGAA allowed only limited access to the camp and began to restrict where and how many workers could gather and what they could discuss.

The MD responded immediately to resolve the problems between contract and noncontract farmworkers and company managers, with Director Rigau taking the workers' side and recommending changes to resolve the problems. Appalled by the migrants' living and working conditions, he believed that the MD was violating Puerto Rican law by promoting migration as a solution to the high unemployment rate in Puerto Rico. META's organizing efforts impressed Rigau, who also wanted to involve workers in contract negotiations, establish a procedure for grievances, and enforce contracts through the courts. Rigau understood the potential conflicts, however, pointing out that if the MD were overzealous in enforcing the contract, growers would not hire Puerto Ricans. Nevertheless, he attempted to bring legal action against employers violating the contract, but the Puerto Rico secretary of labor blocked this action, fearful that the changes workers demanded would lead to the termination of the FLP.

Some high-profile figures in the Puerto Rican government began to see Rigau as "problematic" because of his sympathy for the workers' organizations and the Puerto Rican Legal Defense and Education Fund. In June 1973 a confrontation began among Rigau, Governor Hernández Colón, and Secretary of Labor Luis F. Silva Recio that led to Rigau's dismissal. On July 3, 1973, after only two months in office, Rigau held a press conference accusing the PRDL of tolerating stateside "concentration camps for Puerto Rican migrant workers" to alleviate unemployment in Puerto Rico, noting that the Puerto Rican government had never taken legal action against any employer. After the press conference the secretary of labor summarily fired Rigau, undoing the initial prolabor advances of the Hernández Colón administration. Manuel Bustelo, the new MD director, refused to follow many of Rigau's changes and recommendations, such as including workers in negotiations, arguing that because PRDL was not a labor union, it opposed including workers in negotiations (Papirno 1973a; Young 1975, 181–83).

META's activism intensified after Rigau's firing. On July 18, 1973, the Reverend Wilfredo Vélez and Juan Irizarry challenged the STGAA by going to Camp Windsor at unauthorized hours. When they refused to leave, police arrested them. In the following days journalists and the mayor of Hartford were denied access to the camp. A large demonstration against the STGAA at the entrance to the camp was met with a counterdemonstration, where insults, water, and objects were thrown at demonstrators. On July 26 META filed suit against the STGAA, which the court resolved in META's favor by ordering open access at reasonable hours (Llamas 1977, 32–33).[4] Meanwhile, META was working on establishing a farm-labor union.

META organizers in New Jersey came into conflict with their Connecticut counterparts. According to Gloria Bonilla-Santiago, "religious and social reformers" were prominent in New Jersey's META, while Connecticut's was composed of proindependence advocates and political activists seeking to organize workers. In addition, insular political conflicts were being played out between supporters of the PSP in Connecticut's META and the Puerto Rican Independence Party in New Jersey's. The clashing visions of META, as an advocacy network and religious organization versus a labor union for farmworkers, resulted in its eventual dissolution and incorporation into a new organization, the Agricultural Workers Association (ATA; Asociación de Trabajadores Agrícolas) (1986, 116, 119–20).

On August 5, 1973, around a hundred Puerto Ricans met outside Camp Windsor and created the ATA, the first farmworkers association in the Northeast. The organization received the financial support and endorsement of the Connecticut State Labor Council, the AFL-CIO, and middle-class, white intellectuals from Connecticut (Pappas 1974a, 1974b). Juan Irizarry, the former coordinator of the Connecticut META and a member of the PSP, became ATA's interim president, and the organization's membership grew to 1,500 in New Jersey, Connecticut, and Massachusetts. ATA, joined by the

NEFWC, filed a lawsuit on behalf of workers against the STGAA (Bonilla-Santiago 1986, 96, 122; *CALC Report/TWC Bulletin* 1984, 9–10).

In August 1973 labor organizers circulated a letter addressed to Governor Hernández Colón, signed by more than a thousand Massachusetts and Connecticut tobacco workers, asking for salary increases, overtime payments, unemployment benefits, and better and lower-cost meals in the labor camps. Workers also petitioned for participation in contract negotiations. They complained that Gilberto Camacho, the MD's representative in Hartford, defended the tobacco companies against the interests of migrant workers. Their complaints about the MD were not groundless, as growers' influence on government agencies was strong. A Puerto Rican legislative commission visiting labor camps in 1973 found MD officials indifferent to contract violations and supportive of employers who fired migrants who had become outspoken leaders of work crews (F. Delgado 1973, 19). After Camacho resigned in the fall of 1973, following intense criticism from migrants (*Hartford Courant* 1974a), the MD appointed Juan R. Colón, a former health educator for the STGAA, to lead the Hartford Office.

Governor Hernández Colón pledged to find a way to give workers' representation in contract negotiations, and he informed the NEFWC that his administration would deal immediately with workers' complaints. ATA sought workers' permission to represent them in the contract negotiations. The contract at the time paid $1.90 an hour, provided free room, and required workers to pay $17.50 a week for food (*Hartford Courant* 1973e; Papirno 1973d; PRDL 1973a; Young 1975, 168–69). Seventy workers met during August 1973 to formally recognize ATA as their representative by filling out and signing forms, in Spanish, requesting representation in negotiations. A delegation of workers was selected to take the signed forms to officials in Puerto Rico (Papirno 1973c), but the Puerto Rican government failed to follow up despite Hernández Colón's pledge (Young 1975, 131–36). In response META and the PSP picketed the MD's Hartford Office (*Hartford Courant* 1973b). When ATA and META lobbied the Connecticut General Assembly to get a farmworkers' rights bill, the STGAA threatened to move its operations (Glasser 2005, 182–83).

As a response to ATA and the situation of workers in Connecticut, the Puerto Rican government organized an advisory committee to represent workers in the 1974 contract negotiations with the STGAA. The thirty-two-member committee, composed of workers from twenty-six municipalities throughout Puerto Rico (Muñiz 1973), served as a grievance committee for workers recruited by the STGAA. Workers in fourteen labor camps owned by shade tobacco growers also elected committees (*Hartford Courant* 1973c; PRDL 1973a). During the winter of 1973–74, the Puerto Rican government trained the workers who would participate in the negotiations, and ATA continued its quest to try to negotiate a contract. Community activists began to organize supporting groups in Springfield, Massachusetts; Hartford and Waterbury, Connecticut; Camden, New Jersey; New York City; and Philadelphia (Loperena 1973b, 28). In March 1974 Secretary Silva Recio announced significant gains in the contract for the upcoming season, including wage increases ranging from $0.10 to $0.18 per hour, unemployment insurance after returning to Puerto Rico, paid transportation to the States, the right to paid return at the employer's expense in case of critical illness, new grievance procedures, and guarantees against discrimination. The results of the negotiations also included a recommendation to hire Puerto Rican cooks (PRDL 1974b).

Tensions were high during the fall of 1973, as the STGAA continued its hostile campaign against ATA. In November Vélez and Irizarry were charged with trespassing on the tobacco labor camps (*Hartford Courant* 1973d). In February 1974 a U.S. District Court judge ruled, in a suit filed by META, that the STGAA must recognize the freedom of speech and association rights of the workers and their representatives, but he limited the times visitors could go to the camps, providing open access to Camp Windsor between 10:00 A.M. and 10:00 P.M. daily (1974b).

The NEFWC was also increasing its activism. With the Hartford County Lung Association and assisted by two medical students from Puerto Rico, it attempted to implement a federally funded program that provided physical exams (including free tuberculosis screening), family medical histories, and laboratory tests to farmworkers. After the director of the STGAA barred the group's medical personnel from its camps, activists filed a lawsuit. The conflict was partly over a $400,000 federal grant to create health-care programs for migrant workers that had to be split between the NEFWC and STGAA (Papirno 1973b; Rhinelander 1973; Young 1975, 107–14).

Connecticut's Republican governor, Thomas Joseph Meskill, attacked the NEFWC for its activism among workers. He met with USDL representatives and attempted to bypass the NEFWC by establishing an office for migrant labor within the Connecticut Department of Community Affairs. He accused the NEFWC of ineffectiveness and sought control over its federal funds. Department commissioner Ruben Figueroa accused the NEFWC of causing dissent, claiming that unrest might lead to an exodus of the tobacco industry from Connecticut. When the U.S. Manpower Administration decided to continue providing funds to the NEFWC, Commissioner Figueroa countered that the STGAA or another group should receive the money, while opponents of Governor Meskill's actions indicated that it would be a conflict of interest for the growers to administer the program (Papirno 1974a; Driscoll 1974; Young 1975, 107–14, 173). The NEFWC responded that successful federal reviews showed its capacity to operate the health program.

Growers and government officials rushed to make changes for the 1974 season. The STGAA launched a public-relations campaign, touting improvements in the physical conditions of its labor camps and the addition of recreational facilities. A reader of the *Hartford Courant* expressed some cynicism about these changes: "Yes, things have changed though. Today, instead of buying slaves, we rent them—dirt cheap" (Caldas 1974; Papirno 1974e). Meanwhile, PRDL secretary Silva Recio asked the Amalgamated Meat Cutters to explore the possibility of unionizing migrant workers. While officials worked with the elected representatives of migrant workers to pursue their agenda, the president of the elected workers' committee strongly opposed any official efforts to organize workers, viewing these initiatives as part of a public campaign against ATA rather than a genuine effort to improve workers' living and working conditions (PRDL 1974a).

Since the STGAA still refused labor-organizing efforts, ATA approached each individual grower to organize their workplaces. In the summer of 1974, George M. Zabka, assistant vice president of the Consolidated Cigar Corporation, rejected any bargaining with ATA but agreed to meet with its representatives (Papirno 1974d). Growers sent their allies to distribute anti-union propaganda among workers in hope of breaking up a meeting at Camp Windsor. On July 28, 1974, they sponsored free field trips to interfere with ATA's plan to hold a union general assembly (1974f). Despite growers' resistance, however, ATA was gaining strength among farmworkers.

The 1974 harvest was the largest in two years, so more workers were needed, a gap filled by several Puerto Rican migrant women hired under the FLP contract.[5] They worked in the fields; earned the same wages as men, $2.15 an hour; and lived in similar, but separate, labor camps. Anthony F. Amenta, a representative of the growers, explained that the STGAA had always wanted to recruit women but that the MD did not. The STGAA hired the women because there were not enough local women who could sew tobacco leaves together. Amenta clarified to the press that the recruitment of women had no relation to ATA's efforts in Connecticut (Papirno 1974c).

Pressure from ATA and legal-services organizations led the Puerto Rican government to harden its stance against growers. The STGAA agreed to increase the hourly wage of $2.15 by 13 percent but refused to go higher. This offer contrasted with a 20 percent increase achieved by the MD in negotiations with other stateside growers. In March 1975 Secretary Silva Recio announced that the STGAA's salary offer was unacceptable and, consequently, the MD would recruit no contract workers. In 1975, 12,877 prospective migrants registered with the PRDL, but employers in ten states requested only 5,639 contract workers. The STGAA, with the witting or unwitting help of the MD, had dealt a blow to the FLP (*Hartford Courant* 1975b; PRBES 1975, 8).

By 1975 the Connecticut River Valley tobacco industry was in decline. In their attempts to find an alternative labor source, growers sought a ruling to remove Puerto Rico's contract program from the provisions of the Wagner-Peyser Act of 1933 (Bonilla-Santiago 1986, 128–31). After the Puerto Rican government refused to recruit migrant workers to work for less than $2.58 an hour, growers increased their recruitment efforts among the local population and were flooded with applications (Pollock 1981). But fewer than 400 of the 3,500 workers hired came from Connecticut and Massachusetts, a statistic that contradicted growers' insistence that migrant labor was not essential (*Hartford Courant* 1975a). The reduction of the migrant labor force prompted an article in the *Hartford Courant* criticizing the use of $750,000 in federal grants by government agencies and local organizations serving a migrant workforce of only 175 workers (Papirno 1975). By 1981 Puerto Ricans in the tobacco fields were a rarity. Anastasio was one of the few Puerto Ricans still working on the tobacco farms. His sister was raising his kids in Puerto Rico, and he would send her $45 of every $100 he made (*Hartford Courant* 1981).

Even with the STGAA's hostility, ATA continued to gain the support of farmworkers. By 1976 it had 9,000 members in Connecticut, Massachusetts, and New Jersey; offices in Hartford, Connecticut, and Glassboro and Vineland, New Jersey; and the backing of the AFL-CIO and several labor unions in Connecticut and Puerto Rico (Bonilla-Santiago 1986, 124–27). ATA was becoming so successful that Arthur West, president of the New Jersey Farm Bureau, threatened to withdraw from the 1976 contract negotiations with the Puerto Rican government if a labor union was present. Phillip Alampi, New Jersey secretary of agriculture, also expressed concern about a labor union for

Puerto Rican farmworkers (132; *New York Times* 1976). In a partial concession the PRDL eliminated the contract language requiring farmers to retain legal counsel in Puerto Rico, thus stopping Puerto Rico Legal Services from filing suits against growers in insular courts (Silva Recio 1976a).

Organizing farmworkers was costly, so in 1976 ATA joined with the UFW-Northeast Organizing Committee, which offered financial and logistical support. Juan Irizarry became the northeast regional coordinator of the UFW, which, in 1977, opened an office in Vineland, New Jersey. Before long, however, disputes with the UFW began to take a toll on the ATA. Bonilla-Santiago argues that the disputes were ideological because Irizarry believed in direct, violent confrontation and insurgent actions, in contrast to César Chávez's pacifist and nonviolent stance. Irizarry also accused Chávez of not supporting legislation to organize farmworkers in Massachusetts. Irizarry was explicit that ATA's relationship with the UFW depended on support from Chávez and the UFW. In response, Chávez's support for the ATA decreased and Irizarry eventually left both the ATA and the UFW. Chávez and the UFW were also distracted by a conflict with the Teamsters Union in California. Ángel Domínguez, a former ATA organizer, offered another explanation for the split: the UFW's refusal to pay the salaries of ATA organizers led to the end of their collaboration. ATA was also getting heat from workers who denounced its connections with the PSP (1986, 97, 134–36; Llamas 1977, 35; *New York Times* 1976). This is how the first largest effort of organizing Puerto Rican migrant farmworkers ended, but from which new mobilizations to serve migrant workers emerged.

### LEGAL BATTLES IN THE APPLE ORCHARDS

In September 1976 a New England apple grower fired a group of Puerto Ricans at the beginning of the harvest who, he alleged, did not know how to pick apples. The workers traveled from Maine, without money and unable to communicate in English, after their employer put them on a bus with instructions to go to the MD's Boston Office. The office was closed when they arrived, leaving them stranded. They had been fired after complaining about poor working conditions, wages, meals, and housing (Aldarondo 1976; Kirchheimer 1976).

The decades-long tension over employing Puerto Ricans instead of guest workers came to a head in the apple industry of the eastern United States in the 1970s. Apple growers argued that Puerto Ricans did not know how to pick apples and that the FLP contract was onerous. Migrant legal-services organizations, workers, and the Puerto Rican government waged a legal battle against apple growers who refused to hire Puerto Ricans, litigation that crippled the standing of the MD with employers and the USDL and contributed to the demise of the FLP.

The United States has a long history of importing guest workers for the apple industry. The Immigration and Nationality Act of 1952 embedded this policy in the system of H-2 visas, which required employers to hire any domestic worker who asked for a job in the first half of the apple-picking season before hiring guest workers (Martin 2014, 42–43). Willard Wirtz, secretary of labor under the Johnson administration, restricted the H-2 program to the sugar and apple industries and considered eliminating the importation of guest workers altogether. Nevertheless, by the 1970s H-2 apple workers from the British Caribbean numbered from five thousand to six thousand per year (Hahamovitch 2014, 23).

The Puerto Rican government attempted to negotiate with apple growers through the Farm Labor Executive Committee (FLEC), which represented growers in New England, New York, Virginia, and West Virginia, but the FLEC took the position that the FLP contract was too expensive, and high-ranking officials in the USDL supported their claim (Aders 1976). Migrant Legal Action Programs, in Washington, DC, sued on behalf of Puerto Rican and other domestic workers, arguing that they were being displaced by H-2 workers. Growers insisted that they needed foreign workers because Puerto Ricans were unavailable due to the onerous contract imposed by the Puerto Rican government. In *Galan v. Dunlop* the court ruled in the growers' favor.[6] The government of Puerto Rico joined in an appeal of the ruling while it began negotiating the 1976 contract (PRBES 1975, 3; Turner 1976). In a 1976 congressional hearing to amend the Immigration and Nationality Act, PRDL secretary Silva Recio explained his position:

> No employer is forced to sign our contract. He may seek other domestic workers, but it is obviously wrong to permit an employer to obtain foreign workers by refusing to agree to terms which other American employers have found reasonable and workable. This amounts to permitting foreign workers to tear down the standards already established for American workers. (1976b, 9–10)

During the spring of 1976, the FLEC again began negotiations with the Puerto Rican government, which argued that its contract was very similar to the West Indian contract. The two parties reached an agreement by July that included the placement of a thousand contract workers in the 1976 apple harvest, elimination of a clause requiring employers to provide workers three hot meals daily, the hiring of an adequate number of workers who would be monitored by the Puerto Rican officials, and an agreement to forgo any legal challenges to the importation of H-2 workers (Bustelo 1975).

As of September 2, 1976, the New England Apple Council had not signed the agreement, and growers from New York's Champlain region had not contacted the MD. One grower refused to accept the workers assigned to his farm, and many others were violating the negotiated memorandum of understanding (Vilches 1976). The chair of the FLEC indicated to an MD official that only "over my dead body there would be any Puerto Rican workers picking apples in Wayne County" (Quirós 1977). Other New York growers resigned from the FLEC to avoid complying with the agreement (Green 1976).

The economic recession of the 1970s hit Puerto Rico hard, increasing unemployment. In 1976 the FLP assisted five thousand contract migrant workers, out of ten thousand workers registered for farm-labor jobs (Lovler [1976?]). One of the workers was Reinaldo Hernández Flecha, twenty years old, unemployed, and married, with his wife expecting a second child. He left Puerto Rico on September 13, 1976, expecting to return home with money after eight weeks in a Virginia apple orchard but returned after only two weeks with $14.55 for three days of work.

The FLP contract with the FLEC set a $2.47 minimum wage per hour, but when Hernández Flecha arrived in Virginia, the grower informed him that workers would be paid $0.27 per bushel. After growers' deductions for meals, Social Security, and transportation, workers got checks for $0.25, $0.48, and $1.25. Not only that, Hernández Flecha said, "when we arrived, the barracks living quarters for about 150 men were really dirty and we had to clean it up." He added, "The food was so bad we couldn't eat it. The coffee was coffee in name only. For lunch we got bread with a piece of cheese, mortadella and ham. Dinner was rice that I don't even know what color it was with a piece of chicken that was cold and hard" (Lovler [1976?]). Workers protested and refused to work until the employers paid them hourly wages, provided them with decent meals, and improved the general working and living conditions. The growers reacted by firing dissidents and sending them back to Puerto Rico.

The workers stranded in Boston were in a different situation. Their employer refused to pay for their return tickets. Raymond, a twenty-three-year-old worker, had been told they would be paid $2.69 an hour, but the employer told them that they would be paid a piece rate of $0.35 per bushel. Aurelio, who had been a migrant worker for six years, thought they would receive three meals a day. Instead, the grower gave workers money to buy and cook their own food. The money was only enough to buy milk, cheese, bread, and hamburger meat. When these workers went to talk to the employer, they were told to go back to work. Because they insisted on discussing the problem, the employer fired them for breaking the contract (Kirchheimer 1976).

Trying to account for this turn of events, MD official Lionel de Jesús stated, "Basically, we feel this problem goes back awhile. In the past the growers brought Jamaicans up to pick the apple crop and they were very much at the whim of the growers. They were told to work under difficult conditions—I hate to say this—but, like slave labor" (Kirchheimer 1976). Some growers would put domestic workers to work at piece rates in orchards where harvest yields were lowest, setting aside the best crops to be harvested by H-2 workers (Rola 1977). Growers also provided H-2 workers with better housing conditions and meals. In this way apple growers argued that Puerto Rican pickers' productivity was low and that they could not do quality work. After almost thirty years of the FLP, however, the Puerto Ricans hired for the apple harvest were knowledgeable about the work and the rules, and they were ready to challenge employers.

Puerto Ricans had been harvesting apples since the 1950s (Atwood 1954; *Hartford Courant* 1952), but growers still cited lack of experience as an excuse for not hiring them. Even so, by the early 1970s growers unaffiliated with associations were using a substantial number of Puerto Ricans with no problems, for example, as apple pickers in New York's Hudson and Champlain Valleys and as peach pickers (P. Miller 1972, 29).

Growers found other excuses for not hiring Puerto Ricans. One argument growers used against Puerto Ricans was racial. One stated that "Puerto Ricans aren't able to do apple-picking work. . . . They are physically too small to do this work. . . . The men are used to more low-level work, such as picking berries" (Kirchheimer 1976). Growers deemed tall Jamaicans to be better apple pickers than Puerto Ricans, whose shorter stature made them more suited to harvesting stoop-labor crops (Associated Press 1978, 1983). Another rationalization for discriminating against Puerto Rican workers was their limited English-language fluency. MD official Carlos F. Rola (1982) countered,

FIGURE 16. Worker picking peaches, 1991. Photo by Doel Vázquez. Courtesy of the Records of the Department of Puerto Rican Community Affairs, Archives of the Puerto Rican Diaspora, Centro de Estudios Puertorriqueños, Hunter College, City University of New York.

Some of those veterans and others that have served in our Armed Forces were farmworkers. I mention this because, even though English is not a requirement for employment, one still hears comments such as Puerto Rican workers are not skilled enough to pick apples and that "they" don't speak English. When one contemplates the fact that "they" are able to disassemble and reassemble rifles, etc. blindfolded, among other things, and are able to adapt to the technology of war and peace, such comments are both ridiculous and silly.

Growers complained, too, about Puerto Ricans' low productivity and tendency to refuse to work. But an MD investigation concluded that workers' performance potential had been evaluated before they underwent the sixty hours of training required by the contract. If some workers left jobs voluntarily before the fulfillment of their contracts, this was because they encountered large deductions from their paychecks. Other workers said that they were willing to work but that growers pushed them out (Wagenheim 1976).

The PRDL attempted to transport workers without contracts for the 1977 apple harvest, but legal-services organizations filed a petition to stop the recruitment of noncontract workers for the apple harvest (Bayó 1977; *El Mundo* 1977; *El Vocero* 1977; Ilerio 1977; *San Juan Star* 1977). The same year, in response to the firing of workers during the previous year's apple harvest, legal-services organizations in Puerto Rico and the United States filed a class-action suit on behalf of the workers against the Puerto Rican government, the USDL, and the apple growers. The U.S. First Circuit Court ruled that Puerto Ricans could be considered unavailable if they did not accept the wages offered in the job orders that growers filed with the PRDL. It also ruled that benefits provided to H-2 workers must also be given to domestic workers, but that growers did not have to offer better benefits, as requested by workers.[7] In practice, the court's decision established that the U.S. government, nations sending H-2 workers, and growers could determine the conditions under which domestic workers would be employed, but neither these workers—nor the government of Puerto Rico—could change those conditions (Semler 1983, 215).

Under the new PNP administration of Carlos Romero Barceló (1977–84), the PRDL lobbied U.S. secretary of labor F. Ray Marshall for an amendment to the Wagner-Peyser Act that would include the guarantees provided by the FLP contract (Aldarondo [1977?]; Quirós 1977), but in 1978 the Puerto Rican government accepted the minimum level of benefits set by the USDL, waiving the use of its contract and benefits. In return, the USDL assisted with the hiring of 992 workers from Puerto Rico, paying $275,000 for transportation, housing, and meals. Although many growers took this opportunity to hire Puerto Ricans, many of those workers were quickly dismissed or given poor work opportunities, which led them to leave their jobs voluntarily. Fifteen days after the beginning of the harvest, only 97 Puerto Ricans were still working. By firing the other workers before half of the harvest was complete, growers avoided paying for transportation and subsistence costs (PRES 1978, 3–8). Fearing a repeat of this situation, the Puerto Rican government refused to waive the contract requirements for the 1979 apple harvest, and no Puerto Ricans were hired that year. In the 1980s the government again attempted to place workers in the apple harvest but failed, as apple growers succeeded in maintaining their preference for H-2 workers (Semler 1983, 218–19, 227).

Labor forces are constructed in part by pitting myths about the quality of work and productivity of one ethnic group against others (Griffith 1993, 7), but the firing of workers by apple growers also shows that labor shortages in

U.S. agriculture derive, at least in part, from growers' need for disposable workers. Growers searched for any and all legal maneuvers to get rid of Puerto Ricans because hiring them and other domestic workers meant more complications and less profit. Hiring H-2 workers kept agricultural wages low and saved growers the hassle of withholding income taxes and paying into Social Security. In 1980 eleven of the states using H-2 workers ranked among the bottom fifteen states with the lowest agricultural wages, while growers who did not use H-2 workers paid their workers more (Associated Press 1978, 1983; Semler 1983, 213).

Although eastern apple growers using H-2 workers manipulated the USDL's mechanisms for recruitment and deployment of labor, citing labor shortages and the onerous burden of hiring Puerto Rican and other domestic workers, the ultimate legal battles over farm labor were fought in the district courts, which tended to favor growers (Griffith 1993, 211). Puerto Ricans were imperfect migrant workers for apple growers' associations because their citizenship provided them with rights and access to services. The Puerto Rican government did receive a favorable decision from the courts in July 1982, when the U.S. Supreme Court ruled eight to zero that it could sue to force East Coast apple growers to hire Puerto Ricans instead of Jamaicans. This decision came too late, however, to stop the decline of the FLP (Seaberry 1982; United Press International 1982).

In 1969 the FLP transported 9,463 migrant workers to New Jersey, out of a total workforce of 33,000, but in 1977 New Jersey farmers hired only 2,000 contract workers out of a total workforce of 36,000. With onset of labor organizing in Connecticut and the disputes with apple growers, the total number of contract workers declined by 80 percent, from 21,864 in 1969 to 4,284 in 1977 (Bonilla-Santiago 1988, 11–12). But while the mechanization of agriculture, urbanization, and the reduction in the number of farms reduced the demand for migrant workers, the MD was experiencing increased demand for services in urban communities (Berrios 1981).

## LABOR ORGANIZING IN THE 1980S

In 1978, after working for three days, five hundred Puerto Rican workers with three-month contracts were fired by apple growers in northern New York and replaced by H-2 workers from Jamaica who would work for $1.00 less than the $2.90 per hour required by the FLP contract (Patterson 2012,

9–10). Community organizers established a food bank for the fired workers and negotiated with the growers' association for their return airplane tickets to Puerto Rico. By the late 1970s, however, support for the creation of a farmworkers labor union had waned. The National Labor Relations Act still excluded farmworkers and, with that, their right to unionization (*CALC Report/TWC Bulletin* 1984, 11). Activists were not deterred, however. Some organizers from the struggles of 1973 to 1976 joined the renewed effort, led by Ángel Domínguez, the former ATA organizer and META staff member. Domínguez was working for the organization Philadelphia Farmworkers Opportunities when he was contacted about the plight of Puerto Ricans in the apple harvest. He organized and mobilized a group of supporters, forming the Northeast Farmworkers' Support Committee (NFSC), composed of advocates from farmworker and legal-service organizations (Bonilla-Santiago 1986, 222). After intense debates the NFSC created a workers' committee that traveled to Washington, DC, to meet with representatives of the USDL to explain the situation of migrant apple pickers. The NFSC filed a lawsuit against the growers, which was resolved four years later in the workers' favor, with the payment of three months' wages and airfares to Puerto Rico (*CALC Report/TWC Bulletin* 1984, 10).

During this time the New Jersey State Assembly was considering raising the state minimum wage to the federal minimum. The New Jersey Farm Bureau wanted to exclude farmworkers from such protection, providing fertile ground for organizing efforts in New Jersey. In 1978 farmworkers and advocacy groups demonstrated in front of the New Jersey State House, demanding that farmworkers receive the same minimum wage as other workers (Bonilla-Santiago 1986, 90). The NFSC mobilized between two hundred and three hundred workers and supporters to protest the possible elimination of farmworkers from the bill. Farmers also lobbied the legislature, arguing that because farmworkers worked seasonally, they should be excluded from the new minimum-wage law. Nevertheless, the New Jersey legislature approved the bill and extended coverage to farmworkers. This concession was a victory for the NFSC that spurred the organization of New Jersey farmworkers.

Momentum was lost, however, as many initial members of NFSC lost interest in the hard work of grassroots organizing. With only two members left, the NFSC invited local farmworkers to join in the creation of a new organization. From March through June 1979, the Farmworkers' Organizing Committee distributed questionnaires to 500 farmworkers to learn their priorities and needs and assess their interest in creating a labor union. It became clear that an organization that would educate workers about their rights would be the best option for getting them involved. As a result, an informative assembly was organized, which met with 150 farmworkers present, to discuss pesticide use, housing, wages, and the right to organize.

Moreover, in 1975 the American Civil Liberties Union of New Jersey (ACLU-NJ) established the Farm Workers Rights Project, using $40,000 in grants for legal services. The project opened an office in Glassboro with a small staff who visited farms in Vineland, Bridgeton, and Swedesboro. Initially, the project engaged in litigation to challenge work and housing violations and police abuse and provided legal assistance to workers charged with petty crimes and others who sought help with unemployment-compensation claims (Bonilla-Santiago 1986, 139–42; *CALC Report/TWC Bulletin* 1984, 9–10; Patterson 2012, 57–59).

By 1978 ACLU-NJ's Farm Workers Rights Project had become inactive, but the Farmworkers' Organizing Committee convinced it to redirect the project from legal services to worker education. On August 28, 1979, following a meeting of organizers and twenty-eight farmworkers, the ACLU-NJ's project became the Agricultural Workers Support Committee (CATA), with Ángel Domínguez as project director. CATA organized it first annual assembly from which a support committee emerged, composed of lawyers, clergy, and advocates. In all, CATA comprised an executive committee, a board of directors, staff, and a membership of a thousand farmworkers. From 1979 to 1980 the organization was run by the project director, an administrative assistant, two lawyers, one social worker, administrative support staff, six organizers, two paralegals, one network coordinator, and a group of volunteers. CATA, whose funding came from private and religious foundations and legal-services organizations, was innovative since it placed organizers in Puerto Rico as well as New Jersey. CATA's board of directors met with workers, and the organization held an annual assembly, where members approved all reports and discussed important issues (Bonilla-Santiago 1986, 143–47; *CALC Report/TWC Bulletin* 1984, 11).

During the 1980 harvest, CATA organized workers who struck against Sunny Slope in Gloucester County, New Jersey. The Sunny Slope workers had attempted to resolve their issues by organizing a committee to present their complaints to the company about not having enough time to eat, insufficient drinking water in the fields, and too few rest periods. This committee asked CATA for assistance, but the farmer refused to meet, and after he fired the workers' leaders, all workers went on strike. The growers broke the strike using legal maneuvers and day laborers from Philadelphia, but the strikers and their organization persevered. CATA filed a lawsuit against Sunny Slope, arguing that the workers had been fired because of their attempts to organize. The court ruled in favor of workers, forcing Sunny Slope to reinstate the fired workers. In return, workers agreed not to strike before August 1980 and to avoid any type of violence on the farm (Bonilla-Santiago 1986, 91, 148–49).

After the strike the workers decided to demand a wage increase to $4.00 per hour, additional pay for overtime, and elimination of the $0.45 fee deducted by the Glassboro Service Association (GSA) for employment services. CATA lawyers began negotiations with lawyers for Sunny Slope and the GSA, who took the position that the Puerto Rican contract precluded any negotiation or strikes by workers. After GSA refused to negotiate, fifty farmworkers voted to strike, and on August 13 they staged the first organized strike in New Jersey's agricultural industry. Sunny Slope sued the workers, seeking to evict them from the camps and prohibiting their organizing and picketing. The judge ordered workers out of the labor camp and barred the use of bullhorns by strikers, thus reducing the impact of their demonstration. CATA transported the banished workers, found temporary housing for them, and provided food. Some thirteen migrants returned to work, but thirty-seven remained on the picket line. When the GSA brought in Puerto Rican strikebreakers, CATA sought—and was denied—a federal court order prohibiting the use of replacement workers. After the ruling the USDL did not allow the GSA to negotiate a new contract in Puerto Rico, and CATA concluded that they needed to be financially prepared to support protesting workers (Bonilla-Santiago 1986, 149–51; Janson 1980).

By the 1980s Puerto Rican agriculture was in crisis. Sugarcane cultivation had diminished to the point that rum-producing companies were importing molasses, and the government provided a loan to a large Israeli agribusiness, ignoring the needs of local farmers. Work in agriculture was reduced to the coffee industry and other small operations. As high unemployment pushed people to migrate, it was not unusual to find workers with two or three years of college working on farms in southern New Jersey, some of whom facilitated CATA's organizing among migrants. In 1983 CATA organized a march in Puerto Rico, with more than a thousand migrant farmworkers participating. A year later CATA began to organize self-help support committees on farms in New Jersey and in small towns and neighborhoods in Puerto Rico (Bonilla-Santiago 1986, 90, 156; *CALC Report/TWC Bulletin* 1984, 7–8, 11).

CATA staff identified access to health care as one of the most important problems that workers faced, after finding men in camps with broken legs, lying on their beds for days without seeing a doctor. Alcoholism continued to plague migrants. One worker who had never missed a day on the job during his twenty-year tenure with the same farmer began suffering from depression and drank every night until he died of cirrhosis. When the CATA staff asked the farmer for help with the funeral, he refused, saying it was not his problem and that the deceased worker was one of "their" people (*CALC Report/TWC Bulletin* 1984, 9).

Another health problem stemmed from handling pesticides. In 1984, after a farmer in southern New Jersey sprayed pesticide, six workers in the field at the time suffered rashes, but the farmer did not get them medical attention. CATA helped these workers and filed a complaint with the New Jersey Department of Environmental Protection. Another worker developed an allergy to a pesticide, and his hands became swollen, scaly, and filled with pus. His employer refused to sign a disability-insurance application or provide safety equipment for men working in sprayed areas (*CALC Report/ TWC Bulletin* 1984, 8–9).

While CATA focused on providing social services, a committee of farmworkers, joined by representatives of CATA, ACLU-NJ, and Professor Robert F. Williams of the Rutgers School of Law–Camden, formed Agricultural Workers Organizing Committee (COTA; Comité Organizador de Trabajadores Agrícolas), which the CATA Board of Directors officially recognized as an affiliate on July 20, 1984. For a year COTA attempted to organize more than twenty thousand workers in New Jersey and Pennsylvania. Finally, on September 29, 1985, farmworkers at the Levin Farm in New Jersey gained the right to representation under COTA. At this farm migrant workers had been earning $3.35 per hour for five years, working twelve to fourteen hours a day with no overtime pay or protection against pesticides and living in poor conditions without laundry facilities (CATA [1985?]a, [1985?]b, [1985?]c). In 1986 the owners of Levin Farm refused to sign the agreement with COTA and brought in nonunionized workers. COTA went to court to force the company to negotiate. To avoid imprisonment, the farmers agreed. This incident raised sufficient concern at the New Jersey Farm Bureau that farmers began to raise workers' salaries, offer round-trip tickets, and improve housing conditions (CATA 1985; Domínguez 1985; Knight-Ridder Newspapers 1986). One farmer told a COTA organizer, "If the farmers worked together like the Puerto Ricans, we'd have you licked.

When one of my workers was sick, the rest carried him for six weeks. Farmers are like a chicken house. When one goes down, the others rip them apart. Just go watch them at the Vineland Auction someday!" (COTA 1985).

Farmers enlisted local government officials in their effort to resist COTA. The Cumberland Agricultural Extension agent encouraged farmers to attend a meeting at a government facility to hear from an antilabor attorney about how to fight COTA, but the organization pressed on, organizing workers at the Camsco Produce Company, a subsidiary of Campbell Soup Company, in Pennsylvania (COTA 1985; Bonilla-Santiago 1986, 171). Litigation remained one of COTA's and CATA's most important strategies, including a case brought against farmers that upheld farmworkers' right to collective bargaining under New Jersey's constitution (ACLU-NJ 2010, 3; Patterson 2012, 57–59).[8]

In the 1990s CATA's efforts continued despite a dramatic reduction in the number of Puerto Rican farmworkers and the elimination of the FLP. COTA spearheaded the organization of workers in the mushroom industry in Pennsylvania, and in 1993 workers struck against Kaolin Mushroom Farms. CATA denounced violations of OSHA regulations and the lack of sanitary facilities for workers and sponsored a seminar on labor organizing with the Labor Relations Institute (Instituto de Relaciones del Trabajo) at the University of Puerto Rico (Galafá 1993; *Philadelphia Inquirer* 1993; F. Ramírez 1993a).

## THE DEMISE OF THE FARM LABOR PROGRAM

In 1984 PPD regained power with the election of Rafael Hernández Colón to a second term as governor of Puerto Rico. Seeing the potential for support from Puerto Ricans in the United States, the second Hernández Colón administration (1985–92) transformed the MD, which at its peak had consisted of thirteen offices throughout the United States and the Orientation Program in Puerto Rico. On August 16, 1989, the Puerto Rican legislature enacted public law 58, transferring the MD's functions and resources, including the FLP, to the Department of Puerto Rican Community Affairs in the United States (DPRCA; Departamento de Asuntos de la Comunidad Puertorriqueña en los Estados Unidos). With this law the Puerto Rican government recognized the importance of stateside communities to the vitality of the insular economy. MD director Nydia Velázquez became the secretary of DPRCA (Segundo 1992, 759n4).

The same problems that had plagued the FLP for more than forty years continued into the 1990s. Farmers complained about workers leaving their jobs before the end of their contracts or not arriving to the farms at all, poor performance, and the presence of "troublemakers." Workers complained about unpaid salaries, lack of medical attention, and poor working and living conditions (Peck 1991, 765; Pudlin 1991). The reduction in the number of workers and the DPRCA's new priorities eroded the FLP. By the late 1980s, instead of requiring contracts with individual farmers, MD officials negotiated general contracts with state employment agencies. The continual influx of noncontract workers and the success of the apple growers' challenges also undercut the FLP. As farmers complained that the application and contract process for Puerto Ricans took too long for their needs, MD officials became concerned that agricultural employers would increase their use of the H-2A visa program and avoid hiring Puerto Ricans (Talbot 1988).

The FLP was still important for Puerto Rico. The DPRCA reported that farmworkers earned $9,052,909 for the 1989 season, of which $4,502,382 was earned on GSA member farms (J. López 1990). But H-2A laborers working for Glassboro at this time received the Adverse Effect Wage Rate, which was higher (around $4.85 per hour) than the $3.88 per hour migrants earned for general agricultural work and $4.05 per hour for work in nurseries (Griffith 1991, 1039–40).

In June 1992 the DPRCA met with representatives of the USDL's Boston area Employment and Training Administration, New England state employment agencies, and employers to argue for hiring more migrant workers. Participants concurred on the need for orientation materials in Spanish, Spanish-speaking staff, and cultural-diversity programs. DPRCA agreed to help by sending at least one English speaker with every group of migrant workers, offering legal advice to growers, informing workers about contract provisions and the H-2A program, giving workers a summary of their job descriptions in Spanish, supplying them with a laminated pocket card with emergency call numbers, and providing growers' associations with copies of the health and good-conduct certifications issued to workers during recruitment (DPRCA 1993).

In the November 1992 gubernatorial election, Pedro Roselló González won, ushering in a large PNP majority in the Legislative Assembly. Zaida "Cucusa" Hernández Torres became the Speaker of the Puerto Rico House of Representatives. One of the legislative goals she shared with the new governor was to dismantle offices and programs, such as the DPRCA and the FLP, that facilitated support for the PPD and the autonomous territorial status of Puerto Rico. Under the PNP government, neoliberal considerations and the ideology of statehood superseded the interests of stateside Puerto Ricans.

On March 9, 1993, an MD official stressed the danger in delaying negotiations for the agricultural contract for the 1993 season. Unless negotiations, for which no planning had yet taken place, began soon, it was unlikely that migrant farmworkers would be hired, to the detriment of the rural economy in Puerto Rico. He indicated that Atlantic Blueberry had contracted 59 workers in 1992, who earned $386,143.20. Glassboro had contracted 363 workers, who put in forty-eight hours a week for twenty-eight weeks, earning approximately $2,463,754. The program also helped 74 workers without contracts, who earned $502,253 (F. Ramírez 1993b). As contract negotiations stalled, the GSA, the largest employer of migrant farmworkers throughout the history of the FLP, hired Mexicans for the 1993 season.

On April 15, 1993, the Roselló González administration abolished the DPRCA, transferring some of its duties to the Puerto Rican Federal Affairs Administration (effective July 1, 1993), thereby reducing the number of stateside offices. Demand for Puerto Rican farmworkers in the U.S. Northeast persisted, however. Franklin Mushroom Farms in Connecticut asked the Puerto Rican government for assistance in recruiting migrants, explaining, "We have good Puerto Rican employees. . . . We would like more. We know there are people looking for work in this area. We will caution them of the distance and new job decision. It is to everyone's advantage that we hire long term, successful employees." Franklin Farms paid $5.00 an hour and offered workers medical and life insurance and holiday pay after three months, as well as loans (N. Smith 1992).

Smaller flows of migrant farmworkers from rural communities in Puerto Rico to the States continued after the elimination of the FLP. Anthropologist Elsa Planell Larrinaga documented the migration from Barrio Pezuela, in the municipality of Lares, to Pedricktown, New Jersey. Pezuela was an area with high unemployment and low levels of schooling, so sending migrants to U.S. farms was good for the local economy. Workers migrated for financial reasons, responding to underemployment during the *tiempo muerto* and because they needed to pay debts or buy or improve a house. They could earn an income of $800 to $1,200 a month as farmworkers, compared to $400 to $600 per month in agricultural work in Puerto Rico, making around $14,000 per year, while nonmigrants would earn only between $7,800 to $9,000 per year (1996, 108–9, 226–31). Planell Larrinaga commented on the resources

FIGURE 17. Farmworkers being transported, 1991. Photo by Doel Vázquez. Courtesy of the Records of the Department of Puerto Rican Community Affairs, Archives of the Puerto Rican Diaspora, Centro de Estudios Puertorriqueños, Hunter College, City University of New York.

return migrants put into their property: "It is common to see homes that keep growing from year to year. In these cases, the structure is evidence of the amount of work which the migrant worker has taken up in United States farms and the number of times he has had to turn to migration" (105).

The gains of some workers notwithstanding, the recruitment pool of migrant farmworkers in Puerto Rico had shrunk significantly, from 45.2 percent of agricultural workers in 1940 to 2.8 percent in 1990 (Planell Larrinaga 1996, 220). The number of farmworkers decreased further after the inauguration of the North American Free Trade Agreement, in 1994, led to an explosion of undocumented workers on farms in regions of traditional Puerto Rican seasonal migration. Mexican workers also arrived to work in areas like Chester, Pennsylvania, after getting to know Puerto Rican workers in Michigan who had worked in the Pennsylvania mushroom industry (V. Garcia 1997). Undocumented workers settled for lower wages, worse working conditions, and irregular work schedules, with no need for employers to provide transportation or government aid at the end of the harvest. As a result, many Puerto Ricans stopped migrating (Planell Larrinaga 1996, 102, 106–7).

Litigation against growers was the only alternative that workers grouped in organizations such as META, ATA, and CATA had to fight powerful growers' associations and agribusinesses. Nonetheless, from 1969 on the FLP suffered blows that led to its termination in 1993. During this period the PPD lost its absolute control of the government when the PNP won the governorship in 1968, 1976, 1980, and 1992, and neoliberal policies at the international and federal levels began to erode government-intervention policies, reducing support for managed migration and migrants. The Nixon, Ford, and Reagan administrations curtailed some of the gains achieved by migrant farmworkers, and apple growers effectively blocked the preference for Puerto Ricans over guest workers.

The formal demise of the FLP in 1993 closed an important chapter in the history of Puerto Rican migration to the United States. While governments in other parts of the world began to manage labor migration, leaders of the prostatehood PNP saw any involvement in stateside communities as a confirmation of the existence of a Puerto Rican national identity that undercut their arguments for statehood. Nevertheless, seasonal farm-labor migration remains an alternative for a small number of Puerto Ricans who seek to escape unemployment and uncertainty in times of deep economic crisis and austerity policies in twenty-first-century Puerto Rico.

# *Epilogue*

IMMEDIATELY AFTER HURRICANE MARÍA, in September 2017, I remembered what a Puerto Rican farmworker in southern New Jersey told me in the summer of 2010. He said, "We do this out of necessity. It is not easy to leave your family and come here to work. When there is a family emergency, you are not there for them, and all of the sudden you have to take an airplane to go and help." I could only imagine the anguish of hundreds of farmworkers working in the States during "María" who had no news about their families and could not travel to Puerto Rico. I watched a news report on how, in the aftermath of the hurricane, an elderly woman sent a message to her son who was working on a U.S. farm so he would know she was fine. October and November are when migrant farmworkers usually return to their homes, but after the 2017 season, some of those workers no longer had homes to return to. I am certain that the devastation caused by Hurricane María will force seasonal farmworkers—and many workers new to farmwork—to migrate to the United States for a long time to come.

The hiring of migrant Puerto Rican workers in U.S. agriculture at different historical moments and contexts has depended on their legal status within the U.S. nation, illustrating the intersection of colonialism, citizenship, and immigration in these processes. After Puerto Rico became a U.S. territory in 1898, the U.S. Supreme Court allowed Puerto Ricans into the labor market by defining them as nationals with limited rights. As U.S. nationals, they migrated to Hawaii, Cuba, and other regions on the periphery of the U.S. empire. Colonial labor migration became an option for U.S. sugar corporations trying to avoid restrictive immigration laws, such as the Chinese Exclusion Act and the Foran Act. Since Puerto Rican colonial migrants could not be deported, many local officials and residents objected to their migration, fearing they would become dependent on welfare (García-Colón 2017b). This fear continues to dog migrants in the twenty-first century.

By 1941 Puerto Ricans were deemed to be "native-born" citizens, which led to more intense lobbying by colonial officials for their inclusion in wartime efforts to sustain U.S. agricultural production. Using the Mexican Bracero Program as a model, the Puerto Rican government established the Bureau of Employment and Migration, which housed the Migration Division and the Farm Labor Program (FLP), and encouraged the federal government to give priority to Puerto Ricans over guest workers. These agencies developed a contract system to manage the migration and hiring of seasonal farmworkers in the States. In the 1950s migrants were further integrated into the U.S. labor market through amendments to the Wagner-Peyser Act of 1933, which gave Puerto Ricans preference over guest workers.

Despite these advances, officials regularly confronted employers opposed to hiring Puerto Ricans because they could not be deported, particularly after the Immigration and Nationality Act of 1952 formally acknowledged Puerto Rico as part of the United States and required employers to prove that they could not find U.S. citizens to hire instead of guest workers. Because hiring Puerto Rican farmworkers depended on limiting how many guest workers entered the United States, the number of workers hired under the FLP increased substantially when the Bracero Program ended in 1964 and new restrictions were imposed on guest workers. By 1969 the FLP was transporting more than twenty thousand workers to U.S. farms (García-Colón 2017b).

From the early 1970s through the early 1990s, migrant workers maneuvered within a social field dominated by guest work, neoliberalism, and free trade. Legal battles between labor activists, workers, the government of Puerto Rico, and growers shaped new regulations for the use or rejection of Puerto Ricans in U.S. farm labor. Intense labor organizing among tobacco workers increased their undesirability with growers and farmers in other industries. This sentiment came to a head when apple growers refused to employ Puerto Ricans, leading to legal challenges to both growers and the FLP. For the most part the courts sided with the growers, limiting the applicability of the Wagner-Peyser Act and the preference for Puerto Ricans over guest workers. In Puerto Rico the Roselló González administration (1993–2000) ended the FLP in 1993, a year before the United States became part of North American Free Trade Agreement (NAFTA). Thereafter Mexican migration exploded as large growers and associations began to replace Puerto

Ricans with Mexicans and manufacturers moved their operations from Puerto Rico to Mexico (García-Colón 2017b). Colonial neoliberalism had finally succeeded in eliminating the FLP.

Puerto Rico has experienced dramatic economic and social changes during the first two decades of the twenty-first century. The economic crisis in public finance caused by an unpayable debt of more than $72 billion has propelled the migration of more than half a million residents to the United States. Contemporary migrants come from a U.S. territory where a colonial neoliberal state, controlled by an unelected, presidentially appointed fiscal control board, deepens a long-standing recession by enacting austerity programs that limit workers' rights and benefits. Since 2009 the economic crisis has decimated the construction and banking sectors and led to massive layoffs of government employees and the privatization of public services and corporations, all of which have increased unemployment and impelled farm-labor migration (Caraballo-Cueto and Lara 2018).

At the same time prejudice against Puerto Ricans in the States continues because of the perception that they are "foreigners." The nightly news still reports incidents of discrimination and labor exploitation and complaints about the fate of migrants. Events highlighted in social media show Puerto Ricans targeted by nativists for speaking Spanish and rejection of their Puerto Rican government-issued ID cards (Álvarez and Neal 2018; T. Miller 2018). The nativist, racist, and nationalist climate unleashed by the election of Donald Trump intensified the openness and severity of such incidents. Puerto Ricans experience discrimination on the streets and in jobs, stores, and government offices because of their names and accents or because they are heard speaking Spanish. As this book has shown, this is an old, ongoing story. It is part of my own experience in the United States, even in the classroom. Racism and U.S. colonialism have created an ambiguous citizenship for Puerto Ricans.

The Trump administration's aggressive enforcement of deportation is once again changing how immigration policies affect Puerto Ricans. Anti-immigrant sentiment and fees associated with guest-worker programs are making Puerto Ricans more attractive to the agricultural and food-processing industries (Waugh 2018). In the aftermath of Hurricane María, employers traveled to Puerto Rico in search of workers, although mostly for jobs in food processing and hotels. Headlines in the press about labor migration reveal, however, that the old problems persist. In the summer of 2017, social media and the Puerto Rican newspaper, *El Nuevo Día*, described contract workers as being sold into slavery in Alaska's food-processing factories. After intensive criticism Gov. Ricardo Roselló Nevares announced an investigation into this incident.

Puerto Rican migrants compose a tiny minority of farmworkers compared to the undocumented workers (53 percent) and Mexicans (75 percent) who constitute the majority of the U.S. farm labor force (Alves Pena 2009, 856–57; Gray 2010, 170; Pfeffer and Parra 2005, 4; 2006, 81; USDL 2005, ix).[1] Nonetheless, new workers are becoming part of the migratory flows and deepening the connections between communities in Puerto Rico and U.S. farms. Nowadays the difference is that the colonial neoliberal government—in Puerto Rico and Washington—is not interested in managing migration. The networks, infrastructure, knowledge, and flows established over decades facilitate contemporary migration without the need to foster it. Since 1993 most workers have migrated on their own or through job referrals through the Puerto Rico Department of Labor for the H-2A visa program. The department refers only around 1,000 to 2,000 workers through the interstate clearance system of the U.S. Department of Labor but, in sharp contrast to its practices from the 1940s through the 1980s, does not negotiate contracts or monitor the working and housing conditions of migrant workers (J. Delgado 2014; Santiago Caraballo 2014). Most farmworkers migrate without contracts, using decades-old connections with farmers, counting on only limited institutional support from the government of Puerto Rico and relying instead on the assistance of community and legal-services organizations (Griffith and Kissam 1995, 173–74, 180–82; García-Colón 2008; García-Colón and Meléndez 2013).

In a 2010 survey of 196 Puerto Rican farmworkers in the U.S. Northeast, Edwin Meléndez and I found that 73.6 percent were seasonal migrants. Most were men (97.4 percent) from eighteen to seventy-four years old, coming from rural wards mainly in the municipalities of Villalba, San Lorenzo, Yauco, Isabela, Caguas, Patillas, and San Sebastián. In upstate New York I met a group of migrant workers from Cidra, my hometown, some of whom were in their late forties and had lost jobs in construction. They work in agriculture because they lack formal schooling (64.7 percent have less than a high school diploma or GED) and unemployment is high in Puerto Rico. Almost 85 percent reported few or no English-language skills. These factors affect their ability to find permanent jobs in Puerto Rico, forcing them to migrate, where they encounter work and living conditions like those experienced by earlier generations of farmworkers (García-Colón and Meléndez 2013, 99–105).

Wages rank high in the decision to migrate. Seasonal farmworkers earn from $7.25 to $15.00 per hour, although most are at the lower end of the scale because they work on vegetable farms that pay lower wages. Among these farmworkers, seasonal migrants from Puerto Rico earn an average of $8.33 per hour. Migrants are well aware of the low wages in U.S. agriculture, but they base their decision to migrate on the still lower wages they would likely earn at home. The minimum wage in Puerto Rico is 70 percent of the federal minimum wage for exempted occupations, like agriculture. Many times the only work that they can find is in informal economic activities with even lower pay. The cost of supporting families in Puerto Rico is also higher than in the States (García-Colón and Meléndez 2013, 107–9; PRDL 2018).

The working and living conditions of twenty-first-century Puerto Ricans in U.S. agriculture are similar to those of immigrants and guest workers. Although citizenship provides access to unemployment benefits and legal protections, it does not shield them from discrimination and the inequalities arising from the dynamics of U.S. agriculture. Like other farmworkers, Puerto Ricans, in most states, do not have the right to collective bargaining, rest days, or overtime wages. They also confront a reputation for laziness because they can receive welfare services if they quit their jobs after rejecting unreasonable work routines and conditions (García-Colón and Meléndez 2013, 107–8; Gray and Kreyche 2007, 3, 6–8; Griffith and Kissam 1995, 247). The final irony is that when Puerto Ricans protest or reject the labor conditions offered by stateside farmers, their U.S. citizenship allows those farmers to demonstrate to the U.S. Department of Labor that they have made an effort to hire domestic workers before requesting temporary guest workers through the H-2A visa program.

If workers remain in or return to Puerto Rico, in addition to receiving unemployment benefits, they can often find temporary and off-the-books jobs to supplement their annual incomes and engage in economic activities (such as fishing or cultivating crops) that reduce their expenses. Yet seasonal migration remains their best option because of the limited opportunities to find well-paid, long-term jobs in Puerto Rico. Thus, migrants maintain strong connections to families, friends, and acquaintances in the States. By living in camps, saving money, and sending remittances, they have made seasonal migration a way of life, one that they sustain with the help of coworkers, friends, and family (García-Colón and Meléndez 2013, 107, 109–10; Griffith and Kissam 1995, 169; Griffith and Valdés Pizzini 2002).

Seasonal farmwork is part of migrant workers' hope for a better life. In the summer of 2010, I met a nineteen-year-old worker from San Lorenzo, Puerto Rico, in a labor camp in Vineland, New Jersey, who said that farmwork was his only viable option to earn enough money to support his recently born daughter. In Puerto Rico, after finding only retail jobs that offered twenty hours of work per week, he spoke with one of the older migrants from his neighborhood about migrating. I also talked with a single father from Utuado, Puerto Rico, who migrated with his daughters after he could not find a stable job. Seasonal migration was his only alternative to poverty and welfare dependence (García-Colón and Meléndez 2013, 111–12).

The historical forces and processes described in previous chapters laid the foundation for contemporary migration to stateside farm jobs. Puerto Ricans remain in U.S. agriculture even with its low wages and preference for undocumented and guest labor. Indeed, seasonal migrant farmworkers are part of Puerto Rico's integration into the larger regional and global capitalist order. The contemporary features of low-wage jobs in U.S. agriculture are still linked to flexible capitalist accumulation, free-trade agreements (such as NAFTA), U.S. imperialism and colonialism, and the immigration policies that emerge from these. Nevertheless, while a transnational approach explains certain aspects of migration, it obscures others, in particular the role of U.S. colonialism and citizenship in the history of migration and Puerto Rico's relationship with the federal government (García-Colón and Meléndez 2013, 113–15).

U.S. immigration policies are central to understanding Puerto Rican migrant farm labor, which has fluctuated as a result of guest-worker programs and deportation practices. Contradictorily, U.S. colonialism allowed the government of Puerto Rico to play a strong role in the formation of stateside Puerto Rican communities and to manage migration. It allowed the insertion of Puerto Rican officials into the agencies of the federal government and the establishment of migration offices in the United States. In this regard, the situation of Puerto Ricans is like that of past and present colonial migrants around the world, such as Filipinos in the United States and Algerians in France (García-Colón 2017b, 139–40).

The case of Puerto Rican migrant farm labor reveals that U.S. agriculture and the federal government favor workers who can be easily disposed after the harvest or for attempts to dispute injustice. But Puerto Ricans are not worse off because of undocumented and guest workers, nor are immigrants in a privileged position. Immigrants are not responsible for the loss of farm jobs by U.S. citizens, as nativists like to think. Rather, it is agribusinesses, farmers, and elected officials who choose to maintain unequal opportunities for agricultural laborers. All farmworkers deserve equal pay, living wages, decent working conditions, access to health care, and the right to organize labor unions. They deserve to work without fear of retaliation, getting fired, or being deported for denouncing unjust situations.

The history of farm-labor migration shows that Puerto Ricans are more than U.S. citizens; they are also colonial subjects. Immigration scholars should not indiscriminately compare the experiences of colonial migrants with those of immigrants without looking also at the distinctiveness of their experiences. Scholars of U.S. migrant labor should not forget the presence of Puerto Ricans, since their condition as U.S. colonial subjects reveals the complexity of the definitions and practices of who is a citizen and who is an immigrant in the twenty-first-century United States. That Puerto Rico is a U.S. colony is a matter of concern not only for Puerto Ricans but for all U.S. citizens who pledge allegiance to equality and "life, liberty, and the pursuit of happiness" and for anybody in the world who despises the undemocratic nature of colonialism. Understanding citizenship in an age of massive global migration is an important problem in North American anthropology, where scholars often pursue the study of British, French, and Dutch colonialisms, conveniently forgetting their own backyard.

At the same time scholars of Puerto Rico and Puerto Ricans should not separate the analysis of mid-twentieth-century policies of economic development, political autonomy, and modernity from the study of migration. Looking at the formation of the colonial state and citizenship through the lens of immigration policies demonstrates that the role played by Puerto Ricans in the formulation of U.S. labor policy and the impact of decisions taken by the federal government on them and other U.S. citizens still need to be explained. The problems of Puerto Ricans in the U.S. labor market are not those of incorporation or lack of assimilation. Puerto Ricans' understandings of culture and identity are not an obstacle to social mobility. Rather, inequalities and power have shaped migration, particularly in U.S. farm labor. Immigration policies are part of how states organize these inequalities, shaping not only the lives of immigrants but also the lives of U.S. citizens and colonial subjects.

The large number of Puerto Ricans migrating outside the FLP program from 1947 through 1993 demonstrates both that the government of Puerto Rico was unable to keep up with the demand for jobs on the islands and the ongoing need for Puerto Ricans in U.S. agriculture. The FLP initiated a migratory flow whose scope and unprecedented consequences surpassed the capacity of the government of Puerto Rico to manage them. In promoting migration as an escape valve for unemployment, the FLP raised the hopes and incomes of thousands of migrants. Perhaps the government of Puerto Rico could have developed viable and diverse agricultural production instead of flying unemployed and underemployed Puerto Ricans more than 1,500 miles to work on U.S. farms. Unfortunately, local and global forces facilitated instead the cultivation of inexpensive fruits, vegetables, and tobacco products in the continental United States. In the end, and despite enduring challenges and complaints, migration remains the only alternative for many Puerto Ricans to survive in a colonial regime devastated by economic crisis, government debt and corruption, policies of austerity, and Hurricane María.

# NOTES

## INTRODUCTION

1. In the 1950s farmers began recruiting West Indians through the H-2 visa program, which was established under the Immigration and Nationality Act of 1952 and formalized guest work within U.S. immigration law. The Immigration Reform and Control Act of 1986 replaced the H-2 visa program with the H-2A visa program, which provides temporary legal status to guest workers in agriculture and requires employers to give preference to domestic workers before hiring guest workers (see Griffith 2006).

## CHAPTER ONE. THE MAKING OF COLONIAL MIGRANT FARMWORKERS

1. *Downes v. Bidwell,* 182 U.S. 244 (1901).

2. The Chinese Exclusion Act of 1882 prohibited Chinese immigrants from entering the United States. After the Spanish-American War, the U.S. government extended its application to the Philippines, Puerto Rico, and Guam. The Foran Act, or Alien Contract Labor Law of 1885, prohibited the importation of contract workers from outside the United States in response to the Chinese "coolie" trade (see Baldoz 2011; Jung 2006; Lee 2003).

3. In Puerto Rico the Spanish colonial government had instituted the *libreta de jornaleros,* which required men to be registered with an employer and carry a *libreta,* or notebook, indicating their employment status (Picó 1982). In the U.S. South a pledge-card system was devised by the USES to coerce African American labor, avoid labor shortages, and punish idle workers (Breen 1997; Lee 2003; Torpey 2000).

4. The Foraker Act also provided a government for Puerto Rico, with a governor and an executive council appointed by the U.S. president and with a House of Representatives elected by popular vote among the landowning elites.

5. *Downes,* 182 U.S.

6. *Gonzales v. Williams,* 192 U.S. 1 (1904).

7. In re Giralde, 226 F. 826 (1915) at 3.

8. *Balzac v. People of Porto Rico,* 258 U.S. 298 (1922) at 308, 311.

9. *Downes,* 182 U.S. at 341–42.


## CHAPTER TWO. ESTABLISHING THE FARM
## LABOR PROGRAM

1. All translations from Spanish in the text are mine.

2. After having been part of the U.S. Department of Agriculture for only six months, in 1943 the Farm Placement Program was transferred to the Bureau of Employment Security under the Federal Security Agency. Shortly thereafter, in August 1949, Congress transferred the Bureau of Employment Security to the Department of Labor (Fay and Lippoldt 1999, 31–32; Haber and Kruger 1964, 36–40; Ruttenberg and Gutchess 1970, 4–5; USES 1949, 4).


## CHAPTER THREE. IMPLEMENTING
## CONTRACT MIGRATION

1. These discourses did not go unchallenged. Fred K. Fleagle, in *Social Problems in Porto Rico,* rejects the argument that overpopulation was a problem. Noting that the productive capacity of the land in Puerto Rico was the same as in some of Europe's most populated countries, he argues that the real issue was the low salaries paid to a large segment of the population ([1917] 1975, 19–20).

2. The U.S. Employment Service became part of the U.S. Bureau of Employment Security under the Federal Security Agency between 1948 and 1949. The USBES also oversaw the unemployment-insurance programs. Robert C. Goodwin, director of USES (1945–48), became the director of the USBES (1948–69). In 1949 the USBES was transferred back to the USDL (Goott 1949; USES 1949).

3. In 1948, with the passage of Puerto Rico's public law 25, the BEM emerged from an earlier incarnation of the PRES. After the extension of the Wagner-Peyser Act to Puerto Rico, the PRDL's annual report for 1950–51 referred to the BEM and the PRES, but subsequent reports, from 1952 to 1956, refer only to the BEM. The PRDL initially changed the BEM's name to PRES but changed it back the following year; however, from 1952 to 1956 some documents refer to the office as PRES. What occurred was that the BEM implemented the PRES as a program, assuming all the obligations imposed by its affiliation with the USES and facilitating the allocation of federal funds for employment-service activities (PRDL 1952a, 1952b).

4. In 1956 the Puerto Rican government reorganized the BEM and merged it with the Employment Security Division. The new Puerto Rico Bureau of Employment

Security subsumed the Employment Service division, the MD, and the Unemployment Insurance Division, and the MD took a leading role in the FLP (PRDL 1957).

5. The law did not cover West Indians because Florida growers preferred to continue their importation under the terms of the 1917 immigration law for temporary migrant labor (Briggs 2004).

6. Under the contract with the Glassboro Service Association, workers in New Jersey, Maryland, New York, and Pennsylvania went from earning $0.65 per hour in 1947 to $5.05 in 1992 (J. López 1993; V. Serrano 1991).

7. These contract conditions were not too different from those offered by U.S. growers to Mexican and West Indian guest workers. In 1943 Bahamian workers were paid their passage by the British Colonial Office (which the United States reimbursed) and received free housing and a minimum hourly wage or the prevailing wage in the region, if it were higher. Employers had to guarantee work for three-quarters of the contract period or a daily wage when work was not available (Hahamovitch 2011, 44–45).

## CHAPTER FOUR. *PA'LLA AFUERA* AND THE LIFE EXPERIENCES OF MIGRANTS

1. Mintz (1948–49, file 9, October 13, 1948, 3; file 14, December 31, 1948, 1; file 16, January 5, 1949, 2).

2. Mintz (1948–49, file 8, October 9, 1948, 5).

3. A walk-in worker is someone who shows up at a farm asking for work, in contrast to a worker who migrates with a contract.

4. Mintz (1948–49, file 10, October 28, 1948, 5).

5. Mintz (1948–49, file 8, October 6, 1948, 3; file 8, October 7, 1948, 1).

6. Mintz (1948–49, file 8, October 8, 1948, 1; file 10, October 16, 1948, 2; file 9, October 14, 1948, 1).

7. Mintz (1948–49, file 10, October 28, 1948, 3; file 10, October 16, 1948, 6; file 14, December 29, 1948, 1; file 14, December 21, 1948, 1; file 10, October 28, 1948, 3).

8. Mintz (1948–49, file 13, November 28, 1948, 1; file 10, October 28, 1948, 3; file 13, November 8, 1948, 3).

## CHAPTER FIVE. LABOR CAMPS AS PRISONS IN THE FIELDS

1. Mintz (1948–49, file 14, December 21, 1948, 1).

2. Mintz (1948–49, file 8, October 7, 1948, 1).

3. Unhappiness with the food offered was not restricted to Puerto Ricans. The literature on Mexican and West Indian guest workers registers the same complaint. González (2006, 74) notes that Mexican braceros departing reception centers on the

border were handed white-bread sandwiches that they often threw away because they were unfamiliar with such food. Braceros constantly complained about dinners with pasta and breakfasts of dry cereal, pancakes, scrambled eggs, and other items frequently eaten in the United States but rarely consumed in Mexico (H. Anderson 1976, 96, 100; see also Stouffer et al., 1949).

4. The practices described were pervasive in labor camps throughout the world. Algerian migrants arriving in Marseilles were given medical inspections and photographed. Labor camps were policed by former soldiers and administrators who had served in Algeria, creating a paramilitary environment. The camps separated workers from labor organizing, subversive political ideas, and sex with French women, but they failed to keep migrants in absolute isolation because they could not contain their adventurous spirit and tenacity (MacMaster 1997, 62).

## CHAPTER SIX. PUERTO RICANS IN THE RURAL UNITED STATES

1. The Puerto Rican student population of the summer school in Woodstown, New Jersey, numbered forty-two, out of a total enrollment of sixty-six students (E. Torres 1960d).

2. On July 2, 1960, a similar incident had occurred involving farmworkers and a bar in Durlandville, New York. After a worker was beaten and held in the bar, migrant workers from the area gathered, demanding his release, and a few of them threw rocks at the bar (E. Torres 1960e, 3).

## CHAPTER SEVEN. LABOR ORGANIZING AND THE END OF AN ERA

1. See NAACP, *Western Region v. Brennan*, 360 F. Supp. 1006 (U.S. D.C., D.C. 1973); Employees' Benefits, 20 C.F.R. 651, 653, 658 (1980); and Labor, 29 C.F.R. 42 (1980).

2. See *27 Puerto Rican Migrant Farm Workers v. Shade Tobacco Growers Agricultural Association*, I., 352 F. Supp. 986 (U.S. D.C., D. Conn. 1973).

3. See *Vazquez v. Ferre*, 404 F. Supp. 815 (U.S. D.C., D. N.J. 1975).

4. See *Velez v. Amenta*, 370 F. Supp. 1250 (U.S. D.C., D. Conn. 1974).

5. This was not the first time that the PRDL contracted women to work in the fields (Carlo [1957?]). The General Cigar Company also employed female leaf sewers with contracts in the 1960s (Miranda 1967).

6. See *Galan v. Dunlop*, 411 F. Supp. 268 (U.S. D.C., D.C. 1975).

7. See *Hernandez Flecha et al. v. Quiros*, 567 F.2d 1154, U.S. Court of Appeals (1st Cir. 1977).

8. See *COTA v. Molinelli*, 552 A.2d 1003, 1007–8 (N.J. 1989).

1. Although the American Community Survey (2006–8) estimated that there were 5,274 Puerto Ricans in stateside agriculture-related activities, it is difficult to know exactly how many of them were migrant farmworkers (U.S. Census Bureau 2006–8).

# REFERENCES

## SOURCE ABBREVIATIONS

| | |
|---|---|
| AFL-CIO | American Federation of Labor and Congress of Industrial Organizations |
| AGPR | Archivo General de Puerto Rico (Puerto Rico National Archives; box numbers for records may have changed) |
| ALMM | Archivo Luis Muñoz Marín |
| Centro Archives | Archives of the Puerto Rican Diaspora, Centro de Estudios Puertorriqueños, Hunter College, CUNY (box numbers for records may have changed) |
| GPO | Government Printing Office |
| Kheel Center | Kheel Center for Labor-Management Documentation and Archives, Cornell University |
| NARA | National Archives and Records Administration |
| USDA | U.S. Department of Agriculture |

## SOURCES

ACLU-NJ (American Civil Liberties Union of New Jersey). 2010. *Fifty Years on the Frontlines of Freedom*. Accessed May 28, 2018. www.aclu-nj.org/files/8213/1540/4575/100710AR.pdf.

Aders, Robert O. 1976. Letter to William D. Ford, January 26, 1976. File 2: Correspondence, Memoranda. Box 389. Apple Harvest, 1959–81. Farm Labor Program, 1948–93. Migration Division, Centro Archives.

Aldarondo, Etiony. 1976. Memorandum to Ruben Vilches, October 8, 1976. File 16: Correspondence, October–December 1976. Box 388. Apple Harvest, 1959–81. Farm Labor Program, 1948–93. Migration Division, Centro Archives.

———. [1977?]. Memorandum to Carlos S. Quirós. File 15: Correspondence, New York Regional Office, 1977–78. Box 476. Correspondence. Farm Labor Program, 1948–93. Migration Division, Centro Archives.

Alicea, Miriam. 1969. Letter to Edwin Rivera. File 49. Box 1280. Director's Files, Administration. Migration Division, Centro Archives.

Alvarez, Hector, et al. 1946. "Preliminary Report on Puerto Rican Workers in Chicago," November 1946. File: 9-8-116. Box 1138. Classified Files, 1907–51. Office of Territories. RG 126. NARA.

Álvarez, Johanna A., and David J. Neal. 2018. "Cliente escucha a empleados hablando español y amenaza con llamar al ICE 'para botarlos de mi país.'" *El Nuevo Herald,* May 16, 2018.

Alves Pena, Anita. 2009. "Locational Choices of the Legal and the Illegal: The Case of Mexican Agricultural Workers in the U.S." *International Migration Review* 43 (4): 850–80.

Amador, Emma. 2015. "Organizing Puerto Rican Domestics: Resistance and Household Labor Reform in the Puerto Rican Diaspora after 1930." *International Labor and Working-Class History* 88:67–86.

Anderson, Henry. 1964. *A Harvest of Loneliness: An Inquiry into a Social Problem.* Berkeley, CA: Citizens for Farm Labor.

———. 1976. *The Bracero Program in California.* New York: Arno.

Anderson, Nels. 1940. *Men on the Move.* Chicago: University of Chicago Press.

Aponte, Edwin D., David Bartelt, Luis A. Cortes Jr., and John C. Raines. 1994. *The Work of Latino Ministry: Hispanic Protestant Churches in Philadelphia.* Philadelphia: Pew Charitable Trusts.

Arnold, R. R. 1958. Inter-office communication to William U. Norwood, complaint of Puerto Rican Workers, January 7, 1958. File: Puertorriqueños en Nueva York. Box 2283. Tarea 96–20. Fondo Oficina del Gobernador. AGPR.

Arroyo, Guillermo. 1950. Letter to Comandantes de Zona, Comités de Distrito y Jefes de Negociado y División, Carta Circular 44, April 3, 1950. File: Policía Insular Coronel (de la), 1949–50. Box 165: Correspondencia de la Oficina de la Directora, 1949–50, P a la S. Tarea 61–55. Negociado de Seguridad de Empleo. Fondo Departamento del Trabajo. AGPR.

Asencio Camacho, Luis. 2013. "Migrants Who Never Arrived: The Crash of Westair Transport's N1248N in 1950." *Centro Journal* 25 (11): 120–39.

Asher, Robert, and Charles Stephenson. 1990. *Labor Divided: Race and Ethnicity in United States Labor Struggles, 1835–1960.* Albany: State University of New York Press.

Associated Press. 1978. "Puerto Rican Apple Pickers 'Stranded' Again." *Fort Scott Kansas Tribune,* September 27, 1978, 5.

———. 1983. "Foreign Apple Pickers Stir West Virginia Dispute." *New York Times,* October 23, 1983.

*Atlanta Daily World.* 1943. "Puerto Ricans May Work Farms." August 6, 1943, 1.

Atwood, Frank. 1954. "Connecticut Farm News." *Hartford Courant,* August 4, 1954, 14.

Austin, Diane. 2014. "Guestworkers in the Fabrication and Shipbuilding Industry along the Gulf of Mexico: An Anomaly or a New Source of Labor?" In Griffith 2014, 107–34.

Austin, Diane J. 1983. "Culture and Ideology in the English-Speaking Caribbean: A View from Jamaica." *American Ethnologist* 10 (2): 223–40.

Avilés Lamberty, José Fabián. 1974. "El Programa de colocaciones de trabajadores agrícolas puertorriqueños en Estados Unidos: ¿Una solución al problema de la pobreza?" Master's thesis, Public Administration, University of Puerto Rico, Río Piedras.

Ayala, César. 1996. "The Decline of the Plantation Economy and the Puerto Rican Migration of the 1950s." *Latino Studies Journal* 7 (1): 62–90.

Ayala, César, and Laird W. Bergad. 2002. "Rural Puerto Rico during the Early Twentieth Century Reconsidered: Land and Society, 1899–1915." *Latin American Research Review* 37 (2): 65–99.

Baldoz, Rick. 2011. *The Third Asiatic Invasion: Empire and Migration in Filipino America, 1898–1946.* New York: New York University Press.

Baldwin, Sidney. 1968. *Poverty and Politics: The Rise and Decline of the Farm Security Administration.* Chapel Hill: University of North Carolina Press.

Barr, Mason. 1944a. Letter to Philip Burton, February 29, 1944. File: Emigration. Box 2247. Tarea 96–20. Fondo Oficina del Gobernador. AGPR.

———. 1944b. Memorandum to Rexford G. Tugwell, April 28, 1944. File: Emigration. Box 2247. Tarea 96–20. Fondo Oficina del Gobernador. AGPR.

———. 1944c. Memorandum to the governor, April 18, 1944. File: 9-8-116. Box 1138. Classified Files, 1907–51. Office of Territories. RG 126. NARA.

———. 1946. Memorandum to Arnold, July 22, 1946. File: 9-8-116. Box 1138. Classified Files, 1907–51. Office of Territories. RG 126. NARA.

———. 1947. Letter to Cecil Morales, December 3, 1947. File: Informe del Departamento del Trabajo, Migración de trabajadores puertorriqueños a los Estados Unidos. Box 454. Tarea 96–20. Fondo Oficina del Gobernador. AGPR.

Bayó, Dixie. 1977. "No pueden ir sin contrato: Luz roja a migrantes." *Momento,* September 28, 1977, 3.

Beechert, Edward D. 1985. *Working in Hawaii: A Labor History.* Honolulu: University of Hawai'i Press.

Bender, Daniel E., and Jana K. Lipman. 2015. *Making the Empire Work: Labor and United States Imperialism.* New York: New York University Press.

Benmayor, Rina, Rosa M. Torruellas, and Ana L. Juarbe. 1997. "Cultural Citizenship in East Harlem: 'Si Esto Puede Ayudar a la Comunidad Mía . . .'" In *Latino Cultural Citizenship: Claiming Identity, Space, and Rights,* edited by William V. Flores and Rina Benmayor, 152–209. Boston: Beacon.

Benson, Peter. 2008. "El Campo: Faciality and Structural Violence in Farm Labor Camps." *Cultural Anthropology* 23 (4): 589–629.

Berrios, Julio. 1981. Memorandum to Manuel Amadeo, "Posible disponibilidad de obreros agrícolas no PRs," June 8, 1981. File: Agrícola, 1981. Box 2907. Subject Files, General, Administration. Migration Division, Centro Archives.

Berstein, Michael A. 1989. "Why the Great Depression Was Great: Toward a New Understanding of the Interwar Economic Crisis in the United States." In *The Rise and Fall of the New Deal Order, 1930–1980*, edited by Steve Fraser and Gary Gerstle, 32–54. Princeton: Princeton University Press.

Binford, Arthur Leigh. 2009. "From Fields of Power to Fields of Sweat: The Dual Process of Constructing Mexican Agricultural Contract Workers in Canada and Mexico." *Third World Quarterly* 30 (3): 503–17.

Blair, Alexander, Richard Edwards, Morrison Handsaker, and Fred Schiller. 1954. *Migratory Farm Labor in Pennsylvania, Report of the Lafayette Consulting Group to the Pennsylvania Department of Labor and Industry, December 31*. Easton, PA.

Bonilla-Santiago, Gloria. 1986. "A Case Study of Puerto Rican Migrant Farmworkers Organizational Effectiveness in New Jersey." PhD diss., City University of New York.

———. 1988. "Historical Analysis: Puerto Rican Migrant Workers in New Jersey." In *Proceedings of the Consultation on Farms and Farmworkers, Glassboro State College, September 26, 1988*, edited by New Jersey Council of Churches, 10–22. East Orange, NJ: New Jersey Council of Churches.

Bourdieu, Pierre, and Loïc J. D. Wacquant. 1992. *An Invitation to Reflexive Sociology*. Chicago: University of Chicago Press.

Bowles, Pete. [1966?]. "Reaction Mixed on Petitions to Improve Migrant Camps," newspaper clipping. File 48. Box 1280. Director's Files, Administration. Migration Division, Centro Archives.

Bowman, Georgianne. 2002. *Around North Collins*. Charleston, SC: Arcadia.

Breen, William J. 1997. *Labor Market Politics and the Great War: The Department of Labor, the States, and the First U.S. Employment Service, 1907–1933*. Kent, OH: Kent State University Press.

Briggs, Vernon M. 2004. *Guestworker Programs for Low-Skilled Workers: Lessons from the Past and Warnings for the Future*. Washington, DC: Center for Immigration Studies.

Bronfenbrenner, Kate. 1990. "California Pea Pickers' Strike of 1932." ILR School. Accessed January 16, 1016. http://digitalcommons.ilr.cornell.edu/articles/552/.

*Buffalo Courier-Express*. 1948. "Draft Office Fears Harvest of Trouble from Migrant Workers." June 11, 1948, 6C.

———. 1966. "Migrant Workers Case: Grand Jury Study Asked by Justice." September 27, 1966.

———. 1969. "Fewer Puerto Rican Farm Workers Expected." June 11, 1969.

Burawoy, Michael. 1976. "The Functions and Reproduction of Migrant Labor: Comparative Material from Southern Africa and the United States." *American Journal of Sociology* 81 (5): 1050–87.

———. 1985. *The Politics of Production: Factory Regimes under Capitalism and Socialism*. London: Verso.

Burnett, Christina Duffy. 2008. "'They Say I Am Not an American . . .': The Non-citizen National and the Law of American Empire." *Virginia Journal of International Law* 48 (4): 559–718.

———. 2009. "Empire and the Transformation of Citizenship." In *Colonial Crucible: Empire in the Making of the Modern American State,* edited by Alfred W. McCoy and Francisco A. Scarano, 332–41. Madison: University of Wisconsin Press.

Bustelo, Manuel A. 1975. "Contract Workers for Vermont Growers," memorandum to Ruben Vilches, April 16, 1975. File 15: Correspondence, July–September 1976. Box 388. Apple Harvest, 1959–81. Farm Labor Program, 1948–93. Migration Division, Centro Archives.

Cabán, Pedro A. 1999. *Constructing a Colonial People: Puerto Rico and the United States, 1898–1932.* Boulder, CO: Westview.

Cabranes, Manuel. 1949a. Letter to Fernando Sierra Berdecía, March 25, 1949. File 35: Commissioner of Labor, Fernando Sierra Berdecía. Box 915. Subject and Resource File. Farm Labor Program, 1948–93. Migration Division, Centro Archives.

———. 1949b. Letter to Fernando Sierra Berdecía, May 10, 1949. File 35: Commissioner of Labor, Fernando Sierra Berdecía. Box 915. Subject and Resource File. Farm Labor Program, 1948–93. Migration Division, Centro Archives.

———. 1949c. Letter to Pagán de Colón, March 24, 1949. File: Correspondencia confidencial. Box 163: Correspondencia de la Oficina de la Directora, 1948–50, A y la E. Tarea 61–55. Negociado de Seguridad de Empleo. Fondo Departamento del Trabajo. AGPR.

Calavita, Kitty. 1992. *Inside the State: The Bracero Program, Immigration, and the I.N.S.* New York: Routledge.

*CALC Report/TWC Bulletin.* 1984. "Interview with Angel Dominguez and Juan Ortiz: Organizing Farm Workers in New Jersey." *CALC Report/TWC Bulletin,* October–November 1984, 7–11.

Caldas, Gloria. 1974. "The People's Forum: Slave Status Seen in Tobacco Fields." *Hartford Courant,* July 10, 1974, 12.

Camacho, Gilberto. 1969. Progress report on projects, Adams Nursery, Westfield, MA, report to Francisca Bou, August 6, 1969. File 2: Cases 41–60, 1969–70. Box 464. Correspondence. Farm Labor Program, 1948–93. Migration Division, Centro Archives.

———. 1971. Letter to Robert E. Porter, Adams Nurseries, March 3, 1971. File 25: Adams Nursery, Incorporated, Westfield, Massachusetts, 1971. Box 896. Subject and Resource File. Farm Labor Program, 1948–93. Migration Division, Centro Archives.

Caraballo-Cueto, José and Juan Lara. 2018. "Deindustrialization and Unsustainable Debt in Middle-Income Countries: The Case of Puerto Rico." *Journal of Globalization and Development* 8 (2): 1–11.

Cardona, Francisco José. 1957. Letter to Emerita Cortés, Anchorage, Alaska, April 30, 1957. File: Puertorriqueños en Nueva York. Box 2283. Tarea 96–20. Fondo Oficina del Gobernador. AGPR.

Carlo, Dario. [1957?]. "Sale hacia E.U. la primera mujer que viaja en avión de braceros." *El Diario de Nueva York,* circa March 22, [1957?]. Box 21c. Subject and Correspondence Files. Governor W. Averell Harriman Papers. New York State Archives, Albany.

Carvalho, Joseph. 2015. "The Puerto Rican Community of Western Massachusetts, 1898–1960." *Historical Journal of Massachusetts* 43 (2): 34–62.

Casey, Matthew. 2017. *Empire's Guestworkers: Haitian Migrants in Cuba during the Age of US Occupation.* Cambridge: Cambridge University Press.

Casiano, Miguel E. 1958. Letter to Oficina Central, September 16, 1958. File 1: Claims Complaints to Cases Unpaid Wages. Box 391. Claims and Complaints. Farm Labor Program, 1948–93. Migration Division, Centro Archives.

Castaño, Carlos. 1958. "The Puerto Rican Migratory Program." *Employment Security Review* 25 (3): 31–33.

CATA (Comité de Apoyo a los Trabajadores Agrícolas). 1985. "Histórico convenio entre COTA y farmers." *Siembra* 3 (1): 3. File 9: Comité de Apoyo a los Trabajadores Agrícolas (CATA)–Comité Organizador de Trabajadores Agrícolas (COTA), 1983–94. Box 177. Series 13: Media Unit. Centro Records, Centro Archives.

———. [1985?]a. "An Evening of Solidarity with Puerto Rican and Latino Farmworkers." File 9: Comité de Apoyo a los Trabajadores Agrícolas (CATA)–Comité Organizador de Trabajadores Agrícolas (COTA), 1983–94, Box 177. Series 13: Media Unit. Centro Records, Centro Archives.

———. [1985?]b. Farmworker Support Committee narrative. File 9: Comité de Apoyo a los Trabajadores Agrícolas (CATA)–Comité Organizador de Trabajadores Agrícolas (COTA), 1983–94. Box 177. Series 13: Media Unit. Centro Records, Centro Archives.

———. [1985?]c. "Lack of Field Sanitation Facilities for New Jersey Farmworkers." File 9: Comité de Apoyo a los Trabajadores Agrícolas (CATA)–Comité Organizador de Trabajadores Agrícolas (COTA), 1983–94. Box 177. Series 13: Media Unit. Centro Records, Centro Archives.

Catholic and Protestant Clergy. 1966. "Protests in Migrant Labor Camps—North Collins, New York, Minutes of a Representative Group Called by Action of the Clergy Catholic and Protestant regarding Erie County," July 21, 1966. File 49. Box 1280. Director's Files, Administration. Migration Division, Centro Archives.

*Christian Science Monitor.* n.d. "Puerto Rican Migrant Workers Plunge Eagerly into Study of English." Reprinted from *Christian Science Monitor* by Division of Home Missions, National Council of the Churches of Christ, New York. File 21: Migrant Labor, Pamphlets, and Government-Issued Reports. Box 1. Series 2: Subject Files, National Focus. Collection 5235. National Consumers' League Records. Kheel Center.

*Chronicle Express.* 1952. Photo of newspaper clipping in reference to an event on Puerto Ricans and police violence. File: Migrant Labor, Correspondence, 1954. Box 21. Collection 5307. Consumers' League of New York City Records. Kheel Center.

Clinton Migrant Committee. 1953. Annual report of the Clinton Migrant Committee of the Clinton Council of Church Women. File: 1–32. Box 1. Collection 21–33–1085: Department of Rural Sociology Records, 1920–77. Division of Rare and Manuscript Collections. Cornell University.

Cochrane, Willard W. 1993. *Development of American Agriculture: A Historical Analysis.* Minneapolis: University of Minnesota Press.

Cohen, Deborah. 2011. *Braceros: Migrant Citizens and Transnational Subjects in the Postwar United States and Mexico.* Chapel Hill: University of North Carolina Press.

Cohen, Emil L. 1967. Human Rights Commission report, inv. 2209–66, June 26, 1967. File 49. Box 1280. Director's Files, Administration. Migration Division, Centro Archives.

Coll, Gabriel. 1963. Memorandum to Anthony Vega, Maryland State Employment Service, June 4, 1963. File 10: Monthly Reports, Philadelphia, 1959–90. Box 886. Reports. Farm Labor Program, 1948–93. Migration Division, Centro Archives.

Colón, Jesús. 1993. *The Way It Was and Other Writings: Historical Vignettes about the New York Puerto Rican Community.* Houston: Arte Público.

Colón, Jorge. 1966a. Activity report to Ralph S. Rosas, special report on the situation of North Collins, NY, July 19, 1966. File 41. Box 2367. Subject and Resource File. Farm Labor Program, 1948–93. Migration Division, Centro Archives.

———. 1966b. Activity report to Ralph S. Rosas, visit to Albion, NY, August 3, 1966. File 49. Box 1280. Director's Files, Administration. Migration Division, Centro Archives.

———. 1966c. "Conditions of N. Collins Area: Situation and Developments," progress report on projects, August 24, 1966. File 49. Box 1280. Director's Files, Administration. Migration Division, Centro Archives.

———. 1966d. "English Classes Offered," progress report on projects to Curtis Barn, Mt. Morris Plant, August 24, 1966. File 49. Box 1280. Director's Files, Administration. Migration Division, Centro Archives.

———. 1966e. Progress report on projects, North Collins, NY, August 25, 1966. File 49. Box 1280. Director's Files, Administration. Migration Division, Centro Archives.

———. 1966f. Progress report on projects, North Collins, NY, August 26, 1966. File 49. Box 1280. Director's Files, Administration. Migration Division, Centro Archives.

———. 1966g. Progress report on projects to Carlos Gomez, Strussemberg Bros., Hilton, NY, August 24, 1966. File 49. Box 1280. Director's Files, Administration. Migration Division, Centro Archives.

———. 1966h. Progress report on projects to Raymond Walker and John Colloca, Oswego, NY, August 24, 1966. File 49. Box 1280. Director's Files, Administration. Migration Division, Centro Archives.

———. 1967a. Activity report to Anthony Vega, North Collins Migrant Center, October 20, 1967. File 49. Box 1280. Director's Files, Administration. Migration Division, Centro Archives.

————. 1967b. Letter to Anthony Vega, September 20, 1967. File 49. Box 1280. Director's Files, Administration. Migration Division, Centro Archives.

Commission on Agricultural Workers, ed. 1991. *Report of the Commission on Agricultural Workers.* Washington, DC: GPO.

Concepción de Gracia, Gilberto. 1958. Letter, August 1958. File 1. Box 4. Correspondence, Political Activities, Professional Documents. Gilberto Concepción de Gracia Collection. Centro de Investigaciones Históricas. University of Puerto Rico, Río Piedras.

*Congressional Record.* 1900. 56th Cong. 1st Sess. Vol. 33. Pat. 4.

Consumers' League of New York. 1957. "Migrant Labor in NYS," special newsletter, supplement for June 1957. File C.L. Publications, Migrant Labor Miscellaneous. Box 12. Collection 5307. Consumers' League Records of New York City. Kheel Center.

————. 1960. "Program Agreed on by Action Conference on Migrant Farm Labor in New York State," January 7, 1960. File 20: Migrant Labor, C.L. Action Conference, January 1960. Box 3. Collection 5307. Consumers' League Records of New York City. Kheel Center.

————. n.d. "Crew Leaders," draft chapter. File: C.L. Publications, Migrant Labor Miscellaneous. Box 12. Collection 5307. Consumers' League Records of New York City. Kheel Center.

Cornell University, Department of Rural Sociology. 1948. "Visits to Labor Camps, Orleans County and Others." File 31: Migrant Camps in New York, Cornell. Box 1. Collection 21–33–1085. Department of Rural Sociology Records, 1920–77. Division of Rare and Manuscript Collections. Cornell University.

COTA (Comité Organizador de Trabajadores Agrícolas). 1985. Newsletter, December 1985. File 9: Comité de Apoyo a los Trabajadores Agrícolas (CATA)–Comité Organizador de Trabajadores Agrícolas (COTA), 1983–94, Box 177. Series 13: Media Unit. Centro Records, Centro Archives.

Coudert, Frederic R. 1903. "Our New Peoples: Citizens, Subjects, Nationals or Aliens." *Columbia Law Review* 3 (1): 13–32.

Crafts, Stephen. 1966. "Report from North Collins: 'This Trouble We're Having.'" *Spectrum,* July 29, 1966. File 41. Box 2367. Subject and Resource File. Farm Labor Program, 1948–93. Migration Division, Centro Archives.

Crehan, Kate. 2016. *Gramsci's Common Sense: Inequality and Its Narratives.* Durham, NC: Duke University Press.

Crosby, Alexander. 1952. *Sweatshops in the Sun.* New York: Consumers' League of New York.

Crumbine, Samuel J. 1930. *Porto Rico: An Inquiry into the Health, Nutrition and Social Conditions in Porto Rico as They May Affect Children.* New York: American Child Health Association.

Cruz, José E. 1998. *Identity and Power: Puerto Rican Politics and the Challenge of Ethnicity.* Philadelphia: Temple University Press.

Cunningham, John T. 1957. "Migrants Pose Problems for N.J. Farmers Who Need Them." *Newark Sunday News,* September 1, 1957.

Daniel, Cletus E. 1982. *Bitter Harvest: A History of California Farmworkers: 1870–1941*. Berkeley: University of California Press.

De Genova, Nicholas. 2010. "The Deportation Regime: Sovereignty, Space, and the Freedom of Movement." In De Genova and Peutz 2010, 33–65.

De Genova, Nicholas, and Nathalie Peutz. 2010. *The Deportation Regime: Sovereignty, Space, and the Freedom of Movement*. Durham, NC: Duke University Press.

De Genova, Nicholas, and Ana Y. Ramos-Zayas. 2003. *Latino Crossings: Mexicans, Puerto Ricans, and the Politics of Race and Citizenship*. New York: Routledge.

Degetau y González, Federico. 1903. Brief of Amicus Curiae, October 3, 1903. Submitted in Gonzales v. Williams. 192 U.S. 1 (1904). No. 225.

Delgado, José A. 2014. "Labrador en otras tierras." *El Nuevo Día,* April 6, 2014, 4–5.

———. 2016. "Imputan discriminar contra obreros boricuas." *El Nuevo Día,* June 23, 2016, 14.

Delgado, Federico. 1973. "El infierno de los campamentos de trabajadores agrícolas." *Revista Avance,* July 16, 1973, 19–25.

Del Río, Antonio. 1959a. "Inter-office Report to Eulalio Torres, Meeting with Employment Representative at the Brockton E. S. Office on August 27, 1959." September 2, 1959. File 37: Brockton Employment Security Office, Boston, Massachusetts, 1959. Box 908. Subject and Resource File. Farm Labor Program, 1948–93. Migration Division, Centro Archives.

———. 1959b. Letter to Eulalio Torres, December 2, 1959. File 7: Farmers without Contract, 1959. Box 935. Subject and Resource File. Farm Labor Program, 1948–93. Migration Division, Centro Archives.

———. 1969. "Logan Airport to Meet Workers for United Cape Cod Cranberry, Weston Nurseries, Flerra and A. D. Makepeace," memorandum to Francisca Bou, September 25, 1969. File 33: A. D. Makepeace Company, Wareham, Massachusetts, 1969–73. Box 896. Subject and Resource File. Farm Labor Program, 1948–93. Migration Division, Centro Archives.

DeWind, Josh, Tom Seidl, and Janet Shenk. 1977. "Caribbean Migration: Contract Labor in U.S. Agriculture." *NACLA* 11 (8): 3–37.

*Diario, El.* [1957?]. "Boricuas dicen viven como 'perros' en fincas agrícolas de Pensilvania," circa January 7, [1957?]. Box 21c. Subject and Correspondence Files. Governor W. Averell Harriman Papers. New York State Archives, Albany.

———. 1966. "Policía establece toque de queda para los Boricuas en la aldea de North Collins, N.Y." July 15, 1966, 2.

———. [1969?]. "Ferré se opone a la importación de obreros agrícolas a Puerto Rico," newspaper clipping, May 23, [1969?]. File 36: Ferre Opposes Importing Agricultural Workers to Puerto Rico. Box 935. Subject and Resource File. Farm Labor Program, 1948–93. Migration Division, Centro Archives.

Dietz, James L. 1986. *Economic History of Puerto Rico: Institutional Change and Capitalist Development*. Princeton: Princeton University Press.

Domínguez, Ángel. 1985. "Sembrando." *Siembra* 3 (1): 4. File 9: Comité de Apoyo a los Trabajadores Agrícolas (CATA)–Comité Organizador de Trabajadores

Agrícolas (COTA), 1983–94. Box 177. Series 13: Media Unit. Centro Records, Centro Archives.

DPRCA (Department of Puerto Rican Community Affairs in the United States). 1993. "Follow-Up Action Plan from June 5, 1993, Meeting to Increase the Use of Puerto Rico as a Source of Domestic Agricultural Workers for New England," July 13, 1993. File 4: Farm Labor Program, Supervisor. Box 472. Correspondence. Farm Labor Program, 1948–93. Migration Division, Centro Archives.

Draper, Estella. 1948a. Letter to United Labor Import, August 18, 1948. Case 3 0254. File: 0253–0275, 8/18–8/23/48. Box 2248. Case Files, Social Services. Migration Division, Centro Archives.

———. 1948b. Memorandum to Manuel Cabranes, May 27, 1948. File: Correspondencia confidencial, 1948. Box 163: Correspondencia de la Oficina de la Directora, 1948–50, A y la E. Tarea 61–55. Negociado de Seguridad de Empleo. Fondo Departamento del Trabajo. AGPR.

———. 1950. Letter to Petroamérica Pagán de Colón, June 2, 1950. File: Correspondencia personal, 1949–50. Box 163: Correspondencia de la Oficina de la Directora, 1948–50, A y la E. Tarea 61–55. Negociado de Seguridad de Empleo. Fondo Departamento del Trabajo. AGPR.

Driscoll, Irene. 1974. "Meskill Seeks State Control of Funds for Farmworkers." *Hartford Courant*, March 7, 1974, 6.

Duany, Jorge. 2002. *The Puerto Rican Nation on the Move: Identities on the Island and in the United States*. Chapel Hill: University of North Carolina Press.

———. 2011. "A Transnational Colonial Migration: Puerto Rico's Farm Labor Program." In *Blurred Borders: Transnational Migration between the Hispanic Caribbean and the United States*, 81–103. Chapel Hill: University of North Carolina Press.

DuFresne, Elizabeth J., and John J. McDonnell. 1971. "The Migrant Labor Camps: Enclaves of Isolation in our Midst." *Fordham Law Review* 40 (2): 279–304.

Duke, Michael. 2011. "Ethnicity, Well-Being, and the Organization of Labor among Shade Tobacco Workers." *Medical Anthropology* 30 (4): 409–24.

Dunbar, Tony, and Linda Kravitz. 1976. *Hard Traveling: Migrant Farm Workers in America*. Cambridge, MA: Ballinger.

Dunn, Walter S. 1972. *History of Erie County, 1870–1970*. Buffalo, NY: Buffalo and Erie County Historical Society.

Dyckman, Mary L. 1944. "The Regulation of Labor Camps for Migratory or Seasonal Work in New Jersey," memorandum to the New Jersey State Commission for Post-War Economic Welfare, December 18, 1944. File 21: Migrant Labor, Pamphlets, and Government-Issued Reports. Box 1. Series 2: Subject Files, National Focus. Collection 5235. National Consumers' League Records. Management Documentation and Archives. Kheel Center.

Eastern Airlines. 1956. Memorandum, June 23, 1956. File: The Supervision of the Farm Placement Program. Serie 11: Correspondencia, 1958. División de Migración. Tarea 63–37. Negociado de Seguridad de Empleo. Fondo Departamento del Trabajo. AGPR.

Economic Development Administration. [1950?]. "Capable Hands Can Be Flown to Your Plant from Puerto Rico." *U.S.A. Publicaciones.* Box 1207. Tarea 96–20. Fondo Oficina del Gobernador. AGPR.

Emigration Advisory Committee. 1947. Minutes, September 11, 1947. File: Sección 4. LMM. Sección 4: Presidente del Senado, 1941–48. 195. Emigración 18. ALMM.

Employment Section, Migration Division. 1963. Employment card for Pablo Torres, 1963. Box TBR 2. Migration Division, Centro Archives.

*Employment Service Review.* 1948. "At Press Time." 15 (4): 1–2.

Erman, Sam. 2008. "Meanings of Citizenship in the U.S. Empire: Puerto Rico, Isabel Gonzalez, and the Supreme Court, 1898 to 1905." *Journal of American Ethnic History* 27 (4): 5–33.

———. 2010. "Puerto Rico and the Promise of United States Citizenship: Struggles around Status in a New Empire, 1898–1917." PhD diss., University of Michigan.

———. 2014. "Citizens of Empire: Puerto Rico, Status, and Constitutional Change." *California Law Review* 102 (5): 1181–241.

Esquilín, Félix. 1975. "Medidas de austeridad para el año fiscal 1975–76," memorandum to Directores Auxiliares, September 22, 1975. File 36: Administration, 1973–79. Box 896. Subject and Resource File. Farm Labor Program, 1948–93. Migration Division, Centro Archives.

Fahrmeir, Andreas. 2007. *Citizenship: The Rise and Fall of a Modern Concept.* New Haven: Yale University Press.

Falcón, Luis M., and Dan Gilbarg. 1994. "Mexicans, Puerto Ricans and Cubans in the Labor Market: A Historical Overview." In *Handbook of Hispanic Cultures in the United States,* edited by Félix M. Padilla, Nicolás Kanellos, and Claudio Esteva, 57–79. San Antonio: Arte Público.

Farmer, Paul. 2002. "On Suffering and Structural Violence: A View from Below." In *The Anthropology of Politics: A Reader in the Ethnography, Theory, and Critique,* edited by Joan Vincent, 424–37. Malden: Blackwell.

Farm Placement Division. 1964. "Annual Farm Labor Report." File 12: 1964. Box 3248. Reference, Administration. Migration Division, Centro Archives.

Fay, Robert G., and Douglas Lippoldt. 1999. *The Public Employment Service in the United States.* Paris: Organization for Economic Co-operation and Development.

Fernández, Lilia. 2010. "Of Immigrants and Migrants: Mexican and Puerto Rican Labor Migration in Comparative Perspective, 1942–1964." *Journal of American Ethnic History* 29 (3): 6–39.

Fernández, Matilde. 1958a. "Informe especialista migración en los EEUU," memorandum to Petroamérica Pagán de Colón, August 11 to September 4, September 19, 1958. File: Resumen informes especialistas en migración, 1958. Serie 11: Correspondencia, 1958. División de Migración. Tarea 63–37. Negociado de Seguridad de Empleo. Fondo Departamento del Trabajo. AGPR.

———. 1958b. "Resumen informes de especialistas," memorandum to Petroamérica Pagán de Colón, November 18, 1958. File: Resumen informes especialistas en migración, 1958. Serie 11: Correspondencia, 1958. División de Migración. Tarea

63–37. Negociado de Seguridad de Empleo. Fondo Departamento del Trabajo. AGPR.

———. 1958c. "Resumen semanal especialistas en migración en los Estados Unidos desde el 12 al 28 de julio," memorandum to Petroamérica Pagán de Colón, August 6, 1958. File: Resumen informes especialistas en migración, 1958. Serie 11: Correspondencia, 1958. División de Migración. Tarea 63–37. Negociado de Seguridad de Empleo. Fondo Departamento del Trabajo. AGPR.

Fernós Isern, Antonio. 1944. Letter to Alvin Rucker, August 4, 1944. Box 269. Tarea 96–20. Fondo Oficina del Gobernador. AGPR.

———. 1947a. Letter to Celestina Zalduondo Goodsaid, April 25, 1947. File: Sección 5. LMM, Gobernador de PR. Serie 2: Correspondencia particular. ALMM.

———. 1947b. Letter to Luis Muñoz Marín, April 3, 1947. File: Sección 5. LMM, Gobernador de PR. Serie 2: Correspondencia particular. ALMM.

———. 1947c. Letter to Luis Muñoz Marín, December 4, 1947. File Sección 5. LMM, Gobernador de PR. Serie 2: Correspondencia particular. ALMM.

———. 1947d. Letter to Luis Muñoz Marín, March 12, 1947. File: Sección 5. LMM, Gobernador de PR. Serie 2: Correspondencia particular. ALMM.

———. 1947e. Letter to Luis Muñoz Marín, March 8, 1947. File: Sección 5. LMM, Gobernador de PR. Serie 2: Correspondencia particular. ALMM.

———. 1947f. Letter to Luis Muñoz Marín, October 17, 1947. File: Sección 5. LMM, Gobernador de PR. Serie 2: Correspondencia particular. ALMM.

Figueroa, Tito. 1957. Letter to Clarence Senior, August 13, 1957. File 3: Claims, 1951–59. Box 394. Claims and Complaints. Farm Labor Program, 1948–93. Migration Division, Centro Archives.

Findlay, Eileen. 2014. *We Are Left without a Father Here: Masculinity, Domesticity, and Migration in Postwar Puerto Rico.* Durham, NC: Duke University Press.

Fleagle, Fred K. (1917) 1975. *Social Problems in Porto Rico.* Reprint, New York: Arno.

FLP (Farm Labor Program). 1960. "Oficina de Operaciones de Campo." File 10: Weekly Reports, July 1960–October 1960. Box 892. Reports. Farm Labor Program, 1948–93. Migration Division, Centro Archives.

———. 1964. Report of Intervention Group Insurance Fund for Migrant Farm Workers. File 2: Administrator of Trustees Puerto Rican Agricultural Workers. Box 897. Subject and Resource File. Farm Labor Program, 1948–93. Migration Division, Centro Archives.

Folsom, Josiah C., and Oliver E. Baker. 1937. *A Graphic Summary of Farm Labor and Population: Based Largely on the Census of 1930 and 1935.* Washington, DC: USDA.

Forand, Rebecca. 2015. "N.J. Farm Pays $175K Settlement for Unlawfully Hiring Foreign Workers over U.S. Workers." *South Jersey Times,* January 5, 2015.

Fortas, Abe. 1944. Letter to Marvin Jones, May 27, 1944. File: Emigration. Box 2247. Tarea 96–20. Fondo Oficina del Gobernador. AGPR.

———. 1948a. Letter to Jesús T. Piñero, August 30, 1948. File: Autoridad de transporte, transportación aérea. Box 454. Tarea 96–20. Fondo Oficina del Gobernador. AGPR.

———. 1948b. Letter to Jesús T. Piñero, June 12, 1948. File: Autoridad de transporte, transportación aérea. Box 454. Tarea 96–20. Fondo Oficina del Gobernador. AGPR.

Foucault, Michel. 1982. "The Subject and Power." *Critical Inquiry* 8 (4): 777–95.

Franqui-Rivera, Harry. 2013. "National Mythologies: U.S. Citizenship for the People of Puerto Rico and Military Service." *Memorias: Revista Digital de Historia y Arqueología desde el Caribe* 10 (21): 5–21.

Frías de Hempel, Luisa. 1956. "Viaje oficial a los Estados Unidos," memorandum to Luis Muñoz Marín, November 16, 1956. File: Organización y personal. Box 2254. Tarea 96–20. Fondo Oficina del Gobernador. AGPR.

Frymer, Paul. 2008. *Black and Blue: African-Americans, the Labor Movement, and the Decline of the Democratic Party.* Princeton: Princeton University Press.

Fuller, Varden. 1967. "Farm Manpower Policy." In *Farm Labor in the United States,* edited by Charles E. Bishop, 97–114. New York: Columbia University Press.

Galafá, Félix. 1993. "Visita a Kennett Square: Industria del hongo," memorandum to Fred Ramírez, April 13, 1993. File 5: Farm Labor, Supervisor. Box 472. Correspondence. Farm Labor Program, 1948–93. Migration Division, Centro Archives.

Galarza, Ernesto. 1964. *Merchants of Labor: The Mexican Bracero Story; An Account of the Managed Migration of Mexican Farm Workers in California, 1942–1960.* Charlotte, NC: McNally and Loftin.

———. 1977. *Farm Workers and Agri-business in California, 1947–1960.* Notre Dame, IN: University of Notre Dame Press.

García, Matt. 2002. *A World of Its Own: Race, Labor, and Citrus in the Making of Greater Los Angeles, 1900–1970.* Chapel Hill: University of North Carolina Press.

Garcia, Victor Q. 1997. *Mexican Enclaves in the U.S. Northeast: Immigrant and Migrant Mushroom Workers in Southern Chester County, Pennsylvania.* Research Report 27. East Lansing, MI: Julian Samora Research Institute, Michigan State University.

Garcia Cano, Regina. 2017. "Puerto Ricans Could Ease SD Dairy Labor Shortage." *USA Today,* January 15, 2017.

García-Colón, Ismael. 2006a. "'Buscando Ambiente': Hegemony and Subaltern Tactics of Survival in Puerto Rico's Land Distribution Program." *Latin American Perspectives* 33 (1): 42–65.

———. 2006b. "Playing and Eating Democracy: The Case of Puerto Rico's Land Distribution Program, 1940s–1960s." *Centro Journal* 18 (2): 167–89.

———. 2008. "Claiming Equality: Puerto Rican Farmworkers in Western New York." *Latino Studies* 6 (3): 269–89.

———. 2009. *Land Reform in Puerto Rico: Modernizing the Colonial State, 1941–1969.* Gainesville: University Press of Florida.

———. 2017a. "Confronting the Present: Migration in Sidney Mintz's Journal for *The People of Puerto Rico.*" *American Ethnologist* 44 (3): 403–13.

———. 2017b. "'We Like Mexican Laborers Better': Citizenship and Immigration Policies in the Formation of Puerto Rican Farm Labor in the United States." *Centro Journal* 29 (2): 134–71.

García-Colón, Ismael, and Edwin Meléndez. 2013: "Enduring Migration: Puerto Rican Workers on U.S. Farms." *Centro Journal* 25 (2): 96–119.

García La Torre, Ramón. 1956. Claim-complaint form, October 24, 1956. File 4: Floran–Goitia. Box 391. Claims and Complaints. Farm Labor Program, 1948–93. Migration Division, Centro Archives.

Gautier, Rafael. 1948. "Empleos para puertorriqueños en América Latina," memorandum to governor of Puerto Rico, May 12, 1948. File: Informe del Departamento del Trabajo, migración de trabajadores puertorriqueños a los Estados Unidos. Box 454. Tarea 96–20. Fondo Oficina del Gobernador. AGPR.

Geach, Gwen. 1959. *State Migratory Labor Committees: Their Organization and Problems.* Washington, DC: Bureau of Labor Standards, U.S. Department of Labor.

Geo H. Angle's Sons. 1966. Application for Migrant Labor Registration Certificate, April 20, 1966. File 49. Box 1280. Director's Files, Administration. Migration Division, Centro Archives.

Gillespie, B. R. 1956. Telegram to Fernando Sierra Berdecía, June 27, 1956. File: The Supervision of the Farm Placement Program. Serie 11: Correspondencia, 1958. División de Migración. Tarea 63–37. Negociado de Seguridad de Empleo. Fondo Departamento del Trabajo. AGPR.

Giovannetti-Torres, Jorge L. 2018. *Black British Migrants in Cuba: Race, Labor, and Empire in the Twentieth-Century Caribbean, 1898–1948.* Cambridge: Cambridge University Press.

Glasser, Ruth. 2005. "From 'Rich Port' to Bridgeport: Puerto Ricans in Connecticut." In Whalen and Vázquez-Hernández 2005, 174–99.

Goffman, Erving. 1961. *Asylums: Essays on the Social Situation of Mental Patients and Other Inmates.* New York: Doubleday.

Gomez, Carlos M. 1948. Letter to Manuel Cabranes, August 17, 1948. Case 0254. File: 0253–0275, 8/18–8/23/48. Box 2248. Case Files, Social Services. Migration Division, Centro Archives.

———. 1966a. "Train-Bus Accident," memorandum to Joseph Monserrat and Anthony Vega, February 25, 1966. File 1: Correspondence, Farm Labor Program, Assistant Director. Box 467. Correspondence. Farm Labor Program, 1948–93. Migration Division, Centro Archives.

———. 1966b. "Transfer of Contract Workers to Permanent Employees of Jackson and Perkins," letter from Carlos M. Gomez to John Slagle, September 19, 1966. File 2: Correspondence, Farm Labor Program, Assistant Director. Box 467. Correspondence. Farm Labor Program, 1948–93. Migration Division, Centro Archives.

González, Gilbert G. 1994. *Labor and Community: Mexican Citrus Worker Villages in a Southern California County, 1900–1950.* Urbana: University of Illinois Press.

———. 2006. *Guest Workers or Colonized Labor? Mexican Labor Migration to the United States.* Boulder, CO: Paradigm.

Goodwin, Robert C. 1948. "The Farm Labor Job." *Employment Service Review* 15 (4): 3–4.

————. 1951. Letter to Sierra Berdecía, March 19, 1951. File: U.S. Department of Labor, Robert C. Goodwin. Box 167. Correspondencia de la Oficina de la Directora, T a la V. Tarea 61–55. Negociado de Seguridad de Empleo. Fondo Departamento del Trabajo. AGPR.

————. 1958. "The Challenge That Lies Ahead." *Employment Security Review* 25 (3): 3–4.

Goott, Daniel. 1949. "Employment of Foreign Workers in United States Agriculture." *U.S. Department of State Bulletin* 21 (July 4): 43–46.

Gordillo, Gastón. 2004. *Landscapes of Devils: Tensions of Place and Memory in the Argentinean Chaco.* Durham, NC: Duke University Press.

Gray, Margaret. 2010. "How Latin American Inequality Becomes Latino Inequality: A Case Study of Hudson Valley Farmworkers." In *Indelible Inequalities in Latin America: Insights from History, Politics, and Culture,* edited by Paul Gootenberg and Luis Reygadas, 169–92. Durham, NC: Duke University Press.

Gray, Margaret, and Emma Kreyche. 2007. *The Hudson Valley Farmworker Report: Understanding the Needs and Aspirations of a Voiceless Population.* Annandale: Bard College Migrant Labor Project.

Green, Phillip A. 1976. Letter to Steven Karalekas, September 22, 1976. File 15: Correspondence, July–September 1976. Box 388. Apple Harvest, 1959–81. Farm Labor Program, 1948–93. Migration Division, Centro Archives.

Griffith, David C. 1991. "Seasonal Agricultural Labor and Recruitment Methods in the Eastern United States: An Overview with Special Attention to the Northeast." In Commission on Agricultural Workers 1991, 1035–46.

————. 1993. *Jones's Minimal: Low-Wage Labor in the United States.* Albany: State University of New York Press.

————. 2006. *American Guestworkers: Jamaicans and Mexicans in the U.S. Labor Market.* State College: Pennsylvania State University Press.

————, ed. 2014. *(Mis)managing Migration: Guestworkers' Experiences with North American Labor Markets.* Santa Fe, NM: School for Advanced Research.

Griffith, David, and Ed Kissam. 1995. *Working Poor: Farmworkers in the United States.* With Jeronimo Camposeco, Anna García, Max Pfeffer, David Runsten, and Manuel Valdés Pizzini. Philadelphia: Temple University Press.

Griffith, David, and Manuel Valdés Pizzini. 2002. *Fishers at Work, Workers at Sea: A Puerto Rican Journey through Labor and Refuge.* Philadelphia: Temple University Press.

Grosfoguel, Ramón. 2003. *Colonial Subjects: Puerto Ricans in a Global Perspective.* Berkeley: University of California Press.

Grossman, Jonathan. 1978. "Fair Labor Standards Act of 1938: Maximum Struggle for a Minimum Wage." *Monthly Labor Review* 101 (6): 22–30.

Guerin-Gonzales, Camille. 1994. *Mexican Workers and American Dreams: Immigration, Repatriation, and California Farm Labor, 1900–1939.* New Brunswick, NJ: Rutgers University.

Guerra-Mondragón, Gabriel. 1944. Memorandum to Rexford G. Tugwell, August 7, 1944. Box 269. Tarea 96–20. Fondo Oficina del Gobernador. AGPR.

Haber, William, and Daniel H. Kruger. 1964. *The Role of the United States Employment Service in a Changing Economy*. Kalamazoo: Upjohn Institute for Employment Research.

Haddad, Charles. 1982. "Home's Where the Harvest Is." *Buffalo Courier-Express*, September 19, 1982, 17–19, 21, 25, 27.

Hahamovitch, Cindy. 1997. *The Fruits of Their Labor: Atlantic Coast Farmworkers and the Making of Migrant Poverty, 1870–1945*. Chapel Hill: University of North Carolina Press.

———. 2003. "Creating Perfect Immigrants: Guestworkers of the World in Historical Perspective." *Labor History* 44 (1): 69–94.

———. 2011. *No Man's Land: Jamaican Guestworkers in America and the Global History of Deportable Labor*. Princeton: Princeton University Press.

———. 2014. "Risk the Truck: Guestworker-Sending States and the Myth of Managed Migration." In Griffith 2014, 3–32.

———. 2015. "Slavery's Stale Soil: Indentured Servants, Guestworkers, and the End of Empire." In Bender and Lipman 2015, 227–66.

Ham, William. T. 1940. "Farm Labor in an Era of Change." In *Farmers in a Changing World: The Yearbook of Agriculture*, 907–21. Washington, DC: USDA.

———. 1941. "The Management of Seasonal Labor." *Land Policy Review* 4 (9): 29–34.

Haney López, Ian. 1996. *White by Law: The Legal Construction of Race*. New York: New York University Press.

*Hartford Courant*. 1952. "Puerto Rican Farm Workers Chosen with Extreme Care." May 18, 1952, 23.

———. 1973a. "META Gets $25,000 from Two Churches." April 1, 1973, 25.

———. 1973b. "Migrant Demonstration." August 31, 1973, 36.

———. 1973c. "Puerto Rico Forming Tobacco-Worker Unit." October 6, 1973, 9.

———. 1973d. "Trespassing Nulled for Organizers." November 19, 1973, 22.

———. 1973e. "Will Contact Puerto Rico: Migrants to Petition for Probe." August 3, 1973, 29D.

———. 1974a. "Migrant Office Hires Former Grower Employe [sic]." March 6, 1974, 48.

———. 1974b. "Tobacco Growers Must Open Camps." February 21, 1974, 1B.

———. 1975a. "Residents Discover Work in Area Tobacco Fields." June 25, 1975, 1B.

———. 1975b. "Tobacco Farms in State Lose Labor Supply." March 14, 1975, 8.

———. 1981. "Shrinking Tobacco Fields in State Make Hispanic Farmhand a Rarity." January 11, 1981, A25.

Henderson, Julia. 1945. "Foreign Labor in the U.S. during the War." *International Labor Review* 52 (December): 609–63.

Hepler, A. 1966. "North Collins Labor Camps: A Report on the Erie County Migrant Situation," July 18, 1966. File 41: North Collins Labor Camps. Box 2367. Subject and Resource File. Farm Labor Program, 1948–93. Migration Division, Centro Archives.

Hernández Colón, Rafael. 1973. "El rol de la comunidad puertorriqueña en los Estados Unidos en el desarrollo integral de Puerto Rico." *Revista del Trabajo* 6–7

(24–25): 1–13. December 6, 1973. File 9: Revista del trabajo, July–September 1973. Box 3247. Reference Files, Administration. Migration Division, Centro Archives.

History Task Force, Centro de Estudios Puertorriqueños, ed. 1979. *Labor Migration under Capitalism: The Puerto Rican Experience.* New York: Monthly Review.

———. 1982. *Sources for the Study of Puerto Rican Migration, 1879–1930.* New York: Research Foundation of the City University of New York.

Holden, Christopher. 2002. "Bitter Harvest: Housing Conditions of Migrant and Seasonal Farmworkers." In *The Human Cost of Food: Farmworkers' Lives, Labor, and Advocacy,* edited by Charles D. Thompson Jr. and Melinda F. Wiggins, 169–93. Austin: University of Texas Press.

Holman, Philip A. 1957. "Draft of Text for Orientation on Folder on Climate and Clothing," Memorandum to Pedro Grau, December 20, 1957. File: Adult Education Programs, 1956–57. Box 2907. Subject Files, General, Administration. Migration Division, Centro Archives.

Housing Assistance Council. 1997. *Housing for Families and Unaccompanied Migrant Farmworkers.* Washington, DC: Housing Assistance Council.

Human Relations Council of Greater New Haven. [1959?]. *Su guía a New Haven.* File: *Su guía,* New Haven. Box 3273. Reference, Administration. Migration Division, Centro Archives.

Hurd, T.N. 1953. *New York's Harvest Labor.* Albany, NY: Interdepartmental Committee on Farm and Food Processing Labor.

Ilerio, Pedro. 1977. Activity report to Etiony Aldarondo, September 22, 1977. File 15: Correspondence, New York Regional Office, 1977–78. Box 476. Correspondence. Farm Labor Program, 1948–93. Migration Division, Centro Archives.

*Imparcial, El.* 1947a. "CGT pide discutir el contrato suscrito por obreros que emigran." January 24, 1947, 6.

———. 1947b. "Una emigración desastrosa." May 18, 1947, 10.

———. 1947c. "Géigel pide se reduzcan descuentos a obreros." January 25, 1947, 7.

———. 1947d. "Géigel Polanco relata queja de los obreros boricuas en Chicago." January 24, 1947, 6, 32.

———. 1947e. "No permiten emigración que no se ajuste a lo recomendado por Géigel." February 5, 1947, 4.

———. 1947f. "Senado aprueba proyecto de Géigel reglamentando emigraciones de obreros." April 14, 1947, 6.

———. 1949. "Denuncian mal trato a obreros boricuas," letter to editor, Enrique Custodio, Utuado, October 11, 1949. File: Department of Labor. Box 2254. Tarea 96–20. Fondo Oficina del Gobernador. AGPR.

———. 1958. "Atienda a eso, Señor Sierra Berdecía," August 9, 1958. File 2: Correa–Falcon. Box 391. Claims and Complaints. Farm Labor Program, 1948–93. Migration Division, Centro Archives.

Janson, Donald. 1973. "New Union Is Organizing East's Migrant Workers: Asks Recognition." *New York Times,* November 24, 1973, 66.

———. 1974. "Migrants Have Come Up; There Was Nowhere Else to Go." *New York Times,* July 28, 1974, 163.

————. 1980. "Effects of Jersey Farm Strike Are Spreading." *New York Times,* September 1, 1980, B2.

————. 1982. "Access to Farm Labor Camps Stirs Furor in Jersey." *New York Times,* January 3, 1982, 46.

Johnson, Alfred S., ed. 1901. *The Cyclopedic Review of Current History, 1900.* Vol. 10. Boston: Current History.

Johnson, Howard. 1984. "The Anglo-American Caribbean Commission and the Extension of American Influence in the British Caribbean, 1942–1945." *Journal of Commonwealth and Comparative Politics* 22 (2): 180–203.

Jorgenson, Janet M., David E. Williams, and John H. Burma. 1961. *Migratory Agricultural Workers in the United States.* Grinnell, IA: Grinnell College.

Jung, Moon-Ho. 2006. *Coolies and Cane: Race, Labor, and Sugar in the Age of Emancipation.* Baltimore: Johns Hopkins University Press.

Kassner Minna F. 1954. Letter to Congressman Emanuel Celler, June 8, 1954. File: C.L. Action, Federal, Migrant Labor, Appropriation, 1954. Box 1.1. Collection 5307. Consumers' League Records of New York City. Kheel Center.

Keegan, E.L. 1958. Letter to George S. Pfaus, September 2, 1958. File: New Jersey 411, 1957. Box 17. General Subject Files, 1957–61. Records of the Bureau of Employment Security. RG 183. NARA.

Killie, Willard B. 1943a. Letter to B.W. Thoron, November 15, 1943. File: 9-8-116. Box 1138. Classified Files, 1907–51. Office of Territories. RG 126. NARA.

————. 1943b. Letter to Rexford G. Tugwell, September 27, 1943. File: 9-8-116. Box 1138. Classified Files, 1907–51. Office of Territories. RG 126. NARA.

Kirchheimer, Anne. 1976. "Migrant Pickers Fired, Bused to Boston and Stranded." *Boston Globe,* September 29, 1976.

Kirstein, Peter Neil. 1977. *Anglo over Bracero: A History of the Mexican Worker in the United States from Roosevelt to Nixon.* San Francisco: R and E Research Associates.

Knight-Ridder Newspapers. 1986. "Farm Workers Union Pries Door Open: 1st Pact on East Coast Strengthens Bargaining Position in 2 States." *Chicago Tribune,* May 25, 1986.

Lapp, Michael. 1990. "Managing Migration: The Migration Division of Puerto Rico and Puerto Ricans in New York City, 1948–1968." PhD diss., Johns Hopkins University.

————. 1995. "The Rise and Fall of Puerto Rico as a Social Laboratory, 1945–1965." *Social Science History* 19 (2): 169–99.

Larson, Olaf. 1957. "New York Farm Labor Study." File 15: Farm Labor Study, 1957. Box 27. Migrant Farm Labor Study Papers. Series 5: Migrant Workers. Collection 21-33-1791. Division of Rare and Manuscript Collections. Cornell University.

Lasker, Bruno. 1969. *Filipino Immigration to Continental United States and Hawaii.* New York: Arno.

Latourette, William. 1951. Letter to Teodoro Moscoso, July 26, 1951. Box 2276. Tarea 96–20. Fondo Oficina del Gobernador. AGPR.

Lee, Erika. 2003. *At America's Gate: Chinese Immigration during the Exclusion Era, 1882–1943*. Chapel Hill: University of North Carolina Press.

Li, Tania Murray. 2005. "Beyond 'the State' and Failed Schemes." *American Anthropologist* 107 (3): 383–94.

———. 2007. *The Will to Improve: Governmentality, Development, and the Practice of Politics*. Durham, NC: Duke University Press.

Lianos, Theodore P., and Scott Cauchois Jr. 1972. "The Effect of the 1966 Amendment of the Fair Labor Standards Act on Agricultural Employment in the U.S. South." *Annals of Regional Science* 6 (1): 145–59.

Lillesand, David J. 1973. Letter to Jose A. Rivera, October 16, 1973. File 1: *Vazquez v. Ferre*, Case 31.8. Correspondence, Litigation. Puerto Rican Legal Defense and Education Fund. Centro Archives.

Liss, Samuel. 1941. *Migratory Farm Labor in New Jersey*. Washington, DC: Farm Security Administration, USDA.

Llamas, Frank R. 1977. "Puerto Rican Migrant Farmworkers in Massachusetts and Connecticut: A Case Study of Perceived Training and Service Needs." EdD diss., University of Massachusetts.

Llorente, Elizabeth. 2016. "Puerto Rican Farmworkers Fired for Being Less Productive Than Mexicans, They Claim." *Fox News*. June 27, 2016. www.foxnews.com /world/2016/06/27/puerto-rican-farmworkers-say-were-fired-for-not-being-as-productive-as-mexicans.html.

Loperena, William. 1973a. "El comercio de emigrantes." *Revista Avance,* August 13, 1973, 19–21.

———. 1973b. "Sindicato de migrantes agrícolas intenta negociar contrato." *Revista Avance,* December 17, 1973, 27–28.

López, Ann Aurelia. 2007. *The Farmworker's Journey*. Berkeley: University of California Press.

López, Juan A. 1990. "Ingresos trabajadores agrícolas, 1989," memorandum to Nahro Díaz, April 30, 1990. File 2: Farm Labor Program, Supervisor. Box 472. Correspondence. Farm Labor Program, 1948–93. Migration Division, Centro Archives.

———. 1993. "Comparación de salarios y comidas entre Glassboro Service Association de New Jersey y otros agricultores," memorandum to Arcilio Alvarado, March 31, 1993. File 5: Farm Labor Program, Supervisor. Box 472. Correspondence. Farm Labor Program, 1948–93. Migration Division, Centro Archives.

Lovler, Ronnie. [1976?]. "Heartache at Orchard: Migrant 'Paid' $14.55." *San Juan Star*. File 19: Newspaper Clippings. Box 388. Apple Harvest, 1959–81. Farm Labor Program, 1948–93. Migration Division, Centro Archives.

Low, Robert A., and Joseph Monserrat. 1959. *First Report of Continuations Committee, Third Migration Conference, San Juan, Puerto Rico, Jan. 19–26, 1958*. New York: Committee.

Lumen Román, José. 1957a. "Echan de Glassboro a dos representantes de El Diario." *El Diario de Nueva York,* July 28, 1957.

———. 1957b. "¡Hasta Hambre Pasan en Glassboro! Trabajadores culpan a Muñoz Marín por la despreocupación que muestra por su causa." *El Diario de Nueva York,* July 29, 1957.

Machado, Luis G. 1963. "Vicente Ramos Colón," memorandum to Eulalio Torres, December 11, 1963. File 7: 1963, Rabell-Retamar. Box 420. Claims and Complaints. Farm Labor Program, 1948–93. Migration Division, Centro Archives.

MacLaury, Judson. 1988a. "Carter Administration, 1977–1981." Chapter 8 of *History of the Department of Labor, 1913–1988.* U.S. Department of Labor. Accessed March 16, 2019. www.dol.gov/general/aboutdol/history/dolchp08.

———. 1988b. "Nixon and Ford Administrations, 1969–1977." Chapter 7 of *History of the Department of Labor, 1913–1988.* U.S. Department of Labor. Accessed June 25, 2018. www.dol.gov/general/aboutdol/history/dolchp07.

MacMaster, Neil. 1997. *Colonial Migrants and Racism: Algerians in France, 1900–62.* London: Macmillan.

Maier, Frank H., Sheridan T. Maitland, and Gladys Kleinwort Bowles. 1960. *The Tenure Status of Farmworkers in the United States.* Washington: USDA.

Maldonado, Edwin. 1979. "Contract Labor and the Origins of Puerto Rican Communities in the United States." *International Migration Review* 13 (1): 103–21.

Maldonado Denis, Manuel. 1978. *Puerto Rico y Estados Unidos: Emigración y colonialismo; Un análisis sociohistórico de la emigración puertorriqueña.* Mexico City: Siglo Veintiuno.

Mann, Harold. 1949. Letter to Fernando Sierra Berdecía, April 19, 1949. File: Ordenes. Box 163: Correspondencia de la Oficina de la Directora, 1948–50, A y la E. Tarea 61–55. Negociado de Seguridad de Empleo. Fondo Departamento del Trabajo. AGPR.

———. 1950. Letter to Fernando Sierra Berdecía, July 5, 1950. File: Correspondencia personal, 1949–50. Box 163: Correspondencia de la Oficina de la Directora, 1948–50, A y la E. Tarea 61–55. Negociado de Seguridad de Empleo. Fondo Departamento del Trabajo. AGPR.

Marchán, Rafael. 1918. Statement, October 24, 1918. File 1493. Records of the Bureau of Insular Affairs. RG 350. NARA. Accessed February 26, 2017. http://historymatters.gmu.edu/d/5064.

Marcus, Joseph. 1919. *Labor Conditions in Puerto Rico.* Washington, DC: GPO.

Marín Román, Héctor R. 2009. *¡Llego la gringada! El contexto social-militar estadounidense en Puerto Rico y otros lugares del Caribe hasta 1919.* San Juan: Academia Puertorriqueña de la Historia.

Marshall, Ray. 1981. *The Labor Department in the Carter Administration: A Summary Report.* Washington, DC: U.S. Department of Labor.

Martin, Philip L. 1988. *Harvest of Confusion: Migrant Workers in U.S. Agriculture.* Boulder, CO: Westview.

———. 2002. "Mexican Workers and U.S. Agriculture: The Revolving Door." *International Migration Review* 36 (4): 1124–42.

———. 2003. *Promise Unfulfilled: Unions, Immigration, and the Farm Workers.* Ithaca, NY: Cornell University Press.

———. 2014. "The H-2A Program: Evolution, Impacts, and Outlook." In Griffith 2014, 33–62.

Martínez, Samuel. 1996. "Indifference with Indignation: Anthropology, Human Rights, and the Haitian Bracero." *American Anthropologist* 98 (1): 17–25.

Martínez Matsuda, Verónica. 2009. "Making the Modern Migrant: Work, Community, and Struggle in the Federal Migratory Labor Camp Program, 1935–1947." PhD diss., University of Texas, Austin.

McElroy, Robert C., and Earle E. Gavett. 1965. *Termination of the Bracero Program: Some Effects on Farm Labor and Migrant Housing Needs.* Washington, DC: Economic Research Service, USDA.

McGreevey, Robert C. 2018. *Borderline Citizens: The United States, Puerto Rico, and the Politics of Colonial Migration.* Ithaca, NY: Cornell University Press.

McWilliams, Carey. (1939) 1999. *Factories in the Field: The Story of Migratory Farm Labor in California.* Reprint, Berkeley: University of California Press.

Mejías, Félix. 1946. *Condiciones de vida de las clases jornaleras de Puerto Rico.* Río Piedras: Junta Editora de la Universidad de Puerto Rico.

Meléndez, Edgardo. 2013. "Citizenship and the Alien Exclusion in the Insular Cases: Puerto Ricans in the Periphery of American Empire." *Centro Journal* 25 (1): 106–45.

———. 2017. *Sponsored Migration: The State and Puerto Rican Postwar Migration to the United States.* Columbus: Ohio State University Press.

Meléndez Badillo, Jorell. 2015. "Imagining Resistance: Organizing the Puerto Rican Southern Agricultural Strike of 1905." *Caribbean Studies Journal* 43 (2): 33–82.

Mendez, Bienbenido. 1966. Statement, July 24, 1966. File 49. Box 1280. Director's Files, Administration. Migration Division, Centro Archives.

Mendoza, Roberto. 1959a. Letter to Eulalio Torres, August 28, 1959. File 4: Rosario-Sanchez. Box 393. Claims and Complaints. Farm Labor Program, 1948–93. Migration Division, Centro Archives.

———. 1959b. "Visit to Angelica Nurseries, Mohnton, PA," inter-office report to Eulalio Torres, October 21, 1959. File 29: Angelica Nurseries, Mohnton, Pennsylvania, and Kennedyville, Maryland, 1959. Box 901. Subject and Resource File. Farm Labor Program, 1948–93. Migration Division, Centro Archives.

———. 1966a. Activity report to Anthony Vega, July 15, 1966. File 49. Box 1280. Director's Files, Administration. Migration Division, Centro Archives.

———. 1966b. Activity report to Joseph Monserrat, July 18, 1966. File 49. Box 1280. Director's Files, Administration. Migration Division, Centro Archives.

Meyer, Robert B. 1959. Statement by Governor Meyer to U.S. Senate Sub-committee on Migrant Farm Labor, Trenton, NJ, November 30, 1959. File 14: New Jersey (State of). Box 36. Collection 5307. Consumers' League Records of New York City. Kheel Center.

M. G., Juan. 1952. Letter to government of Puerto Rico, May 29, 1952. Serie 11: Correspondencia, 1952–53. División de Migración. Tarea 63–37. Negociado de Seguridad de Empleo. Fondo Departamento del Trabajo. AGPR.

Migration Division. 1953. *Annual Report.* Annual Reports, 1953–92. Boxes 2733–39. Agency Reports, 1939–92. Administration. Migration Division, Centro Archives.

———. 1954. *Annual Report.* Annual Reports, 1953–92. Boxes 2733–39. Agency Reports, 1939–92. Administration. Migration Division, Centro Archives.

———. 1955. *Annual Report.* Annual Reports, 1953–92. Boxes 2733–39. Agency Reports, 1939–92. Administration. Migration Division, Centro Archives.

———. 1956a. *Annual Report.* Annual Reports, 1953–92. Boxes 2733–39. Agency Reports, 1939–92. Administration. Migration Division, Centro Archives.

———. 1956b. Farm labor newsletter, 56–28, July 13, 1956. File: Farm Labor Newsletter, 1956. Serie 11: Correspondencia, 1958. Division de Migración. Tarea 63–37. Negociado de Seguridad de Empleo. Fondo Departamento del Trabajo. AGPR.

———. 1957. *Annual Report.* Annual Reports, 1953–92. Boxes 2733–39. Agency Reports, 1939–92. Administration. Migration Division, Centro Archives.

———. 1958a. *Annual Farm Labor Report.* File 6: Annual Farm Labor Report, 1958. Box 3248. Reference, Administration. Migration Division, Centro Archives.

———. 1958b. "Registro del movimiento migratorio," Oficina Central (Puerto Rico). File: Registro del movimiento migratorio, 1958. Serie 11: Correspondencia, 1958. Division de Migración. Tarea 63–37. Negociado de Seguridad de Empleo. Fondo Departamento del Trabajo. AGPR.

———. 1959. *A Summary in Facts and Figures.* New York: Puerto Rico Department of Labor.

———. 1961. "Puerto Rico Cracks Down on Illegal Recruitment of Farm Workers, Orders Arrest of Agents of Largest Mainland Recruitment Association," press release, March 13, 1961. File 19: Garden State Service Cooperative Association, Trenton, NJ. Box 938. Subject and Resource File. Farm Labor Program, 1948–93. Migration Division, Centro Archives.

———. 1962. *Annual Report.* Annual Reports, 1953–92. Boxes 2733–39. Agency Reports, 1939–92. Administration. Migration Division, Centro Archives.

———. [1963?]. "Usted en los Estados Unidos: La oportunidad de Pedro y Ramón." File: Correspondence, Farm Labor Program, Director. Box 467. Correspondence. Farm Labor Program, 1948–93. Migration Division, Centro Archives.

———. 1963–69. Various documents. File 10: Florida, 1963–69. Box 936. Subject and Resource File. Farm Labor Program, 1948–93. Migration Division, Centro Archives.

———. 1964. *Annual Report.* Annual Reports, 1953–92. Boxes 2733–39. Agency Reports, 1939–92. Administration. Migration Division, Centro Archives.

———. 1966a. *Annual Report.* Annual Reports, 1953–92. Boxes 2733–39. Agency Reports, 1939–92. Administration. Migration Division, Centro Archives.

———. 1966b. "North Collins Labor Camps," report, July 19, 1966. File 41: North Collins Labor Camp, Special Report on the Situation of North Collins, NY. Box 2367. Subject and Resource File. Farm Labor Program, 1948–93. Migration Division, Centro Archives.

———. 1966c. "Report on Conversation with Mr. Anthony Vega regarding the North Collins Situation," July 15, 1966. File 49. Box 1280. Director's Files, Administration. Migration Division, Centro Archives.

———. 1966d. "Weekend Riot Avoided; Puerto Rican Workers Deprived Civil Liberties; Upstate New York Village Agricultural Workers Exploited," press release, July 13, 1966. File 49. Box 1280. Director's Files, Administration. Migration Division, Centro Archives.

———. 1968. Handwritten notes. File 1: North Collins, New York, 1968. Box 2368. Subject and Resource File. Farm Labor Program, 1948–93. Migration Division, Centro Archives.

———. 1972. Activity report, emergency field report, July 31, 1972. File 33: A.D. Makepeace Company, Wareham, Massachusetts, 1969–73. Box 896. Subject and Resource File. Farm Labor Program, 1948–93. Migration Division, Centro Archives.

———. 1973. "Resumen de evaluaciones temporada interestatal de 1973 por oficinas locales." File 20: Action Plan, Farm Worker Participation in Contract Negotiations, 1973–74. Box 896. Subject and Resource File. Farm Labor Program, 1948–93. Migration Division, Centro Archives.

———. n.d. "Manual of Spanish Phrases: A Service of New Jersey Farm Bureau Supplying Agricultural Labor to New Jersey Farmers." File: Employer's Manual of Spanish Phrases, Glassboro, NJ. Box 3272. Reference, Administration. Migration Division, Centro Archives.

Miller, Martin H. 1942. Letter to Santiago Iglesias Jr., December 21, 1942. Box 269. Tarea 96–20. Fondo Oficina del Gobernador. AGPR.

Miller, Paul F. 1972. *To House the Migrant,* Spring 1972. File: To House the Migrant, NYS Migrant Center. Box 27. Collection 5235. Kheel Center.

Miller, Tom. 2018. "Couple Denied Motel Room after NorCal Clerk Says Puerto Rican License Is Not a U.S. ID." *SFGate,* May 27, 2018. www.sfgate.com/bayarea/article/Couple-denied-motel-room-sacramento-county-id-12947341.php.

Mills, C. Wright, Rose Kohn Goldsen, and Clarence Senior. 1950. *The Puerto Rican Journey: New York's Newest Migrants.* New York: Harper and Brothers.

Mills, Geofrey T., and Hugh Rockoff. 1983. "Business Attitudes towards Wage and Price Controls in World War II." *Business and Economic History* 12:146–57.

Mintz, Sidney W. 1948–49. *The People of Puerto Rico.* Series 4: Journal Entries. Box 2. Research Institute for the Study of Man. New York University Archives.

———. 1998. "The Localization of Anthropological Practice: From Area Studies to Transnationalism." *Critique of Anthropology* 18 (2): 117–33.

Miranda, Antonio. 1967. "Contrato especial 197 cosedoras tabaco viajan a Conecticut." *El Mundo,* September 2, 1967, 1, 22.

Mirengoff, William. 1948. "There Is a Great Recruitment Job Ahead . . . Farm Labor for 354 Million Acres." *Employment Service Review* 15 (4): 6–7.

———. 1954. *Puerto Rican Farm Workers in the Middle Atlantic States.* Washington, DC: U.S. Bureau of Employment Security.

Mirengoff, William, and Mordecai Bail. 1958. "A Decade of Changes in Farm Output and Employment." *Employment Security Review* 25 (3): 5–8.

Mitchell, Don. 1996. *The Lie of the Land: Migrant Workers and the California Landscape.* Minneapolis: University of Minnesota Press.

————. 2012. *"They Saved the Crops": Labor, Landscape, and the Struggle over Industrial Farming in Bracero-Era California.* Athens: University of Georgia Press.

Mitchell, Harry L., and Michael Harrington. 1979. *Mean Things Happening in This Land: The Life and Times of H. L. Mitchell, Co-founder of the Southern Tenant Farmers Union.* Montclair, NJ: Allanheld, Osmun.

Molina, Natalia. 2014. *How Race Is Made in America: Immigration, Citizenship, and the Historical Power of Racial Scripts.* Berkeley: University of California Press.

Monroy, Antonio. 1956. Letter to Eduardo McCormick, March 18, 1956. File: Follow-Up (correspondencia), 1956. Serie 11: Correspondencia, 1958. División de Migración. Tarea 63–27. Negociado de Seguridad de Empleo. Fondo Departamente del Trabajo. AGPR.

Monserrat, Joseph 1957. Weekly report, July 31, 1957. File 4: Director's Weekly Reports. Box 2949. Subject Files, General, Administration. Migration Division, Centro Archives.

Montero, Ann. 1960. "Conversation with Mr. Eulalio Torres of the Puerto Rico Government Labor Department," memorandum to Aaron Cantor, March 23, 1960. File: Commonwealth of Puerto Rico Department of Labor. Box 15. Collection 5307. Consumers' League of New York City Records. Kheel Center.

Montgomery, Paul L. 1966. "Puerto Rican Migrants Upset Upstate Town." *New York Times,* July 17, 1966, 1, 60.

Morales, Julio. 1986. *Puerto Rican Poverty and Migration: We Just Had to Try Elsewhere.* New York: Praeger.

Morales de Cuevas, Idalie. 1954. Aniversario, *Boletín Profesional, International Association Personnel in Employment Security,* IAPES Capitulo de Puerto Rico, 1 (May): 1. File: Correspondencia, 1952–53. Serie 11: Correspondencia, 1952–53. División de Migración. Tarea 63–37. Negociado de Seguridad de Empleo. Fondo Departamento del Trabajo. AGPR.

Morin, Alexander. 1952. *The Organizability of Farm Labor in the United States.* Harvard Studies in Labor in Agriculture 2-HL. Cambridge, MA: Harvard University Press.

Morrisette, W. L. 1956. Telegram to Fernando Sierra Berdecía, June 25, 1956. File: The Supervision of the Farm Placement Program. Serie 11: Correspondencia, 1958. División de Migración. Tarea 63–37. Negociado de Seguridad de Empleo. Fondo Departamento del Trabajo. AGPR.

Moss, Ralph. 1958. Letter to Petroamérica Pagán de Colón, January 8, 1958. File: Puertorriqueños en Nueva York. Box 2283. Tarea 96–20. Fondo Oficina del Gobernador. AGPR.

*Mundo, El.* 1946a. "250 obreros de Puerto Rico en Glassboro, N.J." August 26, 1946, 12.

————. 1946b. "Campamento de boricuas en Nueva Jersey." September 12, 1946, 12.

————. 1946c. "Esta semana saldrán los primeros trabajadores." May 14, 1946, 5, 18.

————. 1946d. "Pérez visitó a trabajadores portorriqueños." October 10, 1946, 12.

————. 1946e. "Pide gobierno auspicie una emigración." August 21, 1946, 1, 20.

———. 1946f. "Reciben buen trato los obreros boricuas en E.U." September 15, 1946, 1, 12.

———. 1946g. "Salen hoy de la Isla con rumbo a fincas y fábricas de Pennsylvania." May 16, 1946, 4.

———. 1946h. "Sorprendió a Piñero queja Marcantonio." August 28, 1946, 1, 22.

———. 1946i. "Trabajadores portorriqueños en Nueva Jersey." August 24, 1946, 7.

———. 1947a. "Hallan desajuste entre las obreras en Chicago." March 6, 1947, 14.

———. 1947b. "Otros dos mil boricuas irán a trabajar a E.U. próximamente." January 20, 1947, 1, 18.

———. 1947c. "Pérez estudia medida sobre la emigración." January 28, 1947, 1.

———. 1947d. "Protestan obreros de la isla llevados a California." March 6, 1947, 1.

———. 1947e. "Sierra Berdecía designado para dirigir Departamento Trabajo." June 30, 1947.

———. 1977. "Secretario de trabajo no enviara obreros a EU sin contrato." September 30, 1977.

Muñiz, Rafael H. 1964. "Suicide Case of Contract Worker," field operations activity report to Eulalio Torres, June 30, 1964. File 12: New Jersey Inter-office Reports, 1964. Box 886. Reports. Farm Labor Program, 1948–93. Migration Division, Centro Archives.

———. 1965. Progress report on projects to Anthony Vega, August 25, 1965. File 26: Adamucci, Nick, Beverly, New Jersey. Box 896. Subject and Resource File. Farm Labor Program, 1948–93. Migration Division, Centro Archives.

———. 1968. "Investigation of Car-Accident Death of Puerto Rican Family in North Carolina," memorandum to Anthony Vega, April 22, 1968. File 4: Car Accident, Puerto Rican Family in North Carolina, 1968. Box 911. Subject and Resource File. Farm Labor Program, 1948–93. Migration Division, Centro Archives.

———. 1973. Letter to Anthony Amenta, November 16, 1973. File 20: Action Plan, Farm Worker Participation in Contract Negotiations, 1973–74. Box 896. Subject and Resource File. Farm Labor Program, 1948–93. Migration Division, Centro Archives.

Muñoz Marín, Luis. 1946. "Foro Público sobre el problema poblacional de P.R., resumen de las soluciones ofrecidas por los ponentes en la sesión de julio 19, 1946." File 16: 1B Office of Information. Serie 2: Gobierno insular. Subserie: Fortaleza, 1946. Sección 4: Presidente del Senado, 1941–48. Subsección 1: Datos y estadísticas, Luis Muñoz Marín. ALMM.

Murrow, Edward R. 1960. *Harvest of Shame*. New York: CBS Television.

Myers, John E. B. 2008. "A Short History of Child Protection in America." *Family Law Quarterly* 42 (3): 449–63.

Narotzky, Susana, and Gavin Smith. 2006. *Immediate Struggles: People, Power and Place in Rural Spain*. Berkeley: University of California Press.

Narváez, Ramón A. 1977. "Obreros migrantes." Master's thesis, Urban Planning, University of Puerto Rico, Río Piedras.

Nash, James, 1973. *Report and Recommendations on Migratory Farmworkers in Massachusetts*. Boston: Massachusetts Council of Churches.

Nelkin, Dorothy. 1970. *On the Season: Aspects of Migrant Labor System*. Ithaca: New York State School of Industrial and Labor Relations, Cornell University.

*New York Amsterdam News*. 1965. "Farmers Lose Cheap Help to Competitors." January 13, 1965.

*New York Times*. 1900. "A Puerto Rican Detained: Citizenship Questioned at Barge Office; An Appeal to Courts." April 4, 1900, 2.

——. 1950. "Alien Farm Labor Is Barred in State." April 5, 1950, 32.

——. 1967. "Jersey May Help Negro Migrants." September 28, 1967.

——. 1976. "Two Farm Unions Agree on Merger, Chavez Joins with Puerto Rican Group in East." June 21, 1976, 52.

Nieves Falcón, Luis. 1975. *El emigrante puertorriqueño*. Río Piedras: Edil.

Ngai, Mae M. 2004. *Impossible Subjects: Illegal Aliens and the Making of Modern America*. Princeton: Princeton University Press.

NJDLI (New Jersey Department of Labor and Industry). 1956. *12th Annual Bureau of Migrant Labor Report*. Trenton: New Jersey Department of Labor and Industry.

——. 1957. *13th Annual Bureau of Migrant Labor Report*. Trenton: New Jersey Department of Labor and Industry.

Norris, Alison Holt, and Eric Worby. 2012. "The Sexual Economy of a Sugar Plantation: Privatization and Social Welfare in Northern Tanzania." *American Ethnologist* 39 (2): 354–70.

North Jersey Office. 1957a. Memorandum to Eulalio Torres, August 19, 1957. File 7: Correspondence, Keyport Regional Office. Box 474. Correspondence. Farm Labor Program, 1948–93. Migration Division, Centro Archives.

——. 1957b. Memorandum to South New Jersey Office, April 29, 1957. File 7: Correspondence, Keyport Regional Office. Box 474. Correspondence. Farm Labor Program, 1948–93. Migration Division, Centro Archives.

——. 1959a. Inter-office report to Eulalio Torres, August 24, 1959. File 6: New Jersey Office, Inter-office Reports, March 1959–July 1959. Box 886. Reports. Farm Labor Program, 1948–93. Migration Division, Centro Archives.

——. 1959b. Inter-office report to Eulalio Torres, March 30, 1959. File 6: New Jersey Office, Inter-office Reports, March 1959–July 1959. Box 886. Reports. Farm Labor Program, 1948–93. Migration Division, Centro Archives.

——. 1959c. Inter-office report to Eulalio Torres, October 8, 1959. File 7: New Jersey Office, Inter-office Reports, August–October 1959. Box 886. Reports. Farm Labor Program, 1948–93. Migration Division, Centro Archives.

——. 1960. Inter-office report to Anthony Vega, August 2, 1960. File 8: New Jersey Office, Inter-office Reports, 1960. Box 886. Reports. Farm Labor Program, 1948–93. Migration Division, Centro Archives.

NYSDL (New York State Department of Labor). 1949. "Child Labor on New York State Farms, 1948," Special Bulletin 227. File 20: Agricultural Labor, Child Labor on Farms. Box 5. Collection 5307. Consumers' League Records of New York City. Kheel Center.

——. 1951. *Farm and Food Processing Labor, 1950 Annual Report*. Rochester, NY: New York State Farm Placement Service.

———. 1955. *Farm and Food Processing Labor, 1954 Annual Report.* Rochester, NY: New York State Farm Placement Service.

———. 1956. *Farm and Food Processing Labor, 1955 Annual Report.* Rochester, NY: New York State Farm Placement Service.

———. 1957. *Annual Agricultural and Food Processing Report.* File: Migrant Labor, NY State Government Reports. Box 39. Collection 5307. Consumers' League Records of New York City. Kheel Center.

———. 1958. *Farm and Food Processing Labor, 1957 Annual Report.* Rochester, NY: New York State Farm Placement Service.

———. 1959. *Farm and Food Processing Labor, 1958 Annual Report.* Rochester, NY: New York State Farm Placement Service.

NYSIC (New York State Interdepartmental Committee on Farm and Food Processing Labor). 1948a. Minutes of meeting, July 1, 1948. File 10: Minutes of Meetings, 1948. Box 1. Collection 21–33–1085: Department of Rural Sociology Records, 1920–77. Division of Rare and Manuscript Collections. Cornell University.

———. 1948b. Newsletter, no. 6, July 7, 1948. File 9: NYS Interdepartmental Committee on Farm and Food Processing Labor Newsletters. Box 1. Collection 21–33–1085: Department of Rural Sociology Records, 1920–77. Division of Rare and Manuscript Collections. Cornell University.

———. 1949. *New York's Harvest Labor.* Albany: NYSIC.

———. 1953. Minutes of meetings, May 19, 1953. File 14: Minutes of Meetings, 1953. Box 1. Collection 21–33–1085: Department of Rural Sociology Records, 1920–77. Division of Rare and Manuscript Collections. Cornell University.

———. 1961. *Migrant Farm Labor in New York State.* Albany: NYSIC.

———. 1963. *Migrant Farm Labor in New York State.* Albany: NYSIC.

NYSJLC (New York State Joint Legislative Committee on Migrant Labor). 1957. *Report of the New York State Joint Legislative Committee on Migrant Labor.* No. 14. Albany: NYSJLC.

———. 1958. *Report of the New York State Joint Legislative Committee on Migrant Labor.* No. 20. Albany: NYSJLC.

———. 1959. *Report of the New York State Joint Legislative Committee on Migrant Labor.* No. 28. Albany: NYSJLC.

———. 1964. *Report of the New York State Joint Legislative Committee on Migrant Labor.* No. 36. Albany: NYSJLC.

O'Connor, Donald J. 1947. "No Panaceas for Puerto Rico," memorandum to Jesús T. Piñero, March 4, 1947. Box 236. Tarea 96–20. Fondo Oficina del Gobernador. AGPR.

———. 1948. Letter to Sierra Berdecía, circa July 1948. File 34: Commissioner of Labor, Fernando Sierra Berdecía. Box 915. Subject and Resource File. Farm Labor Program, 1948–93. Migration Division, Centro Archives.

Oficina del Gobernador, Negociado de Presupuesto, División de Estadísticas. 1952. "Estudio sobre la emigración en Puerto Rico, encuesta en la semana del 21 al 27 de abril de 1952," San Juan, December 1952. Box 1207. Tarea 96–20. Fondo Oficina del Gobernador. AGPR.

OGPRUS (Offices of the Government of Puerto Rico in the United States). 1953–92. Annual reports. Microfilm. Boxes 2733–39. Agency Reports, 1939–92. Migration Division to Department of Puerto Rican Community Affairs in the United States. Administration Program. Migration Division, Centro Archives.

O'Leary, Christopher J., and Randall W. Eberts. 2008. *The Wagner-Peyser Act and U.S. Employment Service: Seventy-Five Years of Matching Job Seekers and Employers.* Report prepared for Center for Employment Security Education and Research, National Association of State Workforce Agencies. December 2008. http://research.upjohn.org/reports/29.

Olmo, José, and Dicxon Valderruten. 1988. *Brief History of Puerto Ricans in Buffalo.* Bronx, NY: IPRUS Institute.

Ortiz, Laura L. 1998. "Disrupting the Colonial Gaze: A Critical Analysis of the Discourses on Puerto Ricans in the United States." PhD diss., City University of New York Graduate Center.

Ortiz, Santiago. 1946. Report to the Office of Puerto Rico, Washington, DC, September 10, 1946. File: 9-8-116. Box 1138. Classified Files, 1907–51. Office of Territories. RG 126. NARA.

Ortíz Cuadra, Cruz Miguel. 2013. *Eating Puerto Rico: A History of Food, Culture, and Identity.* Chapel Hill: University of North Carolina Press.

Padilla, Félix. 1987. *Puerto Rican Chicago.* Notre Dame, IN: University of Notre Dame Press.

Padros Herrero, J. 1956. "Obreros boricuas terminan huelga." *El Mundo,* March 31, 1956, 3.

Pagán de Colón, Petroamérica. 1948. Annual report, 1947–48. File: Annual Reports. Box 163: Correspondencia de la Oficina de la Directora, 1948–50, A y la E. Tarea 61–55. Negociado de Seguridad de Empleo. Fondo Departamento del Trabajo. AGPR.

———. 1949. Letter to Estella Draper, June 23, 1949. File: Correspondencia personal, 1949–50. Box 163: Correspondencia de la Oficina de la Directora, 1948–50, A y la E. Tarea 61–55. Negociado de Seguridad de Empleo. Fondo Departamento del Trabajo. AGPR.

———. 1950a. Letter to Alan F. Perl, January 5, 1950. File: Correspondencia personal, 1949–50. Box 163: Correspondencia de la Oficina de la Directora, 1948–50, A y la E. Tarea 61–55. Negociado de Seguridad de Empleo. Fondo Departamento del Trabajo. AGPR.

———. 1950b. Letter to Bambi, December 14, 1950. File: Correspondencia personal, 1949–50. Box 163: Correspondencia de la Oficina de la Directora, 1948–50, A y la E. Tarea 61–55. Negociado de Seguridad de Empleo. Fondo Departamento del Trabajo. AGPR.

———. 1951. *Annual Report, 1950–1951: Puerto Rico Employment Service.* San Juan: Puerto Rico Department of Labor. Box 163: Correspondencia de la Oficina de la Directora, 1948–50, A y la E. Tarea 61–55. Negociado de Seguridad de Empleo. Fondo Departamento del Trabajo. AGPR.

———. 1955. "Un año que comienza." *Boletín Profesional, International Association Personnel in Employment Security,* IAPES Capitulo de Puerto Rico 2 (1): 1. File: Correspondencia, 1952–53. Serie 11: Correspondencia, 1952–53. División de Migración. Tarea 63–37. Negociado de Seguridad de Empleo. Fondo Departamento del Trabajo. AGPR.

———. 1956a. *Programa de trabajadores migratorios de Puerto Rico a los Estados Unidos.* San Juan: Estado Libre Asociado de Puerto Rico, Departamento del Trabajo.

———. 1956b. "Reclutamiento de trabajadores para Glassboro Service Association, Inc., durante el mes de abril," memorandum to gerentes, March 23, 1956. File: Visitas a las oficinas locales División de Operaciones, 1958. Serie 11: Correspondencia, 1958. División de Migración. Tarea 63–37. Negociado de Seguridad de Empleo. Fondo Departamento del Trabajo. AGPR.

Papirno, Elissa. 1973a. "Ex-Director Berates Farmworkers' Unit." *Hartford Courant,* December 6, 1973, 15.

———. 1973b. "Migrant Camp Chief Adamant on Barring Health Personnel." *Hartford Courant,* August 3, 1973, 27.

———. 1973c. "Puerto Rican Tobacco Workers Decide to Form Organization." *Hartford Courant,* August 6, 1973, 6A.

———. 1973d. "Puerto Rico Said Probing Migrant Workers' Woes." *Hartford Courant,* September 14, 1973, 4.

———. 1974a. "Agency Plans Office for Migrant Labor." *Hartford Courant,* January 22, 1974, 35.

———. 1974b. "Better Migrants' Life Sought." *Hartford Courant,* April 17, 1974.

———. 1974c. "Farm Group Recruits Puerto Rican Women." *Hartford Courant,* August 27, 1974, 2.

———. 1974d. "Growers Reject Bid for Union." *Hartford Courant,* July 6, 1974, 13.

———. 1974e. "State Tobacco Growers Improve Worker Camps." *Hartford Courant,* June 25, 1974, 1.

———. 1974f. "Tobacco Union Says Workers Intimidated." *Hartford Courant,* July 24, 1974, 7.

———. 1975. "$750,000 Serving 175 Workers." *Hartford Courant,* July 20, 1975, 27A.

Pappas, Nancy. 1974a. "Labor Council Backs Tobacco Workers." *Hartford Courant,* August 3, 1974, 19.

———. 1974b. "'Radical Chic' Party Assists Hispanics." *Hartford Courant,* August 26, 1974, 1A.

Paralitici, Ché. 2006. *No quiero mi cuerpo pa' tambor: El servicio militar obligatorio en Puerto Rico.* San Juan: Puerto.

Parker, Carleton Hubbell, and Cornelia Stratton Parker. 1920. *The Casual Laborer and Other Essays.* New York: Harcourt, Brace and Howe.

Parsons, Howard L. 1952. *The Impact of Fluctuations in National Income on Agricultural Wages and Employment.* Harvard Studies in Labor in Agriculture 1-HL. Cambridge, MA: Harvard University Press.

*Paso Herald, El.* 1926. "A. F. of L. Abandons Program to Probe Porto Rican Labor: Suggests That Islands Be Placed under Dept. of Interior." October 13, 1926, 4.

Patterson, Mary Jo. 2012. *On the Frontlines of Freedom: A Chronicle of the First 50 years of the American Civil Liberties Union of New Jersey.* Self-published, iUniverse.

Peck, Marvin C. 1991. "The W. I./H-2A Agricultural Labor Program in the United States with Particular Emphasis on the Northeast, Primarily New England and New York." In Commission on Agricultural Workers 1991, 765–67.

Perales, Cesar. 1973. Letter to Leo Motiuk, July 12, 1973. File 1: *Vazquez v. Ferre,* Case 31.8. Correspondence, Litigation. Puerto Rican Legal Defense and Education Fund. Centro Archives.

Perea, Juan. 2011. "The Echoes of Slavery: Recognizing the Racist Origins of Agricultural and Domestic Worker Exclusion from the National Labor Relations Act." *Ohio State Law Journal* 72 (1): 95–138.

Pérez, Gina M. 2004. *The Near Northwest Side Story: Migration, Displacement, and Puerto Rican Families.* Berkeley: University of California Press.

Pérez, Héctor. 1975. "Visita a Bald Hill Nursery en Exeter Rhode Island," memorandum to Juan R. Colón, July 31, 1975. File 4: Correspondence Boston Office, General, June–November 1975. Box 463. Correspondence. Farm Labor Program, 1948–93. Migration Division, Centro Archives.

Pérez, Manuel A. 1945a. "Emigration of Puerto Ricans to Work in Copper Industry in the United States," memorandum to Rexford G. Tugwell, February 20, 1945. Box 269. Tarea 96–20. Fondo Oficina del Gobernador. AGPR.

———. 1945b. Memorandum to A. Fernós Isern, February 28, 1945. File: Emigration. Box 2247. Tarea 96–20. Fondo Oficina del Gobernador. AGPR.

Pérez, Martín. 1986. "Living History, Vineland New Jersey." In *Extended Roots: From Hawaii to New York/Migración Puertorriqueña a los Estados Unidos,* edited by Oral History Task Force, 19–26. New York: Centro de Estudios Puertorriqueños, Hunter College, CUNY.

Pérez Perález, Gustavo. 1952. Letter to Gustavo Agrait, September 19, 1952. File: Michigan, Accounts. Box 2272. Tarea 96–20. Fondo Oficina del Gobernador. AGPR.

Perl, Alan F., and Eulalio Torres. 1958. Letter to Fernando Sierra Berdecía, June 4, 1958. File: Puerto Rico, 1957. Box 26. General Subject Files, 1957–61. Records of the Employment Security. RG 183. NARA.

Perloff, Harvey S. 1950. *Puerto Rico's Economic Future.* Chicago: University of Chicago Press.

Pfeffer, Max J. and Pilar A. Parra. 2005. *Immigrants and the Community: Former Farmworkers.* Report 3, September 2005. Ithaca, NY: Cornell University.

———. 2006. "New Immigrants in Rural Communities: The Challenges of Integration." *Social Text* 24 (3): 81–98.

*Philadelphia Inquirer.* 1993. "Court Limits Picketing Tactics in Mushroom Workers' Walkout." April 3, 1993. File 5: Farm Labor Program, Supervisor. Box 472. Correspondence. Farm Labor Program, 1948–93. Migration Division, Centro Archives.

Picó, Fernando. 1982. *Libertad y servidumbre en el Puerto Rico del siglo XIX.* Río Piedras: Huracán.

Pierre-Charles, Gérard. 1979. *El Caribe contemporáneo.* Mexico City: Siglo Veintiuno.

Pittman, C. W. E. 1948. "It Can and Has Been Done ... Migration by Appointment." *Employment Service Review* 15 (4): 12–14.

Plá, Jaime. 1959. Inter-office report to Eulalio Torres, July 22, 1959. File 1: Sandoval, Santiago. Box 394. Claims and Complaints. Farm Labor Program, 1948–93. Migration Division, Centro Archives.

Planell Larrinaga, Elsa. 1996. "Puerto Rican Rural Women: Effects of Male Migration on Female Roles, a Case Study of a Puerto Rican Community." PhD diss., Rutgers University.

Plascencia, Luis F. B. 2018. "Get Us Our Privilege of Bringing in Mexican Labor: Recruitment and Desire for Mexican Labor in Arizona, 1917–2016." In *Mexican Workers and the Making of Arizona,* edited by Luis F. B. Plascencia and Gloria H. Cuádraz, 124–78. Tucson: University of Arizona Press.

Pollitt, Daniel. H. 1960. *The Migrant Farm Worker in America: Background Data on the Migrant Worker Situation in the United States Today.* Washington, DC: GPO.

Pollock, Sarah. 1981. "Tobacco Workers Struggle against Poverty, Despair." *Hartford Courant,* August 3, 1981, B1, B3.

Pons, Juan A. 1941. "Cost of Living," memorandum. Box 10. Tarea 63–82. Fondo Autoridad de Tierras. AGPR.

———. 1947. Letter to Teodoro Moscoso, July 14, 1947. File: 9-8-116. Box 1138. Classified Files, 1907–51. Office of Territories. RG 126. NARA.

PPRP (People of Puerto Rico Project). 1946–47. "Nómina y jornal promedio de las distintas actividades de la ciudad de Caguas par el año 1946–47." File 7: Conference and Minutes. Series 1: Correspondence. Research Institute for the Study of Man. New York University Archives.

PRBES (Puerto Rico Bureau of Employment Security). 1975. Annual report. File: Rural Employment and Training Services. Box 3274. Reference, Administration. Migration Division, Centro Archives.

PRDL (Puerto Rico Department of Labor). 1947. *Annual Report of the Commissioner of Labor to the Governor of Puerto Rico, Fiscal Year 1944–45.* San Juan: Printing Division, Service Office of the Government of Puerto Rico.

———. 1948a. *Annual Report of the Commissioner of Labor to the Governor of Puerto Rico, Fiscal Year 1945–46.* San Juan: Printing Division, Service Office of the Government of Puerto Rico.

———. 1948b. *Annual Report of the Commissioner of Labor to the Governor of Puerto Rico, Fiscal Year 1946–47.* San Juan: Printing Division, Service Office of the Government of Puerto Rico.

———. 1949. *Annual Report of the Commissioner of Labor to the Governor of Puerto Rico, Fiscal Year 1947–48.* San Juan: Printing Division, Service Office of the Government of Puerto Rico.

———. 1950. *Annual Report of the Commissioner of Labor to the Governor of Puerto Rico, Fiscal Year 1948–49.* San Juan: Printing Division, Service Office of the Government of Puerto Rico.

———. 1951. *Nineteenth Annual Report of the Commissioner of Labor to the Governor of Puerto Rico, Fiscal Year 1949–50.* San Juan: Printing Division, Service Office of the Government of Puerto Rico.

———. 1952a. *Twentieth Annual Report of the Commissioner of Labor to the Governor of Puerto Rico, Fiscal Year 1950–51.* San Juan: Printing Division, Service Office of the Government of Puerto Rico.

———. 1952b. *Twenty-First Annual Report of the Commissioner of Labor, Fiscal Year 1951–52.* San Juan: Printing Division, Service Office of the Government of Puerto Rico.

———. 1953a. "Conclusions of the Conference on Migration Held in San Juan, Puerto Rico, March 1–7, 1953." File: Publicaciones. Box 1207. Tarea 96–20. Fondo Oficina del Gobernador. AGPR.

———. 1953b. "Salarios y condiciones de trabajo en fincas de caña Puerto Rico," 7 (8), May 1953. Box 2248. Tarea 96–20. Fondo Oficina del Gobernador. AGPR.

———. 1953c. "Salarios y condiciones de trabajo en fincas de piña," 7 (6), August 1953. Box 2248. Tarea 96–20. Fondo Oficina del Gobernador. AGPR.

———. 1954a. "División de Colocaciones en Fincas ayuda a resolver demanda de obreros en cafetal." *Boletín de Información,* DT-168, November 18, 1945. File: Oficina de Relaciones Industriales del Trabajo y Públicas. Box 2248. Tarea 96–20. Fondo Oficina del Gobernador. AGPR.

———. 1954b. "Employment Conditions in Puerto Rico during the First Part of 1954, Second Migration Conference, San Juan, June 21–27, 1954." Box 1207. Tarea 96–20. Fondo Oficina del Gobernador. AGPR.

———. 1954c. "Funcionario de la Guyana Británica visitó el Departamento del Trabajo." *Boletín de Información,* DT-143, September 17, 1954. File: Oficina de Relaciones Industriales del Trabajo y Públicas. Box 2248. Tarea 96–20. Fondo Oficina del Gobernador. AGPR.

———. 1954d. "Industria manufacturera del país tenía en junio 66,300 empleados." *Boletín de Información,* DT-146, September 22, 1954. File: Oficina de Relaciones Industriales del Trabajo y Públicas. Box 2248. Tarea 96–20. Fondo Oficina del Gobernador. AGPR.

———. 1954e. "Jornal promedio en fincas de tabaco fue de 16.6 centavos por hora." *Boletín de Información,* DT-130, August 18, 1954. Box 2248. Tarea 96–20. Fondo Oficina del Gobernador. AGPR.

———. 1954f. "Obreros agrícolas migrantes deben obtener tarjeta de seguro social." *Boletín de Información,* DT-172, March 12, 1954. Box 2248. Tarea 96–20. Fondo Oficina del Gobernador. AGPR.

———. 1957. *Annual Agricultural and Food Processing Report, 1957.* San Juan: Farm Placement Section, Puerto Rico Employment Service.

———. 1958. "División de Migración ha ayudado a colocar a más de 85,000 obreros migrantes desde 1949." *Boletín de Información Departamento,* DT-27, September

10, 1958. File: Boletín Departamento del Trabajo. Serie 11: Correspondencia, 1958. División de Migración. Tarea 63–37. Negociado de Seguridad de Empleo. Fondo Departamento del Trabajo. AGPR.

———. 1973a. "Comité de migrantes asesora departamento trabajo sobre contratos," press release, October 26, 1973. File 20: Part 1, Action Plan Farm Worker Participation in Contract Negotiations, 1973–74. Box 896. Subject and Resource File. Farm Labor Program, 1948–93. Migration Division, Centro Archives.

———. 1973b. "Marco A. Rigau Dirige División de Migración." *Noticias del Trabajo* 33 (430–31): 1. Box 3262. Reference, Administration. Migration Division, Centro Archives.

———. 1974a. Editorial. *Noticias del Trabajo* 35 (441): 1, 6. File: *Noticias del Trabajo,* agosto de 1974. Box 3256. Reference, Administration. Migration Division, Centro Archives.

———. 1974b. "Puerto Rican Secretary of Labor Announces Significant Gains in Agricultural Workers Contracts for New Season," press release, March 26, 1974. File 22: Agriculture, General Information. Box 898. Subject and Resource File. Farm Labor Program, 1948–93. Migration Division, Centro Archives.

———. 2018. *Ley Núm. 180 de 27 de julio de 1998, según enmendada, "Ley de salario mínimo, vacaciones y licencia por enfermedad de Puerto Rico."* Accessed August 14, 2019. www.trabajo.pr.gov/docs/Libreria_Laboral/Leyes/Ley%20180–1998,%20 Ley%20de%20Salario%20M%C3%ADnimo,%20Vacaciones%20y%20Licencia% 20por%20Enfermedad%20de%20Puerto%20Rico.pdf.

*Prensa, La.* 1950. "Regresaron a Puerto Rico 198 obreros de Michigan que se enfermaron." October 22, 1950.

PRES (Puerto Rico Employment Service). 1952. *Puerto Rico Post-Season Farm Labor Report, 1952.* Box 1225. Tarea 96–20. Fondo Oficina del Gobernador. AGPR.

———. 1953. "Informe de la labor desarrollada por el Servicio de Empleos en Puerto Rico como parte del programa de migración recomendado por el gobernador," October 14, 1953. File: Emigración. Box 2272. Tarea 96–20. Fondo Oficina del Gobernador. AGPR.

———. 1954. *Puerto Rico Post Season Farm Labor Report, 1954, San Juan.* File 3: 1954. Box 3248. Reference, Administration. Migration Division, Centro Archives.

———. 1956. "Informe de las visitas hechas a distintas áreas agrícolas de los Estados Unidos en excursión de orientación profesional auspiciada por el Departamento del Trabajo del Estado Libre Asociado de Puerto Rico," October 1956. File: Organización y personal, Servicio de Empleos de Puerto Rico. Box 2254. Tarea 96–20. Fondo Oficina del Gobernador. AGPR.

———. 1978. "Puerto Rico Annual Rural Manpower Report, 1978." Box 3257. Reference, Administration. Migration Division, Centro Archives.

President's Commission on Migratory Labor. 1951. *Migratory Labor in American Agriculture.* Washington, DC: GPO.

Pudlin, Bennet. 1991. Letter to Carmen Vanessa De Vila, October 29, 1991. File: Puerto Rican Agricultural Workers, 1980–92. Box 21. Series 6: Joseph Monserrat Papers. Centro Archives.

Puerto Rico Policy Commission. 1934. *Report of the Puerto Rico Policy Commission (Chardón Plan)*. San Juan: Puerto Rico Policy Commission.

Quirós, Carlos S. 1977. Letter to F. Ray Marshall, June 7, 1977. File 17: Correspondence, 1977. Box 387. Apple Harvest, 1959–81. Farm Labor Program, 1948–93. Migration Division, Centro Archives.

Ramírez, Fred. 1993a. Memorandum to Arcilio Alvarado, huelga trabajadores agrícolas, April 13, 1993. File 5: Migration Specialist. Box 472. Correspondence. Farm Labor Program, 1948–93. Migration Division, Centro Archives.

———. 1993b. Memorandum to Mateo "Herbie" Vélez, March 9, 1993. File 5: Migration Specialist. Box 472. Correspondence. Farm Labor Program, 1948–93. Migration Division, Centro Archives.

Ramírez, Gilbert. 1944. "Importation of Puerto Rican Workers," memorandum, April 29, 1944. File: 9–8-116. Box 1138. Classified Files, 1907–51, Office of Territories. RG 126. NARA.

Ramos, Luis G. 1957. Letter to Luis Muñoz Marín, July 18, 1957. File: Puertorriqueños en Nueva York. Box 2283. Tarea 96–20. Fondo Oficina del Gobernador. AGPR.

Ramos Zayas, Ana Y. 2003. *National Performances: The Politics of Class, Race, and Space in Puerto Rican Chicago*. Chicago: University of Chicago Press.

Rasmussen, Wayne D. 1951. *A History of the Emergency Farm Labor Supply Program, 1943–1947*. Washington, DC: Bureau of Agricultural Economics, USDA.

Reoyo, Paul. 1963. "Field Visit to Dix Brothers Farm, Burlington, NJ," activity report to Anthony Vega, July 18. 1963. File 10: Reports. Box 886. Reports. Farm Labor Program, 1948–93. Migration Division, Centro Archives.

*Revista Avance*. 1973. "Rigau vs. Silva Recio: Beame, los obreros migrantes y una renuncia." July 16, 1973, 5–7.

Rhinelander, David. H. 1973. "TB Tests Blocked at Farm Camp." *Hartford Courant*, July 24, 1973, 1A.

Rios, Angel. 1971. Letter to Carmen H. Correa, September 8, 1971. File 1: Cases 1–40, 1969–70. Box 464. Correspondence. Farm Labor Program, 1948–93. Migration Division, Centro Archives.

Rivera, Bernabé. 1966. Statement, August 15, 1966. File 49. Box 1280. Director's Files, Administration. Migration Division, Centro Archives.

Rivera, Edwin. 1969. "Meeting with Puerto Ricans in North Collins on July 27th, 1969," activity report to Ralph S. Rosas, September 9, 1969. File 49. Box 1280. Director's Files, Administration. Migration Division, Centro Archives.

Rivera, Felipe. 1979. "The Puerto Rican Farmworker: From Exploitation to Unionization." In History Task Force 1979, 239–64.

Rivera, Juan A. 1973. Letter to Juan Reyes, April 23, 1973. File 1: *Vazquez v. Ferre*, Case 31.8. Correspondence, Litigation. Puerto Rican Legal Defense and Education Fund. Centro Archives.

Rivera, Marcia. [1968?]. "Puerto Rican Migrants: A Socio-economic Study." Box 3240. Reference, Administration. Migration Division, Centro Archives.

Rivera, P. 1965a. Memorandum to Jaime A. Plá, January 21, 1965. File 8: Correspondence, Keyport Regional Office. Box 475. Correspondence. Farm Labor Program, 1948–93. Migration Division, Centro Archives.

———. 1965b. Weekly report, memorandum to Jaime A. Plá, February 4, 1965. File 8: Correspondence, Keyport Regional Office. Box 475. Correspondence. Farm Labor Program, 1948–93. Migration Division, Centro Archives.

Rivera de Vicenti, Julia. 1971. *Puerto Rico Rural Manpower Service Report.* Hato Rey: Bureau of Employment Security, Department of Labor, Commonwealth of Puerto Rico.

Rivera Hernández, Dolores. 1956. "Viaje a Estados Unidos," memorandum to Luis Muñoz Marín, November 7, 1956. File: Organización y personal. Box 2254. Tarea 96–20. Fondo Oficina del Gobernador. AGPR.

Robertson, W. M. 1948. Letter to Jesús T. Piñero, June 7, 1948. File: Autoridad de transporte, transportación aérea. Box 454. Tarea 96–20. Fondo Oficina del Gobernador. AGPR.

Robinson, Robert S. 2010. "Taking the Fair Deal to the Fields: Truman's Commission on Migratory Labor, Public Law 78, and the Bracero Program, 1950–1952." *Agricultural History* 84 (3): 381–402.

Rockoff, Hugh. 1984. *Drastic Measures: A History of Wage and Price Controls in the United States.* Cambridge: Cambridge University Press.

Rodríguez, Rafael. 1964. Report to Matilde Pérez de Silva, P. Rivera, L. Jimenez, April 25, 1964. File 5: Correspondence, Keyport Regional Office. Box 475. Correspondence. Farm Labor Program, 1948–93. Migration Division, Centro Archives.

Rojas, Manuel F. n.d. *Hablan las víctimas en las expediciones de trabajadores a E.U.* San Juan.

Rola, Carlos F. 1977. "Non-contract Workers Niagara Orchards," progress report on projects to Manuel Rodríguez Escalera, October 5, 1977. File 35: Niagara Orchards, 1977. Box 3011. Subject Files, General, Administration. Migration Division, Centro Archives.

———. 1982. "Rural Employment Conference, Presentation on the Farm Program Component of the Migration Division," memorandum to New York State Department of Labor, April 7, 1982. File 4: Rochester Regional Office. Box 477. Correspondence. Farm Labor Program, 1948–93. Migration Division, Centro Archives.

Rosario Natal, Carmelo. 2001. *Éxodo puertorriqueño: Las emigraciones al Caribe y Hawaii: 1900–1910.* Río Piedras: Edil.

Roseberry, William. 1989. *Anthropologies and Histories: Essays in Culture, History, and Political Economy.* New Brunswick, NJ: Rutgers University Press.

———. 1994. "Hegemony and the Language of Contention." In *Everyday Forms of State Formation,* edited by Gilbert M. Joseph and Daniel Nugent, 355–66. Durham, NC: Duke University Press.

———. 1996. "Hegemony, Power, and Languages of Contention." In *The Politics of Difference: Ethnic Premises in a World of Power,* edited by Edwin N. Wilmsen and Patrick McAllister, 71–84. Chicago: University of Chicago Press.

———. 2002. "Political Economy in the United States." In *Culture, Economy, Power: Anthropology as Critique, Anthropology as Praxis,* edited by Winnie Lem and Belinda Leach, 59–72. Albany: State University of New York Press.

Ruffini, Gene. 2003. *Harry Van Arsdale, Jr.: Labor's Champion.* Armonk, NY: Sharpe.

Ruiz, Guadalupe. 1957a. Letter to Carlos Martinez, September 18, 1957. File 7: Correspondence, Keyport Regional Office. Box 474. Correspondence. Farm Labor Program, 1948–93. Migration Division, Centro Archives.

———. 1957b. Letter to Felipe Maldonado Rosa, July 30, 1957. File 7: Correspondence, Keyport Regional Office. Box 474. Correspondence. Farm Labor Program, 1948–93. Migration Division, Centro Archives.

———. 1957c. Letter to John Tilelli, August 13, 1957. File 7: Correspondence, Keyport Regional Office. Box 474. Correspondence. Farm Labor Program, 1948–93. Migration Division, Centro Archives.

———. 1957d. Letter to William Venegas, September 24, 1957. File 5: Gonzalez–Guzman. Box 391. Claims and Complaints. Farm Labor Program, 1948–93. Migration Division, Centro Archives.

———. 1959a. Letter to William Venegas, November 20, 1959. File 5: Gonzalez–Guzman. Box 391. Claims and Complaints. Farm Labor Program, 1948–93. Migration Division, Centro Archives.

———. 1959b. Report to the 1959 Post-Season Meeting from Guadalupe Ruiz, November 12, 1959. File 4: Correspondence, Field Representative. Box 475. Correspondence. Farm Labor Program, 1948–93. Migration Division, Centro Archives.

———. 1966. Letter to Joseph Monserrat and Ralph S. Rosas, July 20, 1966. File 49. Box 1280. Director's Files, Administration. Migration Division, Centro Archives.

Ruiz Gutiérrez, Julio. 1959. Letter to Luis Muñoz Marín, circa August 1959. File 4: Rosario–Sanchez. Box 393. Claims and Complaints. Farm Labor Program, 1948–93. Migration Division, Centro Archives.

Rushing, Denton O. 1948. "Must Depend Largely on Direction of Domestic Workers . . . Farm Placement Service—Then and Now." *Employment Service Review* 15 (4): 22.

Ruttenberg, Stanley H., and Jocelyn Gutchess. 1970. *The Federal-State Employment Service: A Critique.* Baltimore: Johns Hopkins University Press.

Sanchez, Paul. 1967. Report of Paul Sanchez, September 2, 1967. File 8: Sanchez, Paul, 1962–67. Box 34. Organizing Department. Records, 1955–75. RG 28–002. AFL-CIO Records. George Meany Memorial AFL-CIO Archive, University of Maryland, College Park.

Sánchez Cappa, Luis F. 1946. "Plan para la emigración de 1,000 obreros." *El Mundo,* May 11, 1946, 1, 32.

*San Juan Star.* 1977. "Labor Agency Admits Illegal Recruiting." September 28, 1977.

Santana Rabell, Leonardo. 1984. *Planificación y política durante la administración de Luis Muñoz Marín.* Santurce: Análisis, Revista de Planificación.

Santiago Caraballo, Yaritza. 2014. "Recogerán melones en Estados Unidos por mejor paga." *El Nuevo Día,* April 6, 2014, 6.

Scarano, Francisco A. 1993. *Puerto Rico: Cinco siglos de historia.* San Juan: McGraw-Hill.

Schiffman, Barry. 1973. "Dissident Migrants Reported Back on Job after Food Strike." *Hartford Courant,* April 14, 1973, 36.

Schlimgen, Veta R. 2010. "Neither Citizens nor Aliens: Filipino 'American Nationals' in the U.S. Empire, 1900–1946." PhD diss., University of Oregon.

School of Public Administration, University of Puerto Rico. 1951. "Organization and Functions of the Department of Labor of Puerto Rico," November 1949. Box 1225. Tarea 96–20. Fondo Oficina del Gobernador. AGPR.

Scruggs, Otey. 1960. "The First Mexican Farm Labor Program." *Arizona and the West* 2 (Winter): 319–26.

———. 1988. *Braceros, "Wetbacks," and the Farm Labor Problem: Mexican Agricultural Labor in the United States, 1942–1954.* New York: Garland.

Seaberry, Jane. 1982. "Court Holds Puerto Ricans May Sue Apple Growers: Court Backs Puerto Rico." *Washington Post,* July 2, 1982, C9.

Seda Bonilla, Eduardo. 1973. *Social Change and Personality in a Puerto Rican Agrarian Reform Community.* Evanston: Northwestern University Press.

Segundo, Aurelio. 1992. "Puerto Rican Migrant Farmworkers Contract Program, 1991." In *Report of the Commission on Agricultural Workers,* edited by the Commission on Agricultural Workers, 758–65. Washington, DC: GPO.

Semler, H. Michael. 1983. "Aliens in the Orchard: The Admission of Foreign Contract Laborers for Temporary Work in U.S. Agriculture." *Yale Law and Policy Review* 1 (2): 187–239.

Senior, Clarence O. 1947. *Puerto Rican Emigration.* Río Piedras: Social Research Center, University of Puerto Rico.

———. 1952a. Letter to Friend [U.S. labor movement leaders], April 7, 1952. File: MLP, Foreign Workers. Box 28. Collection 5307. Consumers' League Records of New York City. Kheel Center.

———. 1952b. Letter to Mason Barr, March 3, 1952. File: Puerto Rico, Population, Central Files, 1951–71. Box 356. Puerto Rico, P–W. Records of the Office of Territories. RG 126. NARA.

———. 1952c. *The Puerto Rican Migratory Farm Workers Program, Testimony of Clarence Senior, Chief, Migration Division, Department of Labor of Puerto Rico before the Labor-Labor Management Relations Sub-committee of the Senate Committee on Labor and Public Welfare,* March 28, 1952. File: MLP, Foreign Workers. Box 28. Collection 5307. Consumers' League Records of New York City. Kheel Center.

———. 1957a. Memorandum to Pagán de Colón, April 17, 1957. File 4: Director's Weekly Reports (Senior), 1957. Box 2949. Subject Files, General, Administration. Migration Division, Centro Archives.

———. 1957b. Memorandum to Sierra Berdecía and Pagán de Colón, weekly report for period ending on March 13, 1957, South Carolina Order. File 4: Director's Weekly Reports (Senior), 1957. Box 2949. Subject Files, General, Administration. Migration Division, Centro Archives.

————. 1957c. Weekly report, May 16, 1957. File 4: Director's Weekly Reports (Senior), 1957. Box 2949. Subject Files, General, Administration. Migration Division, Centro Archives.

————. 1957d. Weekly report, May 22, 1957. File 4: Director's Weekly Reports (Senior), 1957. Box 2949. Subject Files, General, Administration. Migration Division, Centro Archives.

————. 1965. *Puerto Ricans: Strangers Then Neighbors.* Chicago: Quadrangle Books.

Senior, Clarence O., and Don O. Watkins. 1966. "Toward a Balance Sheet of Puerto Rican Migration." In *Status of Puerto Rico: Selected Background Studies,* 689–795. Prepared for the United States–Puerto Rico Commission of the Status of Puerto Rico. Washington, DC: GPO.

Serrano, Susan K. 2017. "Dual Consciousness about Law and Justice: Puerto Ricans' Battle for U.S. Citizenship in Hawai'i." *Centro Journal* 29 (1): 164–201.

Serrano, Víctor. 1991. Letter to Juan Roure, September 13, 1991. File 3: Correspondence, Farm Labor Program Supervisor. Box 472. Correspondence. Farm Labor Program, 1948–93. Migration Division, Centro Archives.

Serrano Molina, Alberto. 1952. Letter to Guadalupe Rodríguez. Serie 11: Correspondencia, 1952–53. División de Migración. Tarea 63–37. Negociado de Seguridad de Empleo. Fondo Departamento del Trabajo. AGPR.

Sheehan, David M. 1974. Letter to José A. Rivera, May 8, 1974. File 1: *Vazquez v. Ferre,* Case 31.8. Correspondence, Litigation. Puerto Rican Legal Defense and Education Fund. Centro Archives.

Shotwell, Louisa Rossiter. 1958–59. "This Is the Migrant." File: Migratory Labor, 1958/08–1959/09. Box 35. Legislation Department Records, 1906–78. AFL-CIO Records. RG 21–001. George Meany Memorial AFL-CIO Archive, University of Maryland, College Park.

Siciliano, Rocco C. 1956. "Puerto Rican Situation in New York City," memorandum to Robert C. Goodwin, March 8, 1956. File: Department of Labor, PCML, Intradeptl., Cte., Misc. Box 11. General Subject Files of Under-Secretary James T. O'Connell, 1954–60. Migratory Labor Operations. Entry 40. Records of the Department of Labor. RG 174. NARA.

Sider, Gerald. 2014. *Skin for Skin: Death and Life for Inuit and Innu.* Durham, NC: Duke University Press.

Sierra Berdecía, Fernando. 1947. "Migración a de trabajadores puertorriqueños a los Estados Unidos," report to Jesús T. Piñero, November 17, 1947. Box 454. Tarea 96–20. Fondo Oficina del Gobernador. AGPR.

————. 1948a. Letter to Alan F. Perl, April 21, 1948. File: Correspondencia confidencial, 1948. Box 163: Correspondencia de la Oficina de la Directora, 1948–50, A y la E. Tarea 61–55. Negociado de Seguridad de Empleo. Fondo Departamento del Trabajo. AGPR.

————. 1948b. Letter to Jesús T. Piñero, April 9, 1948. File: Organización y personal. Box 2244. Tarea 96–20. Fondo Oficina del Gobernador. AGPR.

———. 1948c. Letter to Jorge Font Saldaña, January 8, 1948. File 276. Serie 2: Gobierno insular. Subserie 9b: Correspondencia general. Sección 4: Presidente del Senado, 1941–48. ALMM.

———. 1948d. Letter to Manuel Cabranes, July 23, 1948. File 34: Commissioner of Labor, Fernando Sierra Berdecía. Box 915. Subject and Resource File. Farm Labor Program, 1948–93. Migration Division, Centro Archives.

———. 1948e. Letter to Manuel Cabranes, June 29, 1948. File 34: Commissioner of Labor, Fernando Sierra Berdecía. Box 915. Subject and Resource File. Farm Labor Program, 1948–93. Migration Division, Centro Archives.

———. 1948f. Letter to Manuel Cabranes, May 12, 1948. File 34: Commissioner of Labor, Fernando Sierra Berdecía. Box 915. Subject and Resource File. Farm Labor Program, 1948–93. Migration Division, Centro Archives.

———. 1949a. Letter to Harold Mann, April 12, 1949. File: Ordenes. Box 163: Correspondencia de la Oficina de la Directora, 1948–50, A y la E. Tarea 61–55. Negociado de Seguridad de Empleo. Fondo Departamento del Trabajo. AGPR.

———. 1949b. Letter to Manuel Cabranes, Alan Perl, and Estella Draper, June 1, 1949. File 35: Commissioner of Labor, Fernando Sierra Berdecía. Box 915. Subject and Resource File. Farm Labor Program, 1948–93. Migration Division, Centro Archives.

———. 1949c. Letter to Petroamérica Pagán de Colón, February 6, 1949. File: Correspondencia confidencial, 1948. Box 168. Correspondencia de la Oficina de la Directora, A y la G, 1950–51. Tarea 61–55. Negociado de Seguridad de Empleo. Fondo Departamento del Trabajo, AGPR.

———. 1949d. "Mexican Bracero Contract." File: Correspondencia confidencial, 1948. Box 168. Correspondencia de la Oficina de la Directora, 1950–51, A la G. Tarea 61–55. Negociado de Seguridad de Empleo. Fondo Departamento del Trabajo. AGPR.

———. 1949e. *Protecting Puerto Rico's Labor.* Washington, DC: Office of Puerto Rico.

———. 1950a. Memorandum to Gov. Luis Muñoz Marín, January 3, 1950. File: Legislation and Regulations. Box 2249. Tarea 96–20. Fondo Oficina del Gobernador. AGPR.

———. 1950b. *Un mensaje del comisionado del trabajo a los obreros que desean ir a trabajar en fincas de los Estados Unidos.* San Juan: Administración General de Suministros. Box 1207. Tarea 96–20. Fondo Oficina del Gobernador. AGPR.

———. 1952a. *Frente del trabajo: Hombres y mujeres que laboran y producen.* San Juan: Departamento de Hacienda.

———. 1952b. Letter to Efrén Bernier, December 30, 1952. File: Michigan, Accounts. Box 2272. Tarea 96–20. Fondo Oficina del Gobernador. AGPR.

———. [1952–53?]. "Secretario trabajo insta obreros boricuas que no vayan a Florida." File: Leyes y reglamentos. Box 2249. Tarea 96–20. Fondo Oficina del Gobernador. AGPR.

———. 1953. *Labor Legislation of Puerto Rico.* San Juan: Government of Puerto Rico.

————. 1956a. "Puerto Rican Emigration: Reality and Public Policy," paper read at the Ninth Convention on Social Orientation of Puerto Rico, General Studies, University of Puerto Rico, December 10, 1955. San Juan: Cooperativa de Artes Gráficas Romualdo Real. Box 1207. Tarea 96–20. Fondo Oficina del Gobernador. AGPR.

————. 1956b. Telegram to Clarence O. Senior, June 25, 1956. File: The Supervision of the Farm Placement Program. Serie 11: Correspondencia, 1958. División de Migración. Tarea 63–37. Negociado de Seguridad de Empleo. Fondo Departamento del Trabajo. AGPR.

Sierra Berdecía, Fernando, and Sol Luis Descartes. 1949. "Preparación proyecto establecimiento seguridad de empleo, para la próxima asamblea legislativa," memorandum to governor of Puerto Rico, November 25, 1949. File: Legislation and Regulations. Box 2249. Tarea 96–20. Fondo Oficina del Gobernador. AGPR.

Silva Recio, Luis F. 1975. Letter to Rafael Torregrosa, February 5, 1975. File 28: Additional Funds, 1975. Box 896. Subject and Resource File. Farm Labor Program, 1948–93. Migration Division, Centro Archives.

————. 1976a. "Cláusula de jurisdicción en el contrato de migrantes agrícolas," memorandum to Rafael Hernández Colón, March 24, 1976. File 12: Contract Negotiations. Box 2234. Legal Assistance. Farm Labor Program, 1948–93. Migration Division, Centro Archives.

————. 1976b. Statement of Luis Silva-Recio before Congress, circa August 1976. File 12: Contract Negotiations. Box 2234. Legal Assistance. Farm Labor Program, 1948–93. Migration Division, Centro Archives.

Simpson, David. 1995. "Raymond Williams: Feeling for Structures, Voicing 'History.'" In *Cultural Materialism: On Raymond Williams,* edited by Christopher Prendergast, 29–50. Minneapolis: University of Minnesota Press.

Skeffington, L. B. [1945–50?]a. "Farm Labor Camps to Be Here to Stay." *Democrat and Chronicle.* File 14: Migrant Labor, C. L. Action Conference, 1945–50. Box 3. Collection 5307. Consumers' League Records of New York City. Kheel Center.

————. [1945–50?]b. "Status-Farm Labor Camps." *Democrat and Chronicle.* File 14: Migrant Labor, C. L. Action Conference, 1945–50. Box 3. Collection 5307. Consumers' League Records of New York City. Kheel Center.

Smith, Gavin. 1999. *Confronting the Present: Towards a Politically Engaged Anthropology.* Oxford: Berg.

Smith, Nancy P. 1992. Letter to Luis Roberto Meléndez, April 7, 1992. File 4: Farm Labor Program, Supervisor. Box 472. Correspondence. Farm Labor Program, 1948–93. Migration Division, Centro Archives.

Smith, Rogers M. 1997. *Civic Ideals: Conflicting Visions of Citizenship in U.S. History.* New Haven: Yale University Press.

Social Services Section, Migration Division. 1951a. Case 2144. File: 2139–63, 3/26–4/4/1951. Box 2262. Case Files, Social Services. Migration Division, Centro Archives.

————. 1951b. Case 2179. File: 2179, 4/13/51. Box 2262. Case Files, Social Services. Migration Division, Centro Archives.

———. 1951c. Case 2252. File: 2233–68, 4/19–5/17/1951. Box 2263. Case Files, Social Services. Migration Division, Centro Archives.

———. 1951d. Case 2322. File 3: 2236–334, 3/13–5/23/1951. Box 2264. Case Files, Social Services. Migration Division, Centro Archives.

———. 1951e. Case 2334. File 1: 2335–65, 06/4/6/7/1951. Box 2264. Case Files, Social Services. Migration Division, Centro Archives.

———. 1951f. Case 2372. File 2: 2366–97, 6.27–7.6.51. Box 2264. Case Files, Social Services. Migration Division, Centro Archives.

———. 1951g. Case 2469. File 5: 2460–89, 7/31–8.9.51. Box 2264. Case Files, Social Services. Migration Division, Centro Archives.

Soto, Timoteo, Santos Betancourt, Wenceslao Maldonado, and Pedro. 1952. Letter to Bureau of Employment and Migration, May 6, 1952. Serie 11: Correspondencia, 1952–53. División de Migración. Tarea 63–37. Negociado de Seguridad de Empleo. Fondo Departamento del Trabajo. AGPR.

Spalding, John A. 1948. "Farm Placement Programs in Two Oklahoma Local Offices." *Employment Service Review* 15 (4): 26.

Sparrow, Bartolomeu, and Jennifer Lamm. 2017. "Puerto Ricans and U.S. Citizenship in 1917: Imperatives of Security." *Centro Journal* 29 (1): 284–315.

Stinson Fernández, John H. 1996. "Hacia una antropología de la emigración planificada: El Negociado de Empleo y Migración y el caso de Filadelfia." *Revista de Ciencias Sociales* 1 (June): 112–55.

Stone, D. J. 1958. Police report to Captain E. J. Eimer, August 13, 1958. File 2: Claims, Correa–Falcon. Box 391. Claims and Complaints. Farm Labor Program, 1948–93. Migration Division, Centro Archives.

Stouffer, Samuel, Edward A. Suchman, Leland C. Devinney, Shirley A. Star, and Robin M. Williams Jr. 1949. *The American Soldier: Adjustment during Army Life.* Studies in Social Psychology in World War II. Vol. 1. Princeton: Princeton University Press.

Striffler, Steve. 2007. "Neither Here nor There: Mexican Immigrant Workers and the Search for Home." *American Ethnologist* 34 (4): 674–88.

Talbot, Keith. 1988. "Freedom of Information Request," letter to Felipe del Valle, José A. Santiago, and Apolonio Collazo, September 29, 1988. File 1: Correspondence, Claims, 1988. Box 465. Correspondence. Farm Labor Program, 1948–93. Migration Division, Centro Archives.

Thomas, Lorrin. 2010. *Puerto Rican Citizen: History and Political Identity in Twentieth-Century New York City.* Chicago: University of Chicago Press.

Thomas-Lycklama à Nijeholt, Geertje. 1980. *On the Road for Work: Migratory Workers on the East Coast of the United States.* Boston: Nijhoff.

Thoron, B. W. 1944a. Letter to Rexford G. Tugwell, April 22, 1944. File: Emigration. Box 2247. Tarea 96–20. Fondo Oficina del Gobernador. AGPR.

———. 1944b. Letter to Rexford G. Tugwell, June 19, 1944. Box 269. Tarea 96–20. Fondo Oficina del Gobernador. AGPR.

*Tiempo, El.* 1966a. "Falsos agentes federales provocaron a obreros Boricuas de North Collins." July 19, 1966, 2.

————. 1966b. "Niegan discrimen contra Boricuas en North Collins." August 5, 1966, 3.

————. 1966c. "Suspenden jefe policía de North Collins por actitud agresiva contra los Boricuas." July 20, 1966, 3.

*Times Union.* 1968. "Migrant Hearings Open: Pickets Greet Officials." September 18, 1968.

Torpey, John. 2000. *The Invention of the Passport: Surveillance, Citizenship, and the State.* Cambridge: Cambridge University Press.

Torres, Eulalio. 1956. Letter to Carlos Bartolomei, June 21, 1956. File: Farm Labor Newsletter, 1956. Serie 11: Correspondencia, 1958. División de Migración. Tarea 63–37. Negociado de Seguridad de Empleo. Fondo Departamento del Trabajo. AGPR.

————. 1960a. Letter to Pagán de Colón, November 23, 1960. File 2: Correspondence, Field Representative. Box 474. Correspondence. Farm Labor Program, 1948–93. Migration Division, Centro Archives.

————. 1960b. Letter to Petroamérica Pagán de Colón, August 23, 1960. File 5: Correspondence, Field Operations, Director. Box 473. Correspondence. Farm Labor Program, 1948–93. Migration Division, Centro Archives.

————. 1960c. Letter to Visitación Díaz Virella, October 19, 1960. File 1: Correspondence. Box 474. Correspondence. Farm Labor Program, 1948–93. Migration Division, Centro Archives.

————. 1960d. Weekly report to Joseph Monserrat, August 9, 1960. File 10: Weekly Reports, July–October 1960. Box 892. Reports. Farm Labor Program, 1948–93. Migration Division, Centro Archives.

————. 1960e. Weekly report to Joseph Monserrat, July 18, 1960. File 10: Weekly Reports, July–October 1960. Box 892. Reports. Farm Labor Program, 1948–93. Migration Division, Centro Archives.

————. 1964a. Memorandum to Joseph Monserrat, January 28, 1964. File 6: Correspondence, Farm Labor Program, Director. Box 467. Correspondence. Farm Labor Program, 1948–93. Migration Division, Centro Archives.

————. 1964b. Memorandum to Joseph Monserrat, Pay Rolls-Glassboro Service Association, February 20, 1964. File 6: Correspondence Farm Labor Program, Director. Box 467. Correspondence. Farm Labor Program, 1948–93. Migration Division, Centro Archives.

————. 1964c. "Trip to Yuma, Arizona, and Salinas: Sta. Maria, California," memorandum to Joseph Monserrat, March 9, 1964. File 6: Correspondence Farm Labor Program, Director, January–May 1964. Box 467. Correspondence. Farm Labor Program, 1948–93. Migration Division, Centro Archives.

————. 1966a. "Conditions of Non-contract Puerto Rican Agricultural, Migrant Workers in Chautauqua and Erie Counties, New York," report to Joseph Monserrat, August 18, 1966. File 49. Box 1280. Director's Files, Administration. Migration Division, Centro Archives.

————. 1966b. "Follow-Up to My Report," memorandum to Joseph Monserrat, September 12, 1966. File 49. Box 1280. Director's Files, Administration. Migration Division, Centro Archives.

Torres, Roberto. 1966. Statement, July 24, 1966. File 49. Box 1280. Director's Files, Administration. Migration Division, Centro Archives.

Torres, Rodolfo D., and George Katsiaficas. 1999. Introduction to *Latino Social Movements: Historical and Theoretical Perspectives,* 1–10. New York: Routledge.

Torres Penchi, Israel. 1996. *Sudando la patria (ajena).* New York: Professional Publishing Services.

Trías Monge, José. 1997. *Puerto Rico: The Trials of the Oldest Colony in the World.* New Haven: Yale University Press.

Tugwell, Rexford G. 1944a. Letter to Abe Fortas, October 17, 1944. File: Emigration. Box 2247. Tarea 96–20. Fondo Oficina del Gobernador. AGPR.

———. 1944b. Letter to B. W. Thoron, April 28, 1944. File: 9–8-116. Box 1138. Classified Files, 1907–51. Office of Territories. RG 126. NARA.

———. 1945. Letter to Edwin G. Arnold, September 26, 1945. File: Emigration. Box 2247. Tarea 96–20. Fondo Oficina del Gobernador. AGPR.

———. (1945) 1975 *Puerto Rican Public Papers of R. G. Tugwell Governor.* Reprint, New York: Arno.

Turner, Harry. 1976. "Apple Lift Still Far from Over," newspaper clipping, *Stan Juan Star.* File 16: Correspondence, October–December 1976. Box 387. Apple Harvest, 1959–81. Farm Labor Program, 1948–93. Migration Division, Centro Archives.

United Press International. 1982. "Puerto Rico Has Right to Sue Farmers to Hire Its Citizens." *Baltimore Afro-American,* July 10, 1982, 8.

Urciuoli, Bonnie. 1996. *Exposing Prejudice: Puerto Rican Experiences of Language, Race, and Class.* Boulder, CO: Westview.

U.S. Army, Department of Hawaii, Office of the Assistance Chief of Staff for Military Intelligence. 1930. *A Survey of the Porto Rican in the Territory of Hawaii.* Fort Shafter: Territory of Hawaii.

USBES (U.S. Bureau of Employment Security). 1955. *Puerto Rican Farm Workers in Florida: Highlights of a Study.* Washington, DC: USBES.

U.S. Census Bureau. 1963. *Puerto Ricans in the United States: Social and Economic Data for Persons of Puerto Rican Birth and Parentage.* Washington, DC: GPO.

———. 2006–8. "Three-Years Data for Puerto Rican Farmworkers in the United States, 2006–2008." *American Community Survey.* Accessed on November 10, 2010. www.census.gov/programs-surveys/acs/data/pums.html.

USDA (U.S. Department of Agriculture). 1967. *The Farm Labor Situation in Selected States, 1965–61.* Agricultural Report 110. Washington, DC: Economic Research Service.

USDL (U.S. Department of Labor). 1951. *Mobilizing Labor for Defense: A Summary of Significant Labor Developments in Time of Emergency, Thirty-Ninth Annual Report of the Secretary of Labor for the Fiscal Year ending June 30, 1951.* Washington, DC: GPO.

———. (1959) 1961. *Mexican Farm Labor Program.* Consultant Report, October 1959. Reprinted in U.S. Congress. Senate. Committee on Agriculture and Forestry. Hearings. 87th Cong. 1st Sess. 1961. Washington, DC: GPO.

———. 1975. "A Socio-economic Profile of Puerto Rican New Yorkers," Regional Report 46, July 1975. File: A Socio-economic Profile of Puerto Rican New Yorkers. Box 3240. Reference, Administration. Migration Division, Centro Archives.

———. 1977. "Overview of the Nixon-Ford Administration at the Department of Labor, 1969–1977." Accessed August 12, 2019. www.dol.gov/general/aboutdol/history/webid-nixonford.

———. 2005. "A Demographic and Employment Profile of United States Farm Workers: Findings from the National Agricultural Workers Survey, 2001–2002." Research Report 9. Washington, DC: U.S. Office of Programmatic Policy, Office of the Assistant Secretary for Policy, Department of Labor.

USES (U.S. Employment Service). 1918a. "Arrangements Made to Begin Transportation of Porto Rican Labor." *U.S. Employment Service Bulletin* 1 (25): 9.

———. 1918b. "No Need to Import Chinese and Mexican Labor." *U.S. Employment Service Bulletin* 1 (2): 3.

———. 1918c. "Recruiting of Porto Rican Labor Is Discontinued." *U.S. Employment Service Bulletin* 1 (41): 2.

———. 1918d. "Service Has Placed 10,000 Porto Rican Laborers in Army Construction Work." *U.S. Employment Service Bulletin* 1 (41): 7.

———. 1918e. "To Increase Common Labor Supply with Porto Ricans." *U.S. Employment Service Bulletin* 1 (17): 1.

———. 1949. *Labor Recruitment for Agriculture: The Farm Placement Service in 1948.* Washington, DC: Federal Security Agency/Social Security Administration/Bureau of Employment Security/United States Employment Service.

U.S. Extension Service. 1947. *Preliminary Survey of Major Areas Requiring Outside Agricultural Labor.* Washington, DC: Farm Labor Program, USDA.

U.S. Farm Labor Service. 1957. *This Is How 12 Camps for Migratory Workers in Agriculture Are Operated by Growers, Associations, Counties.* Washington, DC: U.S. Bureau of Employment Security.

U.S. House of Representatives. 1928. *Immigration from Countries of the Western Hemisphere: Hearings before the United States House Committee on Immigration and Naturalization.* 70th Cong. 1st Sess. February 21, 24, 25, 27–29; March 1, 2, 7; April 5, 1928. Washington: U.S. GPO.

———. 1930. *Immigration from Countries of the Western Hemisphere.* House Committee on Immigration and Naturalization Hearings. 71st Cong. 2d Sess. Washington, DC: GPO.

———. 1944. S 1407. *To Amend the Act to Provide a Civil Government for Puerto Rico.* Hearings before the Committee on Insular Affairs. 78th Cong. 2d Sess. Washington, DC: GPO.

———. 1949a. *Disposal of Farm Labor Camps: Hearings before Subcommittee No. 2 of the Committee on Agriculture.* 81st Cong. 1st Sess., on H.R. 2906, H.R. 2970. Serial No. 1. April 4, 1949. Washington, DC: GPO.

———. 1949b. *Importation of Foreign Farm Labor: Hearing before Subcommittee No. 2 of the Committee on Agriculture.* 81st Cong. 1st Sess., on H.R. 5557. July 14, 1949. Washington, DC: GPO.

———. 1949c. *Report on Farm Labor Camps.* Legislative Joint Commission on Farm Labor Housing, House Committee on Agriculture. 80th Cong. 1st Sess. Report 1008. Washington, DC: GPO.

———. 1951a. *Farm Labor: Hearings before the Committee on Agriculture.* 82d Cong. 1st Sess., on H.R. 2955, *A Bill Relating to the Stabilization of Defense Farm Labor;* H.R. 3048, *A Bill to Amend the Agricultural Act of 1949.* March 8, 9, 12, 14, 1950. Serial D. Washington, DC: GPO.

———. 1951b. *Farm Labor Investigations: Hearings before the Subcommittee on Farm Labor of the Committee on Agriculture, House of Representatives.* 81st Cong. 2d Sess., October 2, 4; December 18, 1950. Washington, DC: GPO.

———. 1955. *Hearings before the Subcommittee of the Committee on Appropriations.* 84th Cong. 1st Sess. Departments of Labor and Health, Education, and Welfare Appropriations for 1956. Washington, DC: GPO.

———. 1961. *Migratory Labor: Hearings before the Select Subcommittee on Labor of the Committee on Education and Labor.* 87th Cong. 1st Sess., on H.R. 5288, H.R. 5289, H.R. 5290, H.R. 5291, and related bills, relating to migratory labor, Washington, DC, on May 9, 10; New York City on May 19, 20, 1961. Washington, DC: GPO.

U.S. Office of Territories. [1952?]. *The Potential Contribution of Puerto Rico's Migrant Workers to the Mainland's Need for Workers.* Washington, DC: U.S. Department of Interior. File: Michigan, Accounts. Box 2272. Tarea 96–20. Fondo Oficina del Gobernador. AGPR.

U.S. Senate. 1900a. Jorge Cruz. 56th Cong. 1st Sess. S. Doc. 281.

———. 1900b. Jorge Cruz. 56th Cong. 1st Sess. S. Doc. 311.

———. 1928. *Restriction of Western Hemisphere Immigration. Hearings before the Committee on Immigration.* 70th Cong. 1st Sess., on S. 1296, S. 1437, S. 3019. February 1, 27, 28, 29; March 1, 5, 1928. Washington, DC: GPO.

———. 1941. *Violations of Free Speech and Rights of Labor.* Committee on Education and Labor. Washington, DC: GPO.

———. 1946. *U.S. Employment Service. Hearings before the United States Senate Committee on Education and Labor.* Subcommittee on S. 1456, S. 1510, S. 1848; H.R. 4437. 79th Cong. 2d Sess., on February 18, 20, 21; March 6, 8, 19, 25, 1946. Part 2. Washington, DC: GPO.

———. 1951a. *Farm Labor Program: Hearings before the Committee on Agriculture and Forestry.* 82nd Cong. 1st Sess., on S. 949, S. 984, S. 1106. March 13, 14, 15, 16, 1951. Washington, DC: GPO.

———. 1951b. *Labor-Federal Security Appropriations for 1952 Hearings before the Subcommittee of the Committee on Appropriations.* 82d Cong. 1st Sess. Washington, DC: GPO.

———. 1952a. *Migratory Labor: Hearings before the United States Senate Committee on Labor and Public Welfare, Subcommittee on Labor and Labor-Management Relations.* 82d Cong. 2d Sess. Part 1. Washington, DC: GPO.

———. 1952b. *Migratory Labor: Hearings before the United States Senate Committee on Labor and Public Welfare, Subcommittee on Labor and Labor-Management Relations.* 82d Cong. 2d Sess. Part 2. Washington, DC: GPO.

———. 1962a. *The Migratory Farm Labor Problem in the United States.* 87th Cong. 2d Sess. Senate Report 1225. Washington, DC: GPO.

———. 1962b. *Migratory Labor: Hearings before the Subcommittee on Migratory Labor of the Committee on Labor and Public Welfare.* 87th Cong. 1st and 2d Sess., on S. 1129. Washington, DC: GPO.

———. 1969. *Migrant and Seasonal Farmworker Powerlessness: Hearings before the United States Senate Committee on Labor and Public Welfare, Subcommittee on Migratory Labor.* 91st Cong. 1st Sess., on May 22, 1969. Part 5-B. Washington, DC: GPO.

———. 1970. *Migrant and Seasonal Farmworker Powerlessness. Hearings before the United States Senate Committee on Labor and Public Welfare, Subcommittee on Migratory Labor.* 91st Cong. 1st Sess., on August 8, 1969. Part 4-B. Washington, DC: GPO.

Valdés, Dennis Nodín. 1991. *Al Norte: Agricultural Workers in the Great Lakes Region, 1917–1970.* Austin: University of Texas Press.

Valdés Pizzini, Manuel, Michael González-Cruz, and José Eduardo Martínez-Reyes. 2011. *La transformación del paisaje puertorriqueño y la disciplina del Cuerpo Civil de Conservación, 1933–1942.* San Juan: Centro de Investigaciones Sociales, Universidad de Puerto Rico.

Van Dyne, Frederick. 1904. *Citizenship of the United States.* New York: Lawyer's Cooperative.

Vargas, Claudia. 2010. "The Rev. Charles S. Bean, 76." *Inquirer Daily News,* July 24, 2010. Accessed on April 3, 2018. Philly.com. www.inquirer.com/philly/obituaries /20100724_The_Rev__Charles_S__Bean__76.html.

Vasquez, Joan. 1969. Letter to Edwin Rivera, July 22, 1969. File 49. Box 1280. Director's Files, Administration. Migration Division, Centro Archives.

Vazquez Malavez, Carlos. 1966. Statement, July 24, 1966. File 49. Box 1280. Director's Files, Administration. Migration Division, Centro Archives.

Vega, Anthony. 1966. Memorandum to Joseph Monserrat, July 12, 1966. File 49. Box 1280. Director's Files, Administration. Migration Division, Centro Archives.

———. 1967. "Charles Grave's Farm," memorandum to Ralph Muñiz, July 10, 1967. File 33: Bridgeton, New Jersey, Case of Two Little Girls Poisoned and a Third Girl Dead, 1967. Box 908. Subject and Resource File. Farm Labor Program, 1948–93. Migration Division, Centro Archives.

Venator Santiago, Charles R. 2013. "Extending Citizenship to Puerto Rico: Three Traditions of Inclusive Exclusion." *Centro Journal* 25 (1): 50–75.

———. 2017. "Mapping the Contours of the History of the Extension of U.S. Citizenship to Puerto Rico, 1898–Present." *Centro Journal* 29 (1): 38–55.

Venegas, William. [1958?]. Letter to Guadalupe Ruiz. File 2: Correa–Falcon. Box 391. Claims and Complaints. Farm Labor Program, 1948–93. Migration Division, Centro Archives.

Vialet, Joyce, and Barbara McClure. 1980. *Temporary Worker Programs, Background and Issues: A Report.* Congressional Research Service. Senate Report 55–752. 96th Cong. 2d Sess. Washington, DC: GPO.

Vilar, Gabriel V. 1958. Special report to Eulalio Torres, August 15, 1958. File 2: Correa–Falcon. Box 391. Claims and Complaints. Farm Labor Program, 1948–93. Migration Division, Centro Archives.

———. 1959. Inter-office report to Eulalio Torres, August 14, 1959. File 33: Ferlito, Angelo, Oswego, New York, 1959. Box 935. Subject and Resource File. Farm Labor Program, 1948–93. Migration Division, Centro Archives.

Vilches, Ruben A. 1976. Letter to David Williams, September 2, 1976. File 15: Correspondence, July–September 1976. Box 388. Apple Harvest, 1959–81. Farm Labor Program, 1948–93. Migration Division, Centro Archives.

*Vocero, El.* 1977. "Ilegales se hacen pasar por boricuas y arrebatan el trabajo a los puertorriqueños: Ahora hay que conseguir acta de nacimiento." September 30, 1977.

Vorse, Mary Heaton. 1953. "America's Submerged Class: The Migrants." *Harper's Magazine* 206 (February): 86–93.

Wagenheim, Kal. 1975. *A Survey of Puerto Ricans on the U.S. Mainland in the 1970s.* New York: Praeger.

———. 1976. "Visit to Winchester, Virginia, to Observe Farm Program," memorandum to Rafael Torregrosa, October 18, 1976. File 16: Correspondence, October–December 1976. Box 388. Apple Harvest, 1959–81. Farm Labor Program, 1948–93. Migration Division, Centro Archives.

Waldinger, Roger David, and Michael Ira Lichter. 2003. *How the Other Half Works: Immigration and the Social Organization of Labor.* Berkeley: University of California Press.

Walker, R. C. 1956. "I like Puerto Ricans." *Rural New Yorkers, Journal for the Northern Family,* August 4, 1956, 504.

*Washington Post.* 1944. "Puerto Ricans Recruited," newspaper clipping, April 19, 1944. File: 9-8-116. Box 1138. Classified Files, 1907–51. Office of Territories. RG 126. NARA.

Waugh, Danielle. 2018. "Maine Looks to Puerto Rico for Seasonal Workers." *New England Cable News,* May 29, 2018. www.necn.com/news/business/Maine-Looks-to-Puerto-Rico-for-Seasonal-Workers-483986431.html.

Weber, Devra. 1994. *Dark Sweat, White Gold: California Farm Workers, Cotton, and the New Deal.* Berkeley: University of California Press.

Weir, Margaret 1993. *Politics and Jobs: The Boundaries of Employment Policy in the United States.* Princeton: Princeton University Press.

Weller, Ethelyn. 1941. *North Collins Remembers: A Comprehensive History of North Collins and Vicinity.* Gowanda, NY: Niagara Frontier.

Wesler, Harold. 1959. Letter to the director of Puerto Rican Migration Bureau, Keyport, May 15, 1959. File 3: Correspondence, Field Operations, Director. Box 475. Correspondence. Farm Labor Program, 1948–93. Migration Division, Centro Archives.

Whalen, Carmen Teresa. 2001. *From Puerto Rico to Philadelphia: Puerto Rican Workers and Postwar Economies.* Philadelphia: Temple University Press.

———. 2005. "Colonialism, Citizenship, and the Making of the Puerto Rican Diaspora: An Introduction." In Whalen and Vázquez-Hernández 2005, 1–42.

———. 2009. "Citizens and Workers: African Americans and Puerto Ricans in Philadelphia's Regional Economy since World War II." In *African American Urban History since World War II*, edited by Kenneth L. Kusmer and Joe William Trotter, 98–122. Chicago: University of Chicago Press.

Whalen, Carmen Teresa, and Víctor Vázquez-Hernández. 2005. *The Puerto Rican Diaspora: Historical Perspectives*. Philadelphia: Temple University Press.

WHD (Wage and Hour Division). n.d. *History of Changes to the Minimum Wage Law*. U.S. Department of Labor. Accessed July 19, 2017. www.dol.gov/whd /minwage/coverage.htm.

Whitcomb, Emmons J. 1947. *A Report of Puerto Rico Air Transportation Service and Its Importance to the Development of Tourism*, November 22, 1947. File: Autoridad de transporte, transportación aérea. Box 454. Tarea 96–20. Fondo Oficina del Gobernador. AGPR.

Whitney A. F. 1943. Letter to A. W. Motley, February 19, 1943. Box 269. Tarea 96–20. Fondo Oficina del Gobernador. AGPR.

Williams, Raymond. 1977. *Marxism and Literature*. Oxford: Oxford University Press.

Wolf, Eric R. 2001. *Pathways of Power: Building an Anthropology of the Modern World*. Berkeley: University of California Press.

Woytinsky, Wladimir J. 1946. "Postwar Economic Perspectives II: Prewar Experience; The Labor Force and Employment." *Social Security Bulletin* 9 (1): 8–16.

Young, Bruce. 1975. "The New England Farm Workers' Council: A Case Study of a Community Service Organization." EdD diss., University of Massachusetts.

Yuh, Ji-Yeon. 2002. *Beyond the Shadow of Camptown: Korean Military Brides in America*. New York: New York University.

Zeno, Fernando M. 1952. Letter to Concepción Diaz. Serie 11: Correspondencia, 1952–53. División de Migración. Tarea 63–37. Negociado de Seguridad de Empleo. Fondo Departamento del Trabajo. AGPR.

Zeno, Tulio N. 1958a. "Visita a la Oficina Local de Caguas el día 31 de julio 1958," memorandum to Petroamérica Pagán de Colón, August 4, 1958. File: Visitas a las oficinas locales División de Operaciones, 1958. Serie 11: Correspondencia, 1958. División de Migración. Tarea 63–37. Negociado de Seguridad de Empleo. Fondo Departamento del Trabajo. AGPR.

———. 1958b. "Visita de supervisión a la Oficina Local de Humacao," letter to Petroamérica Pagán de Colón, March 20, 1958. File: Visitas a las oficinas locales División de Operaciones, 1958. Serie 11: Correspondencia, 1958. División de Migración. Tarea 63–37. Negociado de Seguridad de Empleo. Fondo Departamento del Trabajo. AGPR.

Zgodnik, Joseph. 1966. Letter from Joseph Zgodnik to Migration Division, circa September 20, 1966. File 2: Correspondence, Farm Labor Program, Assistant Director. Box 467. Correspondence. Farm Labor Program, 1948–93. Migration Division, Centro Archives.

Zorrilla, Frank. 1962. *Secretario del Trabajo se dirige a la Convención Anual del Sindicato de Trabajadores Packinghouse*. San Juan: Departamento del Trabajo, Estado Libre Asociado de Puerto Rico.

# INDEX

Note: Page numbers in *italics* indicate illustrations or tables.

Clements, George P., 37–38

Cleveland, Ohio, 64, 75

Coalición, La (The Coalition), 41–42, 48

coffee production, 29, 40, 51, 108, 109, 116–17, 118, 123, 215

cohabitation of migrants: and labor camps, 110; the MD assigning blame for, 185; welfare assistance denied due to, 185; and women of other ethnicities, 110, 175, 180. *See also* families; marriages

Cold War, and autonomy of Puerto Rico, 12

Colombia, 59

colonial migration: overview, 22, 222; and contract farm labor, emergence of, 22; distinguished from immigration, 228; early twentieth-century regulation by colonial governments, 24–25; early twentieth-century status as lower-cost alternative to foreign workers, 29; global trend to modernization of, 13; and international convention requiring colonial subjects to be admitted without restrictions, 22, 26; and Manifest Destiny, 30; transportation modes and trade networks as facilitating, 29

colonial relationship of Puerto Rico to the United States: and incorporation of Puerto Ricans into the U.S. labor market, 9–11, 26–27, 29; and insertion of Puerto Rican officials into U.S. government, 7–8, 11–13, 14, 72, 83, 227; legitimacy of U.S. rule, questioning of, 41–42; migratory field of, 26; resistance of Puerto Ricans to second-class status imposed by, 164–65, 187; and statehood, politics of, 219, 221

colonial state, modern (Puerto Rico): overview, 12–14, 227–28; agency of Puerto Rican and colonial officials and, 16, 17; autonomy/self-government of, 12, 66, 69, 71; contemporary colonial neoliberal state, 224, 225; as global trend, 13; and infrastructure of the FLP, 72; insertion of Puerto Rican officials into the sphere of the federal government and, 11–13, 227; land reform, 69; population control, 69; PPD regulation

of labor markets and migration and, 48; state formation and development of, 9, 13, 15–16; stateside Puerto Ricans as important asset of, 69; tax exemptions for labor-intensive manufacturing, 69; and World War II agricultural production, 12. *See also* neoliberal policies

Colón, Jesús, 134, 159

Colón, Jorge, 144, 159, 177–78, 180, 185

Colón, Juan R., 202

Colón Torres, Ramón, 63

Colorado, 64

Columbia University study, 65

commodity production: expansion in Puerto Rico, 50–51; research into crop yields, 44

common-law unions. *See* cohabitation

communities of Puerto Ricans on the mainland: expansion of, and social problems, 185; as farmers, 165; migrants settling among, 164; moving to nearby cities to be among, 185; organizing events at labor camps, 139–40, 165; property ownership and, 165; solidarity among, 164–65; summer farm work as supplementing income of, 167. *See also* population of Puerto Ricans in the mainland U.S.; settlement of Puerto Rican migrant farmworkers stateside; *specific cities and towns*

Community Action Organization, 175, 182

community organizations: access to labor camps, 156; and civil rights movement, 165–66; contemporary Puerto Rican migrants and reliance on, 225; Ferré administration and hostility toward, 193; food banks for fired workers, 213; formation of, after Ferré administration, 197; formation of, in the wake of the North Collins incident, 182, 184, 188; legal services to migrants, generally, 197; opposition to Bracero Program, 169; return airplane tickets, negotiation for, 213. *See also* labor organizers and organizing

complaints by employers of Puerto Rican migrant workers: as continuing into the 1990s, 218; of FLP as onerous, 207, 218;

language barrier, 81; physical unpreparedness due to illness or disability, 65; preference for insular vs. those residing in NYC, 126–27; and preference for West Indian guest workers, 127–28; reduction of, following institution of FLP, 87; workers leaving before the end of harvest, 120, 218

complaints by Puerto Rican migrant workers: bullying and machismo, 149; crew leader abuses, 157; desire to take leave from labor camp, 150; for farmers pushing workers beyond endurance, 149–50; firing of workers for making complaints, 206, 208; food not to Puerto Rican standards, 151–55, 208; in Hawaii, 31; housing conditions, 145, 218; lack of health care, 218; lack of work hours, 121; letters written to MD for, 145; MD collaboration with state agencies, 145; by noncontract workers, 145; overcharging for food or housing, 121, 153; on PPD, 118–19; and private contractor job sites, 60–61; reduction of, following institution of FLP, 87; as stimulating Puerto Rican government management of migrant labor, 14; U.S. government request for paid person to handle, 64; wages, 195, 209, 218; work week not allowing time to shop or post letters, 148. *See also* quitting the job

Comprehensive Employment and Training Act (CETA), 192

Concepción de Gracia, Gilberto, 119

Connecticut: ATA in, 201; and contemporary Puerto Rican farmworkers, 3; as destination for Puerto Rican farmworkers, 66, 111, 194, 219; labor organizing in, 197, 198, 199–205, 212; local farmworkers, 205; META branch in, 201; in migratory routes, 46; and noncontract workers, 128; preference for deportable workers, 82; Puerto Rican settlement in, 163–64; religious ministry to Puerto Ricans, 165; USES barring entrance of guest workers into, 73; wages in, 194

Connecticut Department of Community Affairs, 203–4

Connecticut General Assembly, 202

Connecticut River Valley, 2, 193, 199, 205

Connecticut State Labor Council, 201

Consolidated Cigar Corporation, 199–200, 204

Consolidated Cigar Division of Gulf and Western Industries, 199

construction jobs, 108, 125, 195, 224, 225

Consumers League of New Jersey, 86

consumption: as aspirational, 125; modern colonial subjects and, 13

contemporary Puerto Rican farmworkers: colonial neoliberal government and, 224, 225; composition of the U.S. farm labor force, 3, 225, 235n1; continued migration of, 2–3, 4, 224–25, 227; demographics of, 225; economic crisis (2009) and migration of populace, 224; facing similar issues as in the North Collins incident, 188; fear of migrants getting welfare benefits, 223; and H-2A visa program, 3, 225, 226; and hope, 227; modern labor camps, 2–3, 21, 141–42; networks of, 225, 226; noncontract workers as most common, 3, 225; remittances, 3, 226; Trump administration and nativist, racist, and nationalist climate, 224; unemployment and underemployment and, 225, 226

contract farmworkers, Puerto Rican. *See* fired workers; FLP (Puerto Rico Farm Labor Program); labor camps; migrant farmworkers, Puerto Rican; migrant farmworkers, Puerto Rican, numbers of; noncontract farmworkers, Puerto Rican; quitting the job (Puerto Rico workers)

Contract Labor Act (1864), 23

contract-labor regulation. *See* regulation of contract-labor migration

Convention of the Fruit Growers of California, 37–38

corn production, 120

Costa Rica, 42

cost of living: and falling wages (1951), 117; the Great Depression and, 40–41, 51; as higher in Puerto Rico, 226

cotton industry, 37, 57

"Puerto Rican problem," 81; racialization and, 81, 209; in sites of social reproduction, 179–80; social relationships and dating, 180; for speaking Spanish, 224; white denial of, 178–79, 180, 183; and World War II, 57. *See also* nativism; North Collins incident; racial segregation; racism

disease and illness: and alcohol abuse, 146; employer complaints about, 65; firing of workers for, 119–20; grower fear of Puerto Rican workers about, 80–81; and mortality rate, 41; persistence of, 40; rejection of workers on arrival at labor camps due to, 111; return to Puerto Rico and, 119–20, 123; sudden death of workers, 158. *See also* health care; injured workers

disposable labor, 21, 186, 211–12

dissatisfaction. *See* complaints; quitting the job (Puerto Rico workers)

Dollenberg, Fred P., 60, 93

domesticity, discourses of, 51

domestic service, 60, 61, 113

domestic workers: court order to accept the same benefits as H-2 workers, 211; extension of Bracero Program guarantees to, proposal for, 169; extension of FLP contract provisions to all, proposals for, 169, 171, 186, 211; guest worker reforms and increase in demand for (1964–65), 169–71; guest workers as preferred over, 77–78; recognition of Puerto Ricans as, 73. *See also* labor shortages; local labor; migrant farmworkers, Puerto Rican

Domínguez, Ángel, 156, 206, 213, 214

Dominican Republic: proposed guest-worker migration to Puerto Rico, 192; Puerto Rican emigration to, 34, 42, 59; Puerto Rican labor migration to, 23, 31–32, 34, 35; U.S. occupation of, 35

Dover, New Jersey, 185

*Downes v. Bidwell*, 23, 27–28

DPRCA. *See* Department of Puerto Rican Community Affairs

Draper, Stella, 77–78, 79, 81

driver's license, driving without, 159

DTIP. *See* U.S. Division of Territories and Island Possessions

dual frame of reference, 123–24

Dunkirk, New York, 174, 181

Dunn, Walter S., 14–15

Durkin, New York, 184

Durlandville, New York, 234n2

Durst Brothers Ranch, 25–26

Durst, Ralph, 25

Dust Bowl, 44

Eastern Airlines, 96, 97, 114

eastern European immigrants: and transition from slavery to free labor, 23; whiteness of, 24

economic development of Puerto Rico: contrary and disorganized effects of, 49; FLP as tool of, 12, 69–70, 72; migration as prominent feature of, 69–70, 72, 91; New Deal plan for, 42–43

economy of Puerto Rico: aftermath of the Spanish-American War and weakness of, 29; agriculture, 215; crisis of (1970s), 191, 196, 208; crisis of (2009), 224; industrialization, 13, 42, 71; as reason for migrating, 108, 109. *See also* coffee production; manufacturing; neoliberal policies; sugar sector in Puerto Rico

Ecumenical Farmworkers Ministry (META): creation of, 198; dissolution of, 201; and lawsuits to enforce the FLP contract, 198–99, 221; and migrant workers strikes and protests, 198, 200, 201, 202; offices of, 198; political split of, 201. *See also* Agricultural Workers Association (ATA)

Eden, New York, 173, 175–76, 177, 183

education: adult, in labor camps, 89, *90*, 136, 139, 140, 183–84; of children of migrant workers, 65, 166, 174, 180, 234n1; demographics of migrant workers, 194, 225; of farmworkers, labor organizing and, 213–14; formal credentials in, and migrant agricultural jobs, 83, 215; limited, and the fine print of the contracts, 84

eligibility to work, rise of requirement for, 24

emigration of Puerto Ricans: contemporary numbers due to economic crisis of 2009, 224; government of Puerto Rico as supporting, 30, 34; the Great Depression and decrease of, 41; in interwar period, 37, 39, 40, 41, 43; New Deal plan for, 42; permanent resettlement, U.S. officials and support for, 76; protested by the business sector, 35; protested by the press and agricultural interests, 29–30; viewed as internal U.S. migratory pattern, 78; viewed as solution to overpopulation, poverty, and hunger, 13–14, 34, 36, 41; vs. investment in Puerto Rican agriculture as path not taken, 229

empires, global trend to modern colony formation, 13

employment in nonfarm labor: desire to settle stateside and flexibility in, 164; winter jobs, 167; winter jobs found by farmers to retain labor force, 167. *See also* manufacturing jobs; service sector jobs

English language: classes in, and labor recruitment, 89–90, *90*; classes in, at labor camps, 89, *90*, 139, 140, 184; FLP contracts in Spanish and, 84; knowledge of, and job opportunities, 109. *See also* language barrier; Spanish language

enticements to migrate: overview, 10, 106; complementary harvest seasons as, 109; FLP contract as, 87; maintenance and renewal and, 106; serving Puerto Rico–style food, 155

Episcopal Church, 165, 197, 198

Erie County Department of Welfare, 185

Erie County Health Department, 184

Erie, New York, 174

estrangement of migrants, 107, 131–33, 142, 147, 161, 162

ethnicity: farmers ignoring differences in, and complaints about food, 152; food as terrain of struggle over, 151; interaction among ethnicities in the field, 148, 149, 150–51; pitting ethnicities against each other, 211; and rural power relations between Puerto Ricans and white

residents, 164–65; succession of, in northeastern U.S. agriculture, 165

eugenics, 24

Europe: and citizenship as based on common descent, 23; and gatekeeping/deportation regimes, 25; interwar period and labor migrants from, 51; postwar period and slowing of immigrants from, 58; post–World War I immigration restrictions on, 36; and transition from slavery to free labor, 23; World War I and decrease of migration from, 33; World War II and guest workers from, 57

expendable labor, 21, 186

experience of migration: overview, 105–7, 122, 196; ban on working in Jim Crow states, 79, 101, 114, 116; and boundaries, crossing of, 107; criticism of younger workers, 196; demographics of migrant workers, 108, 163, 166–67, 194, 225; and dual frame of reference, 123–24; estrangement and, 107, 131–33, 142, 147, 161, 162; and families, problems within, 110–11, 124–25; fear of not being selected, 106; homesickness, 151, 158; hope and, 105–6, 131–32, 227, 229; hurricane damage as reason to migrate, 222; personal problems as reason to migrate, 108, 110–11, 114; and place, construction of, 106–7; political persecution as reason to migrate, 108, 109; rejection of applicants, 111; relationships between farmers and workers, 116, 133, 134, 165; silence about the hardships, 123; unemployment and underemployment as incentive to migrate, 108–9; voting rights and, 123; wages as reason to migrate, 31, 124, 194, 219, 226. *See also* agency of Puerto Rican migrants; air transportation of Puerto Rican workers; depression; discrimination; disease and illness; ethnicity; families; fired workers; food; injured workers; labor camps; quitting the job (Puerto Rico workers); racism; recruitment of labor; remittances; return migration to Puerto Rico; settlement of Puerto Rican

numbers of, *170*; Puerto Rican experience as similar to, 11, 21, 227; as "unassimilable foreigners," 21; as U.S. nationals, 37

Fineberg, Richard A., 171

fired workers: the apple industry and, 206, 208, 211, 212–13; for complaining about living and working conditions, 206, 208; for illness, 119–20; for labor organizing, and court order to reinstate, 214–15; no written termination letter given, 99; for protesting lowered wage, 121–22

Fitchie, Thomas, 27

Fleagle, Fred K., 232n1

Florida: accident during transport to fields, 148, 154; banning of, as destination for Puerto Rican workers, 115; and contemporary Puerto Rican farmworkers, 3; as destination for Puerto Rican seasonal farmworkers, 2, 111; families of migrants in, 166, 167; and the Great Depression, 40; grower testimonials on behalf of, 115–16; and informal/illegal hiring, 114–16; labor camps in, 136, 145, 148, 154, 155; in migratory routes, 46; noncontract workers and, 100, 111; number of Puerto Ricans employed in, 82; Puerto Rican settlement in, 163–64; and racism, 114, 116; sending migrant workers into the labor stream, 195; USES information station for migrants, 83; and World War II, 56

FLP. *See* Farm Labor Program (FLP)

food: and air transport, 95; complaints about, 151–55, 208; cook-manager recommended to remedy issues about, 155; crew leaders in control of, 157; deductions from paychecks for, 86, 181, 208; dislike for, and weight loss, 151; as enticement to migrate, 155; ethnic differences in, farmers ignoring, 152; farmers overcharging for, 121, 153, 181; FLP contract requirements for, 86, 152–53, 198, 200; guest workers and complaints about, 233–34n3; identity and, 151; noncontract workers and, 118; Puerto Rican officials finding the food

unacceptable, 152; Puerto Rican traditional diet, 151; workers cooking their own meals in small camps, 152. *See also* cost of living

food insecurity in Puerto Rico: Great Depression and price increases in food, 40–41, 51; and mortality rate, 41; persistence of, 40

food-processing plants: contract workers sold into slavery in Alaska, 224–25; hiring Puerto Ricans who settle stateside, 108, 122; hiring Puerto Rican workers, 2, 56, 126–27, 127, 224–25; NLRA as applying to, 45; numbers of Puerto Rican workers hired, 126; as off-season job, 174; Puerto Ricans as preferring work in, 127; in Puerto Rico, and complementary harvest seasons, 109; as second job, 174; women as noncontractor workers in, 113

Foraker Act (1900), 27, 231n4

Foraker, Joseph B., 27

Foran Act (1885, Alien Contract Labor Law), 23, 222, 231n2

Ford, Gerald, administration of, 221

Ford Motor Company, 98

Ford, Richard "Blackie," 25–26

Fortas, Abe, 57

France: Algerian migrant workers in, 11, 24, 25, 26, 227, 234n4; experience of West Indian colonial migrants in, 11; labor camps as prisons in, 234n4; regulation of colonial migrant labor by, 25

Franklin Mushroom Farms, 219

Free Federation of Labor (FLT, Federación Libre de Trabajadores), 35

Friedman, Samuel, 60, 93–94

FSA. *See* U.S. Farm Security Administration

Gage, Lyman J., 27

*Galan v. Dunlop,* 207

Garcia, Joseph, 197

Garden State Service Cooperative Association (GSSCA), 80, 83–84, 94, 98–99, 114, 127–28, 138

Gary, Indiana, Puerto Rican community established in, 185

Gowanda, New York, 173

grape production, 173

Great Depression: cost of living increases and, 40–41, 51; immigration restrictions instituted during, 39; and labor regulation, need for, 44; massive unemployment and, 40, 44, 51, 52–53; and migrant labor, rise of, 44. *See also* New Deal

Green Giant Company, 2

Grosfoguel, Ramón, 26

growers: mobility of workers, practices to limit, 30–31, 43, 54; prevailing wage determined by, 52, 70, 84, 85, 118; in Puerto Rico, protesting emigration of farmworkers, 29–30; resentment of PRDL regulations, 87, 119, 207, 218; testimonials on behalf of Puerto Rican workers, 115–16, 128–29, 219; U.S. government request to have paid person to deal with, 64. *See also* citizenship of Puerto Ricans (U.S.) as undesirable to the agricultural-labor market; complaints by employers of Puerto Rican migrant workers

growers' associations: overview, 83–84; FLP contracts for, 84; and illegal hiring, MD efforts to curtail, 114; lobbying for, and World War II guest workers, 54; MD and relationships with, 83–84, 133, 184; preference for offshore workers, 126; prevailing wages as set by, 52, 70, 84, 85, 118

Guam, 22, 231n2

Guánica Central, 34

Guayama, Puerto Rico, 87, 114

Gue, Stanley, 62

guest-worker programs: Adverse Effect Wage Rate, 218; the apple industry and, 207, 209, 211–12; decertifying, Puerto Rican interest in, 64, 118; and deportation as threat, 24; and depression of wages for domestic labor, 70, 85–86, 168, 212; housing requirements, 233n7; as influence on Puerto Rican programs, 67; interwar period and shelving of, 36; limitations imposed on employers by, and preference for Puerto Ricans, 84; male immigrants as preferred, 51, 107; postwar period and termination of, 59; in Puerto Rico (proposed), 192; racist/nativist context of establishing, 24; as threat to BEM, 76; Trump administration and, 224; wages and wage requirements, 167, 218, 233n7; work guarantees, 233n7. *See also* H-2 visa program; H-2A visa program; transportation of migrants to work locations

guest workers: federal requirement for labor shortage of domestic workers to be demonstrated before hiring, 1, 73, 223, 226, 231n1; growers' cooperatives as preferring, 126; numbers of, *170*, 172, *172*, 207; as "perfect immigrants," 2; postwar period and continued prioritization of, 58, 127–28, 129; Puerto Rican officials lobbying for Puerto Rican workers instead of, 12; reduction in numbers of (late 1950s), 127; rejection of Puerto Rican workers in favor of, 1, 4; USES barring entrance into the Northeast, 73; World War II and, 51–54, 56–58. *See also* British West Indian migrant workers; deportability of guest workers preferred by agricultural-labor market; *specific countries*

*Guía del viajero* (radio program), 89

Guyanas, 59

H-2 visa program: apple growers' preference for workers through, 207, 209, 211–12; domestic workers ordered to accept same benefits as, 211; limited to the sugar and apple industries, 207; replaced with H-2A visas, 231n1; West Indians and, 207, 231n1

H-2A visa program: Adverse Effect Wage Rate, 218; charges for violation of rules, 1; contemporary Puerto Rican workers and, 3, 225; domestic workers must be given preference prior to hiring guest workers, 1, 226, 231n1; GSA member farms and, 218; MD decline and concern farmers would increasingly turn to, 218; and repeal of public law 78 (Bracero Program termination), 172; as replacing H-2 visas, 231n1

Hadley, Massachusetts, 120
Hahamovitch, Cindy, 2
Haiti, 192
Hamburg, New York, 173, 176
Hamburg, Pennsylvania, MD office in, 75
Hardwick, Arthur Jr., 183
Harris, William, 38
Hartford, Connecticut: and Camp Windsor protests, 201; labor organizing in, 203, 205; MD office in, 75, 154–55, 193, 202; Puerto Rican community in, 164, 185
Hartford County Lung Association, 203
Hart, Fred J., 38–39
*Harvest of Shame* (CBS documentary), 168, 169
Harvey, Illinois, 91
Hatt, Paul, 63
Hawaii: Filipino migration to, 29, 38; Puerto Rican migration to, 12, 29, 30–31, 36, 37, 38, 58, 67, 142; as U.S. territory, 22, 31
Hawaiian Sugar Producers Association, 30
head tax-entry fee for immigrants, 33
health care: contract laborers as more likely to receive, 86; discrimination in, 180; and families of migrant workers, 166, 167; federal and state funding for clinics and projects for, 167, 182, 203–4; labor camps and access to, 21, 203, 216; and labor organizing, 203–4, 216; and Mexican migrant workers, 21; in Puerto Rico, 21. *See also* disease and illness; injured workers
health certificates: ensuring employers get copies of, 218; and illegal recruitment, 101; possession of, and rejection for health issues, 111; workers turned away at airport without, 96
health insurance: farmer failure to pay for, 180; farmers complaints about paying for, 98; FLP contract requirements for, 86, 98
Henderson, Max, 91
Hernández Colón, Rafael, administration of, 196–97, 200–201, 202, 217
Hernández Flecha, Reinaldo, 208
Hernández Torres, Zaida "Cucusa," 218–19

Hoffman, Jeffrey, 186
Holmdel, New Jersey, 153–54
Holyoke, Massachusetts, 164
home communities, income activities in, as subsidizing stateside employers, 10–11
home ownership, migrants and, 165, 185–86, 194, 219–20
homesickness, 151, 158
homosexual activity in labor camps, 147
hope as inspiring migration, 105–6, 131–32, 227, 229
hotel work, 167, 224
hours of work, lack of adequate: complaints about, 121, 181; Operation Farmlift and, 97
hours of work, laws on, 66, 108–9, 169
House Committee on Immigration and Naturalization, 38–39
housing: discrimination in, 139, 181, 184; and families of migrants, 166, 181; farmers overcharging for, 121; farmers providing year-round, to entice return to the fields, 167; FLP contract requirements for, 86; guest worker requirements for, 233n7; loans and subsidies for farmers to improve, 182; noncontract workers and, 10, 118; OSHA standards for, 197–98; racist belief in Puerto Ricans' lesser need for good housing, 178–79; for rural people Puerto Rico, 41. *See also* labor camps
Housing Assistance Council, 142
Hudson Valley (New York), 2, 127, 209
Hughes, Richard, 167
Humacao, Puerto Rico, 87, 108
Hunt, William H., 31
Hurff Soup Canning Company, 56
Hurricane María (2017), 222, 224, 229
Hurricane San Ciprián (1932), 41
Hurricane San Ciriaco (1899), 29
Hurricane San Felipe (1928), 40

Ickes, Harold L., 55
identification cards (Puerto Ricans), 101, 224
identity: food and, 151; as no obstacle to social mobility, 228
Idlewild Airport, 128, 166

Iglesia Cristiana Pentecostal, 165
Iglesia Discípulos de Cristo, 165
Iglesias, Santiago Jr., 55–56
illegal aliens, as concept, 24
illegal hiring. *See* informal and illegal
hiring practices
Illinois: complaints of employers in, 91;
cooperation on Puerto Rican unemployment benefits, 122; as destination of
Puerto Rican farmworkers, 111; Puerto
Rican migrant workers in, 92; Puerto
Rican settlement in, 163–64
Immigration and Nationality Act (1952),
207, 231n1; hearing to amend (1976), 207
Immigration and Naturalization Act
(1965), 171
immigration policies of the United States:
the Great Depression and restrictions
in, 39–40; head tax-entry fee, 33; and
inequality, organization of, 227–28;
literacy tests, 33; and organized labor as
threat to agricultural interests, 26;
quotas, 33, 36; recruitment of colonial
workers as circumvention of, 26; restrictions in the interwar period as favoring
Puerto Rican migrants, 36–37; restrictions on the use of noncitizen guest
workers for temporary farm labor
(1965), 171; restrictions proposed in
interwar period on Puerto Rican and
Filipino workers, 38–39; World War I
and relaxation of, 33; World War II and
favoring of guest workers, 51–54. *See
also* deportability of guest workers
preferred by agricultural-labor market;
deportation; guest-worker programs;
Mexican Bracero Program; regulation;
U.S. Department of Labor (USDL);
*specific laws, agencies, and departments*
Immigration Reform and Control Act
(1986), 231n1
immigration to the U.S.: annual population movement between Puerto Rico
and U.S., 163; distinguished from
colonial migration, 227–28; net migration (1950–60), 163
imperialism, 22; annexation of territories
and questions of citizenship, 22, 27–29.

*See also* colonial migration; colonial
relationship of Puerto Rico to the
United States; colonial state, modern
(Puerto Rico)
Imperial Valley Farmers' Association, 79
independent farmers: FLP contract for, 84;
preference for local workers and southern
African Americans, 126. *See also* growers
India, migrant workers from, 23
industrialization of Puerto Rico, 13, 42, 71.
*See also* manufacturing
industrial labor, and World War I, 33, 34–35
Industrial Mission of Puerto Rico (Misión
Industrial de Puerto Rico), 197
infant mortality rate, 41
informal and illegal hiring practices: overview, 99; FLP as facilitating, 113–14;
and health certificates, 101; and migrant
networks, 99, 114; North Collins, New
York and, 179; prosecution of illegal
recruiters, 100, 114; recruitment, unauthorized, 99, 100–101, 114; San Juan
airport and intervention in, 100; as
springboard to better opportunities,
100; unscrupulous practices and, 100,
101; wages for, as generally lower than
contract workers, 100
infrastructure, colonial government building, 40, 42
injured workers: handling case from Puerto
Rico, 93; lack of treatment for, 216; MD
assisting, 120–21; from pesticides,
166–67, 216; physician refusal to treat
migrants, 180. *See also* disease and
illness; health care; workers compensation (Puerto Rico)
*In Re Giralde,* 29
Insular Cases, 27–29
Insular Labor Relations Act (1945), 46
Insular Passport Act (1902), 28
insular possessions, defined, 29
insurance: Agricultural Group Insurance
(life insurance and benefits for accidents
or illness), 169; Puerto Rico Agricultural Insurance Fund, 86, 169; Puerto
Rico State Insurance Fund, 86. *See also*
health insurance; unemployment insurance; workers compensation

labor organizers and organizing *(continued)*
Rico, 55; World War II labor shortages
as overshadowing, 52. *See also* labor
organizers and organizing, and litigation; strikes and public protests of
farmworkers; United Farm Workers
Union of America (UFW)

labor organizers and organizing, and litigation: overview, 221; the apple industry
and, 207, 211, 212, 213, 223; to enforce
FLP contract, 198; to enforce labor law,
198–99; as important strategy, 217; legal
services for migrants, generally, 197; and
Sunny Slope strike, 215; threat of, as
yielding results, 216–17; upholding the
right to collective bargaining, 217

Labor Relations Institute (Instituto de
Relaciones del Trabajo), 217

labor shortages: artificial, and need for
disposable workers, 211–12; artificial,
due to low wages, 117; demonstration of
domestic workers shortage prior to
recruitment of guest workers, 73, 223,
226; H-2A visas and requirement of
preference for domestic workers prior to
hiring guest workers, 1, 226, 231n1;
Korean War and, 70, 77, 81; postwar,
58–59, 173; World War I and, 33–34;
World War II and, 36, 52–53, 136

labor unions. *See* labor organizers and
organizing

Lancaster, Pennsylvania, 164

Landisville, New Jersey, 165

landlessness of Puerto Rican population,
40, 51, 69

land reform, 13, 42, 48, 69, 71, 108

*Land Reform in Puerto Rico* (García-
Colón), 15

language barrier: claimed to be a problem
by employers, 57; and contemporary
Puerto Rican migrants, 225; discrimination based on, 178–79, 180, 209–10; and
due process, denial of, 179; and extension agent wage data collection, 85;
grower complaints about, 81; and labor
camps as prisons, 155, 157; and legal
rights, ignorance of, 157; migration to
neighboring Latin American republics

and lack of, 32; and school officials, 65;
and welfare officials, 65

Lapp, Michael, 7

Lares, Puerto Rico, 121, 219

La Romana, Dominican Republic, 34

Latin America: Chinese migrant workers
in, 23; proposals for resettling Puerto
Ricans in, 63; Puerto Rican migration
to, ease of, 32; and transition from
slavery to free labor, 23

Latin American Democratic Club, 184

LatinoJustice PRLDEF (Puerto Rican
Legal Defense and Education Fund),
1–2, 198–99, 200

Latourette, William G., 80

laundry workers, 125

leaving the job early. *See* quitting the job

Legislative Assembly. *See* Puerto Rican
legislature

Lehman, Herbert H., 80

Leserson, William M., 33–34

Levin Farm (New Jersey), 216

*libreta de jornaleros* employment registration system, 231n3

Lichter, Michael Ira, 123–24

life expectancy, 41

Li, Tania Murray, 11–12

literacy tests for immigrants, 33

litigation. *See* labor organizers and organizing, and litigation

local communities surrounding labor
camps: and ethnic conflicts as occurring
in sites of social reproduction, 179–80;
health conditions in camps, as low
priority for, 144; impersonal relationships of migrants and, 133; isolation of
migrant workers from, 147; marriage
and ties to, 175; perception of slave-like
treatment of migrant workers, 133–34;
Puerto Rican communities organizing
events in labor camps, 139–40, 165;
refusing to rent to Puerto Ricans, 139,
181, 184; refusing to serve Puerto
Ricans, 160, 175–76, 177, 180. *See also*
discrimination; networks of migration;
North Collins incident; racism; relationships between farmers and migrant
workers

local labor: as day labor, 194; decreases in availability of, 127, 128, 129; and farm work as springboard to better opportunities, 167; increases in availability of, 127; preferred by small farmers, 126; tobacco industry and, 205. *See also* domestic workers

Lock Joint and Pipe Company, 56

Long Island Fruit Company, 56

Long Island, New York, 2, 46, 124, 127, 183

López, William D., 67, 92

Lorain, Ohio, Puerto Rican community established in, 185

Louisiana, labor camps in, 35

McGreevey, Robert C., 6

machismo. *See* manliness/manhood (machismo)

McIntyre, Frank, 34

Maine, 46, 206

maintenance and renewal, 106

Malthusian crisis of overpopulation, 71, 232n1

management of labor migration by the Puerto Rican government: backlash against Puerto Ricans feared, 64; and insertion of colonial officials into the federal government, 12–13; as modern colonial trend, 13; negative experiences of migrants as stimulating, 14; proposals for (1947), 62–66; special advisory committee on (1947), 63; staff for, U.S. government request to hire, 64. *See also* regulation of contract-labor migration by Puerto Rican government

Manifest Destiny, 30

manliness/manhood (machismo): bullying/harassment for perceived lack of, 149, 158; and competition in the field, 149; traditional Puerto Rican diet associated with, 151

Mann, Harold M., 81, 92, 98

manufacturing jobs: abandonment of farm labor in favor of, 43, 102, 125, 185–86; and decimation of sugarcane industry, 108; FLP contracts as springboard to, 165, 167; government of Puerto Rico and development of, 11, 71, 108; and loss of off-season employment to farmworkers, 43; moved to Mexico, 224; OSHA and, 197–98; Puerto Rican labor and, 59, 60, 195; and Puerto Rican migrants who settle in the U.S., 108, 164, 174–75; replacement of farm labor in favor of, 71; return to Puerto Rico to work in, 194; scarcity of, and migration stateside vs. rural-to-urban, 48; urban concentration of, 43, 122–23; wages in, 117, 125; as winter job, 167; World War II migrant labor and, 55, 56

Marcantonio, Vito, 61

marijuana, 196

Marlboro, New Jersey, 120

marriages: and demographics of migrant workers, 194; by men who settle stateside, 110; problems in, created by migration, 110–11, 124–25; with women of other ethnicities, 110, 175, 180. *See also* cohabitation; families

Marshall, Ray, 211

Martínez, Carlos, 133

Martínez, Juan Cancio, 30

Maryland: as destination for Puerto Rican farmworkers, 2, 111; GSSCA membership and, 84; labor camps in, 145; Puerto Rican settlement in, 163–64; USES information station for migrants, 83; wages in, 233n6

masculinity. *See* manliness/manhood (machismo)

Massachusetts: ATA in, 201; and contemporary Puerto Rican farmworkers, 3; decline in number and size of farms in, 191; as destination for Puerto Rican farmworkers, 66, 111, 194; labor camps in, 155; labor organizing in, 198, 202, 206; local farmworkers, 205; MD regional office in, 92; in migratory routes, 46; noncontract workers in, 193; and overstatement of contract workers being sent to, 195; Puerto Rican settlement in, 163–64; religious ministry to Puerto Ricans, 165–66; seasonal noncontract migration in, 114

Massachusetts Employment Service, 92

Michigan Field Crops Association, 91

Mid-Atlantic states, number of Puerto Ricans employed in, 82

Middletown, New York, MD office in, 75

midwestern United States: and problematic beet harvest, 98; racism and, 101

migrant farmworkers, Puerto Rican: age range of, 3, 108, 163; agricultural experience of, 108; demand for, continuing after demise of the FLP, 219–20; demographics of, 108, 163, 166–67, 194, 225; emigration of as protested, 29–30, 35; emigration of as supported, 30, 34, 35, 76, 80; enthusiasm for migration, and rejection of applicants, 111; as expendable and disposable, 21, 186; grower testimonials on behalf of, 115–16, 128–29, 219; interwar period and, 37–40; as percentage of rural population, 163; postwar period and, 173–75; racial hybridity of, 38; racialization of, and discrimination by employers, 81; treated as deportable immigrants, 82; World War I and hiring of, 33; World War II and, 50, 55–58, 223. *See also* citizenship of Puerto Ricans (U.S.) as undesirable to the agricultural-labor market; contemporary Puerto Rican farmworkers; experience of migration; migrant farmworkers, Puerto Rican, numbers of; networks of migration; noncontract farmworkers, Puerto Rican; relationships between farmers and migrant workers; settlement of Puerto Rican migrant farmworkers stateside; transportation of migrants to work locations

migrant farmworkers, Puerto Rican, numbers of: in the 1950s, 102, 125–27; in the 1990s, 220; BEM implementation and, 94; contemporary, 3, 225, 235n1; drops in, 78, 114, 126–27, 167, 193–94, 212; and Florida, 115; FLP placements, table of, *171*; graphs and tables illustrating, *4*, *170–73*; vs. guest-worker placements, *170*, *172*; and New York state, 174–75; at peak of migration (late 1960s to early 1970s), 3, 167, 172, 193–94; as percentage of all travelers, 108; and termination of

the Mexican Bracero Program, 169–71, 223; in tobacco production, 200; as varying from year to year, 126; in World War II, 58

Migrant Legal Action Programs, 207

migrant workers: aftermath of Hurricane Maria and demand for, 224–25; Great Depression and, 44; and maintenance and renewal, 106; and the modern colonial state, 13; New Deal programs for, 45; postwar period and, 59; and the transition from slavery to free trade, 23, 51; unintended consequences of, 102; voting rights of, 123; World War I and, 33, 34–35. *See also* guest-worker programs; migrant farmworkers, Puerto Rican; undocumented labor

Migration Division (MD): and accidents in transportation, 148; as agency operating in the U.S., 7–8; blaming the victims of bullying and harassment, 158; blaming the victims of discrimination (on moral grounds), 185; crew leaders designated by, 114; and death of migrants workers, 148, 158; demise of, 218–19; employer appreciation of benefits of working with, 84; English-language classes in labor camps, 89, *90*, 184; establishment of, 5, 74, 223; and the Ferré administration, 192–93; field representatives of, 92, 101, 193; and FLP demise, 205; funding for, 74, 75, 193, 196, 211; guest workers as threat to, 76, 77; Hernández Colón administration and, 196, 200–201, 202; inspections of farms, 119; inspections of labor camps, 142–44, 145, 153–55, *153–54*, 156, 157; and labor concerns, indifference to, 202; and labor-management relations, 91; and labor organizing, 200–201; management problems with, 195; and mediation of problems, 98–99, 161, 176–77, 180, 185; migration specialists of, 92–93, 196; New York Office of, 74, 126; and the New York State Employment Service, 74; noncontract workers placed by, 126; and the North Collins incident (1966), 177–78, 180, 182, 183–84, 185, 186–87; offices of, 75,

National Labor Relations Act (NLRA, 1935), 45–46; extension to Puerto Rico, 46; farmworkers excluded from, 45, 213

National Labor Relations Board, 45

National Migrant Ministry, 198

Native American migrant workers: from Canada, 46; in history of U.S. farm labor, 3, 51; Puerto Rican experience as similar to, 21; as "unassimilable foreigners," 21

Native Americans, dating and relationships with Puerto Rican migrant workers, 175, 180

nativism: belief that immigrants are responsible for loss of farm jobs, 227–28; contemporary discrimination for speaking Spanish, 224; and ethnic and racial citizenship, 23–24, 27; hostility to Puerto Rican labor in the interwar period, 36, 37–39; regulation of contract-labor migration and, 23, 26, 231n2; temporary migration of U.S. colonial subjects as unable to be legally opposed by, 25; World War I priorities as overcoming interests of, 33

Nazario, Ruben, 167

Nebraska, cooperation on Puerto Rican unemployment benefits, 122

NEFWC. See New England Farm Workers Council

neoliberal policies, 221, 223–24; austerity policies of, 224; contemporary migration and colonial neoliberal government, 224, 225; Ferré administration, 192–93, 196, 197; Roselló González administration, 218–19

Netherlands, West Indian migrants in, 11

networks of migration: contemporary, 225, 226; informal hiring practices and development of, 99, 114; leaving the labor camp and need for, 160; low-wage jobs and difficulty of establishing, 172, 173; between stateside and insular communities, 185

New Deal: BEM as modeled on, 5, 49; extension to farmworkers, 70; farmworkers generally excluded from protections of, 45, 46; governance and reform

as focus in Puerto Rico, 42–43, 48–49; and initial leadership of autonomous Puerto Rico, 12; political opposition to, in Puerto Rico, 41–42, 192; political support for, in Puerto Rico, 46, 48; postwar extension of, 70; regulation of labor, 44–46, 49; regulation of labor camps, 144; transformation of agricultural-labor regimes, 44; and USES, revival of, 36

New England: apple industry, 207; as destination of Puerto Rican farmworkers, 2

New England Apple Council, 208

New England Farm Workers Council (NEFWC): overview, 194, 197; attacked by Republican governor of Connecticut, 203–4; and health care for workers, 203–4; lawsuit on behalf of workers against the STGAA, 201–2

Newfoundland, 46

New Hampshire, 114

New Jersey: and African American migrant workers, 171; ATA in, 201; bullying and harassment in labor camps, 158; contemporary Puerto Rican farmworkers and, 2–3, 227; contract workers leaving job before end of contract, 128; Cumberland County, 2; as destination of Puerto Rican farmworkers, 66, 82, 105, 108, 111; education of migrant children in, 234n1; families of migrants in, 166–67, 234n1; FLP perceived as beneficial to agriculture in, 80; Gloucester County, 2, 56, 214–15; and health care access, 21; illness of workers and firing of, 119–20; justice system and discrimination in, 179; labor camps in, 137–42, 137, 143, 153–54, 156, 158, 159, 165 (see also Farmers and Gardeners Association labor camp; Glassboro labor camp); labor organizing in, 197, 198–99, 203, 205–6, 213–17; META branch in, 201; in migratory routes, 46; minimum wage law, 213; numbers of contract workers in, 194, 212; Passaic County, 165; postwar labor shortage in, 80; postwar Puerto Rican contract workers in, 60; property

population growth and Puerto Rico: early-twentieth century, 40; negative growth rate (1952–53), 78; ongoing expectations of (1947), 63

population of Puerto Ricans in the mainland U.S.: in New York City, 163; in rural areas, 163; in states consistently hiring Puerto Rican workers, 163–64; total involved in agriculture-related activities, 235n1; total stateside population, 163

Portuguese migrant workers, 57

postcolonial countries, wages and worker rights compared to modern colonies, 13

postwar period: and decrease in number of farms and farmworkers, 125, 167; and establishment of BEM and MD, 5, 65–66; and global trend to modern colony formation, 13; labor shortages and, 58–59, 173; and migration as solution to overpopulation, 13–14; New Deal extension, 70; New York state agricultural economy and need for migrant workers, 173–75; Puerto Rican migrant farmworkers and, 173–75; reform of labor conditions, 66–67. *See also* Bureau of Employment and Migration (BEM); Farm Labor Program (FLP); Migration Division (MD)

potato production, 2, 120, 124, 166, 173

poverty: difficulty of escaping, 187; emigration viewed as solution to, 13–14, 34, 36, 41; extreme problems with, 40; immigration policy as shaping inequality, 227–28; labor camps and the image of farmworkers as destitute and oppressed, 134; low wages viewed as source of, 36, 172–73, 232n2; and mortality rate, 41; overpopulation viewed as source of, 34, 46

PPD. *See* Popular Democratic Party (PPD)

PRDL. *See* Puerto Rico Department of Labor

President's Commission on Migratory Labor in American Agriculture, 70, 77, 85, 98

press coverage: criticizing use of federal grants for small number of migrant workers, 205; of the living and working conditions of Puerto Rican farmworkers, 197; New York City "Puerto Rican problem," 64–65, 81; and North Collins incident, 175–76, 178; and perception of Puerto Ricans as foreigners, 79; postwar labor shortages, causes of, 58–59; praise for Puerto Ricans in, 186; in Puerto Rico, attacks on emigration of farmworkers, 29–30; and recruitment campaigns for farmworkers, 87; slavery, contract workers sold into, 224–25; Wheatland Hop Riot (1913), 26

PRES. *See* Puerto Rico Employment Service

prevailing wage, 76, 233n7; growers as setting, 52, 70, 84, 85, 118

prisoners of war, 54, 59

private labor contractors: acting as travel agents, 60, 96; BEM granting licenses to, 93–94; BEM organization based on experiences of, 66; bonding requirements, 87; fees and costs charged by, 60; and illegal hiring, 179; and northeastern U.S., 174, 175, 179; overbooking job sites with workers, 60, 181; postwar recruitment of Puerto Ricans, 59, 60; price gouging by, 60–61, 62, 65; promoting migration of Puerto Ricans to other countries, 59; regulation of, 93–94; unscrupulous practices of, 62, 93; World War I and preeminence of, 34

privatization, 192, 224

PRLDEF (Puerto Rican Legal Defense and Education Fund), 1–2, 198–99, 200

Protestant churches: aiding Puerto Rican migrants, 120; and migration recruitment, 87; ministry in labor camps, 140–41; ministry to Puerto Ricans, 165; and North Collins incident, 180

Protestant status, citizenship and, 23–24

Prussia, 24

PSP. *See* Puerto Rican Socialist Party

public opinion, support for improved working and living conditions for farmworkers, 87, 134, 168, 169, 204

public-relations campaigns: against non-contract labor, 114, 115; recruitment of labor, 87–88, 106, 133 public-sector jobs: neoliberal layoffs of, 224; Puerto Rican government policy creating, 108

Puerto Rican Farmworkers Ministry, 198

Puerto Rican Federal Affairs Administration, 219

Puerto Rican Independence Party (PIP, Partido Independentista Puertorriqueño), 109, 119, 197, 201

Puerto Rican legislature: act 12 (1950), 73; act 19 (1919), 60; act 54 (1936), 60, 62; Act to Regulate Emigration from Porto Rico (1919), 36; air transportation regulation, 94; establishment of, 32; postwar labor legislation passed by, 66–67; public law 2 (1956), 75; public law 25 (1947), 66, 67, 70, 132, 232n3; public law 58 (1989), 217; public law 77 (1958), 86; public law 87 (1962), 99, 168; public law 89 (1947), 62, 67, 70, 99, 168; public law 108 (1958), 89; public law 111 (1951), 87; public law 417 (1947), 62

Puerto Rican Liberal Party (Partido Liberal Puertorriqueño), 46

Puerto Rican Migrant Support Committee (CAMP, Comité de Apoyo al Migrante Puertorriqueño), 197, 198

Puerto Rican migrant workers, Chinese Exclusion Act (1882) applied to, 231n2

Puerto Rican problem, 64–65, 81

Puerto Rican Senate Labor Committee, 61

Puerto Rican Social Club, 184

Puerto Rican Socialist Party (PSP), 190, 197, 198, 201, 202, 206

Puerto Rican studies, political economy and, 9

Puerto Rico: ceded to the U.S., 22, 27, 29; internal migration within, 40, 41. *See also* colonial migration; colonial relationship of Puerto Rico to the United States; colonial state, modern (Puerto Rico); culture of Puerto Rico; economy of Puerto Rico; emigration of Puerto Ricans; government of Puerto Rico; interwar period; migrant farmworkers, Puerto Rican; postwar period; Spanish American War; World War I; World War II

Puerto Rico Agricultural Insurance Fund, 86, 169

Puerto Rico Bureau of Employment Security (PRBES), 75, 83, 99, 100, 118, 232n2

Puerto Rico Bureau of Labor Standards, 87–88

Puerto Rico Department of Education, 89

Puerto Rico Department of Health, 61

Puerto Rico Department of Labor (PRDL): and BEM administration of PRES, 232n3; bonding of workers, requirements for, 86–87; and contemporary workers, 3; decentralization of, 191; and discrimination, interest in preventing, 101; Ferré administration and, 193; funding from USES, 73; funding of MD, 74; grower discomfort with regulations of, 87; H-2A visa program job referrals by, 225; and impersonal relationships of migrants and employers, 133; and labor organizing, 204; lobbying federal officials for recruitment of Puerto Rican laborers, 73; Mediation and Conciliation Service, 65; and migration to other countries, 59; and migration to the U.S., 59, 62–63; Orientation and Information Section, 87; on policy favoring domestic workers, 207; and private contractors, 60, 61; reduction of costs for worker transportation, food, and medical care, 87; World War II and, 56. *See also* Farm Labor Program (FLP)

Puerto Rico Division of Employment Placement, 105–6

Puerto Rico Division of Public Welfare, 61, 110

Puerto Rico Economic Development Bank, 137

Puerto Rico Emergency Relief Administration, 43, 45

Puerto Rico Employment Office, 65

Puerto Rico Employment Security Division, 232–33n4

Puerto Rico Employment Service (PRES): and agriculture as focus of migrant labor, 72; BEM as administering, 73, 232n3; earlier incarnation of (1948),

Rath Camp, *141*
Read, Arthur, 156
Reagan, Ronald, administration of, 221
Reck, Daisy D., 63
recruitment of labor: overview, 10, *88*; BEM
and, 87–92, 133; decentralization of, 96;
English-language classes, 89–90, *90*;
English speakers included with groups
of workers, 218; improvements to system
(1992), 218; interpretive information on
Puerto Rico culture given to farmers
and communities, 91–92, 133; literature
distribution, 89–91; MD and, 115;
networking, 87–88; preseason estimates
of labor needs and, 83; public campaigns, 87–88, 106, 133; regulation by
Puerto Rican government, 62, 67, 70,
87, 89, 99, 168; romanticization of
worker-employer relationship, 89; and
Spanish-speaking staff, need for, 218;
undertaken by the Puerto Rico government, 14; World War I and, 34–35. *See
also* enticements to migrate; informal
and illegal hiring practices; private
labor recruiters; transportation of
migrants to work locations
Red Wind Company camp, 157
regulation (labor): of company stores, 156;
of crew leaders, 148–49; of labor camps,
135–36, 139, 143–44, 156; large-scale
agricultural operations and need for,
44; of modern colonies vs. postcolonial
countries, 13; New Deal and, 44–46,
49, 144; New Deal laws excluding
farmworkers, 45, 46; opening of "closed
camps," 156; OSHA, 197–98, 217. *See
also* Wagner-Peyser Act
regulation of contract-labor migration: and
colonial migrant workers as marginal
category, 25; early twentieth-century
colonial governments and, 24–25,
31–32; expansion of citizens' privileges
and increase in, 24; and racist/nativist
context, 23, 24, 25, 231n2
regulation of contract-labor migration by
Puerto Rican government: as collective
product of colonial and Puerto Rican
officials and stakeholders, 49; initial

grower discomfort with, 87; and private
labor contractors, 61–62; vision of
migratory flows (1947), 48–49. *See also*
Bureau of Employment and Migration
(BEM); Farm Labor Program (FLP);
Migration Division (MD); Puerto
Rican legislature
relationships between farmers and migrant
workers: experience of migrants and,
116, 133, 134, 165; public relations campaigns and romanticization of, 89;
testimonies of farmers on benefits of,
115–16, 128–29, 219. *See also* networks of
migration
religious ministry: in labor camps, 140–41,
147, 165–66; labor organizing, 197, 198;
to Puerto Rican communities, 165–66.
*See also* Catholic Church; Protestant
churches
remittances: amounts of, 111; contemporary
practices of, 3, 226; contract for payment at end of season and difficulties
with, 98; and destitution of worker if
anything goes wrong, 121; and family
problems, 111; as goal of most migrants,
105; money orders for, sold in labor
camps, 111; and postwar proposals for
migrants, 63–64; tobacco workers and,
205; USES mandatory requirement for,
and problems with, 58, 61
Republican Union Party (Partido Unión
Republicana), in La Coalición with
the Socialist Party (Partido Socialista),
42, 48
resistance by Puerto Rican workers: to
discrimination (North Collins incident), 164–65, 181, 187–88; to exploitation in Hawaii, 30–31; to second-class
status as colonial subjects, 164–65, 187;
to violence, 177, 234n2. *See also* agency
of Puerto Rican migrants
rest days, farmworkers have no right to, 226
retail workers, 125, 227
return migration to Puerto Rico: overview,
122–25; ambivalence about, 124–25;
complaints of workers, 124; farm labor
as expectation for, 194; and the Great
Depression, 41, 43; and home owner-

southwestern United States: Filipino labor migration to, 29; and labor camps, 142; Mexican migrants as predominant immigrant labor force in, 54, 172; proposed as location for Puerto Rican migrant relocation, 64; Puerto Rican labor migration to, 29; wages in, 85; World War I and labor shortages in, 33

Spain: loss of Spanish market for Puerto Rican coffee, 29. *See also* Spanish-American War (1898); Spanish colonial government of Puerto Rico

Spanish American Organization, 182, 184, 185

Spanish-American War (1898), 22, 27, 29

Spanish Caribbean, 23

Spanish colonial government of Puerto Rico, *libreta de jornaleros* employment registration system, 231n3

Spanish Harlem, 67

Spanish language: classes in, for farmers, 139; FLP contracts in English and, 84; growers speaking and learning, 116, 128, 129, 139. *See also* English language; language barrier

Special Committee on Importation of Mexican Labor, 54

Springfield, Massachusetts, 102, 164, 185, 203

Stanley, Oliver, 101

state departments of health, inspecting labor camps, 144, 197–98

state departments of labor, overseeing labor camps, 144

state employment services: BEM made similar to, 73; data collection of FLP and, 83; extending unemployment benefits to Puerto Rican migrants, 122; general FLP contract negotiated with, 218; the PRES and, 73, 74–75; as siding with farmers, 119; World War II and, 53–54

state formation: ethnic and racial citizenship and, 24; and gatekeeping/deportation regimes, 25; nationalism and, 24

state formation of Puerto Rico: the BEM and MD as tools of, 7; constitution, 13, 66; and modern colony, development as, 9, 13, 15–16

statehood of Puerto Rico, politics of, 219, 221

state migration programs, 68; BEM as following example of, 68–69; World War II and federal funding of, 68–69

staying in the U.S. *See* settlement of Puerto Rican migrant farmworkers stateside

stereotypes, negative, 57, 186, 188. *See also* discrimination; racism

STGAA. *See* Shade Tobacco Growers Agricultural Association

Stoolewell Company, 151

Striffler, Steve, 107

strikebreakers, 35, 77, 215

strikes, prevalence in Puerto Rico, 41

strikes and public protests of farmworkers: emigration from Puerto Rico viewed as solution for, 34; Japanese workers in Hawaii, 31; Mexican braceros prohibited from, 77; migrants in Connecticut, 198; migrants in New Jersey, 118, 214–15; pea pickers (California 1932), 39; and wage improvements, 118, 215

structural power, 8–9

structural violence in labor camps, 142–47

sugar sector: in Dominican Republic, 34; and guest worker programs, 207; in Hawaii, 30–31, 38, 222; Puerto Rican, decimation of, 108; Puerto Rican labor migration and, 30–31, 34, 35; Puerto Rican migrant demographics and, 108; and transition from slavery to free labor, 23

sugar sector in Puerto Rico: decline of, 215; exports, 40, 50–51; "fleeing the cane," 109; guest-workers brought to Puerto Rico, proposal for, 192; harvest season as complementary to northeastern U.S., 59, 65–66, 109; regions grown in, 51; and rice in the diet, 151; *tiempo muerto* (before and after the harvest), 36, 108–9; unemployment and underemployment in, 36, 41, 108–9; U.S. corporate interests and, 30, 40, 50; wages in, 41, 50, 116–17, 194

Sunny Slope, 214–15

Swedesboro camp, 137, 214

Syracuse, New York, 164

Taft, William Howard, 32

tariffs, 29, 50

Cassaday Farms for rejecting Puerto
Rican migrant workers and hiring guest
workers, 1; and public-employment
exchange, 34; Puerto Rican officials
inserted into, 7–8; report on guest-
worker wages as depressing domestic
workers' wages, 168; unemployment
viewed as structural problem requiring
governmental intervention by, 34; and
World War I labor shortages/recruit-
ment, 33, 35; and World War II labor
shortages, investigation of, 52–53. *See
also* U.S. Employment Service (USES)
U.S. Department of State, 54, 64, 79
U.S. Department of War, 34, 54
U.S. Division of Territories and Island
Possessions (DTIP), 42, 50, 55, 56, 64, 71
USDL. *See* U.S. Department of Labor
U.S. Emergency Farm Labor Supply Program, 52, 136
U.S. Employment Service (USES): as
barring entrance of guest workers into
the Northeast, 73; BEM as modeled
after, 5, 49, 67–68; BEM officially
incorporated into, 98; and complaints
by noncontract workers, 145; creation
of, 33–34; extension into Puerto Rico,
45, 55, 73; funding for PRDL, 73; information stations for migrant workers, 83;
interwar period and reduction of scope
of, 36; New Deal reorganization of, 45;
pledge-card system of, 231n3; postwar
labor management by, 67–68; postwar
pressure to hire Puerto Ricans by,
127–28; and prevailing wage as determined by growers, 70, 84, 85; private
labor recruiters and agribusinesses as
preeminent vs., 34; and Region 2, membership in, 74; remittances withheld
from wages, 58; and return migration to
Puerto Rico, assurances for, 78, 80; and
state employment-service offices, 68–69;
under USBES (1948–49), 232n2; Washington D.C. Office, 74–75; and World
War I labor shortages and recruitment,
33–35; and World War II employment-
service offices, 68–69; and World War
II guest worker recruitment, 53; and

World War II labor shortages and
recruitment, 136; and World War II
labor shortages, investigation of, 52
U.S. Equal Opportunity Commission, 2
USES. *See* U.S. Employment Service
U.S. Farm Security Administration (FSA),
45, 46, 49, 53, 67–68, 69, 136
U.S. Federal Security Agency, 69, 80,
232nn2,2
U.S. First Circuit Court, 211
U.S. Immigration and Naturalization
Service (INS), 53, 54, 76–77, 82
U.S. Manpower Administration, 191, 204
U.S. Office of Economic Opportunity, 197
U.S. public law 45 (1943), 54, 76
U.S. public law 78 (1951), 70, 85, 77; termi-
nation of (1964), 169, 172
U.S. Republican Party: Charles H. Allen
and, 30; and labor organizing, 203–4;
migrant workers in platform of (1960),
190; the PNP and, 192, 196; the Repub-
lican Union Party (Partido Unión
Republicana) as affiliated with, 42, 48
U.S. Resettlement Administration (RA),
45, 46, 136
U.S. Supreme Court: apple growers and
guest workers, 212; *Balzac v. People of
Porto Rico,* 32; *Downes v. Bidwell,* 23,
27–28; *Galan v. Dunlop,* 207; *Gonzales
v. Williams,* 28–29; Insular Cases,
27–29
U.S. Training and Employment Service, 191
U.S. Virgin Islands, 35, 74
U.S. War Emergency Committees, 51–52
U.S. War Emergency Program (WEP), 53,
54, 56, 58
U.S. War Food Administration (WFA), 53,
55, 57
U.S. War Manpower Commission
(WMC), 51–52, 53, 54, 55–56, 57
U.S. War Trade Board, 35
Utah, 165
Utah Copper Mines, 56
Utuado, Puerto Rico, 153, 167, 227

vagrancy charges on migrant workers, 115,
155, 160
Vega, Anthony, 174

maintain, 35, 43, 51, 52–53, 181; refusal of migrants to work for, 117; as source of poverty, 36, 172–73, 232n2; and workers leaving the camps, 159

Wagner-Peyser Act (1933), 44–45, 46, 67–68, 205, 211, 223; extension to Puerto Rico (1950), 73, 74, 75, 232n3

Waldinger, Roger David, 123–24

Waldorf Astoria Hotel, 111

Walker, R. C., 128–29

Waltham, Massachusetts, Puerto Rican community established in, 185

Wareham, Massachusetts, 147

Washington state, 2, 111, 170

Waterbury, Connecticut, 203

Watts, Fred, 118

weather, 124, 133, 140–41

Weiss, Bernard, 180

welfare benefits: expansion of, and increased regulation of migrants, 24; fear of migrant workers seeking, 80–81, 222–23; health insurance requirements as lessening fear of migrants using, 86; migrants not seeking, 65; migrants resorting to, 65, 185; nativist hostility toward nondeportable Puerto Ricans receiving, 37, 38; noncontract workers and, 115; reputation for laziness because of eligibility for, 226

WEP. See U.S. War Emergency Program

Westair Corporation, 96

West, Arthur, 205

Westfield, New York, 174, 185

West Indians. See British West India (Caribbean); British West Indian migrant workers

West Virginia, apple industry, 207

WEVM radio station, 89

Whalen, Carmen Teresa, 9

Wheatland Hop Riot (California), 25–26

white migrant workers: and ethnic succession of farmworkers, 165; interwar period and, 51; sent to the U.S. South, 59; violence in labor camps and, 145

whiteness: as basis of citizenship, 23–24. See also nativism; racism

whites: Puerto Rico migrant men dating white women, 180; World War I and migration from rural South to industrial North, 33. See also discrimination; North Collins incident; racial segregation

white supremacy. See racism

Whitney, A. F., 55

Wickards, Claude R., 55

Williams, Harrison A., 169

Williams, Robert F., 216

will to improve, 12, 48

Wilson, Malcolm, 182–83

Windsor, Connecticut, 199

Wirtz, Willard, 167, 172, 207

WMC. See U.S. War Manpower Commission

Wolf, Eric, 8

women: contracts for domestic work by, 66; and domestic work, 61; government programs creating gender-based jobs for, 108; and marriage difficulties, 110–11; men as preferred workers, 51, 71, 107, 173; as noncontract workers, 113; postwar departure from war industries, 59; as test subjects for birth-control pills and mass sterilization, 71; in tobacco production, 204–5; wages made by, compared to men's, 41

Woodcliff Lake, New Jersey, 117–18

Woodstown, New Jersey, 234n1

workers compensation (Puerto Rico): establishment of, 66–67; in FLP contracts, 86; MD officials reporting, 119; noncontract workers not covered by, 175; and public law 87, 168. See also injured workers

work permits, 24

World War I: and agricultural-labor shortages, 33–34; contract farm labor as emerging during, 22, 34; industrial labor for mobilization for, 33, 34–35; IWW and, 26; passing of Jones Act and granting of naturalized U.S. citizenship, 32; and rural migration from the South to the North, 33. See also interwar period

AMERICAN CROSSROADS

Edited by Earl Lewis, George Lipsitz, George Sánchez, Dana
Takagi, Laura Briggs, and Nikhil Pal Singh